THE POEMS OF EDWARD TAYLOR

THE POEMS OF

Edward Taylor

EDITED BY

Donald E. Stanford

UNIVERSITY OF NORTH CAROLINA PRESS

Chapel Hill and London

The paper in this book meets the guidelines for
permanence and durability of the Committee on
Production Guidelines for Book Longevity of the
Council on Library Resources.

Printed in the United States of America

97 96 95 94 93   5 4 3 2

Library of Congress Cataloging-in-Publication Data

Taylor, Edward, 1642–1729.
  The poems of Edward Taylor.

  Reprint, with new introd. Originally published: Poems.
New Haven: Yale University Press, c1960.
  I. Stanford, Donald E., 1913–   . II. Title.
PS850.T2A6   1989   811′.1   88-40555
ISBN 0-8078-4248-6 (alk. paper)

FOR YVOR WINTERS

Among the first and farthest

Contents

Preface

This edition of Edward Taylor's poetry was inspired by Yvor Winters's lectures on American literature at Stanford University in the early 1940s. In commenting on Thomas H. Johnson's then recent publications of Taylor's poems, Winters stated that the discovery of Taylor was important and that he would eventually be considered America's first major poet. I resolved to prepare an edition of all of Taylor's poems (then extant), which would include the minor poems as well as "Gods Determinations" and the more than two hundred "Preparatory Meditations" of which Johnson had published only thirty-one under the title "Sacramental Meditations." The edition was completed as a doctoral dissertation directed by Winters at Stanford University in 1953, and a few years later it was accepted for publication by the Yale University Press. Upon further consideration, however, it was decided that an edition that would necessarily run to two volumes would be difficult to market and that the best of Taylor could be confined to one volume. That Yale edition, first published in 1960, included a brief introduction by me and a longer foreword by Louis L. Martz in which he convincingly demonstrated the influence of the Christian meditative tradition on Taylor's "Preparatory Meditations." It included all the "Preparatory Meditations," "Gods Determinations," and what I considered to be the best of the minor poems. Critical and scholarly response exceeded expectations as did sales. I wrote a new introduction for an abridged paperback edition that was issued by the Yale University Press in 1963. The present volume is a reprint of the 1963 edition.

My introduction contains evidence I had discovered in Leicester, England, concerning Taylor's parentage and an assessment of Taylor's religious beliefs that had become a controversial issue. My position was and still is that Taylor was, like his contemporary Michael Wigglesworth (author of the *Day of Doom*) and like the later Jonathan Edwards (author of "Sinners in the Hands of an Angry God"), a thorough and complete Calvinist. It was the position of a number of scholars, including Samuel Eliot Morison, Perry Miller, and Thomas H. Johnson, that Taylor was not a complete Calvinist. The reader who wishes to pursue the matter further will find a detailed discussion of the question in the long introduction to my doctoral dissertation and in my entry on Taylor in the *Dictionary of Literary Biography*, vol. 24 (1984). Karen E. Rowe's impressive *Saint and Singer: Edward Taylor's Typology and the Poetics of Meditation* (1986) brings the controversy up to date. In common with a number of scholars today, Rowe argues that Taylor's religious beliefs are not truly Calvinistic but are modified by "Covenant Theology," which she defines (in part) as follows: "Rather than stress the impotence of the believer who is subject to predestination, covenant theology encourages assurance by accentuating the free will with which man participates in the contract [with God]" (p. 18). A careful examination of "Gods Determinations" should convince the reader that Covenant Theology thus defined is not the theology of Taylor. In this poem, which is a versified treatise on the poet's religious beliefs, humankind has no free will—note, for example, the word *determinations* in the title. Humans are "cripples," completely impotent until "God's Selecting Love in the Decree" saves a few fortunate individuals. Such was the belief of both Calvin and Taylor.

For Further Reading

Valuable scholarly aids are Constance J. Gefvert, *Edward Taylor: An Annotated Bibliography, 1668–1970* (Kent, Ohio: Kent State University Press, 1971), and Gene Russell, *A Concordance to the Poems of Edward Taylor* (Washington, D.C.: Microcard Editions, 1973). Varied critical insights into Taylor's poetry will be found in Karen Rowe's 1986 work, mentioned above, and in the following: E. F. Carlisle, "The Puritan Structure of Edward Taylor's Poetry," *American Quarterly* 20 (1968): 147–63; Michael J. Colacurcio, "Gods Determinations Touching Half-Way Membership: Occasion and Audience in Edward Taylor," *American Literature* 39 (November 1967): 298–314; *Early American Literature*, special issue 4, no. 3 (Winter 1969–70); Clark Griffith, "Edward Taylor and the Momentum of Metaphor," *ELH* 33

(1966): 448–60; Allen B. Howard, "The World as Emblem: Language and Vision in the Poetry of Edward Taylor," *American Literature* 44 (November 1972): 359–84; Barbara Kiefer Lewalski, "Edward Taylor: Lisps of Praise and Strategies for Dispraise," in *Protestant Poetics and the Seventeenth Century Religious Lyric* (Princeton, N.J.: Princeton University Press, 1979), pp. 388–426; and Donald E. Stanford, "Edward Taylor," in *Major American Writers of Early American Literature*, edited by Everett Emerson (Madison: University of Wisconsin Press, 1972), pp. 59–91.

D. E. S.
Baton Rouge, La.
July 1988

Other Writings of Edward Taylor

In addition to the poems in this collection, the following volumes of Edward Taylor's writings have been published:

The Poems of Edward Taylor. Edited by Donald E. Stanford. New Haven, Conn.: Yale University Press, 1960. The fuller collection on which this volume is based.

Edward Taylor's Christographia. Edited by Norman S. Grabo. New Haven, Conn.: Yale University Press, 1962. Fourteen sacrament-day sermons.

Edward Taylor's Metrical History of Christianity. Edited by Donald E. Stanford. Cleveland, Ohio: Micro Photo, Inc., 1962. Reprint. Ann Arbor: Books on Demand: University Microfilms International, 1977. A poem of 21,500 lines.

The Diary of Edward Taylor. Edited by Francis Murphy. Springfield, Mass.: Connecticut Valley Historical Museum, 1964.

Edward Taylor's Treatise Concerning the Lord's Supper. Edited by Norman S. Grabo. East Lansing: Michigan State University Press, 1965. Eight sermons.

Edward Taylor's "Church Records" and Related Sermons. Edited by Thomas M. and Virginia L. Davis. Boston: Twayne Publishers, 1981. Vol. 1 of "The Unpublished Writings of Edward Taylor."

Edward Taylor vs. Solomon Stoddard: The Nature of the Lord's Supper. Edited by Thomas M. and Virginia L. Davis. Boston: Twayne Publishers, 1981. Vol. 2 of "The Unpublished Writings of Edward Taylor."

Edward Taylor's Minor Poetry. Edited by Thomas M. and Virginia L. Davis. Boston: Twayne Publishers, 1981. Vol. 3 of "The Unpublished Writings of Edward Taylor." Includes six poems first edited and published by Donald E. Stanford in *American Literature* 32 (May 1960): 136–51 and *New York History* 40 (January 1959): 47–61.

Edward Taylor's Harmony of the Gospels. Edited by Thomas M. and Virginia L. Davis. 4 vols. Delmar, N.Y.: Scholars' Facsimiles and Reprints, 1983.

Upon the Types of the Old Testament. Edited by Charles W. Mignon. Lincoln: University of Nebraska Press, forthcoming. Sermons.

Abbreviations

C   "Christographia." A manuscript by Edward Taylor in the Yale University Library.

Cent.   *The Century Dictionary and Cyclopedia,* 12 vols. New York, Century,
Dict.   1889–1911.

Conj.   Conjectural reading.

CP   "Commonplace Book." A manuscript by Edward Taylor in the Massachusetts Historical Society Collection of manuscripts.

CR   Westfield "Church Record." A manuscript by Edward Taylor in the Westfield Athenaeum.

DAE   *A Dictionary of American English,* ed. Sir William A. Craigie and James R. Hulbert, Chicago, University of Chicago Press, 1938–44.

DB   Sir William Smith, *Dr. William Smith's Dictionary of the Bible,* rev. and ed. by H. B. Hackett, New York, Hurd and Houghton, 1868–70.

DTP   "Diary, Theological Notes, and Poems." A manuscript by Edward Taylor in the Redwood Athenaeum.

EDD   *The English Dialect Dictionary,* 6 vols. London, Henry Frowde, 1898–1905.

ETG   Thomas H. Johnson, "Some Edward Taylor Gleanings," *New England Quarterly, 16* (1943), 280–96.

ETP   Thomas H. Johnson, "Edward Taylor: A Puritan 'Sacred Poet,'" *New England Quarterly, 10* (1937), 290–322.

HG   "Harmony of the Gospels." A manuscript by Edward Taylor in the Redwood Athenaeum.

MGG   Morris A. Neufeld, "A Meditation upon the Glory of God," *Yale University Library Gazette, 25* (1951), 110–11.

orig: Originally (used in textual notes to indicate words canceled by Taylor).

PET   Barbara Damon Simison, "Poems by Edward Taylor," *Yale University Library Gazette, 28* (1954), 93–102, 161–70; *29* (1954), 25–34, 71–80.

PW   The "Poetical Works" of Edward Taylor. Manuscript in the Yale University Library.

SMT   Donald E. Stanford, "Sacramental Meditations by Edward Taylor," *Yale University Library Gazette, 31* (1956), 61–75.

UPT   Donald E. Stanford, "Nineteen Unpublished Poems by Edward Tay-
        lor," *American Literature, 29* (1957), 18–46.

W   Thomas H. Johnson, *The Poetical Works of Edward Taylor,* Rock-
        land Editions, 1939; Princeton University Press, 1943.

WDB   *The Westminster Dictionary of the Bible,* Philadelphia, Westminster
        Press, 1944.

WNI   *Webster's New International Dictionary,* Springfield, Mass., Merriam,
        1956.

Z   Copies of poems by Edward Taylor found in the binding of the
        "Poetical Works."

Introduction

The poems in this collection were written over a period of approximately forty years by the "Venerable, Learned, and Pious Pastor of the Church of Christ" in the small frontier town of Westfield, Massachusetts. Here the Congregational minister Edward Taylor labored from 1671 until his retirement in 1725, ministering to the souls and the bodies of his parishioners (he was a physician as well as a preacher of the gospel), helping to organize defenses against Indian attack, farming to provide for his large family, preaching lengthy sermons at least once a week, and writing thousands of lines of poetry. His best verses are a kind of secret diary, a record of his spiritual experiences, his communion with God. Like his New England spiritual heir, Emily Dickinson, he did not write for publication. Indeed, there was a tradition among his descendants that he forbade publication of his poems.[1]

Edward Taylor was born in Sketchley, Leicestershire, England, during the English civil wars, probably in the year 1642. There is no entry in the Burbage parish church register concerning his birth or baptism and it is probable that none will be discovered. The Burbage register, which includes the records for Sketchley, is incomplete. During the civil disturbances of the sixteen forties, church records were frequently destroyed or not kept at all. However, the wills of Taylor's father, William Taylor, and of his eldest brother, Richard, are extant, and they provide us with information concerning the poet's childhood and early youth.[2] He was brought up in the family of a midland yeoman farmer who was somewhat more prosperous than the average man of his class. The poet's father owned a two-story house with barn and garden. At the time

1. There is no document by Taylor to prove the truth of this tradition. Perry Miller's statement in *The American Puritans* (New York, 1956), p. 302, that Taylor "left instructions in his will that nothing ever be published" is incorrect. Taylor died intestate. See Francis Murphy, "Edward Taylor's Attitude Toward Publication: A Question Concerning Authority," *American Literature, 34* (1962), 393–94.

2. See Donald E. Stanford, "The Parentage of Edward Taylor," *American Literature, 33* (1961), 215–21.

of his death in 1658 he possessed fifty sheep as well as hogs, pigs, calves, horses, bees, and a store of barley, malt, corn, and peas. Taylor undoubtedly took an active part in the independent hardy life of the seventeenth-century English yeoman. The Taylor family brewed their own ale, sheared and spun their own wool, raised their own honey, poultry, meat, milk, and vegetables. The village of Sketchley, a hamlet of less than forty inhabitants, lay in the beautiful green rolling fields of Leicestershire which maintain much of their rural character to this day, and where the spire of the Burbage parish church still dominates the landscape. The images of farm life and rural landscape which appear in Taylor's poetry written long after he left England are probably, in part, recollections of his Leicestershire childhood. Also, frequent references of the poet to the art of weaving and a score or so of technical terms used in weaving suggest his familiarity with the new industry of the neighboring town of Hinckley, where frame knitting began in 1640 and where the hosiery industry flourished after 1670. It is probable that Taylor worked in a Hinckley weaver's shop.

Leicestershire was a hotbed of non-conformity during the seventeenth century, and dissenters of the generation of the poet's father had vivid memories of the Cavalier Prince Rupert's storming of Leicester in 1645. Taylor's dislike of Anglicanism began early. He was educated under a non-conformist schoolmaster, receiving a good foundation in theology and in the learned languages. The typical curriculum of that time included the Westminster Catechism, Calvin's *Institutes* and *Epistles*, the New Testament in Greek, Augustine's *Soliloquies* in Latin, elementary Hebrew, and studies in Job and Canticles. Verse writing in Latin was standard practice for grammar school students, but English poets were also studied—Francis Quarles and George Herbert being considered particularly suitable for Leicestershire students.[3] Thus Taylor was introduced at an early age to two of his favorite poets, who were to have a lasting influence on him—the author of Canticles and the author of *The Temple,* George Herbert.

3. See Foster Watson, *The English Grammar Schools to 1660: Their Curriculum and Practice,* Cambridge, 1908; M. Claire Cross, *The Free Grammar School of Leicester,* Leicester, 1953.

At the time of the Restoration in 1660 Taylor was about eighteen years old. His puritan character and convictions had been formed during the regime of Oliver Cromwell. With the return of Charles II to the throne of England, the young man faced a bleak future. He was qualified to teach, and for a short time he kept a school at Bagworth, Leicestershire. But he would not subscribe to the Act of Uniformity of 1662.[4] His religious convictions prevented him from taking the oaths necessary to procure a license to continue his teaching. This refusal was the turning point of his career. He could not preach, teach, or attend the universities of Cambridge or Oxford. He and his friends were harried and persecuted. Their difficulties are hinted at in the diary Taylor kept on his voyage to America:

> After dinner, I reading the fourth chapter of John in Greek, was so sleepy that when I had done I lay down, and dropping into a sleep, and dreaming of my brethren, was so oppressed with sorrow that I had much to do to forbear weeping out.[5]

On April 26, 1668, Taylor embarked from Execution Dock, Wapping, for a new country and a more hopeful life. Delayed for many days by unfavorable winds, Taylor's ship did not reach the open sea until the 21st of May. During the rough ocean journey, the poet "exercised" from Scripture for the edification of the passengers, read his New Testament in Greek, and kept a journal which is a curious mixture of religious piety, "scientific" observation, and folk superstition:

> We saw a pair of sunfish lie flapping on the water. They say that this kind of fish is thus that it cannot sink while the sun shines.

Land was sighted on July 4th with "Plymouth on the left, and Salem on the right." On July 5th, seventy days after he boarded ship at Execution Dock, he disembarked at Boston.

---

4. See Taylor's obituary in the *Boston News Letter* for August 7–14, 1729.
5. Taylor's diary is in the Redwood Library and Athenaeum, Newport, R.I. It has been published in *Proceedings of the Massachusetts Historical Society, 18* (1880), 5–18.

Taylor was well received in Boston. He lodged for two nights with the famous Increase Mather and for over two weeks with John Hull, mintmaster and one of Boston's most important merchants, before enrolling as an upperclassman in Harvard College; there he was invited to stay over night in the house of the president of the college, Charles Chauncy. During his three years at Harvard, Taylor was the college butler, responsible for keeping account of kitchen and dining room utensils, for providing candles for prayer and supper, and for collecting weekly payments for food and drink. The position was usually given to a mature and responsible upperclassman. The award of this position and his favorable reception by Mather, Hull, and President Chauncy indicate that Taylor was held in good repute by his superiors. When he graduated in 1671, he was chosen one of four seniors to declaim in College Hall. His declamation was a long poem full of fantastic conceits and diction which was supposed to demonstrate the superiority of English to the learned languages.

After his graduation, Taylor decided to remain at Harvard. In the fall of 1671 he settled in college and was instituted scholar of the house. However, the arrival of Thomas Dewey from Westfield changed his plans. Dewey, upon the advice of Increase Mather, offered the pastorship of the Congregational Church of Westfield to Taylor who, after considerable hesitation, accepted the call. On November 27 Dewey and Taylor set out on horseback on the difficult hundred-mile journey through deep snow to the frontier town near the Connecticut River, reaching it four days later.

The settlement in which the new minister took up his duties was a farming community of about twenty-five or thirty families occupying a township of forty square miles in the valley of the Westfield River. Each family was given allotments of meadowland and plowland. Taylor eventually received at least three separate lots and a parsonage built, in all probability, of unhewn logs. The first meeting house in which he preached and administered the Lord's Supper was a fortified building, square in shape, with a pyramidal roof, on top of which was a turret used as a watch tower during Indian troubles. His congregation was summoned to worship by the roll of a drum.

This congregation was made up of housewives and farmers of

little learning. Of the original settlers, only two were distinguished in the Westfield town records by the term "Mr." Only one "library" is mentioned—that of John Root, who owned twenty-two books with such titles as *Groans of the Damned, Thirsty Sinner,* and *Heavenly Passtime.*[6] After the intellectual companionship he enjoyed at Harvard, Taylor must have felt somewhat isolated in his new environment. He was discouraged with the task of organizing a church in a frontier town, and in 1673 several members of his congregation requested that David Wilton, a distinguished citizen of Northampton, be allowed to settle in Westfield "for further encouraging of Mr. Taylor." Solomon Stoddard, Northampton's pastor, refused the request.[7]

In 1674 Taylor married Elizabeth Fitch, daughter of the Reverend James Fitch of Norwich, Connecticut. During their fifteen years of married life she bore him eight children, five of whom died in infancy. Mrs. Taylor died in 1689. Approximately three years later, Taylor married Ruth Wyllis of Hartford, Connecticut. They had six children, all of whom grew to maturity. One of his daughters, Keziah, married Isaac Stiles of New Haven. She was the mother of Ezra Stiles, who became president of Yale College.

Shortly after Taylor's first marriage, in 1675, King Philip's War broke out. Upon the shoulders of the minister fell much of the responsibility for organizing the defense against Indian raids. It was probably Taylor who was instrumental in making the decision to keep the townspeople in Westfield rather than to remove them to Springfield or Hartford for their protection. The decision turned out to be the right one. Westfield survived as an independent town, and although there was widespread devastation throughout the Bay Colony, Westfield suffered very little from Indian attacks.

With the termination of King Philip's War, Taylor was at long last able to organize his congregation into "a church state." Foundation services were held on August 27, 1679. Taylor was ordained minister, and he then preached his foundation sermon, "A Particular Church is God's House."

6. John H. Lockwood, *Westfield and Its Historic Influences* (2 vols. Springfield, Mass., 1922), *1*, 98.

7. Donald E. Stanford, *The Poems of Edward Taylor* (New Haven, 1960), p. 513.

For the next forty-six years, Taylor carried on his public duties as a small town minister, preaching sermons with learned allusions that few in his congregation could understand,[8] and in the secrecy of his study (which contained a substantial library)[9] writing poems in the metaphysical style of a previous generation. He retired in 1725, an invalid, worn out with his labors. No extant poems bear a date later than this year. According to the testimony of his life-long friend, the diarist and witchcraft judge, Samuel Sewall, and according to a family tradition, Taylor was almost completely incapacitated, mentally and physically, during his final years. He died June 24, 1729, and was interred in the old burying ground at Westfield where his tombstone still stands.

Ezra Stiles was only two years old when his grandfather Edward Taylor died, and he therefore could not have remembered him. However, Stiles collected considerable information about his ancestor and composed the best description we have of Taylor. He says that Taylor was "a man of small stature, but firm; of quick Passions, yet serious and grave. Exemplary in Piety, and for a very sacred Observance of the Lord's Day." He was "Very curious in Botany, Minerals and Natural History. He was an incessant student. He was a vigorous Advocate for Oliver Cromwell, civil and religious Liberty. A Congregationalist in opposition to Presbyterian Church Discipline." He "greatly detested King James [II], Sir Edmond Andross, and Randolph: gloried in King William and the Revolution of 1688."[10] Taylor's diary, letters, and sermons substantiate Stiles' description. In a curious love letter in which he tells his first wife that he cannot give her all his heart because the greater part of it is promised to Christ, Taylor pushes piety to the verge of the ludicrous.[11] His later years were disturbed by difficulties with his townsmen which reveal Taylor to have been a stubborn disciplinarian, set in his ways. In a sermon on church

8. See Norman Grabo, *Edward Taylor's Christographia* (New Haven, 1962).

9. Books in Taylor's library are listed in Thomas H. Johnson, *The Poetical Works of Edward Taylor* (Princeton, 1943), pp. 204–20.

10. Written by Ezra Stiles in blank leaves of Taylor's manuscript book "Metallographia," in the Yale Library.

11. See W. B. Goodman, "Edward Taylor Writes His Love," *New England Quarterly*, 27 (1954), 510–15.

discipline preached in 1713 he relates how he sternly suppressed a faction in his church by withholding the sacrament of the Lord's Supper, and admonishing them as follows:

> I here in the name and Magisty of Christ Commande you to repent of these your Sins and greate Evill, And to manifest your Repentance to the Church in due time that you may beg them to forgive you, and this I charge you to do upon your perill as you shall answer it at the day of Jesus Christ.[12]

We learn from Sewall's diary and from the town records that there was a long protracted struggle concerning the location of the new Westfield meeting house. When the matter was settled and the church completed in 1721–22 Taylor put up considerable resistance to preaching in it. He preferred the location of the old meeting house and wanted to preach there.[13] Stephen Williams, pastor of Longmeadow Church, who knew Taylor during his declining years, refers in his journal to a dispute that Taylor had with his townspeople over the choice of a constable. "Old Mr. Taylor is very fond of his own thoughts and I am afraid will make a very great difficulty and division in the town." Taylor's stubbornness caused "a mournfull countenance among the people again. Their Spirits Seem to be quite Sunk and depressed, and I fear the ruine (i.e. in a great measure) of Town and church by reason of the old Gentleman's resolution."[14]

Taylor, then, seems to have been endowed with most of those qualities usually connoted by the word *puritan*. He was learned, grave, severe, stubborn, and stiff-necked. He was very, very pious. But his piety was sincere. It was fed by a long continuous spiritual experience arising, so he felt, from a mystical communion with Christ. The reality and depth of this experience is amply witnessed by his poetry.

12. In the Prince Collection, Boston Public Library, p. 66.
13. "The Letter Book of Samuel Sewall," *Collections of the Massachusetts Historical Society*, 6th ser., 2 (1886–88), 145–46.
14. See Alexander Medlicott, Jr., "Notes on Edward Taylor from the Diaries of Stephen Williams," *American Literature*, 34 (1962), 270–74.

II

Taylor's first poems, composed in England, copied into a com-
monplace book, and bound up with the manuscript of his diary,
are of biographical and historical interest but of little literary
value.[15] A letter to his brother Joseph expresses commonplace
pious ejaculations in the ingenious acrostic form which fascinated
seventeenth-century poets: it is the first of a series of acrostic poems
by Taylor. "The Lay-man's Lamentation" attacks the Act of Uni-
formity of 1662; a poem on Maypole dancing attacks that custom
as being both pagan and Popish; another poem places the respon-
sibility for the London fire of 1666 on the Catholics. Taylor's life-
long aversion to the church of Rome is expressed in hundreds of
lines of verse in his *Metrical History of Christianity,* a poem of
over 21,000 lines, paraphrased mainly from the Latin of the Prot-
estant church history of the sixteenth century known as the Magde-
burg Centuries.[16]

Taylor is at his best, however, when, instead of attacking others,
he is expressing his own doctrine in *Gods Determinations,* and his
spiritual experience of communion with Christ in the *Preparatory
Meditations.* These are the poems which have established Taylor
as America's first major poet and as the last important representa-
tive of the metaphysical school of poetry founded by John Donne
and continued by George Herbert, Richard Crashaw, and Henry
Vaughan. The doctrine which informs Taylor's verse is funda-
mentally Calvinistic. It is in accord with the Westminster Cate-
chism and Confession, Calvin's *Institutes,* the sermons of the
Mather dynasty, and Michael Wigglesworth's *Day of Doom.*
Taylor, in the age of Newton and Locke, still believed in the God
of Calvin—an all powerful sovereign deity who, before the founda-
tions of the world were laid, arbitrarily decided to save and glorify
certain souls (the elect) from the just punishment of original sin.
Christ, God's only begotten son, purchased by his active and pas-

15. See Donald E. Stanford, "The Earliest Poems of Edward Taylor," *Ameri-
can Literature, 32* (1960), 136–51.

16. See Donald E. Stanford, "Edward Taylor's Metrical History of Christian-
ity," *American Literature, 33* (1961), 279–95; *A Transcript of Edward Taylor's
Metrical History of Christianity* (Cleveland, Micro Photo Inc., 1962).

sive obedience, salvation for the elect. In his relationship with man, God operated under two covenants: the covenant of works and the covenant of grace. Under the covenant of works, man was to be saved if he obeyed the law of God. This covenant was broken by the disobedience of Adam and Eve, but God out of his mercy instituted a new covenant, the covenant of grace, which became operative immediately after the fall. Taylor considered himself and his congregation to be under the covenant of grace, by means of which salvation was achieved by faith in Christ, and not by works, this faith being made possible by God's free gift of saving grace. In this relationship between God and man, Taylor emphasized again and again the worthlessness of natural man contrasted with the majesty of God, but he also emphasized the spiritual exaltation of the elect (as contrasted with the misery of the damned) as they contemplate their eventual glorification in heaven. Into the meeting house of frontier Westfield came God himself, calling his humble farmer saints to salvation as Taylor preached in his church foundation sermon in 1679, "A Particular Church is God's House":

> He calls you all to open the doore of your hearts, and he will Come, and banquet therein with you: Hee opens the doore of his House and calls you to his royall Banquet that he hath prepared. He opens the Golden doore of Glory, and calls you, saying, Come up hither! Come up hither! He hath Riches, Honour and Glory, and Eternall Life to bestow upon you: and urges them upon you: Now this is he that is Come and hath set up his Habitation among you . . . Oh then Sing praise to God, Sing praise, Sing praise to our King, Sing praise.[17]

The words of the sermon are echoed seven years later in one of the poet's finest poems, Meditation 1.20:

> God is Gone up with a triumphant Shout
> The Lord with sounding Trumpets melodies.

17. Page 78 of the MS in the Prince Collection.

> Sing Praise, sing Praise, sing Praise, sing Praises out,
>> Unto our King sing praise seraphickwise.
>> Lift up your Heads ye lasting Doore they sing
>> And let the King of Glory Enter in.

They are echoed three years later in the first meditation Taylor wrote after the death of his wife, 1.34:

> Say I am thine, My Lord: Make me thy bell
>> To ring thy Praise. Then Death is mine indeed
> A Hift to Grace, a Spur to Duty; Spell
>> To Fear; a Frost to nip each naughty Weede.
>> A Golden doore to Glory. Oh I'le sing
>> This Triumph o're the Grave! Death where's thy Sting?

The spiritual exaltation arising from his conviction of being one of the elect, of having received saving grace, enables him to conquer his grief and to triumph over death itself.

Taylor's successful communication of this intense sustaining spiritual experience over a period of many years is the great poetic achievement of the *Preparatory Meditations*. The experience was real, and Taylor's expression of it moves us, in spite of frequent and obvious lapses in style and taste. These poems are meditations, spiritual exercises to prepare the minister for the administration of the Lord's Supper—a sacrament which Taylor took very seriously. The Lord's Supper was not a mere commemorative ritual. As Samuel Willard wrote in his *Sacramental Meditations*, a copy of which was in Taylor's library:

> What! nothing but a Ceremony? Nothing but a meer historical Representation of the Death of Christ? Oh no! It is a Sacrament that I am come to the Celebration of.[18]

Taylor believed that during his administration of the Lord's Supper he was experiencing a union with Christ, whose spirit was actually present in the elements. Taylor's attitude was identical with Calvin's as interpreted by J. K. S. Reid: "He puts aside the view that the elements of the Holy Supper are bare signs, figures,

18. *Some Brief Sacramental Meditations Preparatory for Communion at the Great Ordinance of the Supper*, 2d ed. (Boston, 1743), p. 30.

or symbols. He affirms a true and real presence of Christ in the elements."[19] Calvin himself wrote:

> Therefore, if, by the breaking of the bread, the Lord truly represents the participation of his body, it ought not to be doubted that he truly presents and communicates it. If it be true that the visible sign is given to us to seal the donation of the invisible substance, we ought to entertain a confident assurance, that in receiving the symbol of his body, we at the same time truly receive the body itself.[20]

This view of the sacrament inspired a feeling which might not improperly be called mystical. So Cotton Mather wrote:

> I did spend no small part of the Day, in Praeparations, for the *Eucharist;* which on the Morrow, I was to administer. And in the Administration of it, when the Time arrived, I enjoy'd rapturous Communications from Heaven.[21]

To express this mystical feeling of communion with Christ at what Taylor was pleased to call the "royall banquet," Taylor searched his memory for appropriate figures of speech. He sometimes refers to the elements of the sacrament as "dainties"; the bread is of the finest wheat baked by angel's hands; it is heaven's sugar cake; it is soul bread. Closely associated with images derived from the other element of the sacrament, wine, are the many figures of speech comparing saving grace to liquids: clear spring water, aqua vitae, beer, olive oil—liquids which are conveyed from the God-head to the soul by buckets, casks, channels, and golden pipes.

> Oh! Grace, Grace, Grace! this Wealthy Grace doth lay
>   Her Golden Channells from thy Fathers throne,
> Into our Earthen Pitchers to Convay
>   Heavens Aqua Vitae to us for our own.

19. J. K. S. Reid, ed., *Calvin: Theological Treatises* (London, 1954), p. 140.
20. John Allen, trans., *Institutes of the Christian Religion by John Calvin* (2 vols. Philadelphia, 1936), 2, 651; Donald E. Stanford, "Edward Taylor and the Lord's Supper," *American Literature*, 27 (1955), 172–78.
21. "Diary of Cotton Mather," *Collections of the Massachusetts Historical Society*, 7th ser., 7 (1911), part 1, 232–33.

> O! let thy Golden Gutters run into
> My Cup this Liquour till it overflow.   (1.32)

Besides the overwhelming experience of receiving God's grace, the contemplation of the infinite majesty of God is a recurrent theme:

> The Silver Candlesticks of th'heaven bright,
> Bearing the Blazing torches round about
> The Moon and Sun the Worlds bright Candle's light
> These Candles flames thy Glory blows all out.
> These Candle flames lighting the World as tapers,
> Set in thy Sunshine seem like smokie vapors.   (2.101)

In contrast is the worthlessness of sinful natural man. He may be punished by a terrifying deity:

> Proud Sinners now that ore Gods Children crow
> Would if they could creep into Augur holes,
> Thy Lightening Flashing in their faces so,
> Melts down their Courage, terrifies their Souls.   (2.92)

To this deity Taylor prays:

> I'm but a Flesh and Blood bag: Oh! do thou
> Sill, Plate, Ridge, Rib, and Rafter me with Grace.   (1.30)

And because God is capable of infinite love as well as wrath, the poet receives assurance:

> But listen, Soule, here seest thou not a Cheate.
> Earth is not heaven: Faith not Vision. No.
> To see the Love of Christ on thee Compleate
> Would make heavens Rivers of joy, earth overflow.
> This is the Vale of tears, not mount of joyes.
> Some Crystal drops while here may well suffice.   (2.96)

The mystical communion with Christ at the Lord's Supper, the sweetness of saving grace and of the knowledge that one is of the elect, the glory, mercy, and terror of God, the baseness of natural sinful man, and God's hatred of sin are the subjects which dominate the *Preparatory Meditations*.

These meditations are *preparatory,* written to prepare the preacher to administer and to receive the sacrament. The puritans stressed the need of preparation. Thomas Doolittle wrote, in his *Treatise Concerning the Lord's Supper,* "We should approach to the Lord's Supper, after painful and serious Preparation. *No preparation, no participation.*"[22] In his diary, the Reverend William Cooper of Boston wrote "I tried myself by the rules that Mr. Doolittel lays down in his book of the Lords Supper. . . . At noon this day, prostrate on the chamber floor, I renewed my covenant with almighty God. . . . I retir'd for preparatory work. I was very dull and drowsy at first, when I was reading; but the glorious God graciously quickened. me."[23] Taylor also stressed the need for preparation. In a sermon preached in 1693 he devoted several pages to the need of preparing for the "wedding supper."

> Not to prepare is a Contempt of the Invitation; and of the Wedden. It is to fall short of the end of the Invitation to you which is nextly your preparation. Wherefore Consider of this. It is to abide in a Sordid, and filthy, wicked, and Sinfull State. It is to abide without the Wedden Garment, which is a right beautifull Garment. It is therefore to abide graceless, and Damnable. And what Shame is this? Oh! to strive to avoid this Shame by preparing for this Wedden Supper.[24]

"To avoid this Shame by preparing for this Wedden Supper" was the work of meditation. As Louis Martz has pointed out,[25] Taylor was working within a long established meditative tradition which provided him with an orderly procedure for his "preparatory work." The method of meditation which Taylor may have derived from the fourth part of Richard Baxter's *The Saints Everlasting Rest* involved three faculties of the soul: memory, understanding, and will. The subject matter, heavenly doctrine, is supplied by the memory; it is analyzed by the reason or understanding; once understood, the "affections of the Will (the emotions) are aroused

---

22. *A Treatise Concerning the Lord's Supper,* 9th ed. (London, 1675).

23. Page 10 of Cooper's diary which is bound up with his *Beatifick Vision* (Boston, 1734).

24. Sermon 1 of the 1693–94 sermons, pp. 17–18. MS in the Prince Collection.

25. In his Foreword to *The Poems of Edward Taylor,* pp. xxiv ff.

in the following order: Love, Desire, Hope, Courage (Resolution) and Joy." Professor Martz has analyzed Meditation 1.29 as an application of this method. Such a procedure gave the poet a logical order for his poem, whereby he moved from doctrine or image illustrative of doctrine to analysis and understanding to emotional response (usually love, praise, or joy) motivated by the understanding.

Baxter's methods, however, even in his own time did not go unchallenged. On October 16, 1656, John Eliot, the apostle to the Indians, wrote from Roxbury to Richard Baxter expressing his satisfaction upon reading *The Saints Everlasting Rest* and urging Baxter to undertake the composition of a series of practical meditations. Baxter replied, saying that he did not have time to do so and suggesting that there might be some opposition to orderly meditations, just as there was opposition to set prayers.[26] Later, in *The Duty of Heavenly Meditation* (1671) Baxter defends the practice of set and orderly meditation against the attacks of Giles Firmin in *The Real Christian* (1670). Firmin's position seemed to be that meditation is difficult or impossible unless *first* "the affections . . . be much enlarged." "But when we come only to *thinking, meditating,* who will fix this Quicksilver?" "The mind of a man is like a Spannel that runs before his Master." Firmin's argument is that strong emotion must precede meditation. "If the heart be laden with sorrows, or filled with fears, it can fix the mind upon the Objects which cause these fears or sorrows."[27] Firmin argues that feeling precedes form, Baxter that form precedes feeling. Firmin's argument is one aspect of the beginning of the romantic revolt against reason and form. Taylor may have been influenced, to some extent, by this reaction against order and reason in meditative verse; he may have deliberately avoided that closely knit logical development that we find in the best poetry of Donne and Herbert. From Crashaw to Vaughan to Taylor we find increasing looseness of structure and an increasing irrationality which suggests the decadence of the great meditative tradition which achieved its finest expression in the poetry of Donne and Herbert.

---

26. The Baxter-Eliot correspondence is in Dr. Williams' Library, London.
27. Giles Firmin, *The Real Christian* (London, 1670), p. 13.

Taylor sometimes employs the method described by Firmin, beginning his poems with a surge of emotion, then finding in doctrine reasons for the correct adjustment of his feeling. Thus his two meditations on his family losses (1.34 and 2.40) begin with his feeling of grief.

> Under thy Rod, my God, thy smarting Rod
> That hath off broke my James, that Primrose, Why?   (2.40)

Instead of searching the memory for heavenly doctrine, he begins with a surge of grief that has to be controlled during the act of meditation. Similarly, Meditation 2.69 begins with a feeling of melancholy which must be overcome before the poet can undertake "preparatory work":

> Dull! Dull! my Lord, as if I eaten had
> A peck of Melancholy: or my Soule
> Was lockt up by a Poppy key, black sad.

In many of his meditations, then, Taylor sometimes followed the method of Baxter, sometimes that of Firmin.

It need hardly be said that Taylor was thoroughly familiar with the Old and New Testaments not only in various English translations but also in the ancient tongues. Canticles (as he called the Song of Solomon) was his favorite text, and in many of his meditations one need look no further for poetic influence. Taylor, like other Christians of his time, believed that the love song of Solomon was a symbolic type anticipating the spiritual marriage between Christ and the elect. Hence in Taylor's poems, Christ is the bridegroom and the members of the church, singly or collectively, are the bride. Taylor had in his library two sermons by the early church father Origen, untitled in the inventory of his estate, but very likely the two famous homilies on Canticles. He was also probably familiar with Origen's commentary on Canticles in which Origen stresses the union of Christ and the individual soul more than the marriage between Christ and the church as a whole. This mystical tendency in Origen found a response in Taylor's own mystical temperament. Union between himself and Christ is sometimes expressed in the sensuous language of love borrowed from the Song of Solomon, with suggestions perhaps from James Durham's *Clavis Cantici: or, an Exposition of the Song of Solomon* (a copy of which was in Taylor's library) which opens with a long epistle to Margaret Durham in the language of Song of Songs:

> Those love-restings, and reposings on the arme, and on the bosome of one another . . . those feastings, feedings and banquetings on all manner of pleasant fruits, etc. etc.[28]

Thomas Wilson's *A Christian Dictionary* (also in Taylor's library) explains in detail the allegorical meanings of this sensuous love language. For example, the *two breasts* of the bride refer to the Old and New Testaments, the *lips like lilies* refer to the words of Christ, sweet to the elect, and the *navel* refers to the spiritual nourishment conveyed to the children of the church. Every phrase or image taken from Canticles probably had some such allegorical meaning for Taylor.

Analogy deriving from Christian typology, from the belief that persons, objects, events recorded in the Old Testament foreshadowed those in the New Testament is frequently employed by Taylor. Christ, the "anti-type," was preceded by many types, the chief being Adam, Noah, Jonah, the ram sacrificed in place of Isaac, Moses, Aaron, Joseph, and Jacob. Similarly, the Jewish Passover was the "type" of the Lord's Supper, and the Jewish custom of circumcision was the type of Christian Baptism. The first thirty meditations of the second series are devoted to this typology.

Christ was also symbolized by objects such as gold (used as a restorative in seventeenth-century medicine), cordial, the Rose of Sharon, medicine made of the rose, a pearl or other jewel (usually in a cabinet), the brazen serpent of the Old Testament, grapes—particularly the bunch of grapes found by the scouts in Canaan, and wine pressed from the grapes. The red robes of Bozrah foreshadowed the robe of blood that Christ wore at the passion; Joseph's coat represented Christ's flesh, as did the priestly garments of Aaron. The pit in which Joseph was concealed represented hell

28. James Durham, *Clavis Cantici: or an Exposition of the Song of Solomon* (Edinburgh, 1668), "Epistle Dedicatory" (pages unnumbered).

or the grave of Jesus. The whale which swallowed Jonah repre-sented the tomb of Jesus.

This habit of finding meaning in Old Testament events by reading into them analogies with the New Testament was similar to the puritan habit of finding supernatural significance in events and objects from the greatest to the most trivial. Richard Baxter advised his followers:

> You can open your Bibles, and read there of God and of Glory: O learn to open the creatures, and to open the several passages of providence, to reade of God and Glory there. Cer-tainly by such a skilful industrious improvement, we might have a fuller taste of Christ and heaven, in every bit of bread that we eat, and in every draught of Beer that we drink, then most men have in the use of the Sacrament.[29]

This puritan tendency to invest all aspects of life with religious meaning had a profound and often unfortunate effect on Taylor's choice of images. Taylor saw nothing incongruous in using an image from everyday life (such as beer) to illustrate a serious theo-logical idea (such as grace). Taylor had little concern with incon-gruous connotations. He saw resemblances rather than differences.

In seeking a style suitable for expressing his deepest spiritual experiences, Taylor undoubtedly was influenced by the Anglican priest and poet, George Herbert, whose series of poems entitled *The Temple* was highly respected by the puritans in spite of their opposition to Anglicanism. Passages from *The Temple* were quoted with approval by Richard Baxter, a copy of *The Temple* was in the library of Taylor's friend, President Chauncy of Har-vard, and, as we have already noted, Herbert's poems were recom-mended reading for grammar school students in Taylor's native Leicestershire. Taylor adopted for his meditations the six-line stanza of "The Church-porch" which is the introductory poem of *The Temple,* he echoed a number of Herbert's lines and phrases, and, like Herbert, he expressed the metaphysical sensibility of Donne, Crashaw, and Vaughan, the sensibility and style defined by

29. Richard Baxter, *The Saints Everlasting Rest* (London, 1653), part 4, pp. 135–36.

Samuel Johnson in his life of Cowley and by T. S. Eliot in his famous essay "The Metaphysical Poets." Taylor draws his figures of speech from all levels of human experience. His vocabulary includes the specialized diction of the learned theologian, the technical terms of the weaver's trade, the colloquial phrases of the Leicestershire and New England farmer, the poetic diction of Canticles. The rhythms of his verse range from the stately cadence of the King James Bible to the homely expostulations of the semi-literate farmer. The metaphysical poets, of whom Taylor is the last great representative, had an appetite for almost all human experience, and they had the sensibility to express this great range of experience in their verse.

In evaluating Herbert's influence on Taylor, we must also note certain differences between the verse of the Anglican priest and that of the puritan parson. Taylor's meditations are personal and private; they are between himself and God. Many of the poems of *The Temple* are also "private ejaculations" as they are called on the title page of the first edition. However, the "Church-porch," which probably suggested the stanza form of the *Preparatory Meditations,* is frankly didactic: "A verse may finde him, who a sermon flies." This gnomic quality is quite lacking in the *Preparatory Meditations.* Furthermore, there is a difference in tone. Taylor's verse is often crude, rhetorical, powerful, and grim. Herbert's is frequently harmonious, subtle, and subdued. Taylor is obsessed with the thought of original sin under which the whole creation groans. Herbert also believes in original sin, of course, but he never approaches the morbid preoccupation of Taylor. Herbert had the flexible mind of an Anglican priest whose early training and temperament would have fitted him to become a courtier; Taylor had the rigid mind of a puritan parson who chose to live in the wilderness rather than submit to the Anglican Act of Uniformity. The harshness and the isolation of frontier life probably increased rather than diminished Taylor's stubborn dogmatism.

Taylor was sensitive to the dangers of religious beliefs which might threaten the New England way of Calvinistic Congregationalism. His verses and his sermons are loaded with attacks on Anglicanism, Catholicism, Presbyterianism, Quakerism, Sherlockism, Sabellianism, Socinianism, and Stoddardeanism, to name a few of the "heresies" as Taylor called them. Sherlockism, Sabellianism and Socinianism over-emphasized (according to Taylor's view) either Christ's humanity or his divinity. In Meditations 33–56 of the second series, Taylor expounds the doctrine of "Theanthropie," that Christ is God-Man, with distinct yet unified human and divine natures. The nature of Christ's person was also the subject of the group of fourteen sermons entitled *Christographia* which Taylor preached at Westfield from 1701 to 1703.

The "heresy" which moved Taylor's most prolonged disapproval was one which developed close to home in the neighboring town of Northampton where Solomon Stoddard, the grandfather of Jonathan Edwards, was preaching and practicing the doctrine that the Lord's Supper was a regenerating ordinance, and that therefore all church members not leading scandalous lives should be admitted to it, even though they might consider themselves to be in an unregenerate condition. Taylor considered Stoddardeanism, as it was called, to be a degradation of the sacrament. He argued that the Lord's Supper should be restricted to regenerate members only, that is to those who felt themselves to be in a state of grace. Taylor continuously attacked Stoddard over a period of many years, beginning with his foundation sermon of 1679, which appears to contain oblique references to Stoddard's intentions, to 1720 when Stephen Williams reported that Taylor "preached from Hosea 9.12. Twas a good Sermon . . . He seemed too sharp (in my apprehension) against Some that hold that persons may lawfully wait upon Christ in the ordinance of the Supper if they have not Grace."[30] Taylor's long crusade included a letter to Stoddard (1688), a series of eight sermons on the Lord's Supper (1693–94), "Animadversions" (covering thirty-four pages of manuscript in answer to one of Stoddard's sermons), and a long tract entitled *The Appeal Tried* (c. 1709–10) in answer to Stoddard's *An Appeal to the Learned* (1709).[31] Taylor also attacked the Northampton heresy in poetry. Meditations 102–111, written from

30. Medlicott, "Notes," 271.

31. See Norman Grabo, *Edward Taylor* (New York, 1961), pp. 31–39; " 'The Appeale Tried': Another Edward Taylor Manuscript," *American Literature, 34* (1962), 394–400.

June 10, 1711 to December 7, 1712, explicate Taylor's doctrine of the Lord's Supper and vigorously attack the Catholic belief in transubstantiation, the Lutheran belief in consubstantiation, and Stoddardeanism. Stoddard, in administering the sacrament to the unregenerate, is compared with a child who feeds oats to his wooden horse:

> The Dead don't eate, Though Folly childish dotes
> In th'Child that gives his Hobby horses oates.

Gods Determinations has affinities with John Bunyan's *The Holy War* (1682), Michael Wigglesworth's *The Day of Doom* (1662), and Lorenzo Scupoli's *The Spiritual Conflict* (1589, translated into English 1613). *The Holy War* and Taylor's poem present the combat between God (or Christ) and the Devil for the souls of men; both works are Calvinistic; both are allegorical. Because the date of Taylor's poem cannot be established, the influence of Bunyan is doubtful. *The Day of Doom,* however, was most certainly in Taylor's mind as he composed his own poem on the destiny of man. (His wife used to recite Wigglesworth's verses to him.) Taylor's description of Christ, the Devil, and hell may have been influenced by Wigglesworth. *The Spiritual Conflict,* which directly or indirectly influenced Donne, Herbert, and Marvell, defines the conflict as the conquest of the self, as a battle between the higher and the lower will:

> Hereupon all our spiritual Battell principally consisteth in this, that this superior will being placed as in the midst between the divine wil, which stands above, and the inferior, which is that of the sence, continually assaulted by the one and the other, whilst either of these assaieth to draw it and make it subject, and obedient unto them.

The central idea of *The Spiritual Conflict* is the necessity of overcoming the passions, "but if the wil have once placed th'affection, the understanding then, doth not discover the thing as it is." The passions darken the understanding and the understanding then presents the object in false colors to the will, which is brought to love it more ardently. In Shakespeare's phrase "Reason panders will." The same notions are evident in Taylor's lines:

> The Understandings dark, and therefore Will
> Account of Ill for Good, and Good for ill.
> As to a Purblinde man men oft appeare
> Like Walking Trees within the Hemisphere.
> So in the judgment Carnall things Excell:
> Pleasures and Profits beare away the Bell.
> The Will is hereupon perverted so,
> It laquyes after ill, doth good foregoe.
> The Reasonable Soule doth much delight
> A Pickpack t'ride o'th'Sensuall Appitite.

This psychological and theological conflict is externalized and described in terms of war. William Ames in his *Conscience with the Power and Cases thereof* (a copy of which was in Taylor's library) states that temptations should be considered a battle between the Devil and the castle of man's soul. This is the battle of *Gods Determinations*. Battle imagery and scenes came naturally to the puritan poet. He was born in the midst of the turmoil of the Civil War, and as he grew up he probably heard many stories of armed conflict. He came to maturity during the militant puritanism of Cromwell's regime, and the foundation of his church in Westfield was postponed by the turmoil of King Philip's War. Furthermore, the church embattled, the Church Militant, was central to all puritan thinking. "To hew Agag in pieces before the Lord is to his mind not the least attractive of religious duties"[32] was truly said of Edward Johnson, the author of *Wonder-Working Providence*. A chapter of this book bears the title "How the People of Christ ought to behave themselves in War-like Discipline": "See then," says Johnson, "you store yourselves with all sorts of weapons for war, furbish up your Swords, Rapiers, and all other piercing weapons. As for great Artillery, seeing present meanes falls short, waite on the Lord Christ, and hee will stir up friends to provide for you: and in the meane time spare not to lay

32. J. Franklin Jameson, ed., *Johnson's Wonder-Working Providence 1628–1651* (New York, 1952), p. 16.

out your coyne for Powder, Bullets, Match, Armes of all sorts, and all kinde of Instruments for War."[33] Johnson frequently compares the puritans of New England to that other embattled and chosen people, the Israelites, and the zest for battle is one aspect of the Hebraism of our New England ancestors. In describing the "Elects Combat," then, Taylor is not only writing from experiences close to him in England and New England, but also out of that puritan obsession with the notion of the battle between the chosen people of God and the Devil, a notion which was fostered in the Bay Colony by the Mathers and others to whom it seemed that the climax of the drama of salvation was being enacted between the dark forces of the Devil and the wilderness on the one hand and the small body of Saints on the other—with the final scene, the Judgment Day, only a few years in the future. "His Coming in Flaming Fire, is not far off."[34]

Much of *Gods Determinations* is in dramatic dialogue, a form which came naturally to Taylor after his probable study in grammar school of Latin *Colloquies*, of the *Terentius Christianus* of Cornelius Schonaeus which are a collection of plays in Latin based on Bible stories, the *Dialogues* of Sebastien Castellion based on scripture, and the dialogues of the Calvinist Maturinus Corderius on Christian doctrine.[35] The literature of religious controversy of the seventeenth century was frequently written in verse dialogue. Taylor copied into his commonplace book a "play," *The Recantation of a Penitent Proteus* by Robert Wild which had been acted at St. Mary's in Cambridge and at St. Paul's in London, and early in his career he wrote "A Dialogue between the Writer and a Maypole Dresser," "An Answer to a Popish Pamphlet" (in dialogue), and "The Lay-mans Lamentation," which is a dialogue between a prelate and a "poor professour."[36] Also in his youth he may have seen the Corpus Christi procession near Coventry and have thus become interested in the medieval drama. In the dialogue between Justice and Mercy in Taylor's poem, there may be echoes of the medieval debate of the heavenly graces, and the

33. Ibid., p. 11.
34. Increase Mather, *The Glorious Throne* (Boston, 1702), p. 118.
35. Watson, *English Grammar Schools*, pp. 315–39.
36. Stanford, "Earliest Poems of Edward Taylor," pp. 136–51.

struggle of Christ and Satan for the soul of man in *Gods Determinations* may have been influenced by the morality conflicts of vices and virtues.[37]

Taylor's drama of salvation depicts in Calvinistic terms the ways of God in bringing the elect to glory. At the beginning of the poem all mankind are divided into two groups—the damned who go to hell and the elect who eventually ride to glory in God's coach. The elect are subdivided into the Saints (those who have sinned little and who receive grace quickly and easily) and the Converts (those who come to Christ through varying degrees of difficulty and who eventually become Saints). These Converts are divided into three ranks. The first rank is captured by God's Mercy; the second and third ranks are captured, after considerable difficulty, by God's Justice. "The Preface," which contains some of Taylor's best and most famous poetry, describes the creation of the universe out of nothing by an infinite God. The universe is maintained by the sustaining presence of God, who can return it to nothing in an instant. The insignificance of man, his corruption by original sin, and, conversely, the glory and the terror of God are emphasized. The entire passage reverberates with echoes of Job 38: 4–8 "Who laid the corner stone thereof; when the morning stars sang together, and all the sons of God sang for joy? Or who shut up the sea with doors?"

The action of the entire poem may be summarized as follows. As a result of original sin, man finds God his enemy. Justice and Mercy, personified attributes of God, debate man's destiny. They decide that Mercy, incarnate in Christ, shall satisfy Justice by suffering as scapegoat for the sins of men. The elect shall then be saved by Mercy's free gift of inherent grace and saving faith. Justice too will continue to aid in the salvation of the elect by frequent reminders of the danger of hell fire.

The rest of the poem depicts the working out of God's decrees. A feast is prepared for the sinful sons of men and all are called to it, but only those who in addition to the general call receive also the special call accept the invitation. The rest refuse and are con-

37. Nathalia Wright, "The Morality Tradition in the Poetry of Edward Taylor," *American Literature, 18* (1946), 1–17.

demned, and thus "All mankinde splits in a Dicotomy." Those
chosen by God's "Selecting Love" are brought to salvation in
various ways. Some find their hearts softened quickly by recogni-
tion of God's infinite Mercy. Others, holding out against Mercy's
terms, sorely tempted by Satan, are eventually subdued by the
threats of Justice, and, after receiving comfort and assurance from
one of the Saints, throw themselves on God's Mercy. Satan's
temptations of the second and third ranks are presented with con-
siderable subtlety by means of arguments suggested, probably, by
the spiritual difficulties of members of Taylor's congregation as
well as by Taylor's reading in such books as William Ames' *Cases
of Conscience*. With all difficulties finally overcome, God's pre-
destined elect sing hymns as they ride to glory in God's coach.

A series of eight numbered poems on "occurants" i.e. a rain-
storm, a fly caught in a spider's net, a wasp numbed with cold,
his wife spinning (two poems), the death of children, the act of
lighting a fire by flint and steel, and a flood illustrate Taylor's
habit of investing events, from the most trivial to the most signifi-
cant, with religious significance. In "[When] Let by rain" the
decision of whether or not to make a journey during a rainstorm
suggests the difficulties of a more important decision concerning
his calling as a preacher. It may have been written in 1671 when
he was hesitating about accepting the call to Westfield, or in 1673
when he was perhaps considering giving up his ministry. In "Upon
a Spider Catching a Fly," the spider is a symbol of the Devil and
the insects he is snaring are symbols of men who may be saved
only if by the grace of God the web is broken. The charming
"Upon a Wasp Child with Cold" describes a wasp numbed by the
northern blast being warmed back to life by the sun, and ends
with the obvious parallel of the poet being saved in a similar
fashion by God. In the two poems on "Huswifery," the arts of
spinning and weaving provide the basic images for a prayer to
God to make the poet his "spinning wheel" and his "loom," the
resulting cloth to be used to adorn him and to glorify God. The
moving lament for his dead children "Upon Wedlock and Death
of Children" ends on a triumphant note, with the conviction that
they have gone to heaven to the glory of themselves, himself and

God: "I piecemeale pass to Glory bright in them." "The Ebb and Flow" expresses one of Taylor's recurrent themes, the fear that his heart has grown cold toward God, and the hope that, through God's grace, his affections will be warmed. In "Upon the Sweeping Flood" Taylor indulges in a kind of speculation habitual with himself and his puritan contemporaries, the relationship between a human event and a natural event. The poet suggests that the sin of carnal love "physicked" the heavens so that they poured out a cloudburst on the sinners' "lofty heads."

These "occurants" are charming (and sometimes puzzling) minor poems. There are, of course, passages of much greater poetry in *Gods Determinations*. Satan's accusations and his "Sophestry" are expressed with considerable verve and with psychological and theological subtlety. "Christ's Reply"—"I am a Captain to your Will"—is a fine statement in the plain style of the perseverance of the saints, of God's predestined elect:

> You found me Gracious, so shall still,
> Whilst that my Will is your Design.

But it is to the *Preparatory Meditations* that we turn to find the poems on which Taylor's eventual reputation will rest. The quiet Herbertian piety of Meditation 1.6, the spiritual exaltation of Meditation 1.20, the powerful statements of the atonement and the victory over death in Meditation 2.112, will remain permanent contributions to our heritage of devotional poetry. There is nothing to equal the *Preparatory Meditations* in American poetry until the time of Bryant, and they are not unworthy of the metaphysical school of which they are the last representatives.

DONALD E. STANFORD

Baton Rouge, Louisiana
January 1963

Prologue

Lord, Can a Crumb of Dust the Earth outweigh,
  Outmatch all mountains, nay the Chrystall Sky?
Imbosom in't designs that shall Display
  And trace into the Boundless Deity?
  Yea hand a Pen whose moysture doth guild ore   5
  Eternall Glory with a glorious glore.

If it its Pen had of an Angels Quill,
  And Sharpend on a Pretious Stone ground tite,
And dipt in Liquid Gold, and mov'de by Skill
  In Christall leaves should golden Letters write   10
  It would but blot and blur yea jag, and jar
  Unless thou mak'st the Pen, and Scribener.

I am this Crumb of Dust which is design'd
  To make my Pen unto thy Praise alone,
And my dull Phancy I would gladly grinde   15
  Unto an Edge on Zions Pretious Stone.
  And Write in Liquid Gold upon thy Name
  My Letters till thy glory forth doth flame.

Let not th'attempts breake down my Dust I pray
  Nor laugh thou them to scorn but pardon give.   20
Inspire this Crumb of Dust till it display
  Thy Glory through't: and then thy dust shall live.
  Its failings then thou'lt overlook I trust,
  They being Slips slipt from thy Crumb of Dust.

Thy Crumb of Dust breaths two words from its breast,   25
  That thou wilt guide its pen to write aright
To Prove thou art, and that thou art the best
  And shew thy Properties to shine most bright.
  And then thy Works will shine as flowers on Stems
  Or as in Jewellary Shops, do jems.   30

1 *outweigh*,] PW outweigh   10 *In Christall leaves*] orig: And golden letters
in   13 *which*] orig: and   29 *Works will shine as flowers on Stems*] orig:
Glorious Works as flowers on Stems

1

Preparatory Meditations before my
Approach to the Lords Supper. Chiefly
upon the Doctrin preached upon
the Day of administration

1. Meditation

Westfield 23. 5m [July] *1682*. Pub. ETP, W.

What Love is this of thine, that Cannot bee
    In thine Infinity, O Lord, Confinde,
Unless it in thy very Person see,
    Infinity, and Finity Conjoyn'd?
    What hath thy Godhead, as not satisfide   5
    Marri'de our Manhood, making it its Bride?

Oh, Matchless Love! filling Heaven to the brim!
    O're running it: all running o're beside
This World! Nay Overflowing Hell; wherein
    For thine Elect, there rose a mighty Tide!   10
    That there our Veans might through thy Person bleed,
    To quench those flames, that else would on us feed.

Oh! that thy Love might overflow my Heart!
    To fire the same with Love: for Love I would.
But oh! my streight'ned Breast! my Lifeless Sparke!   15
    My Fireless Flame! What Chilly Love, and Cold?
    In measure small! In Manner Chilly! See.
    Lord blow the Coal: Thy Love Enflame in mee.

2. Meditation on Can. 1.3. Thy Name is an Ointment poured out.

12. 9m [Nov.] *1682*. Pub. PET.

My Dear, Deare, Lord I do thee Saviour Call:
    Thou in my very Soul art, as I Deem,

At the top of the page in PW: "Sacramental Meditations for 35 y. from 1682 to 1725. Preparatory Meditations before my Approach to the Lords Supper. Chiefly upon the Doctrin preached upon the Day of administration." The original date *1717* has been crossed out and changed to "1725." The figure *35* has not been corrected. On the same page: "By Rev. Edward Taylor A.M. Attest Ezra Stiles his Grandson 1786." The words "Sacramental Meditations for 35 y. from 1682 to 1717" are in the hand of Ezra Stiles. The correction "1725" is in another hand.   Med. *2, 2 Soul art, as I Deem,*] orig: Soul indeed art I Deem,

Soe High, not High enough, Soe Great; too small:
   Soe Deare, not Dear enough in my esteem.
Soe Noble, yet So Base: too Low; too Tall: 5
   Thou Full, and Empty art: Nothing, yet ALL.

A Precious Pearle, above all price dost 'bide.
   Rubies no Rubies are at all to thee.
Blushes of burnisht Glory Sparkling Slide
   From every Square in various Colour'd glee   10
   Nay Life itselfe in Sparkling Spangles Choice.
   A Precious Pearle thou art above all price.

Oh! that my Soul, Heavens Workmanship (within
   My Wicker'd Cage,) that Bird of Paradise
Inlin'de with Glorious Grace up to the brim   15
   Might be thy Cabbinet, oh Pearle of Price.
   Oh! let thy Pearle, Lord, Cabbinet in mee.
   I'st then be rich! nay rich enough for thee.

My Heart, oh Lord, for thy Pomander gain.
   Be thou thyselfe my sweet Perfume therein.   20
Make it thy Box, and let thy Pretious Name
   My Pretious Ointment be emboxt therein.
   If I thy box and thou my Ointment bee
   I shall be sweet, nay, sweet enough for thee.

Enough! Enough! oh! let me eat my Word.   25
   For if Accounts be ballanc'd any way,
Can my poore Eggeshell ever be an Hoard,
   Of Excellence enough for thee? Nay: nay.
   Yet may I Purse, and thou my Mony bee.
   I have enough. Enough in having thee.   30

---

3 *Soe High*] orig: Too high   *Soe Great*] orig: too Great   4 *Soe*] orig: Too
in] orig: to   23 *thy box*] Z the box   PW orig: the box   *my Ointment*] Z the
Ointment   27 *an Hoard*] Z a Hord   29 *my Mony*] Z the Money

17–18: Cf. Herbert's "To All Angels and Saints," line 14: "Thou art the
cabinet where the jewell lay." Cf. also Herbert's "Ungratefulness," lines 7–12.
19–20: Herbert's "Odour" describes the sweetness of Christ's name "My
Master" in terms of perfumes. This poem may be the origin of Taylor's many
figures involving perfumes.

3. Meditation. Can. 1.3. Thy Good Ointment

11. 12m [Feb.] *1682.* Pub. ETG.

How sweet a Lord is mine? If any should
    Guarded, Engarden'd, nay, Imbosomd bee
In reechs of Odours, Gales of Spices, Folds
      Of Aromaticks, Oh! how sweet was hee?
      He would be sweet, and yet his sweetest Wave   5
      Compar'de to thee my Lord, no Sweet would have.

A Box of Ointments, broke; sweetness most sweet.
    A surge of spices: Odours Common Wealth,
A Pillar of Perfume: a steaming Reech
      Of Aromatick Clouds: All Saving Health.   10
      Sweetness itselfe thou art: And I presume
      In Calling of thee Sweet, who art Perfume.

But Woe is mee! who have so quick a Sent
    To Catch perfumes pufft out from Pincks, and Roses
And other Muscadalls, as they get Vent,   15
      Out of their Mothers Wombs to bob our noses.
      And yet thy sweet perfume doth seldom latch
      My Lord, within my Mammulary Catch.

Am I denos'de? or doth the Worlds ill sents
    Engarison my nosthrills narrow bore?   20
Or is my smell lost in these Damps it Vents?
      And shall I never finde it any more?
      Or is it like the Hawks, or Hownds whose breed
      Take stincking Carrion for Perfume indeed?

4 *was hee*] Z were hee   7 *Ointments*] Z Ointment   19 *denos'de*] Z benosde
Worlds ill sents] Z world with sents   20 *Engarison*] Z Ingarrison'd
narrow bore] Z or bore   21 *it Vents*] Z the vents   24 *Take*] Z Count

18 ff.: Johnson suggests (ETG, p. 285) that Taylor uses *mammulary*
throughout the poem to refer to the olfactory system, but there is no evi-
dence for a meaning other than the normal 'nipples' or 'breasts.'

This is my Case. All things smell sweet to mee: 25
    Except thy sweetness, Lord. Expell these damps.
Breake up this Garison: and let me see
    Thy Aromaticks pitching in these Camps.
    Oh! let the Clouds of thy sweet Vapours rise,
    And both my Mammularies Circumcise.   30

Shall Spirits thus my Mammularies suck?
    (As Witches Elves their teats,) and draw from thee
My Dear, Dear Spirit after fumes of muck?
    Be Dunghill Damps more sweet than Graces bee?
    Lord, clear these Caves. These Passes take, and keep.   35
    And in these Quarters lodge thy Odours sweet.

Lord, breake thy Box of Ointment on my Head;
    Let thy sweet Powder powder all my hair:
My Spirits let with thy perfumes be fed
    And make thy Odours, Lord, my nosthrills fare.   40
    My Soule shall in thy sweets then soar to thee:
    I'le be thy Love, thou my sweet Lord shalt bee.

The Experience.

Undated. Pub. ETP, *W*.

Oh! that I alwayes breath'd in such an aire,
    As I suckt in, feeding on sweet Content!
Disht up unto my Soul ev'n in that pray're
    Pour'de out to God over last Sacrament.
    What Beam of Light wrapt up my sight to finde   5
    Me neerer God than ere Came in my minde?

Most strange it was! But yet more strange that shine
    Which filld my Soul then to the brim to spy
My Nature with thy Nature all Divine
    Together joyn'd in Him thats Thou, and I.   10

30 *Mammularies*] Z Mammilaries   31 *Mammularies*] Z Mammilaries
35 *These*] PW these   38 *all*] Z well   40 *And make thy Odours, Lord,*] Z Thine
Odors set to be   42 *I'le*] Z I'st   8 *spy*] Z see   10 *I*] Z me

Flesh of my Flesh, Bone of my Bone. There's run
  Thy Godhead, and my Manhood in thy Son.

Oh! that that Flame which thou didst on me Cast
  Might me enflame, and Lighten ery where.
Then Heaven to me would be less at last   15
    So much of heaven I should have while here.
    Oh! Sweet though Short! Ile not forget the same.
    My neerness, Lord, to thee did me Enflame.

I'le Claim my Right: Give place, ye Angells Bright.
  Ye further from the Godhead stande than I.   20
My Nature is your Lord; and doth Unite
    Better than Yours unto the Deity.
    Gods Throne is first and mine is next: to you
    Onely the place of Waiting-men is due.

Oh! that my Heart, thy Golden Harp might bee   25
  Well tun'd by Glorious Grace, that e'ry string
Screw'd to the highest pitch, might unto thee
    All Praises wrapt in sweetest Musick bring.
    I praise thee, Lord, and better praise thee would
    If what I had, my heart might ever hold.   30

The Return.

Undated.

Inamoring Rayes, thy Sparkles, Pearle of Price
  Impearld with Choisest Gems, their beams Display
Impoysoning Sin, Guilding my Soule with Choice
    Rich Grace, thy Image bright, making me pray,
    Oh! that thou Wast on Earth below with mee   5
    Or that I was in Heaven above with thee.

11 *There's*] PW there's   15 *Heaven to me would be*] Z heaven would be heaven
less   *less at last*] Z to me at last   26 *tun'd*] Z tuned   *Glorious*] Z thy
27 *to the highest*] Z up to th'highest   28 *Praises wrapt in*] Z praise rapt up in
PW orig: Praises wrapt up in   30 *might*] Z did   4 *thy*] Z thine

Thy Humane Frame, with Beauty Dapled, and
    In Beds of Graces pald with golden layes,
Lockt to thy Holy Essence by thy hand,
      Yields Glances that enflame my Soul, that sayes   10
      Oh! that thou wast on Earth below with mee!
      Or that I was in Heaven above with thee.

All Love in God, and's Properties Divine
    Enam'led are in thee: thy Beauties Blaze
Attracts my Souls Choice golden Wyer to twine   15
      About thy Rose-sweet selfe. And therefore prayes
      Oh! that thou wast on Earth below with mee!
      Or, that I was in Heaven above with thee.

A Magazeen of Love: Bright Glories blaze:
    Thy Shine fills Heaven with Glory; Smile Convayes   20
Heavens Glory in my Soule, which it doth glaze
      All ore with amoring Glory; that she sayes,
      Oh! that thou wast on Earth below with mee!
      Or, that I was in Heaven above with thee!

Heavens Golden Spout thou art where Grace most Choice   25
    Comes Spouting down from God to man of Clay.
A Golden Stepping Stone to Paradise
    A Golden Ladder into Heaven! I'l pray
    Oh! that thou wast on Earth below with mee
    Or that I was in Heaven above with thee.   30

Thy Service is my Freedom Pleasure, Joy,
    Delight, Bliss, Glory, Heaven on Earth, my Stay,
In Gleams of Glory thee to glorify.
      But oh! my Dross and Lets. Wherefore I say
      Oh! that thou wast on Earth below with mee: 35
      Or that I was in Heaven above with thee.

If off as Offall I be put, if I
    Out of thy Vineyard Work be put away:
Life would be Death: my Soule would Coffin'd ly,
    Within my Body; and no longer pray   40

7 *with*] PW whith   16 *And*] PW and   38 *Out of*] PW Outed

Oh! that thou wast on Earth below with mee:
But that I was in Heaven above with thee.

But I've thy Pleasant Pleasant Presence had
    In Word, Pray're, Ordinances, Duties; nay,
And in thy Graces, making me full Glad,   45
        In Faith, Hope, Charity, that I do say,
        That thou hast been on Earth below with mee.
        And I shall be in Heaven above with thee.

Be thou Musician, Lord, Let me be made
    The well tun'de Instrument thou dost assume.   50
And let thy Glory be my Musick plaide.
        Then let thy Spirit keepe my Strings in tune,
        Whilst thou art here on Earth below with mee
        Till I sing Praise in Heaven above with thee.

4. Meditation. Cant. 2.1. I am the Rose of Sharon.

22. 2m [April] *1683.*

My Silver Chest a Sparke of Love up locks:
    And out will let it when I can't well Use.
The gawdy World me Courts t'unlock the Box,
        A motion makes, where Love may pick and choose.
        Her Downy Bosom opes, that pedlars Stall,   5
        Of Wealth, Sports, Honours, Beauty, slickt up all.

Love pausing on't, these Clayey Faces she
    Disdains to Court; but Pilgrims life designs,
And Walkes in Gilliads Land, and there doth see
        The Rose of Sharon which with Beauty shines.   10
        Her Chest Unlocks; the Sparke of Love out breaths
        To Court this Rose: and lodgeth in its leaves.

53 *Whilst*] Z While   PW orig: While   54 *with*] Z to   2 *out will let it when I
can't well Use*] Z will bring't out when I it well can use   3 *gawdy*] Z gilded
t'unlock] Z t'unscrew   4 *A*] Z And   7 *on't*] Z here   11 *Her Chest*] Z The
Chest 12 *lodgeth*] Z lodges

No flower in Garzia Horti shines like this:
    No Beauty sweet in all the World so Choice:
It is the Rose of Sharon sweet, that is   15
    The Fairest Rose that Grows in Paradise.
    Blushes of Beauty bright, Pure White, and Red
    In Sweats of Glory on Each Leafe doth bed.

Lord lead me into this sweet Rosy Bower:
    Oh! Lodge my Soul in this Sweet Rosy bed: 20
Array my Soul with this sweet Sharon flower:
    Perfume me with the Odours it doth shed.
    Wealth, Pleasure, Beauty Spirituall will line
    My pretious Soul, if Sharons Rose be mine.

The Blood Red Pretious Syrup of this Rose   25
    Doth all Catholicons excell what ere.
Ill Humours all that do the Soule inclose
    When rightly usd, it purgeth out most clear.
    Lord purge my Soul with this Choice Syrup, and
    Chase all thine Enemies out of my land.   30

The Rosy Oyle, from Sharons Rose extract
    Better than Palma Christi far is found.
Its Gilliads Balm for Conscience when she's wrackt
    Unguent Apostolorum for each Wound.
    Let me thy Patient, thou my Surgeon bee.   35
    Lord, with thy Oyle of Roses Supple mee.

18 *on*] orig: of   23 *line*] orig: live
24 *pretious*] Z Deare deare   27 *Soule inclose*] Z Soul up grace [?] inclose
28 *usd*] Z tooke   *most*] Z full   30 *my land*] Z that Land
land] orig: hand   33 *when she's wrackt*] Z Pains, exact
34 *each*] Z its   PW orig: all   36 *thy*] Z this

    25 ff.: The rose as a symbol of Christ, of Christ's blood, and of Christ's
grace is common in Christian typology. The notion of Christ's blood as a
medicine or cordial is also common. The rose and other flowers were used as
purges and medicines in the seventeenth century. For the church considered
as a rose see Herbert's "Church-rents and schismes." For the rose and other
flowers as purges see Herbert's "The Rose," line 18; "Providence," line 78;
"Life," line 15. For Christ's blood or Christ's grace considered as a cordial
see Herbert's "The Sacrifice," line 159; "The Glance," line 6; "Whitsunday,"
line 18; "The Odour," line 9; "Sighs and Groans," line 28.

No Flower there is in Paradise that grows
    Whose Virtues Can Consumptive Souls restore
But Shugar of Roses made of Sharons Rose
    When Dayly usd, doth never fail to Cure.   40
    Lord let my Dwindling Soul be dayly fed
    With Sugar of Sharons Rose, its dayly Bread.

God Chymist is, doth Sharons Rose distill.
    Oh! Choice Rose Water! Swim my Soul herein.
Let Conscience bibble in it with her Bill.   45
    Its Cordiall, ease doth Heart burns Causd by Sin.
    Oyle, Syrup, Sugar, and Rose Water such.
    Lord, give, give, give; I cannot have too much.

But, oh! alas! that such should be my need
    That this Brave Flower must Pluckt, stampt, squeezed bee,
And boyld up in its Blood, its Spirits sheed,   51
    To make a Physick sweet, sure, safe for mee.
    But yet this mangled Rose rose up again
    And in its pristine glory, doth remain.

All Sweets, and Beauties of all Flowers appeare   55
    In Sharons Rose, whose Glorious Leaves out vie
In Vertue, Beauty, Sweetness, Glory Cleare,
    The Spangled Leaves of Heavens cleare Chrystall Sky.
    Thou Rose of Heaven, Glory's Blossom Cleare
    Open thy Rosie Leaves, and lodge mee there.   60

My Dear-Sweet Lord, shall I thy Glory meet
    Lodg'd in a Rose, that out a sweet Breath breaths.
What is my way to Glory made thus sweet,
    Strewd all along with Sharons Rosy Leaves.
    I'le walk this Rosy Path: World fawn, or frown   65
    And Sharons Rose shall be my Rose, and Crown.

37 *there is in Paradise*] Z in Paradise there is
40 *usd, doth never fail*] Z usen never fails
42 *its*] Z as   46 *ease doth*] Z eases   50 *must*] Z should   53 *Rose*] orig: flower
rose up again] Z rose after this   54 *And in its pristine*] Z In'ts Pristine
doth remain] Z beautifull it is   56 *Glorious*] Z beautious
57 *Beauty, Sweetness, Glory*] Z glory, Sweetness, breadth, and Beauty
Cleare,] PW Cleare.   58 *cleare*] Z broad   59 *Blossom Cleare*] Z blossom so
cleare   61 *Glory*] Z beauty   63 *Glory*] Z heaven

The Reflexion.

Undated. Pub. ETP, *W*.

Lord, art thou at the Table Head above
    Meat, Med'cine, sweetness, sparkling Beautys to
Enamour Souls with Flaming Flakes of Love,
    And not my Trencher, nor my Cup o'reflow?
    Be n't I a bidden Guest? Oh! sweat mine Eye.   5
    Oreflow with Teares: Oh! draw thy fountains dry.

Shall I not smell thy sweet, oh! Sharons Rose?
    Shall not mine Eye salute thy Beauty? Why?
Shall thy sweet leaves their Beautious sweets upclose?
    As halfe ashamde my sight should on them ly?   10
    Woe's me! for this my sighs shall be in grain
    Offer'd on Sorrows Altar for the same.

Had not my Soule's thy Conduit, Pipes stopt bin
    With mud, what Ravishment would'st thou Convay?
Let Graces Golden Spade dig till the Spring   15
    Of tears arise, and cleare this filth away.
    Lord, let thy spirit raise my sighings till
    These Pipes my soule do with thy sweetness fill.

Earth once was Paradise of Heaven below
    Till inkefac'd sin had it with poyson stockt   20
And Chast this Paradise away into
    Heav'ns upmost Loft, and it in Glory Lockt.
    But thou, sweet Lord, hast with thy golden Key
    Unlockt the Doore, and made, a golden day.

Once at thy Feast, I saw thee Pearle-like stand   25
    'Tween Heaven, and Earth where Heavens Bright glory all

2 *Beautys*] Z beauty
to] orig: show   5 *Guest*] PW Guess   6 *with Teares: Oh! draw thy fountains dry.*] Z my Cup with tears *** pass by?   7 *smell thy sweet, oh!*] Z catch the sweet of   8 *not mine Eye salute thy Beauty? Why?*] Z I not greet thy Beauty with mine eye   9 *Beautious sweets*] Z Beauty bright   23 *hast*] Z do
24 *Unlockt*] PW Unlock   *made*] Z make   25 *Pearle-like*] PW Pearle like

In streams fell on thee, as a floodgate and,
    Like Sun Beams through thee on the World to Fall.
    Oh! sugar sweet then! my Deare sweet Lord, I see
    Saints Heavens-lost Happiness restor'd by thee.   30

Shall Heaven, and Earth's bright Glory all up lie
    Like Sun Beams bundled in the sun, in thee?
Dost thou sit Rose at Table Head, where I
    Do sit, and Carv'st no morsell sweet for mee?
    So much before, so little now! Sprindge, Lord,   35
    Thy Rosie Leaves, and me their Glee afford.

Shall not thy Rose my Garden fresh perfume?
    Shall not thy Beauty my dull Heart assaile?
Shall not thy golden gleams run through this gloom?
    Shall my black Velvet Mask thy fair Face Vaile?   40
    Pass o're my Faults: shine forth, bright sun: arise
    Enthrone thy Rosy-selfe within mine Eyes.

5. Meditation. Cant. 2.1. The Lilly of
the Vallies.

    2.7m [Sept.] *1683.*

My Blessed Lord, art thou a Lilly Flower?
    Oh! that my Soul thy Garden were, that so
Thy bowing Head root in my Heart, and poure
    Might of its Seeds, that they therein might grow.
    Be thou my Lilly, make thou me thy knot:
    Be thou my Flowers, I'le be thy Flower Pot.   5

My barren heart thy Fruitfull Vally make:
    Be thou my Lilly floeurishing in mee:

37 *my*] orig: thy   40 *fair Face Vaile*] Z face up vale   4 *Seeds, that they therein might*] Z Lillie *** therein to

Oh Lilly of the Vallies. For thy sake,
    Let me thy Vally, thou my Lilly bee.   10
    Then nothing shall me of thyselfe bereave.
    Thou must not me, or must thy Vally leave.

How shall my Vallie's Spangling Glory spred,
    Thou Lilly of the Vallies Spangling
There springing up? Upon thy bowing Head   15
    All Heavens bright Glory hangeth dangling.
    My Vally then with Blissfull Beams shali shine,
    Thou Lilly of the Vallys, being mine.

[6.] Another Meditation at the same time.

Undated. Pub. *W*.

Am I thy Gold? Or Purse, Lord, for thy Wealth;
    Whether in mine, or mint refinde for thee?
Ime counted so, but count me o're thyselfe,
    Lest gold washt face, and brass in Heart I bee.
    I Feare my Touchstone touches when I try   5
    Mee, and my Counted Gold too overly.

Am I new minted by thy Stamp indeed?
    Mine Eyes are dim; I cannot clearly see.
Be thou my Spectacles that I may read
    Thine Image, and Inscription stampt on mee.   10
    If thy bright Image do upon me stand
    I am a Golden Angell in thy hand.

Lord, make my Soule thy Plate: thine Image bright
    Within the Circle of the same enfoile.
And on its brims in golden Letters write   15
    Thy Superscription in an Holy style.
    Then I shall be thy Money, thou my Hord:
    Let me thy Angell bee, bee thou my Lord.

Another Meditation] PW Another Mediation
4 *and*] Z but   15 *brims*] Z brim

7. Meditation. Ps. 45.2. Grace in thy
lips is poured out.

10.12m [Feb.] *1683.* Pub. ETP, *W.*

Thy Humane Frame, my Glorious Lord, I spy,
    A Golden Still with Heavenly Choice drugs filld;
Thy Holy Love, the Glowing heate whereby,
      The Spirit of Grace is graciously distilld.
      Thy Mouth the Neck through which these spirits still.   5
      My Soul thy Violl make, and therewith fill.

Thy Speech the Liquour in thy Vessell stands,
    Well ting'd with Grace a blessed Tincture, Loe,
Thy Words distilld, Grace in thy Lips pourd, and,
      Give Graces Tinctur in them where they go.   10
      Thy words in graces tincture stilld, Lord, may
      The Tincture of thy Grace in me Convay.

That Golden Mint of Words, thy Mouth Divine,
    Doth tip these Words, which by my Fall were spoild;
And Dub with Gold dug out of Graces mine   15
      That they thine Image might have in them foild.
      Grace in thy Lips pourd out's as Liquid Gold.
      Thy Bottle make my Soule, Lord, it to hold.

2 *Heavenly Choice drugs filld*] Z Heavens sweet drugs is filld   *filld;*] PW filld
10 *Give*] Z Carry
13 *Words,*] PW Words   *Divine,*] PW Divine   16 *thine*] Z thy
18 *Thy Bottle make my Soule, Lord, it to hold*] Z Lord, make my heart thy
Bottle this *** to hold

16. foild (see also Glossary). Taylor hopes his words will be adorned with
the golden image of Christ.

8. Meditation. Joh. 6.51. I am the
Living Bread.

8. 4m [June] *1684*. Pub. ETP, *W*.

I kening through Astronomy Divine
    The Worlds bright Battlement, wherein I spy
A Golden Path my Pensill cannot line,
    From that bright Throne unto my Threshold ly.
    And while my puzzled thoughts about it pore   5
    I finde the Bread of Life in't at my doore.

When that this Bird of Paradise put in
    This Wicker Cage (my Corps) to tweedle praise
Had peckt the Fruite forbad: and so did fling
    Away its Food; and lost its golden dayes;   10
    It fell into Celestiall Famine sore:
    And never could attain a morsell more.

Alas! alas! Poore Bird, what wilt thou doe?
    The Creatures field no food for Souls e're gave.
And if thou knock at Angells dores they show   15
    An Empty Barrell: they no soul bread have.
    Alas! Poore Bird, the Worlds White Loafe is done.
    And cannot yield thee here the smallest Crumb.

In this sad state, Gods Tender Bowells run
    Out streams of Grace: And he to end all strife   20
The Purest Wheate in Heaven, his deare-dear Son
    Grinds, and kneads up into this Bread of Life.
    Which Bread of Life from Heaven down came and stands
    Disht on thy Table up by Angells Hands.

Did God mould up this Bread in Heaven, and bake,   25
    Which from his Table came, and to thine goeth?
Doth he bespeake thee thus, This Soule Bread take.

2 *Battlement*] Z Battlements   8 *Wicker*] Z vitall
22 *Grinds, and kneads up*] Z Doth knead up there
this] Z the   23 *came*] Z comes   27 *Doth he bespeake*] Z And there bespeakes

Come Eate thy fill of this thy Gods White Loafe?
Its Food too fine for Angells, yet come, take
And Eate thy fill. Its Heavens Sugar Cake.   30

What Grace is this knead in this Loafe? This thing
    Souls are but petty things it to admire.
Yee Angells, help: This fill would to the brim
    Heav'ns whelm'd-down Chrystall meele Bowle, yea and
        higher.
    This Bread of Life dropt in thy mouth, doth Cry.   35
    Eate, Eate me, Soul, and thou shalt never dy.

9. Meditation. Joh. 6.51. I am the Living Bread.

7.7m [Sept.] *1684.*

Did Ever Lord such noble house mentain,
    As my Lord doth? Or such a noble Table?
'T would breake the back of kings, nay, Monarchs brain
    To do it. Pish, the Worlds Estate's not able.
    I'le bet a boast with any that this Bread   5
    I eate excells what ever Caesar had.

Take earth's Brightst Darlings, in whose mouths all flakes
    Of Lushous Sweets she hath do croude their Head,
Their Spiced Cups, sweet Meats, and Sugar Cakes
    Are but dry Sawdust to this Living Bread.   10
    I'le pawn my part in Christ, this Dainti'st Meate,
    Is Gall, and Wormwood unto what I eate.

The Boasting Spagyrist (Insipid Phlegm,
    Whose Words out strut the Sky) vaunts he hath rife
The Water, Tincture, Lozenge, Gold, and Gem,   15

28 *Come Eate*] Z Eate, Soule   4 *Pish,*] PW Pish. Z nay
9 *Cups, sweet*] Z Cups and sweet   *Meats, and Sugar*] Z Meats, Sugar
11 *this*] Z his

Of Life itselfe. But here's the Bread of Life.
I'le lay my Life, his Aurum Vitae Red
Is to my Bread of Life, worse than DEAD HEAD.

The Dainti'st Dish of Earthly Cookery
    Is but to fat the body up in print.   20
This Bread of Life doth feed the Soule, whereby
    Its made the Temple of Jehovah in't.
        I'le Venture Heav'n upon't that Low or High
        That eate this Living Bread shall never dy.

This Bread of Life, so excellent, I see   25
    The Holy Angells doubtless would, if they
Were prone unto base Envie, Envie't mee.
        But oh! come, tast how sweet it is. I say,
        I'le Wage my Soule and all therein uplaid,
        This is the sweetest Bread that e're God made.   30

What wonder's here, that Bread of Life should come
    To feed Dead Dust? Dry Dust eate Living Bread?
Yet Wonder more by far may all, and some
    That my Dull Heart's so dumpish when thus fed.
        Lord Pardon this, and feed mee all my dayes,   35
        With Living Bread to thy Eternall Prayse.

10. Meditation. Joh. 6.55. My Blood is
        Drinke indeed.

26. 8m [Oct.] *1684.* Pub. ETG.

Stupendious Love! All Saints Astonishment!
    Bright Angells are black Motes in this Suns Light.
Heav'ns Canopy the Paintice to Gods tent
        Can't Cover't neither with its breadth, nor height.
        Its Glory doth all Glory else out run,   5
        Beams of bright Glory to't are motes i'th'sun.

My Soule had Caught an Ague, and like Hell
    Her thirst did burn: she to each spring did fly,
But this bright blazing Love did spring a Well
    Of Aqua-Vitae in the Deity,   10
      Which on the top of Heav'ns high Hill out burst
      And down came running thence t'allay my thirst.

But how it came, amazeth all Communion.
    Gods onely Son doth hug Humanity,
Into his very person. By which Union   15
    His Humane Veans its golden gutters ly.
      And rather than my Soule should dy by thirst,
      These Golden Pipes, to give me drink, did burst.

This Liquour brew'd, thy sparkling Art Divine
    Lord, in thy Chrystall Vessells did up tun,   20
(Thine Ordinances,) which all Earth o're shine
    Set in thy rich Wine Cellars out to run.
      Lord, make thy Butlar draw, and fill with speed
      My Beaker full: for this is drink indeed.

Whole Buts of this blesst Nectar shining stand   25
    Lockt up with Saph'rine Taps, whose splendid Flame
Too bright do shine for brightest Angells hands
    To touch, my Lord. Do thou untap the same.
      Oh! make thy Chrystall Buts of Red Wine bleed
      Into my Chrystall Glass this Drink-Indeed.   30

How shall I praise thee then? My blottings Jar
    And wrack my Rhymes to pieces in thy praise.
Thou breath'st thy Vean still in my Pottinger
    To lay my thirst, and fainting spirits raise.
      Thou makest Glory's Chiefest Grape to bleed   35
      Into my cup: And this is Drink-Indeed.

Nay, though I make no pay for this Red Wine,
    And scarce do say I thank-ye-for't; strange thing!
Yet were thy silver skies my Beer bowle fine

19 *brew'd*,] PW brew'd.   29 *Oh!*] orig: And

I finde my Lord, would fill it to the brim.   40
Then make my life, Lord, to thy praise proceed
For thy rich blood, which is my Drink-Indeed.

11. Meditation. Isai. 25.6. A Feast
         of Fat things.

31.3m [Mar.] *1685.*

A Deity of Love Incorporate
     My Lord, lies in thy Flesh, in Dishes stable
Ten thousand times more rich than golden Plate
     In golden Services upon thy Table,
         To feast thy People with. What Feast is this!   5
         Where richest Love lies Cookt in e'ry Dish?

A Feast, a Feast, a Feast of Spiced Wine
     Of Wines upon the Lees, refined well
Of Fat things full of Marrow, things Divine
     Of Heavens blest Cookery which doth excell.   10
         The Smell of Lebanon, and Carmell sweet
         Are Earthly damps unto this Heavenly reech.

This Shew-Bread Table all of Gold with white
     Fine Table Linen of Pure Love, 's ore spred
And Courses in Smaragdine Chargers bright   15
     Of Choicest Dainties Paradise e're bred.
         Where in each Grace like Dainty Sippits lie
         Oh! brave Embroderies of sweetest joy!

Oh! what a Feast is here? This Table might
     Make brightest Angells blush to sit before.   20
Then pain my Soule! Why wantst thou appitite?
     Oh! blush to thinke thou hunger dost no more.
         There never was a feast more rich than this:
         The Guests that Come hereto shall swim in bliss.

21 *Why*] PW why   24 *Guests*] PW Guess

Hunger, and Thirst my Soule, goe Fasting Pray,
    Untill thou hast an Appitite afresh:
And then come here; here is a feast will pay
    Thee for the same with all Deliciousness.
    Untap Loves Golden Cask, Love run apace:
    And o're this Feast Continually say Grace.   30

12. Meditation. Isai. 63.1. Glorious
in his Apparell.

19. 5m [July] *1685.* Pub. *W.*

This Quest rapt at my Eares broad golden Doores
    Who's this that comes from Edom in this shine
In Died Robes from Bozrah? this more ore
    All Glorious in's Apparrell; all Divine?
    Then through that Wicket rusht this buss there gave,   5
    Its I that right do speake mighty to save.

27 *here;*] PW here.

    3: Died Robes from Bozrah? Probably, robes of wool from Bozrah sheep,
dyed red. The red robe representing Christ's blood at the Passion was a com-
mon symbol in Christian typology; it derives from Isa. 63:1 ff.: "Who is this
that cometh from Edom, with dyed garments from Bozrah? . . . I have trod-
den the winepress alone; and of the people there was none with me: for I will
tread them in mine anger, and trample them in my fury; and their blood
shall be sprinkled upon my garments, and I will stain all my raiment." Cf.
Herbert's "The Sacrifice," lines 157–60: "Then with a scarlet robe they me
array; / Which shews my bloud to be the onely way / And cordiall left to
repair mans decay; / Was ever grief like mine?" Cf. also Herbert's "The
Agonie," line 10, and Crashaw's "On our crucified Lord Naked, and bloody"
(L. C. Martin, ed., *Crashaw's Poetical Works*, Oxford, 1927), p. 100:

        Th'have left thee naked Lord, O that they had;
           This Garment too I would they had deny'd,
        Thee with thy selfe they have too richly clad,

        Opening the purple wardrobe of thy side.
           O never could bee found Garments too good
           For thee to weare, but these, of thine owne blood.

I threw through Zions Lattice then an Eye
    Which spide one like a lump of Glory pure
Nay, Cloaths of gold button'd with pearls do ly
    Like Rags, or shooclouts unto his he wore.   10
    Heavens Curtains blancht with Sun, and Starrs of Light
    Are black as sackcloth to his Garments bright.

One shining sun guilding the skies with Light
    Benights all Candles with their flaming Blaze
So doth the Glory of this Robe benight   15
    Ten thousand suns at once ten thousand wayes.
    For e'ry thrid therein's dy'de with the shine
    Of All, and Each the Attributes Divine.

The sweetest breath, the sweetest Violet
    Rose, or Carnation ever did gust out   20
Is but a Foist to that Perfume beset
    In thy Apparell steaming round about:
    But is this so? My Peuling soul then pine
    In Love untill this Lovely one be thine.

Pluck back the Curtains, back the Window Shutts: 25
    Through Zions Agate Window take a view;
How Christ in Pinckted Robes from Bozrah puts
    Comes Glorious in's Apparell forth to Wooe.
    Oh! if his Glory ever kiss thine Eye,
    Thy Love will soon Enchanted bee thereby.   30

Then Grieve, my Soul, thy vessell is so small
    And holds no more for such a Lovely Hee.
That strength's so little, Love scarce acts at all.
    That sight's so dim, doth scarce him lovely see.
    Grieve, grieve, my Soul, thou shouldst so pimping bee,   35
    Now such a Price is here presented thee.

All sight's too little sight enough to make
    All strength's too little Love enough to reare
All Vessells are too small to hold or take
    Enough Love up for such a Lovely Deare.   40

16 *ten thousand wayes*] PW ten thosand wayes

How little to this Little's then thy ALL.
For Him whose Beauty saith all Love's too small?

My Lovely One, I fain would love thee much
But all my Love is none at all I see,
Oh! let thy Beauty give a glorious tuch   45
Upon my Heart, and melt to Love all mee.
Lord melt me all up into Love for thee
Whose Loveliness excells what love can bee.

13. Meditation. Col. 2.3. All the
            Treasures of Wisdom.

27.7m [Sept.] *1685*. Pub. PET.

Thou Glory Darkning Glory, with thy Flame
Should all Quaint Metaphors teem ev'ry Bud
Of Sparkling Eloquence upon the same
It would appeare as dawbing pearls with mud.
Nay Angells Wits are Childish tricks, and like   5
The Darksom night unto thy Lightsom Light.

Oh! Choicest Cabbinet, more Choice than gold
Or Wealthist Pearles Wherein all Pearls of Price
All Treasures of Choice Wisdom manifold
Inthroned reign. Thou Cabinet most Choice   10
Not scant to hold, not staind with cloudy geere
The Shining Sun of Wisdom bowling there.

Thou Shining Golden Lanthorn with pain'd Lights
Of Chrystall cleare, thy golden Candles flame,
Makes such a Shine, as doth the Sun benights.   15
Its but a Smoaky vapor to the Same.
All Wisdom knead into a Chrystall Ball,
Shines like the Sun in thee, its azure Hall.

Thou rowling Eye of Light, to thee are sent
 All Dazzling Beams of Shine the Heavens distill. 20
All Wisdoms Troops do quarter in thy Tents
 And all her Treasures Cabin in thy tills.
 Be thou, Lord, mine: then I shall Wealthy bee,
 Enricht with Wisdoms Treasures, Stoughd in thee.

That little Grain within my golden Bowle, 25
 Should it attempt to poise thy Talent cleare,
It would inoculate into my Soule,
 As illookt Impudence as ever were.
 But, loe, it stands amaizd, and doth adore,
 Thy Magazeen of Wisdom, and thy Store. 30

14. Meditations. Heb. 4.14. A Great
15.   High Priest.

14. 9m [Nov.] *1685. 10. 11m* [Jan.] *1685.*

Raptures of Love, surprizing Loveliness,
 That burst through Heavens all, in Rapid Flashes,
Glances guilt o're with smiling Comliness!
 (Wonders do palefac'd stand smit by such dashes).
 Glory itselfe Heartsick of Love doth ly 5
 Bleeding out Love o're Loveless mee, and dy.

Might I a glance of this bright brightness shew;
 Se it in him who gloriously is dresst:
A Gold Silk Stomacher of Purple, blew
 Blancht o're with Orient Pearles being on his Breast: 10
 And all his Robes being answerable, but
 This glory seen, to that unseen's a Smut.

Yea, Beauteous Hee, in all his Glory stands,
 Tendring himselfe to God, and Man where hee
Doth Justice thus bespeake, Hold out thy hands: 15
 Come, take thy Penworths now for mine of mee.

I'le pay the fine that thou seest meet to set
Upon their Heads: I'le dy to cleare their debts.

Out Rampant Justice steps in Sparkling White,
    Him rends in twain, who on her Altar lies   20
A Lump of Glory flaming in her bright
    Devouring Flames, to be my Sacrifice
    Untill her Fire goes out well Satisfide:
    And then he rose in Glory to abide.

To Heav'n went he, and in his bright Throne sits   25
    At Gods right hand pleading poor Sinners Cases.
With Golden Wedges he of Promise, splits
    The Heav'ns ope, to shew what Glory 'braces.
    And in its thickness thus with Arms extended,
    Calls, come, come here, and ever be befriended.   30

Frost bitten Love, Frozen Affections! Blush;
    What icy Chrystall mountain lodge you in?
What Wingless Wishes, Hopes pinfeatherd tush!
    Sore Hooft Desires hereof do in you spring?
    Oh hard black Kirnell at the Coare! not pant?   35
    Encastled in an heart of Adamant!

What strange Congealed Heart have I when I
    Under such Beauty shining like the Sun
Able to make Frozen Affection fly,
    And Icikles of Frostbitt Love to run.   40
    Yea, and Desires lockt in an heart of Steel
    Or Adamant, breake prison, nothing feel.

Lord may thy Priestly Golden Oares but make
    A rowing in my Lumpish Heart, thou'lt see
My Chilly Numbd Affections Charm, and break   45
    Out in a rapid Flame of Love to thee.
    Yea, they unto thyselfe will fly in flocks
    When thy Warm Sun my frozen Lake unlocks.

Be thou my High Priest, Lord; and let my name
    Ly in some Grave dug in these Pearly rocks   50

40 *Frostbitt*] orig: Frostbitten

Upon thy Ephods Shoulder piece, like flame
    Or graved in thy Breast Plate-Gem: brave Knops.
    Thou'lt then me beare before thy Fathers Throne
    Rowld up in Folds of Glory of thine own.

One of these Gems I beg, Lord, that so well   55
    Begrace thy Breast Plate, and thy Ephod cleaver
To stud my Crown therewith: or let me dwell
    Among their sparkling, glancing Shades for ever.
    I'st then be deckt in glory bright to sing
    With Angells, Hallelujahs to my King.   60

16. Meditation. Lu. 7.16. A Greate
Prophet is risen up.

6. 1m [Mar.] *1685/6*. Pub. UPT.

Leafe Gold, Lord of thy Golden Wedge o'relaid
    My Soul at first, thy Grace in e'ry part
Whose peart, fierce Eye thou such a Sight hadst made
    Whose brightsom beams could break into thy heart
    Till thy Curst Foe had with my Fist mine Eye   5
    Dasht out, and did my Soule Unglorify.

I cannot see, nor Will thy Will aright.
    Nor see to waile my Woe, my loss and hew
Nor all the Shine in all the Sun can light
    My Candle, nor its Heate my Heart renew.   10
    See, waile, and Will thy Will, I must, or must
    From Heavens sweet Shine to Hells hot flame be thrust.

Grace then Conceald in God himselfe, did rowle
    Even Snow Ball like into a Sunball Shine
And nestles all its beams buncht in thy Soule   15
    My Lord, that sparkle in Prophetick Lines.
    Oh! Wonder more than Wonderfull! this Will
    Lighten the Eye which Sight Divine did spill.

What art thou, Lord, this Ball of Glory bright?
 A Bundle of Celestiall Beams up bound   20
In Graces band fixt in Heavens topmost height
  Pouring thy golden Beams thence, Circling round
  Which shew thy Glory, and thy glories Way
  And ery Where will make Celestiall Day.

Lord let thy Golden Beams pierce through mine Eye   25
 And leave therein an Heavenly Light to glaze
My Soule with glorious Grace all o're, whereby
  I may have Sight, and Grace in mee may blaze.
  Lord ting my Candle at thy Burning Rayes,
  To give a gracious Glory to thy Prayse.   30

Thou Lightning Eye, let some bright Beames of thine
 Stick in my Soul, to light and liven it:
Light, Life, and Glory, things that are Divine;
  I shall be grac'd withall for glory fit.
  My Heart then stufft with Grace, Light, Life, and Glee
  I'le sacrifice in Flames of Love to thee.

17. Meditation. Rev. 19.16. King of Kings.

13.4m [June] *1686.*

A King, a King, a King indeed, a King
 Writh up in Glory! Glorie's glorious Throne
Is glorifide by him, presented him.
  And all the Crowns of Glory are his own.
  A King, Wise, Just, Gracious, Magnificent.   5
  Kings unto him are Whiffles, Indigent.

What is his Throne all Glory? Crown all Gay?
 Crown all of Brightest Shine of Glory's Wealth?
This is a Lisp of Non-sense. I should say,
  He is the Throne, and Crown of Glory 'tselfe.   10

21 *fixt in*] orig: fixt up in

Should Sun beams come to gilde his glory they
    Would be as 'twere to gild the Sun with Clay.

My Phancys in a Maze, my thoughts agast,
    Words in an Extasy; my Telltale Tongue
Is tonguetide, and my Lips are padlockt fast   15
    To see thy Kingly Glory in to throng.
    I can, yet cannot tell this Glory just,
    In Silence bury't, must not, yet I must.

This King of King's Brave Kingdom doth Consist
    Of Glorious Angells, and Blesst Saints alone   20
Or Chiefly. Where all Beams of Glory twist,
    Together, beaming from, lead to his throne
    Which Beams his Grace Coiles in a Wreath to Crown
    His, in the End in Endless Bright Renown.

His Two-Edg'd Sword, not murdering Steel so base,   25
    Is made of Righteousness, unspotted, bright
Imbellisht o're with overflowing Grace
    Doth killing, Cure the Sinner, kills Sin right.
    Makes milkwhite Righteousness, and Grace to reign,
    And Satan and his Cubs with Sin ly slain.   30

Were all Kings deckt with Sparkling Crowns, and arm'd
    With flaming Swords, and firy Courage traind
And led under their King Abaddon, Charmd
    In battell out against their foes disdaind
    One smiling look of this bright Shine would fell   35
    Them and their Crowns of Glory all to Hell.

Thou art my king: let me not be thy Shame.
    Thy Law my Rule: my Life thy Life in Mee.
Thy Grace my Badge: my Glory bright thy Name.
    I am resolv'd to live and dy with thee.   40
    Keep mee, thou King of Glory on Record.
    Thou art my King of Kings, and Lord of Lords.

11 *gilde*] orig: guilde   12 *gild*] orig: guild   20 *Saints*] PW Saint
35 *smiling*] PW smiting[?]

18. Meditation. Isai. 52.14. His Vissage
       was marr'd more than any man.

29. 6m [Aug.] *1686*. Pub. UPT.

Astonisht stand, my Soule; why dost not start
    At this surprizing Sight shewn here below?
Oh! let the twitch made by my bouncing Heart
    Gust from my breast this Enterjection, Oh!
    A Sight so Horrid, sure its Mercies Wonder   5
    Rocks rend not at't, nor Heavens split asunder.

Souls Charg'd with Sin, Discharge at God, beside
    Firld up in Guilt, Wrapt in Sins Slough, and Slime.
Wills wed to Wickedness, Hearts Stonifide
    Flinty Affections, Conscience Chalybdine   10
    Flooding the World with Horrid Crimes, arise
    Daring Almighty God Contemptuouswise.

Hence Vengeance rose with her fierce Troops in Buff,
    Soul-piercing Plagues, Heart-Aching Griefs, and Groans,
Woes Pickled in Revenges Powdering Trough: 15
    Pain fetching forth their Proofs out of the boanes.
    Doth all in Flames of Fire surround them so
    Which they can ne're o'recome, nor undergo.

In this sad Plight the richest Beauty Cleare
    That th'bravest Flower, that bud was big with, wore,   20
Did glorify those Cheeks, whose Vissage were
    Marr'd more than any mans, and Form spoild more.
    Oh! Beauty beautifull, not toucht with vice!
    The fairest Flower in all Gods Paradise!

Stept in, and in its Glory 'Counters all.   25
    And in the Belly of this Dismall Cloud,
Of Woes in Pickle is gulpht up, whose Gall
    He dranke up quite. Whose Claws his Face up plow'd.

Yet in these Furrows sprang the brightest Shine
That Glory's Sun could make, or Love Enshrine.   30

Then Vengeance's Troops are routed, Pickled Woe
Heart-aching Griefes, Pains plowing to the boanes,
Soul piercing Plagues, all Venom do foregoe.
The Curse now Cures, though th'Griefe procureth groans.
As th'Angry Bee doth often lose her Sting,   35
The Law was Cursless made in Cursing him.

And now his shining Love beams out its rayes
My Soul, upon thy Heart to thaw the same:
To animate th'Affections till they blaze;
To free from Guilt, and from Sins Slough, and Shame.   40
Open thy Casement wide, let Glory in,
To Guild thy Heart to be an Hall for him.

My Breast, be thou the ringing Virginalls:
Ye mine Affections, their sweet Golden Strings,
My Panting Heart, be thou for Stops, and Falls: 45
Lord, let thy quick'ning Beams dance o're the Pins.
Then let thy Spirit this sweet note resume,
ALTASCHATH MICHTAM, in Seraphick Tune.

19. Meditation. Phil. 2.9. God hath
       highly exalted him.

14.9m [Nov.] *1686.* Pub. *W.*

Looke till thy Looks·look Wan, my Soule; here's ground.
The Worlds bright Eye's dash't out: Day-Light so brave
Bemidnighted; the sparkling sun, palde round
With flouring Rayes lies buri'de in its grave
The Candle of the World blown out, down fell.   5
Life knockt a head by Death: Heaven by Hell.

Alas! this World all filld up to the brim
With Sins, Deaths, Divills, Crowding men to Hell.

For whose reliefe Gods milkwhite Lamb stept in
    Whom those Curst Imps did worry, flesh, and fell.   10
    Tread under foot, did Clap their Wings and so
    Like Dunghill Cocks over their Conquourd, Crow.

Brave Pious Fraud; as if the Setting Sun:
    Dropt like a Ball of Fire into the Seas,
And so went out. But to the East come, run: 15
    You'l meet the morn Shrinde with its flouring Rayes.
    This Lamb in laying of these Lyons dead;
    Drank of the brooke: and so lift up his Head.

Oh! sweet, sweet joy! These Rampant Fiends befoold:
    They made their Gall his Winding sheete; although   20
They of the Heart-ach dy must, or be Coold
    With Inflamation of the Lungs, they know.
    He's Cancelling the Bond, and making Pay:
    And Ballancing Accounts: its Reckoning day.

See, how he from the Counthouse shining went,   25
    In Flashing Folds of Burnisht Glory, and
Dasht out all Curses from the Covenant
    Hath Justices Acquittance in his hand
    Pluckt out Deaths Sting, the Serpents Head did mall
    The Bars and Gates of Hell he brake down all.   30

The Curse thus Lodgd within his Flesh, and Cloyde,
    Can't run from him to his, so much he gave.
And like a Gyant he awoke, beside,
    The Sun of Righteousness rose out of's Grave.
    And setting Foot upon its neck I sing   35
    Grave, where's thy Victory? Death, Where's thy Sting?

9 *milkwhite*] PW mikewhite

20. Meditation. Phil. 2.9. God hath
highly Exalted him.

9.11m [Jan.] *1686.* Pub. *W.*

View all ye eyes above, this sight which flings
    Seraphick Phancies in Chill Raptures high,
A Turffe of Clay, and yet bright Glories King
      From dust to Glory Angell-like to fly.
      A Mortall Clod immortalizde, behold,   5
      Flyes through the Skies swifter than Angells could.

Upon the Wings he of the Winde rode in
    His Bright Sedan, through all the Silver Skies
And made the Azure Cloud his Charriot bring
      Him to the Mountain of Celestiall joyes.   10
      The Prince o'th'Aire durst not an Arrow spend
      While through his Realm his Charriot did ascend.

He did not in a Fiery Charriot's Shine,
    And Whirlewinde, like Elias upward goe.
But th'golden Ladders Jasper rounds did climbe   15
      Unto the Heavens high from Earth below.
      Each step trod on a Golden Stepping Stone
      Of Deity unto his very Throne.

Methinks I see Heavens sparkling Courtiers fly,
    In flakes of Glory down him to attend: 20
And heare Heart Cramping notes of Melody,
      Surround his Charriot as it did ascend
      Mixing their Musick making e'ry string
      More to inravish as they this tune sing.

God is Gone up with a triumphant Shout   25
    The Lord with sounding Trumpets melodies.

13–18: The figure of God ascending to heaven on a ladder is inconsistent
with the figure of God ascending in a chariot in the preceding and following
stanzas.

Sing Praise, sing Praise, sing Praise, sing Praises out,
    Unto our King sing praise seraphickwise.
    Lift up your Heads ye lasting Doore they sing
    And let the King of Glory Enter in.   30

Art thou ascended up on high, my Lord,
    And must I be without thee here below?
Art thou the sweetest Joy the Heavens afford?
    Oh! that I with thee was! what shall I do?
    Should I pluck Feathers from an Angells Wing,   35
    They could not waft me up to thee my King.

Lend mee thy Wings, my Lord, I'st fly apace.
    My Soules Arms stud with thy strong Quills, true Faith,
My Quills then Feather with thy Saving Grace,
    My Wings will take the Winde thy Word displai'th.   40
    Then I shall fly up to thy glorious Throne
    With my strong Wings whose Feathers are thine own.

21. Meditation. Phil. 2.9. God hath
Highly Exalted Him.

13. 1m [Mar.] 1686/7. Pub. MGG.

What Glory's this, my Lord? Should one small Point
    Of one small Ray of't touch my Heart 'twould spring
Such joy as would an Adamant unjoynt
    If in't, and tare it, to get out and sing.
    T'run on Heroick golden Feet, and raise   5
    Heart Ravishing Tunes, Curld with Celestiall praise.

Oh! Bright! Bright thing! I fain would something say:
    Lest Silence should indict me. Yet I feare
To say a Syllable lest at thy day
    I be presented for my Tattling here.   10

32 *below?*] PW below   41 *up to*] orig: unto

Course Phancy, Ragged Faculties, alas!
And Blunted Tongue don't Suit: Sighs Soile the Glass.

Yet shall my mouth stand ope, and Lips let run
    Out gliding Eloquence on each light thing?
And shall I gag my mouth, and ty my Tongue,   15
    When such bright Glory glorifies within?
    That makes my Heart leape, dancing to thy Lute?
    And shall my tell tale tongue become a Mute?

Lord spare I pray, though my attempts let fall
    A slippery Verse upon thy Royall Glory.   20
I'le bring unto thine Altar th'best of all
    My Flock affords. I have no better Story.
    I'le at thy Glory my dark Candle light:
    Not to descry the Sun, but use by night.

A Golden Throne whose Banisters are Pearles,   25
    And Pomills Choicest Gems: Carbuncle-Stayes
Studded with Pretious Stones, Carv'd with rich Curles
    Of Polisht Art, sending out flashing Rayes,
    Would him surround with Glory, thron'de therein.
    Yet this is to thy Throne a dirty thing.   30

Oh! Glorious Sight! Loe, How Bright Angells stand
    Waiting with Hat in hand on Him alone
That is Enthron'de, indeed at Gods right hand:
    Gods Heart itselfe being his Happy Throne.
    The Glory that doth from this Person fall,   35
    Fills Heaven with Glory, else there's none at all.

22. Meditation. Phil. 2.9. God hath
        Highly Exalted him.

12. 4m [June] 1687. Pub. PET.

When thy Bright Beams, my Lord, do strike mine Eye,
    Methinkes I then could truely Chide out right

My Hide bound Soule that stands so niggardly
    That scarce a thought gets glorified by't.
    My Quaintest Metaphors are ragged Stuff,   5
    Making the Sun seem like a Mullipuff.

Its my desire, thou shouldst be glorifi'de:
    But when thy Glory shines before mine eye,
I pardon Crave, lest my desire be Pride.
    Or bed thy Glory in a Cloudy Sky.   10
    The Sun grows wan; and Angells palefac'd shrinke,
    Before thy Shine, which I besmeere with Inke.

But shall the Bird sing forth thy Praise, and shall
    The little Bee present her thankfull Hum?
But I who see thy shining Glory fall   15
    Before mine Eyes, stand Blockish, Dull, and Dumb?
    Whether I speake, or speechless stand, I spy,
    I faile thy Glory: therefore pardon Cry.

But this I finde; My Rhymes do better suite
    Mine own Dispraise than tune forth praise to thee.   20
Yet being Chid, whether Consonant, or Mute,
    I force my Tongue to tattle, as you see.
    That I thy glorious Praise may Trumpet right,
    Be thou my Song, and make Lord, mee thy Pipe.

This shining Sky will fly away apace,   25
    When thy bright Glory splits the same to make
Thy Majesty a Pass, whose Fairest Face
    Too foule a Path is for thy Feet to take.
    What Glory then, shall tend thee through the Sky
    Draining the Heaven much of Angells dry?   30

What Light then flame will in thy Judgment Seate,
    'Fore which all men, and angells shall appeare?
How shall thy Glorious Righteousness them treate,

13–14: Cf. Herbert's "Employment (1)," lines 17–20: "All things are busie;
onely I / Neither bring hony with the bees, / Nor flowers to make that, nor
the husbandrie / To water these." Cf. also Herbert's "Praise (1)," lines 17–20:
"O raise me then! Poore bees, that work all day, / Sting my delay, / Who
have a work, as well as they, / And much, much more."

Rend'ring to each after his Works done here?
Then Saints With Angells thou wilt glorify: 35
And burn Lewd Men, and Divells Gloriously.

One glimps, my Lord, of thy bright Judgment day,
    And Glory piercing through, like fiery Darts,
All Divells, doth me make for Grace to pray,
        For filling Grace had I ten thousand Hearts.   40
        I'de through ten Hells to see thy Judgment Day
        Wouldst thou but guild my Soule with thy bright Ray.

23. Meditation. Cant. 4.8. My Spouse.

21. 6m [Aug.] *1687*. Pub. UPT.

Would God I in that Golden City were,
    With Jaspers Walld, all garnisht, and made swash,
With Pretious Stones, whose Gates are Pearles most cleare
    And Street Pure Gold, like to transparent Glass.
        That my dull Soule, might be inflamde to see   5
        How Saints and Angells ravisht are in Glee.

Were I but there, and could but tell my Story,
    'Twould rub those Walls of Pretious Stones more bright:
And glaze those Gates of Pearle, with brighter Glory;
        And pave the golden Street with greater light.   10
        'Twould in fresh Raptures Saints, and Angells fling.
        But I poore Snake Crawl here, scarce mudwalld in.

May my Rough Voice, and my blunt Tongue but spell
    My Tale (for tune they can't) perhaps there may
Some Angell catch an end of't up, and tell   15
    In Heaven, when he doth return that way,
    He'l make thy Palace, Lord, all over ring,
    With it in Songs, thy Saint, and Angells sing.

8 *'Twould*] PW T'would   11 *'Twould*] PW T'would

I know not how to speak't, it is so good:
    Shall Mortall, and Immortall marry? nay,   20
Man marry God? God be a Match for Mud?
        The King of Glory Wed a Worm? mere Clay?
        This is the Case. The Wonder too in Bliss.
        Thy Maker is thy Husband. Hearst thou this?

My Maker, he my Husband? Oh! strange joy!   25
    If Kings wed Worms, and Monarchs Mites wed should,
Glory spouse Shame, a Prince a Snake or Fly
        An Angell Court an Ant, all Wonder would.
        Let such wed Worms, Snakes, Serpents, Divells, Flyes.
        Less Wonder than the Wedden in our Eyes.   30

I am to Christ more base, than to a King
    A Mite, Fly, Worm, Ant, Serpent, Divell is,
Or Can be, being tumbled all in Sin,
        And shall I be his Spouse? How good is this?
        It is too good to be declar'de to thee.   35
        But not too good to be believ'de by mee.

Yet to this Wonder, this is found in mee,
    I am not onely base but backward Clay,
When Christ doth Wooe: and till his Spirit bee
        His Spokes man to Compell me I deny.   40
        I am so base and Froward to him, Hee
        Appears as Wonders Wonder, wedding mee.

Seing, Dear Lord, its thus, thy Spirit take
    And send thy Spokes man, to my Soul, I pray.
Thy Saving Grace my Wedden Garment make: 45
        Thy Spouses Frame into my Soul Convay.
        I then shall be thy Bride Espousd by thee
        And thou my Bridesgroom Deare Espousde shalt bee.

26 *Worms*] PW Worm   27 *Shame,*] PW Shame   48 *shalt bee*] orig: by mee

24. Meditation. Eph. 2.18. Through him we have—an Access—unto the Father.

6.9m[Nov.] *1687*. Pub. PET.

Was there a Palace of Pure Gold, all Ston'de
    And pav'de with Pearles, whose Gates Rich Jaspers were,
And Throne a Carbuncle, whose King Enthronde
    Sat on a Cushion all of Sunshine Cleare;
    Whose Crown a Bunch of Sun Beams was: I should   5
    Prize such as in his favour shrine me Would.

Thy Milke white Hand, my Glorious Lord, doth this:
    It opes this Gate, and me Conducts into
This Golden Palace whose rich Pavement is
    Of Pretious Pearles: and to this King also.   10
    Thus Thron'de, and Crown'd: whose Words are 'bellisht all
    With brighter Beams, than e're the Sun let fall.

But oh! Poore mee, thy sluggish Servant, I
    More blockish than a block, as blockhead, stand.
Though mine Affections Quick as Lightning fly   15
    On toys, they Snaile like move to kiss thy hand.
    My Coal-black doth thy Milke white hand avoide,
    That would above the Milky Way me guide.

What aim'st at, Lord? that I should be so Cross.
    My minde is Leaden in thy Golden Shine.   20
Though all o're Spirit, when this dirty Dross
    Doth touch it with its smutting leaden lines.
    What shall an Eagle t'catch a Fly thus run?
    Or Angell Dive after a Mote ith'Sun?

What Folly's this? I fain would take, I thinke,   25
    Vengeance upon myselfe: But I Confess,
I can't. Mine Eyes, Lord, shed no Tears but inke.
    My handy Works, are Words, and Wordiness.

Earth's Toyes ware Knots of my Affections, nay,
Though from thy Glorious Selfe they're Stoole away.   30

Oh! that my heart was made thy Golden Box
Full of Affections, and of Love Divine
Knit all in Tassles, and in True-Love Knots,
To garnish o're this Worthy Worke of thine.
This Box and all therein more rich than Gold,   35
In sacred Flames, I to thee offer would.

With thy rich Tissue my poore Soule array:
And lead me to thy Fathers House above.
Thy Graces Storehouse make my Soule I pray.
Thy Praise shall then ware Tassles of my Love.   40
If thou Conduct mee in thy Fathers Wayes,
I'le be the Golden Trumpet of thy Praise.

25. Meditation. Eph. 5.27. A Glorious Church.

22. 11m [Jan.] *1687*. Pub. ETP, *W*.

Why should my Bells, which Chime thy Praise, when thou
My Shew-Bread, on thy Table wast, my King,
Their Clappers, or their Bell-ropes want even now?
Or those that can thy Changes sweetly ring?
What is a Scar-Fire broken out? No, no.   5
The Bells would backward ring if it was so.

Its true: and I do all things backward run,
Poor Pillard I have a sad tale to tell:
My soule starke nakt, rowld all in mire, undone.
Thy Bell may tole my passing Peale to Hell.   10
None in their Winding sheet more naked stay
Nor Dead than I. Hence oh! the Judgment Day.

When I behold some Curious Piece of Art,
Or Pritty Bird, Flower, Star, or Shining Sun,

Poure out o'reflowing Glory: oh! my Heart   15
    Achs seing how my thoughts in Snick-Snarls run.
    But all this Glory to my Lord's a spot
    While I instead of any, am all blot.

But, my sweet Lord, what glorious robes are those
    That thou hast brought out of thy Grave for thine?   20
They do outshine the Sun-Shine, Grace the Rose.
    I leape for joy to thinke, shall these be mine?
    Such are, as waite upon thee in thy Wars,
    Cloathd with the Sun, and Crowned with twelve Stars.

Dost thou adorn some thus, and why not mee?   25
    Ile not believe it. Lord, thou art my Chiefe.
Thou me Commandest to believe in thee.
    I'l not affront thee thus with Unbeliefe.
    Lord, make my Soule Obedient: and when so,
    Thou saist Believe, make it reply, I do.   30

I fain the Choicest Love my soule Can get,
    Would to thy Gracious selfe a Gift present
But cannot now unscrew Loves Cabbinet.
    Say not this is a Niggards Complement.
    For seing it is thus I choose now rather   35
    To send thee th'Cabbinet, and Pearle together.

26. Meditation. Act. 5.31. To Give—
Forgiveness of Sins.

15. 1m [Mar.] *1688.* Pub. PET.

My Noble Lord, thy Nothing Servant I
    Am for thy sake out with my heart, that holds,
So little Love for such a Lord: I Cry

      .   .   .   .   .   .

31 *Choicest*] PW Coicest   4 This line is missing in PW

How should I be but angry thus to see   5
My Heart so hidebound in her Acts to thee?

Thou art a Golden Theame: but I am lean,
    A Leaden Oritor upon the same.
Thy Golden Web excells my Dozie Beam:
    Whose Linsy-Wolsy Loom deserves thy blame.   10
    Its all defild, unbiasst too by Sin:
    An hearty Wish for thee's scarce shot therein.

It pitties mee who pitty Cannot show,
    That such a Worthy Theame abusd should bee.
I am undone, unless thy Pardons doe   15
    Undoe my Sin I did, undoing mee.
    My Sins are greate, and grieveous ones, therefore
    Carbuncle Mountains can't wipe out their Score.

But thou, my Lord, dost a Free Pardon bring.
    Thou giv'st Forgiveness: yet my heart through Sin,   20
Hath naught but naught to file thy Gift up in.
    An hurden Haump doth Chafe a Silken Skin.
    Although I pardons beg, I scarce can see,
    When thou giv'st pardons, I give praise to thee.

O bad at best! what am I then at worst?   25
    I want a Pardon: and when pardon'd, want
A Thankfull Heart: Both which thou dost disburst.
    Giv'st both, or neither: for which Lord I pant.
    Two such good things at once! methinks I could
    Avenge my heart, lest it should neither hold.   30

Lord tap mine Eyes, seing such Grace in thee,
    So little doth affect my Graceless Soule.
And take my teares in lue of thanks of mee,
    New make my heart: then take it for thy tole.
    Thy Pardons then will make my heart to sing   35
    Its Michtam-David: With sweet joy Within.

11 *Its all defild*] orig: That all defild

27. Meditation. Col. 1.19. In Him
should all Fulness Dwell.

1. 5m [July] *1688.*

Oh! Wealthy Theam! Oh! Feeble Phancy: I
    Must needs admire, when I recall to minde,
That's Fulness, This it's Emptiness, though spy
    I have no Flowring Brain thereto inclinde.
    My Damps do out my fire. I cannot, though   5
    I would Admire, finde heate enough thereto.

What shall I say? Such rich rich Fullness would
    Make stammering Tongues speake smoothly, and Enshrine
The Dumb mans mouth with Silver Streams like gold
    Of Eloquence making the Aire to Chime.   10
    Yet I am Tonguetide stupid, sensless stand,
    And Drier drain'd than is my pen I hand.

Oh! Wealthy Box: more Golden far than Gold
    A Case more Worth than Wealth: a richer Delph,
Than Rubies; Cabbinet, than Pearles here told   15
    A Purse more glittering than Glory 'tselfe
    A Golden Store House of all Fulness: Shelfe,
    Of Heavenly Plate. All Fulness in thyselfe.

Oh! Godhead Fulness! There doth in thee flow
    All Wisdoms Fulness; Fulness of all Strength: 20
Of Justice, Truth, Love, Holiness also
    And Graces Fulness to its upmost length
    Do dwell in thee. Yea and thy Fathers Pleasure.
    Thou art their Cabbinet, and they thy Treasure.

All Office Fulness with all Office Gifts   25
    Imbossed are in thee, Whereby thy Grace,
Doth treat both God, and Man, brings up by hifts
    Black Sinner and White Justice to imbrace.

3 *That's*] PW Thats   22 *to*] orig: unto

Making the Glory of Gods Justice shine:
And making Sinners to Gods glory Climbe. 30

All Graces Fulness dwells in thee, from Whom
    The Golden Pipes of all Convayance ly,
Through which Grace to our Clayie Panchins Come.
    Fullness of Beauty, and Humanity.
        Oh! Glorious Flow're, Glory, and Sweetness splice, 35
        In thee to Grace, and sweeten Paradise!

But, oh! the Fathers Love! herein most vast!
    Angells engrave't in brightest Marble, t'see
This Flower that in his Bosom sticks so fast,
    Stuck in the Bosom of such stuffe as wee 40
    That both his Purse, and all his Treasure thus,
    Should be so full, and freely sent to us.

Were't not more than my heart can hold, or hord,
    Or than my Tongue can tell; I thus would pray,
Let him in Whom all Fulness Dwells, dwell, Lord 45
    Within my Heart: this Treasure therein lay.
    I then shall sweetly tune thy Praise, When hee
    In Whom all Fulness dwells, doth dwell in mee.

28. Meditation. Joh. 1.16. Of His Fulness
wee all receive: and Grace—

2. 7m [Sept.] *1688*. Pub. *W*.

When I Lord, send some Bits of Glory home,
    (For Lumps I lack) my Messenger, I finde,
Bewildred, lose his Way being alone
    In my befogg'd Dark Phancy, Clouded minde.
    Thy Bits of Glory packt in Shreds of Praise 5
    My Messenger doth lose, losing his Wayes.

3 *lose*] orig: and lose

Lord Cleare the Coast: and let thy sweet sun shine.
    That I may better speed a second time:
Oh! fill my Pipkin with thy Blood red Wine:
    I'l drinke thy Health: To pledge thee is no Crime.   10
    Although I but an Earthen Vessell bee
    Convay some of thy Fulness into mee.

Thou, thou my Lord, art full, top full of Grace,
    The Golden Sea of Grace: Whose springs thence come,
And Pretious Drills, boiling in ery place.   15
    Untap thy Cask, and let my Cup Catch some.
    Although its in an Earthen Vessells Case,
    Let it no Empty Vessell be of Grace.

Let thy Choice Caske, shed, Lord, into my Cue
    A Drop of Juyce presst from thy Noble Vine.   20
My Bowl is but an Acorn Cup, I sue
    But for a Drop: this will not empty thine.
    Although I'me in an Earthen Vessells place,
    My Vessell make a Vessell, Lord, of Grace.

My Earthen Vessell make thy Font also: 25
    And let thy Sea my Spring of Grace in't raise.
Spring up oh Well. My Cup with Grace make flow.
    Thy Drops will on my Vessell ting thy Praise.
    I'l sing this Song, when I these Drops Embrace.
    My Vessell now's a Vessell of thy Grace.   30

29. Meditation. Joh. 20.17. My Father,
        and your Father, to my God,
        and your God.

11.9m [Nov.] *1688.* Pub. *W*.

My shattred Phancy stole away from mee,
    (Wits run a Wooling over Edens Parke)

21 *My*] PW By   27 *My*] PW my

And in Gods Garden saw a golden Tree,
> Whose Heart was All Divine, and gold its barke.
> Whose glorious limbs and fruitfull branches strong   5
> With Saints, and Angells bright are richly hung.

Thou! thou! my Deare-Deare Lord, art this rich Tree
> The Tree of Life Within Gods Paradise.
I am a Withred Twig, dri'de fit to bee
> A Chat Cast in thy fire, Writh off by Vice.   10
> Yet if thy Milke white-Gracious Hand will take mee
> And grafft mee in this golden stock, thou'lt make mee.

Thou'lt make me then its Fruite, and Branch to spring.
> And though a nipping Eastwinde blow, and all
Hells Nymps with spite their Dog's sticks thereat ding   15
> To Dash the Grafft off, and it's fruits to fall,
> Yet I shall stand thy Grafft, and Fruits that are
> Fruits of the Tree of Life thy Grafft shall beare.

I being grafft in thee there up do stand
> In us Relations all that mutuall are.   20
I am thy Patient, Pupill, Servant, and
> Thy Sister, Mother, Doove, Spouse, Son, and Heire.
> Thou art my Priest, Physician, Prophet, King,
> Lord, Brother, Bridegroom, Father, Ev'ry thing.

I being grafft in thee am graffted here   25
> Into thy Family, and kindred Claim
To all in Heaven, God, Saints, and Angells there.
> I thy Relations my Relations name.
> Thy Father's mine, thy God my God, and I
> With Saints, and Angells draw Affinity.   30

My Lord, what is it that thou dost bestow?
> The Praise on this account fills up, and throngs
Eternity brimfull, doth overflow
> The Heavens vast with rich Angelick Songs.
> How should I blush? how Tremble at this thing,   35
> Not having yet my Gam-Ut, learnd to sing.

4 *Divine,*] PW Divine.   12 *make mee*] mee Conj.   29 *Father's*] PW Fathers

But, Lord, as burnish't Sun Beams forth out fly
    Let Angell-Shine forth in my Life out flame,
That I may grace thy gracefull Family
      And not to thy Relations be a Shame.   40
      Make mee thy Grafft, be thou my Golden Stock.
      Thy Glory then I'le make my fruits and Crop.

30. Meditation. 2 Cor. 5.17.—He is
a New Creature.

6. 11m [Jan.] *1688.* Pub. *W.*

The Daintiest Draught thy Pensill ever Drew:
    The finest vessell, Lord, thy fingers fram'de:
The statelist Palace Angells e're did view,
      Under thy Hatch betwixt Decks here Contain'd
      Broke, marred, spoild, undone, Defild doth ly   5
      In Rubbish ruinde by thine Enemy.

What Pittie's this? Oh Sunshine Art! What Fall?
    Thou that more Glorious wast than glories Wealth!
More Golden far than Gold! Lord, on whose Wall
      Thy scutchons hung, the Image of thyselfe!   10
      Its ruinde, and must rue, though Angells should
      To hold it up heave while their Heart Strings hold.

But yet thou stem of Davids stock when dry
    And shrivled held, although most green was lopt
Whose sap a sovereign Sodder is, whereby   15
      The breach repared is in which its dropt.
      Oh Gracious Twig! thou Cut off? bleed rich juyce
      T'Cement the Breach, and Glories shine reduce?

Oh Lovely One! how doth thy Loveliness
    Beam through the Chrystall Casements of the Eyes   20
Of Saints, and Angells sparkling Flakes of Fresh

1 *ever*] PW every

Heart Ravishing Beauty, filling up their joyes?
And th'Divells too; if Envies Pupills stood
Not peeping there these sparkling Rayes t'exclude?

Thou Rod of Davids Root, Branch of his Bough   25
  My Lord, repare thy Palace, Deck thy Place.
I'm but a Flesh and Blood bag: Oh! do thou
    Sill, Plate, Ridge, Rib, and Rafter me with Grace.
    Renew my Soule, and guild it all within:
    And hang thy saving Grace on ery Pin.   30

My Soule, Lord, make thy Shining Temple, pave
  Its Floore all o're with Orient Grace: thus guild
It o're with Heavens gold: Its Cabbins have
    Thy Treasuries with Choicest thoughts up filld.
    Pourtray thy Glorious Image round about   35
    Upon thy Temple Walls within, and Out.

Garnish thy Hall with Gifts, Lord, from above
  With that Rich Coate of Male thy Righteousness,
Truths Belt, the Spirits Sword, the Buckler Love
    Hopes Helmet, and the Shield of Faith kept fresh.   40
    The Scutchons of thy Honour make my Sign
    As Garland Tuns are badges made of Wine.

New mould, new make me thus, me new Create
  Renew in me a spirit right, pure, true.
Lord make me thy New Creature, then new make   45
    All things to thy New Creature here anew,
    New Heart, New thoughts, New Words, New wayes likewise.
    New Glory then shall to thyselfe arise.

39 *Spirits*] orig: Plate

31. Meditation. 1 Cor. 3.21.22. All
things are yours.

17. 12m [Feb.] *1688.* Pub. UPT.

Begracde with Glory, gloried with Grace,
    In Paradise I was, when all Sweet Shines
Hung dangling on this Rosy World to face
    Mine Eyes, and Nose, and Charm mine Eares with Chimes.
    All these were golden Tills the which did hold   5
    My evidences wrapt in glorious folds.

But as a Chrystall Glass, I broke, and lost
    That Grace, and Glory I was fashion'd in
And cast this Rosy World with all its Cost
    Into the Dunghill Pit, and Puddle Sin.   10
    All right I lost in all Good things, each thing
    I had did hand a Vean of Venom in.

Oh! Sad-Sad thing! Satan is now turnd Cook:
    Sin is the Sauce he gets for ev'ry Dish.
I cannot bite a bit of Bread or Roote   15
    But what is sopt therein, and Venomish.
    Right's lost in what's my Right. Hence I do take
    Onely what's poison'd by th'infernall Snake.

But this is not the Worst: there's worse than this.
    My Tast is lost; no bit tasts sweet to mee,   20
But what is Dipt all over in this Dish
    Of Ranck ranck Poyson: this my Sauce must bee.
    Hell Heaven is, Heaven hell, yea Bitter Sweet:
    Poison's my Food: Food poison in't doth keep.

What e're we want, we cannot Cry for, nay,   25
    If that we could, we could not have it thus.
The Angell's can't devise, nor yet Convay

4 *Nose,*] PW Nose.   21 *Dish*] PW Dish.

Help in their Golden Pipes from God to us.
But thou my Lord, (Heart leape for joy and sing)
Hast done the Deed: and't makes the Heavens ring.   30

By mee all lost, by thee all are regain'd.
    All things are thus fall'n now into thy hande.
And thou steep'st in thy Blood what Sin had stain'd
        That th'Stains, and Poisons may not therein stand.
        And having stuck thy Grace all o're the same   35
        Thou giv'st it as a Glorious Gift again.

Cleare up my Right, my Lord, in thee, and make
    Thy Name stand Dorst upon my Soule in print,
In grace I mean, that so I may partake
        Of what I lost, in thee, and of thee in't.   40
        I'l take it then, Lord, at thy hand, and sing
        Out Hallelujah for thy Grace therein.

32. Meditation. 1 Cor. 3.22. Whether
Paul or Apollos, or Cephas.

28. 2m [Apr.] *1689*. Pub. PET.

Thy Grace, Dear Lord's my golden Wrack, I finde
    Screwing my Phancy into ragged Rhimes,
Tuning thy Praises in my feeble minde
        Untill I come to strike them on my Chimes.
        Were I an Angell bright, and borrow could   5
        King Davids Harp, I would them play on gold.

But plung'd I am, my minde is puzzled,
    When I would spin my Phancy thus unspun,
In finest Twine of Praise I'm muzzled.
        My tazzled Thoughts twirld into Snick-Snarls run.   10
        Thy Grace, my Lord, is such a glorious thing,
        It doth Confound me when I would it sing.

Eternall Love an Object mean did smite
    Which by the Prince of Darkness was beguilde,
That from this Love it ran and sweld with spite   15
    And in the way with filth was all defilde
    Yet must be reconcild, cleansd, and begrac'te
    Or from the fruits of Gods first Love displac'te.

Then Grace, my Lord, wrought in thy Heart a vent,
    Thy Soft Soft hand to this hard worke did goe,   20
And to the Milke White Throne of Justice went
    And entred bond that Grace might overflow.
    Hence did thy Person to my Nature ty
    And bleed through humane Veans to satisfy.

Oh! Grace, Grace, Grace! this Wealthy Grace doth lay   25
    Her Golden Channells from thy Fathers throne,
Into our Earthen Pitchers to Convay
    Heavens Aqua Vitae to us for our own.
    O! let thy Golden Gutters run into
    My Cup this Liquour till it overflow.   30

Thine Ordinances, Graces Wine-fats where
    Thy Spirits Walkes, and Graces runs doe ly
And Angells waiting stand with holy Cheere
    From Graces Conduite Head, with all Supply.
    These Vessells full of Grace are, and the Bowls   35
    In which their Taps do run, are pretious Souls.

Thou to the Cups dost say (that Catch this Wine,)
    This Liquour, Golden Pipes, and Wine-fats plain,
Whether Paul, Apollos, Cephas, all are thine.
    Oh Golden Word! Lord speake it ore again.   40
    Lord speake it home to me, say these are mine.
    My Bells shall then thy Praises bravely chime.

13 *an*] orig: did an
24 *bleed*] orig: bled   26 *Golden*] PW Goldens   27 *Pitchers*] PW Pilchers
37 *that Catch*] orig: Catching

    38: Golden Pipes. The figure probably comes from Zech. 4:12. Cf. Herbert's
"The Pearl," lines 1–2, and "Whitsunday," lines 17–18.

33. Meditation. 1 Cor. 3.22. Life is
youres.

7. 5m [July] *1689*. Pub. *W.*

My Lord my Life, can Envy ever bee
    A Golden Vertue? Then would God I were
Top full thereof untill it colours mee
    With yellow streaks for thy Deare sake most Deare,
    Till I be Envious made by't at myselfe,   5
    As scarcely loving thee my Life, my Health.

Oh! what strange Charm encrampt my Heart with spite
    Making my Love gleame out upon a Toy?
Lay out Cart-Loads of Love upon a mite?
    Scarce lay a mite of Love on thee, my Joy?   10
    Oh, Lovely thou! Shalt not thou loved bee?
    Shall I ashame thee thus? Oh! shame for mee!

Nature's amaz'de, Oh monstrous thing Quoth shee,
    Not Love my life? What Violence doth split
True Love, and Life, that they should sunder'd bee?   15
    She doth not lay such Eggs, nor on them sit.
    How do I sever then my Heart with all
    Its Powers whose Love scarce to my Life doth crawle.

Glory lin'de out a Paradise in Power
    Where e'ry seed a Royall Coach became   20
For Life to ride in, to each shining Flower.
    And made mans Flower with glory all ore flame.
    Hells Inkfac'de Elfe black Venom spat upon
    The same, and kill'd it. So that Life is gone.

Life thus abusde fled to the golden Arke,   25
    Lay lockt up there in Mercie's seate inclosde:
Which did incorporate it whence its Sparke
    Enlivens all things in this Arke inclosde.

Oh, glorious Arke! Life's Store-House full of Glee!
  Shall not my Love safe lockt up ly in thee?   30

Lord arke my Soule safe in thyselfe, whereby
  I and my Life again may joyned bee.
That I may finde what once I did destroy
  Again Conferde upon my soul in thee.
    Thou art this Golden Ark; this Living Tree   35
    Where life lies treasurde up for all in thee.

Oh! Graft me in this Tree of Life within
  The Paradise of God, that I may live.
Thy Life make live in mee; I'le then begin
  To bear thy Living Fruits, and them forth give.   40
    Give mee my Life this way; and I'le bestow
    My Love on thee my Life, and it shall grow.

34. Meditation. 1 Cor. 3.22. Death is
           Yours.

25. 9m [Nov.] *1689.* Pub. PET.

My Lord I fain would Praise thee Well but finde
  Impossibilities blocke up my pass.
My tongue Wants Words to tell my thoughts, my Minde
  Wants thoughts to Comprehend thy Worth, alas!
    Thy Glory far Surmounts my thoughts, my thoughts   5
    Surmount my Words: Hence little Praise is brought.

But seing Non-Sense very Pleasant is
  To Parents, flowing from the Lisping Child,
I Conjue to thee, hoping thou in this
  Will finde some hearty Praise of mine Enfoild,   10
    But though my pen drop'd golden Words, yet would
    Thy Glory far out shine my Praise in Gold.

Poor wretched man Deaths Captive stood full Chuffe
  But thou my Gracious Lord didst finde reliefe,

14 *reliefe,*] PW reliefe

Thou King of Glory didst, to handy cuff   15
    With King of Terrours, and dasht out his Teeth,
    Plucktst out his sting, his Poyson quelst, his head
    To pieces brakest. Hence Cruell Death lies Dead.

And still thou by thy gracious Chymistry
    Dost of his Carkass Cordialls make rich, High,   20
To free from Death makst Death a remedy:
    A Curb to Sin, a Spur to Piety.
    Heavens brightsom Light shines out in Death's Dark Cave.
    The Golden Dore of Glory is the Grave.

The Painter lies who pensills death's Face grim   25
    With White bare butter Teeth, bare staring bones,
With Empty Eyeholes, Ghostly Lookes which fling
    Such Dread to see as raiseth Deadly groans,
    For thou hast farely Washt Deaths grim grim face
    And made his Chilly finger-Ends drop grace.   30

Death Tamde, Subdude, Washt fair by thee! Oh Grace!
    Made Usefull thus! thou unto thine dost say
Now Death is yours, and all it doth in't brace.
    The Grave's a Down bed now made for your clay.
    Oh! Happiness! How should our Bells hereby   35
    Ring Changes, Lord, and praises trust with joy.

Say I am thine, My Lord: Make me thy bell
    To ring thy Praise. Then Death is mine indeed
A Hift to Grace, a Spur to Duty; Spell
    To Fear; a Frost to nip each naughty Weede.   40
    A Golden doore to Glory. Oh I'le sing
    This Triumph o're the Grave! Death where's thy Sting?

15 *didst*,] PW didst   18 *Hence*] PW hence   23 *Death's*] PW Death
26 *Teeth*,] PW Teeth   31 *Washt*] PW Whasht   40 *naughty*] Conj.

    34: The Grave's a Down bed . . . Cf. Herbert's "Death," lines 21–24:

        Therefore we can go die as sleep, and trust
            Half that we have
         Unto an honest faithfull grave;
        Making our pillows either down, or dust.

35. Meditation. 1 Cor. 3.22. Things Present.

19. 11m [Jan.] *1689*. Pub. PET.

Oh! that I ever felt what I profess.
   'Twould make me then the happi'st man alive.
Ten thousand Worlds of Saints can't make this less
   By living on't, but it would make them thrive.
   These Loaves and Fishes are not lessened   5
   Nor Pasture over stock, by being fed.

Lord am I thine? art thou, Lord, mine? So rich!
   How doth thy Wealthy bliss branch out thy sweets
Through all things Present? These the Vent-holes which
   Let out those Ravishing Joys our Souls to greet?   10
   Impower my Powers sweet Lord till up they raise
   My 'Fections that thy glory on them blaze.

How many things are there now, who display'th?
   How many Acts each thing doth here dispense?
How many Influences each thing hath?   15
   How many Contraries each Influence?
   How many Contraries from Things do flow?
   From Acts? from Influences? Who can show?

How Glorious then is he that doth all raise
   Rule and Dispose and make them all Conspire   20
In all their Jars, and Junctures, Good-bad wayes
   To meliorate the self same Object higher?
   Earth, Water, Fire, Winds, Herbs, Trees, Beasts and Men,
   Angells, and Divells, Bliss, Blasts, advance one stem?

Hell, Earth, and Heaven with their Whole Troops come   25
   Contrary Windes, Grace, and Disgrace, Soure, Sweet,
Wealth, Want, Health, Sickness, to Conclude in Sum
   All Providences Works in this good meet?

4 *on't*,] PW on't.

Who, who can do't, but thou, my Lord? and thou
Dost do this thing. Yea thou performst it now.   30

Oh, that the Sweets of all these Windings, spoute
      Might, and these Influences streight, and Cross,
Upon my Soule, to make thy Shine breake out
      That Grace might in get and get out my dross!
      My Soule up lockt then in this Clod of Dust   35
      Would lock up in't all Heavenly Joyes most just.

But oh! thy Wisdom, Lord! thy Grace! thy Praise!
      Open mine Eyes to see the same aright.
Take off their film, my Sins, and let the Rayes
      Of thy bright Glory on my peepholes light.   40
      I fain would love and better love thee should,
      If 'fore me thou thy Loveliness unfold.

Lord, Cleare my Sight, thy Glory then out dart.
      And let thy Rayes beame Glory in mine eye
And stick thy Loveliness upon my heart,   45
      Make me the Couch on which thy Love doth ly.
      Lord make my heart thy bed, thy heart make mine.
      Thy Love bed in my heart, bed mine in thine.

36. Meditation. 1 Cor. 3.22. Things
          to come yours.

16. 1m [Mar.] *1689*. Pub. UPT.

What rocky heart is mine? My pincky Eyes
      Thy Grace spy blancht, Lord, in immensitie.
But finde the Sight me not to meliorize,
      O Stupid Heart! What strang-strange thing am I?
      I many months do drown in Sorrows Spring   5
      But hardly raise a Sigh to blow down Sin.

30 *Yea*] PW yea   5 *Spring*] orig: Springs   6 *Sin*] orig: Sins

To find thee Lord, thus overflowing kinde,
    And t'finde mee thine, thus overflowing vile,
A Riddle seems onrivetted I finde.
       This reason saith is hard to reconcile.   10
       Dost Vileness choose? Or can't thy kindness shown
       Me meliorate? Or am I not thine own?

The first two run thy glory would to Shame:
    The last plea doth my Soule to hell Confine.
My Faith therefore doth all these Pleas disdain.   15
       Thou kindness art, it saith, and I am thine.
       Upon this banck it doth on tiptoes stand
       To ken o're Reasons head at Graces hand.

But Did I say, I wonder, Lord, to spie
    Thy Selfe so kind; and I so vile yet thine?   20
I eate my Word: and wonder more that I
       No viler am, though all ore vile do shine.
       As full of Sin I am, as Egge of meate.
       Yet finde thy golden Rod my Sin to treate.

Nay did I say, I wonder t'see thy Store   25
    Of kindnesses, yet me thus vile with all?
I now Unsay my Say: I wonder more
       Thou dash me not to pieces with thy maule,
       But in the bed, Lord, of thy goodness lies
       The Reason of't, which makes my Wonders rise.   30

For now I wonder t'feele how I thus feele.
    My Love leapes into Creatures bosoms; and
Cold Sorrows fall into my Soule as Steel,
       When faile they, yet I kiss thy Love's White hand.
       I scarce know what t'make of myselfe. Wherefore   35
       I crave a Pardon, Lord, for thou hast Store.

How wondrous rich art thou? Thy Storehouse vast
    Holdes more ten thousand fold told ore and ore
Than this Wide World Can hold. The doore unhasp.
       And bring me thence a Pardon out therefore.   40
       Thou Stoughst the World so tite with present things
       That things to Come, though crowd full hard, cant in.

30 *of't*,] PW of't   34 *I kiss*] Conj.   39 *Wide*] Conj.

These things to Come, tread on the heels of those.
  The presents breadth doth with the broad world run.
The Depth and breadth of things to come out goes   45
  Unto Times End which bloweth out the Sun.
  These breadth and length meate out Eternity.
  These are the things that in thy Storehouse ly.

A Cockle Shell contains this World as well
  As can this World thy Liberallness contain.   50
And by thy Will these present things all fell
  Unto thy Children for their present gain;
  And things to Come too, to Eternity.
  Thou Willedst them: they're theirs by Legacy.

But am I thine? Oh! what strange thing's in mee?   55
  Enricht thus by thy Legacy? yet finde
When one small Twig's broke off, the breach should bee
  Such an Enfeebling thing upon my minde.
  Then take a pardon from thy Store, and twist
  It in my Soule for help. 'Twill not be mist.   60

I am asham'd to say I love thee do.
  But dare not for my Life, and Soule deny't.
Yet wonder much Love's Springs should lie so low
  Thy loveliness its Object shines so bright.
  Shall all the Beams of Love upon me shine?   65
  And shall my Love Love's Object still make pine?

I'me surely made a Gazing Stock to all.
  The Holy Angells Wonder: and the Mock
Of Divells (pining that they misse it all)
  To see these beams gild me a Stupid Stock.   70
  Thy Argument is good, Lord point it, come
  Let't lance my heart, till True Loves Veane doth run.

But that there is a Crevice for one hope
  To creep in, and this Message to Convay
That I am thine, makes me refresh. Lord ope   75

46 *Times*] orig: the End of Times 66 *Love Love's*] orig: Love's Object
70 *gild*] orig: guild

The Doore so wide that Love may Scip, and play.
My Spirits then shall dance thy Praise. I'me thine.
And Present things with things to come are mine.

37. Meditation. 1 Cor. 3.23. You are
Christ's.

4.3m [May] *1690*. Pub. ETG.

My Soule, Lord, quailes to thinke that I should bee
    So high related, have such colours faire
Stick in my Hat, from Heaven: yet should see
    My Soule thus blotcht: Hells Liveries to beare.
    What Thine? New-naturizd? Yet this Relation   5
    Thus barren, though't 's a Priviledg-Foundation?

Shall I thy Vine branch be, yet grapes none beare?
    Grafft in thy Olive stand: and fatness lack?
A Shackeroon, a Ragnell, yet an Heire?
    Thy spouse, yet, oh! my Wedden Ring thus slack?   10
    Should Angel-Feathers plume my Cap, I should
    Be swash? but oh! my Heart hereat grows Cold.

What is my Title but an empty Claim?
    Am I a fading Flower within thy Knot?
A Rattle, or a gilded Box, a Flame   15
    Of Painted Fire, a glorious Weedy Spot?
    The Channell ope of Union, the ground
    Of Wealth, Relation: yet I'me barren found?

What am I thine, and thou not mine? or dost
    Not thou thy Spouse joyn in thy Glory Cleare?   20
Is my Relation to thee but a boast?
    Or but a blustring say-so, or spruice jeere?
    Should Roses blow more late, sure I might get,
    If thine, some Prim-Rose or sweet Violet?

9 *Ragnell,*] PW Ragnell.   15 *gilded*] orig: guilded

Make me thy Branch to bare thy Grapes, Lord, feed   25
    Mee with thy bunch of Raisins of the Sun.
Mee stay with apples; let me eate indeed
    Fruits of the tree of Life: its richly hung.
    Am I thy Child, Son, Heir, thy Spouse, yet gain
    Not of the Rights that these Relations claim?   30

Am I hop't on thy knees, yet not at ease?
    Sunke in thy bosom, yet thy Heart not meet?
Lodgd in thine Arms? yet all things little please?
    Sung sweetly, yet finde not this singing sweet?
    Set at thy Table, yet scarce tast a Dish   35
    Delicious? Hugd, yet seldom gain a Kiss?

Why? Lord, why thus? Shall I in Question Call
    All my Relation to thyselfe? I know
It is no Gay to please a Child withall
    But is the Ground whence Priviledges flow.   40
    Then ope the sluce: let some thing spoute on me.
    Then I shall in a better temper bee.

38. Meditation. 1 Joh. 2.1. An Advocate
With the Father.

6. 5m [July] *1690.* Pub. ETP, *W.*

Oh! What a thing is Man? Lord, Who am I?
    That thou shouldst give him Law (Oh! golden Line)
To regulate his Thoughts, Words, Life thereby.
    And judge him Wilt thereby too in thy time.
    A Court of Justice thou in heaven holdst   5
    To try his Case while he's here housd on mould.

How do thy Angells lay before thine eye
    My Deeds both White, and Black I dayly doe?

28 *Fruits of the*] PW Fruits the
3 *Words*] orig: his Words   8 *I dayly*] orig: before***

How doth thy Court thou Pannellst there them try?
    But flesh complains. What right for this? let's know.   10
    For right, or wrong I can't appeare unto't.
    And shall a sentence Pass on such a suite?

Soft; blemish not this golden Bench, or place.
    Here is no Bribe, nor Colourings to hide
Nor Pettifogger to befog the Case   15
    But Justice hath her Glory here well tri'de.
    Her spotless Law all spotted Cases tends.
    Without Respect or Disrespect them ends.

God's Judge himselfe: and Christ Atturny is,
    The Holy Ghost Regesterer is founde.   20
Angells the sergeants are, all Creatures kiss
    The booke, and doe as Evidences abounde.
    All Cases pass according to pure Law
    And in the sentence is no Fret, nor flaw.

What saist, my soule? Here all thy Deeds are tri'de.   25
    Is Christ thy Advocate to pleade thy Cause?
Art thou his Client? Such shall never slide.
    He never lost his Case: he pleads such Laws
    As Carry do the same, nor doth refuse
    The Vilest sinners Case that doth him Choose.   30

This is his Honour, not Dishonour: nay
    No Habeas-Corpus gainst his Clients came
For all their Fines his Purse doth make down pay.
    He Non-Suites Satan's Suite or Casts the Same.
    He'l plead thy Case, and not accept a Fee.   35
    He'l plead Sub Forma Pauperis for thee.

My Case is bad. Lord, be my Advocate.
    My sin is red: I'me under Gods Arrest.
Thou hast the Hint of Pleading; plead my State.
    Although it's bad thy Plea will make it best.   40
    If thou wilt plead my Case before the King:
    I'le Waggon Loads of Love, and Glory bring.

39 *Hint*] PW Hit

39. Meditation. from 1 Joh. 2.1. If any man sin, we have an Advocate.

9.9m [Nov.] *1690.* Pub. PET.

My Sin! my Sin, My God, these Cursed Dregs,
    Green, Yellow, Blew streakt Poyson hellish, ranck,
Bubs hatcht in natures nest on Serpents Eggs,
    Yelp, Cherp and Cry; they set my Soule a Cramp.
    I frown, Chide, strik and fight them, mourn and Cry   5
    To Conquour them, but cannot them destroy.

I cannot kill nor Coop them up: my Curb
    'S less than a Snaffle in their mouth: my Rains
They as a twine thrid, snap: by hell they're spurd:
    And load my Soule with swagging loads of pains.   10
    Black Imps, young Divells, snap, bite, drag to bring
    And pick mee headlong hells dread Whirle Poole in.

Lord, hold thy hand: for handle mee thou may'st
    In Wrath: but, oh, a twinckling Ray of hope
Methinks I spie thou graciously display'st.   15
    There is an Advocate: a doore is ope.
    Sin's poyson swell my heart would till it burst,
    Did not a hope hence creep in't thus, and nurse't.

Joy, joy, Gods Son's the Sinners Advocate
    Doth plead the Sinner guiltless, and a Saint.   20
But yet Atturnies pleas spring from the State
    The Case is in: if bad its bad in plaint.
    My Papers do contain no pleas that do
    Secure mee from, but knock me down to, woe.

I have no plea mine Advocate to give: 25
    What now? He'l anvill Arguments greate Store
Out of his Flesh and Blood to make thee live.
    O Deare bought Arguments: Good pleas therefore.

17 *swell*] PW 'swell   22 *plaint*] PW paint

Nails made of heavenly Steel, more Choice than gold
Drove home, Well Clencht, eternally will hold.   30

Oh! Dear bought Plea, Deare Lord, what buy't so deare?
What with thy blood purchase thy plea for me?
Take Argument out of thy Grave t'appeare
And plead my Case with, me from Guilt to free.
These maule both Sins, and Divells, and amaze   35
Both Saints, and Angells; Wreath their mouths with praise.

What shall I doe, my Lord? what do, that I
May have thee plead my Case? I fee thee will
With Faith, Repentance, and obediently
Thy Service gainst Satanick Sins fulfill.   40
I'l fight thy fields while Live I do, although
I should be hackt in pieces by thy foe.

Make me thy Friend, Lord, be my Surety: I
Will be thy Client, be my Advocate:
My Sins make thine, thy Pleas make mine hereby.   45
Thou wilt mee save, I will thee Celebrate.
Thou'lt kill my Sins that cut my heart within:
And my rough Feet shall thy smooth praises sing.

40. Meditation. 1 Joh. 2.2. He is a
Propitiation for our Sin.

12m [Feb.] *1690/1*. Pub. ETG.

Still I complain; I am complaining still.
Oh! woe is me! Was ever Heart like mine?
A Sty of Filth, a Trough of Washing-Swill
A Dunghill Pit, a Puddle of mere Slime.
A Nest of Vipers, Hive of Hornets; Stings.   5
A Bag of Poyson, Civit-Box of Sins.

2: *Was ever Heart like mine?* This question, repeated several times, is probably an echo of the refrain in Herbert's "The Sacrifice": "Was ever grief like mine?"

Was ever Heart like mine? So bad? black? Vile?
  Is any Divell blacker? Or can Hell
Produce its match? It is the very Soile
  Where Satan reads his Charms, and sets his Spell.   10
  His Bowling Ally, where he sheeres his fleece
  At Nine Pins, Nine Holes, Morrice, Fox and Geese.

His Palace Garden where his courtiers walke.
  His Jewells Cabbinet. Here his Caball
Do sham it, and truss up their Privie talk   15
  In Fardells of Consults and bundles all.
  His shambles, and his Butchers stale's herein.
  It is the Fuddling Schoole of every sin.

Was ever Heart like mine? Pride, Passion, fell.
  Ath'ism, Blasphemy, pot, pipe it, dance   20
Play Barlybreaks, and at last Couple in Hell.
  At Cudgells, Kit-Cat, Cards and Dice here prance.
  At Noddy, Ruff-and-trumpt, Jing, Post-and-Pare,
  Put, One-and-thirty, and such other ware.

Grace shuffled is away: Patience oft sticks   25
  Too soon, or draws itselfe out, and's out Put.
Faith's over trumpt, and oft doth lose her tricks.
  Repentance's Chalkt up Noddy, and out shut.
  They Post, and Pare off Grace thus, and its shine.
  Alas! alas! was ever Heart like mine?   30

Sometimes methinks the serpents head I mall:
  Now all is still: my spirits do recreute.
But ere my Harpe can tune sweet praise, they fall
  On me afresh, and tare me at my Root.
  They bite like Badgers now nay worse, although   35
  I tooke them toothless sculls, rot long agoe.

My Reason now's more than my sense, I feele
  I have more Sight than Sense. Which seems to bee
A Rod of Sun beams t'whip mee for my steele.
  My Spirits spiritless, and dull in mee   40

17 *stale's*] orig: stall's   26 *Put*] orig: Putsh   40 *and dull*] orig: abide

For my dead prayerless Prayers: the Spirits winde
Scarce blows my mill about. I little grinde.

Was ever Heart like mine? My Lord, declare.
 I know not what to do: What shall I doe?
I wonder, split I don't upon Despare.   45
  Its grace's wonder that I wrack not so.
  I faintly shun't: although I see this Case
  Would say, my sin is greater than thy grace.

Hope's Day-peep dawns hence through this chinck. Christs name
 Propitiation is for sins. Lord, take   50
It so for mine. Thus quench thy burning flame
  In that clear stream that from his side forth brake.
  I can no Comfort take while thus I see
  Hells cursed Imps thus jetting strut in mee.

Lord take thy sword: these Anakims destroy: 55
 Then soake my soule in Zions Bucking tub
With Holy Soap, and Nitre, and rich Lye.
  From all Defilement me cleanse, wash and rub.
  Then wrince, and wring mee out till th'water fall
  As pure as in the Well: not foule at all.   60

And let thy Sun, shine on my Head out cleare.
 And bathe my Heart within its radient beams:
Thy Christ make my Propitiation Deare.
  Thy Praise shall from my Heart breake forth in streams.
  This reeching Vertue of Christs blood will quench   65
  Thy Wrath, slay Sin and in thy Love mee bench.

49 *Hence* canceled at beginning of line   50 *sins*] orig: our sins
take] orig: take it   56–7 Two lines written between 56 and 57 have been
canceled: Oh! wash mee well and all my Sin out rub, / Then rince, and wring
mee cleare out: till th' water f●●●.   62 *its*] orig: these

41. Meditation. Joh. 14.2. I go to
prepare a Place for you.

24. 3m [May] *1691*. Pub. UPT.

A Clew of Wonders! Clusterd Miracles!
    Angells, come whet your sight hereon. Here's ground.
Sharpen your Phansies here, ye Saints in Spiricles.
    Here is enough in Wonderment to drownd's.
    Make here the Shining dark or White on which   5
    Let all your Wondring Contemplations pitch.

The Magnet of all Admiration's here.
    Your tumbling thoughts turn here. Here is Gods Son,
Wove in a Web of Flesh, and Bloode rich geere.
    Eternall Wisdoms Huswifry well spun.   10
    Which through the Laws pure Fulling mills did pass.
    And so went home the Wealthy'st Web that was.

And why thus shew? Hark, harke, my Soule. He came
    To pay thy Debt. And being come most Just
The Creditor did sue him for the same,   15
    Did winn the Case, and in the grave him thrust.
    Who having in this Prison paid the Debt.
    And took a Quittance, made Death's Velvet fret.

He broke her Cramping tallons did unlute
    The sealed Grave, and gloriously up rose.   20
Ascendeth up to glory on this Sute,
    Prepares a place for thee where glorie glowes.
    Yea yea for thee, although thy griefe out gush
    At such black Sins at which the Sun may blush.

What Wonder's here? Big belli'd Wonders in't   25
    Remain, though wrought for Saints as white as milk.
But done for me whose blot's as black as inke.
    A Clew of Wonders finer far than Silke.

3 *Saints*] PW Saint   *Spiricles*] PW Spirit'les   **25** *in't*] PW in't.

Thy hand alone that wound this Clew I finde
Can to display these Wonders it unwinde.   30

Why didst thou thus? Reason stands gasterd here.
   She's overflown: this Soares above her Sight.
Gods onely Son for Sinners thus appeare,
     Prepare for Durt a throne in glory bright!
     Stand in the Doore of Glory to imbrace   35
     Such dirty bits of Dirt, with such a grace!

Reason, lie prison'd in this golden Chain.
   Chain up thy tongue, and silent stand a while.
Let this rich Love thy Love and heart obtain
     To tend thy Lord in all admiring Style.
     Lord screw my faculties up to the Skill   40
     And height of praise as answers thy good Will.

Then while I eye the Place thou hast prepar'de
     For such as I, I'le sing thy glory out
Untill thou welcome me, as 'tis declar'de   45
     In this sweet glory runing rounde about.
     I would do more but can't, Lord help me so
     That I may pay in glory what I owe.

42. Meditation. Rev. 3.22. I will give Him to sit with me in my Throne.

2. 6m [Aug.] *1691.* Pub. *W.*

Apples of gold, in silver pictures shrin'de
   Enchant the appetite, make mouths to water.
And Loveliness in Lumps, tunn'd, and enrin'de
     In Jasper Cask, when tapt, doth briskly vaper:
     Brings forth a birth of Keyes t'unlock Loves Chest,   5
     That Love, like Birds, may fly to't from its nest.

38 *silent*] PW silence   41 *screw*] orig: screw up
42 *thy*] orig: this   45 *me, as*] orig: me there, as   Med. *42, me*] PW we
2 *appetite,*] PW appetite.   6 *Love*] orig: new Love

Such is my Lord, and more. But what strang thing
    Am I become? Sin rusts my Lock all o're.
Though he ten thousand Keyes all on a string
      Takes out, scarce one, is found, unlocks the Doore.   10
      Which ope, my Love crincht in a Corner lies
      Like some shrunck Crickling: and scarce can rise.

Lord ope the Doore: rub off my Rust, Remove
    My sin, And Oyle my Lock. (Dust there doth shelfe).
My Wards will trig before thy Key: my Love   15
      Then, as enliven'd, leape will on thyselve.
      It needs must be, that giving handes receive
      Again Receivers Hearts furld in Love Wreath.

Unkey my Heart; unlock thy Wardrobe: bring
    Out royall Robes: adorne my Soule, Lord: so,   20
My Love in rich attire shall on my King
      Attend, and honour on him well bestow.
      In Glory he prepares for his a place
      Whom he doth all beglory here with grace.

He takes them to the shining threshould cleare   25
    Of his bright Palace, cloath'd in Grace's flame.
Then takes them in thereto, not onely there
      To have a Prospect, but possess the same.
      The Crown of Life, the Throne of Glorys Place,
      The Fathers House blancht o're with orient Grace.   30

Can'an in golden print enwalld with jems:
    A Kingdome rim'd with Glory round: in fine
A glorious Crown pal'de thick with all the stems
      Of Grace, and of all Properties Divine.
      How happy wilt thou make mee when these shall   35
      As a bless't Heritage unto mee fall?

Adorn me, Lord, with Holy Huswifry.
    All blanch my Robes with Clusters of thy Graces:
Thus lead me to thy threshold: give mine Eye
      A Peephole there to see bright glories Chases.   40
      Then take mee in: I'le pay, when I possess,
      Thy Throne, to thee the Rent in Happiness.

43. Meditation. Rev. 2.10. A Crown
of Life.

8. 9m [Nov.] *1691*. Pub. PET.

Fain I would sing thy Praise, but feare I feign.
    My Sin doth keepe out of my heart thy Feare,
Damps Love: defiles my Soule. Old Blots new stain.
    Hopes hoppled lie, and rusty Chains worn cleare.
    My Sins that make me stand in need of thee,   5
    Do keep me back to hugge all Sin I see.

Nature's Corrupt, a nest of Passion, Pride,
    Lust, Worldliness, and such like bubs: I pray,
But struggling finde, these bow my Heart aside.
    A Knot of Imps at barly breaks in't play.   10
    They do inchant me from my Lord, I finde,
    The thoughts whereof proove Daggers in my minde.

Pardon, and Poyson them, Lord, with thy Blood.
    Cast their Curst Karkasses out of my Heart.
My Heart fill with thy Love: let Grace it dub.   15
    Make this my Silver Studs by thy rich art.
    My Soule shall then be thy sweet Paradise.
    Thou'st be its Rose, and it thy Bed of Spice.

Why mayn't my Faith now drinke thy Health, Lord, ore,
    The Head of all my Sins? And Cast her Eye,   20
In glorifying glances, on the Doore
    Of thy Free Grace, where Crowns of Life do lie?
    Thou'lt give a Crown of Life to such as bee
    Faithfull to Death. And shall Faith faile in mee?

A Crown of Life, of Glory, Righteousness,   25
    Thou wilt adorn them with, that will not fade.
Shall Faith in mee shrinke up for Feebleness?
    Nor take my Sins by th'Crown, till Crownless made?

2 *Feare,*] PW Feare.

Breath, Lord, thy Spirit on my Faith, that I
    May have thy Crown of Life, and Sin may dy.   30

How Spirituall? Holy shall I shine, when I
    Thy Crown of Righteousness ware on my Head?
How Glorious when thou dost me glorify
    To ware thy Crown of Glory pollished?
      How shall I when thy Crown of Life I ware   35
      In lively Colours flowrish, fresh, and fair?

When thou shalt Crown me with these Crowns I'l bend
    My Shallow Crown to crown with Songs thy Name.
Angels shall set the tune, I'le it attend:
      Thy Glory'st be the burden of the same.   40
      Till then I cannot sing, my tongue is tide.
      Accept this Lisp till I am glorifide.

44. Meditation. 2 Tim. 4.8. A Crown
     of Righteousness.

17. 11m [Jan.] *1691.*

A Crown, Lord, yea, a Crown of Righteousness.
    Oh! what a Gift is this? Give Lord I pray
An Holy Head, and Heart it to possess
    And I shall give thee glory for the pay.
      A Crown is brave, and Righteousness much more.   5
      The glory of them both will pay the score.

A Crown indeed consisting of fine gold
    Adherent, and Inherent Righteousness,
Stuck with their Ripe Ripe Fruits in every fold
    Like studded Carbuncles they do it dress.   10
      A Righteous Life doth ever ware renown
      And thrusts the Head at last up in this Crown.

41 *then*] PW when

A Milk whit hand sets't on a Righteous Head.
    An hand Unrighteous can't dispose it nay
It's not in such an hande. Such hands would bed   15
    Black Smuts on't should they fingers on it lay.
    Who can the Crown of Righteousness suppose
    In an Unrighteous hand for to dispose.

When once upon the head its ever green
    And altogether Usde in Righteousness,   20
Where blessed bliss, and blissfull Peace is seen,
    And where no jar, nor brawler hath access.
    Oh! blessed Crown what hold the breadth of all
    The State of Happiness in Heavens Hall.

A Crown of Righteousness, a Righteous Head,   25
    Oh naughty man! my brain pan turrit is
Where Swallows build, and hatch: Sins black and red.
    My head and heart do ach, and frob at this.
    Lord were my Turret cleansd, and made by thee
    Thy Graces Dovehouse turret much might bee.   30

Oh! make it so: then Righteousness pure, true
    Shall Roost upon my boughs, and in my heart
And all its fruits that in Obedience grew
    To stud this Crown like jems in every part.
    Ist then be garnisht for this Crown, and thou   35
    Shalt have my Songs to diadem thy brow.

Oh! Happy me, if thou wilt Crown me thus.
    Oh! naughty heart! What swell with Sin? fy, fy.
Oh! Gracious Lord, me pardon: do not Crush
    Me all to mammocks: Crown and not destroy.   40
    Ile tune thy Prayses while this Crown doth come.
    Thy Glory bring I tuckt up in my Songe.

13 *on a*] orig: upon   34 *To stud*] orig: T'bestud   *this*] orig: thy

45. Meditation. 1 Pet. 5.4. Ye shall
receive a Crown of Glory.

24. 2m [Apr.] *1692.* Pub. UPT.

A Crown of Glory! Oh! I'm base, its true.
    My Heart's a Swamp, Brake, Thicket vile of Sin.
My Head's a Bog of Filth; Blood bain'd doth spew
    Its venom streaks of Poyson o're my Skin.
        My Members Dung-Carts that bedung at pleasure,   5
        My Life, the Pasture where Hells Hurdloms leasure.

Becrown'd with Filth! Oh! what vile thing am I?
    What Cost, and Charge to make mee Meddow ground?
To drain my Bogs? to lay my Frog-pits dry?
    To stub up all my brush that doth abound?   10
        That I may be thy Pasture fat and frim,
        Where thy choice Flowers, and Hearbs of Grace shine trim?

Vast charge thus to subdue me: Wonders play
    Hereat like Gamesters; 'bellisht Thoughts dresst fine,
In brave attire, cannot a finger lay   15
    Upon it that doth not besmut the Shine.
        Yet all this cost and more thou'rt at with me.
        And still I'm sad, a Seing Eye may see.

Yet more than this: my Hands that Crown'd thy Head
    With sharpest thorns, thou washest in thy Grace.   20
My Feet that did upon thy Choice Blood tread
    Thou makest beautifull thy Way to trace.
        My Head that knockt against thy head, thou hugg'st
        Within thy bosom: boxest not, nor lugg'st.

Nay more as yet: thou borrow'st of each Grace   25
    That stud the Hearts of Saints, and Angells bright

5 *bedung*] orig: with filth bedung   *pleasure,*] PW pleasure
14 *Gamesters;*] PW Gamesters   23 *hugg'st*] PW hugg' with
end of word worn away

Its brightest beams, the beams too of the place
    Where Glory dwells: and all the Beames of Light
    Thy, and thy Fathers Glorious Face out spread,
    To make this Crown of Glory for my head.   30

If it was possible the thoughts that are
    Imbellisht with the riches of this tender
Could torment such as do this bright Crown Ware,
    Their Love to thee Lord's lac'de so streight, and slender.
    These beams would draw up Griefe to cloude this Glory,   35
    But not so then; though now Grace acts this Story.

My Pen enravisht with these Rayes out strains
    A sorry Verse: and when my gold dwells in
A Purse guilt with the glory bright that flames
    Out from this Crown, I'le tune an higher pin.   40
    Then make me Lord heir of this Crown. Ile sing
    And make thy Praise on my Heroicks ring.

46. Meditation. Rev. 3.5. The same shall be cloathed in White Raiment.

17. 5m [July] *1692.* Pub. PET.

Nay, may I, Lord, believe it? Shall my Skeg
    Be ray'd in thy White Robes? My thatcht old Cribb
(Immortal Purss hung on a mortall Peg,)
    Wilt thou with fair'st array in heaven rig?
    I'm but a jumble of gross Elements   5
    A Snaile Horn where an Evill Spirit tents.

A Dirt ball dresst in milk white Lawn, and deckt
    In Tissue tagd with gold, or Ermins flush,
That mocks the Starrs, and sets them in a fret
    To se themselves out shone thus. Oh they blush.   10
    Wonders stand gastard here. But yet my Lord,
    This is but faint to what thou dost afford.

27 *brightest*] PW brighest   34 *Lord's*] PW Lord,s

I'm but a Ball of dirt. Wilt thou adorn
    Mee with thy Web wove in thy Loom Divine
The Whitest Web in Glory, that the morn   15
    Nay, that all Angell glory, doth ore shine?
    They ware no such. This whitest Lawn most fine
    Is onely worn, my Lord, by thee and thine.

This Saye's no flurr of Wit, nor new Coin'd Shape
    Of frollick Fancie in a Rampant Brain.   20
It's juyce Divine bled from the Choicest Grape
    That ever Zions Vinyarde did mentain.
    Such Mortall bits immortalliz'de shall ware
    More glorious robes, than glorious Angells bare.

Their Web is wealthy, wove of Wealthy Silke   25
    Well wrought indeed, its all brancht Taffity.
But this thy Web more white by far than milke
    Spun on thy Wheele twine of thy Deity
    Wove in thy Web, Fulld in thy mill by hand
    Makes them in all their bravery seem tand.   30

This Web is wrought by best, and noblest Art
    That heaven doth afford of twine most choice
All brancht, and richly flowerd in every part
    With all the sparkling flowers of Paradise
    To be thy Ware alone, who hast no peere   35
    And Robes for glorious Saints to thee most deare.

Wilt thou, my Lord, dress my poore wither'd Stump
    In this rich web whose whiteness doth excell
The Snow, though 'tis most black? And shall my Lump
    Of Clay ware more than e're on Angells fell?   40
    What shall my bit of Dirt be deckt so fine
    That shall Angelick glory all out shine?

Shall things run thus? Then Lord, my tumberill
    Unload of all its Dung, and make it cleane.
And load it with thy wealthi'st Grace untill   45
    Its Wheeles do crack, or Axletree complain.

19 *flurr*] orig: flux[?]

I fain would have it cart thy harvest in,
Before its loosed from its Axlepin.

Then screw my Strings up to thy tune that I
    May load thy Glory with my Songs of praise.   50
Make me thy Shalm, thy praise my Songs, whereby
    My mean Shoshannim may thy Michtams raise.
        And when my Clay ball's in thy White robes dresst
        My tune perfume thy praise shall with the best.

47. Meditation on Matt. 25.21. Enter thou into the joy of thy Lord.

9. 8m [Oct.] *1692*. Pub. ETG.

Strang, strang indeed. It rowell doth my heart
    With pegs of Greefe, and tents of greatest joy:
When I wore Angells Glory in each part
    And all my skirts wore flashes of rich die
        Of Heavenly Colour, hedg'd in with rosie Reechs,   5
        A spider spit its Vomit on my Cheeks.

This ranckling juyce bindg'd in its cursed stain
    Doth permeat both Soul and Body: soile
And drench each Fibre, and infect each grain.
    Its ugliness swells over all the ile.   10
        Whose stain'd mishapen bulk's too high, and broad
        For th'Entry of the narrow gate to God.

Ready to burst, thus, and to burn in hell:
    Now in my path I finde a Waybred spring
Whose leafe drops balm that doth this venom quell   15
    And juyce's a Bath, that doth all stains out bring
        And sparkling beauty in the room convay.
        Lord feed me with this Waybred Leafe, I pray.

53 *dresst*] PW dress   54 *best*] Conj.

7: *bindg'd* (see also Glossary): The spider vomit enters soul and body,
drenching and swelling each fiber.

My stain will out: and swelling swage apace.
    And holy Lusters on my shape appeare.   20
All Rosie Buds: and Lilly flowers of grace
      Will grace my turfe with sweet sweet glory here.
      Under whose shades Angells will bathing play
      Who'l guard my Pearle to glory, hous'd in clay.

Those Gates of Pearle, porter'd with Seraphims,   25
    On their carbuncle joynts will open wide.
And entrance give me where all glory swims
      In to the Masters Joy, e're to abide.
      O sweet sweet thought. Lord take this praise though thin.
      And when I'm in't Ile tune an higher pin.   30

48. Meditation on Matt. 25.21. Enter into the Joy of thy Lord.

10m ? [Dec.] *1692*. Pub. UPT.

When I, Lord, eye thy Joy, and my Love, small,
    My heart gives in: what now? Strange! Sure I love thee!
And finding brambles 'bout my heart to crawl
      My heart misgives mee. Prize I ought above thee?
      Such great Love hugging them, such small Love, thee!   5
      Whether thou hast my Love, I scarce can see.

My reason rises up, and chides my Cup
    Bright Lovelinesse itselfe. What not love thee!
Tumbling thy Joy, Lord, ore, it rounds me up.
      Shall loves nest be a thorn bush: not thee bee?   10
      Set Hovells up of thorn kids in my heart!
      Avant adultrous Love. From me depart.

The Influences my vile heart sucks in
    Of Puddle Water boyld by Sunn beams till

22 *sweet sweet*] orig: sweetest   12 *From*] PW from

Its Spiritless, and dead, nothing more thin   15
    Tasts wealthier than those thou dost distill.
    This seems to numb my heart to think that I
    Should null all good to optimate a toy.

Yet when the beamings, Lord, of thy rich Joys,
    Do guild my Soule, meethinks I'm sure I Love thee.   20
They Calcine all these brambly trumperys
    And now I'm sure that I prize naught above thee.
    Thy beams making a bonefire of my Stack
    Of Faggots, bring my Love to thee in'ts pack.

For when the Objects of thy Joy impress   25
    Their shining influences on my heart
My Soule seems an Alembick doth possess
    Love stilld into rich Spirits by thy Art.
    And all my pipes, were they ten thousand would
    Drop Spirits of Love on thee, more rich than gold.   30

Now when the world with all her dimples in't
    Smiles on me, I do love thee more than all:
And when her glory freshens, all in print,
    I prize thee still above it all. And shall.
    Nay all her best to thee, do what she can,   35
    Drops but like drops dropt in a Closestoole pan.

The Castings of thy Joy, my Lord therefore
    Let in the Cabbin of my Joy rise high,
And let thy Joy enter in mee before
    I enter do into my masters joy.   40
    Thy joyes in mee will make my Pipes to play
    For joy thy Praise while teather'd to my clay.

22 *prize*] orig: love   32 *Smiles*] PW Smile
37 *Castings*] conj.   41 *make*] PW makes

49. Meditation. Matt. 25.21. The joy
of thy Lord.

26. 12m [Feb.] *1692.* Pub. *W.*

Lord, do away my Motes: and Mountains great.
    My nut is vitiate. Its kirnell rots:
Come, kill the Worm, that doth its kirnell eate
    And strike thy sparkes within my tinderbox.
    Drill through my metall-heart an hole wherein   5
    With graces Cotters to thyselfe it pin.

A Lock of Steel upon my Soule, whose key
    The serpent keeps, I fear, doth lock my doore.
O pick't: and through the key-hole make thy way
    And enter in: and let thy joyes run o're.   10
    My Wards are rusty. Oyle them till they trig
    Before thy golden key: thy Oyle makes glib.

Take out the Splinters of the World that stick
    Do in my heart: Friends, Honours, Riches, and
The Shivers in't of Hell whose venoms quick   15
    And firy make it swoln and ranckling stand.
    These wound and kill: those shackle strongly to
    Poore knobs of Clay, my heart. Hence sorrows grow.

Cleanse, and enlarge my kask: It is too small:
    And tartarizd with worldly dregs dri'de in't.   20
It's bad mouth'd too: and though thy joyes do Call
    That boundless are, it ever doth them stint.
    Make me thy Chrystall Caske: those wines in't tun
    That in the Rivers of thy joyes do run.

Lord make me, though suckt through a straw or Quill,   25
    Tast of the Rivers of thy joyes, some drop.

11 *Wards*] orig: Oyl   18 *Hence*] PW hence   22 *are,*] PW are.

'Twill sweeten me: and all my Love distill
　　　Into thy glass, and me for joy make hop.
　　　'Twill turn my water into wine: and fill
　　　My Harp with Songs my Masters joyes distill.　　　30

28 *glass*,] PW glass.

Preparatory Meditations

1. Meditation. Col. 2.17. Which are Shaddows of things to come and the body is Christs.

[16] *93.*

Oh Leaden heeld. Lord, give, forgive I pray.
    Infire my Heart: it bedded is in Snow.
I Chide myselfe seing myselfe decay.
    In heate and Zeale to thee, I frozen grow.
    File my dull Spirits: make them sharp and bright: 5
    Them firbush for thyselfe, and thy delight.

My Stains are such, and sinke so deep, that all
    The Excellency in Created Shells
Too low, and little is to make it fall
    Out of my leather Coate wherein it dwells.   10
    This Excellence is but a Shade to that
    Which is enough to make my Stains go back.

The glory of the world slickt up in types
    In all Choise things chosen to typify,
His glory upon whom the worke doth light,   15
    To thine's a Shaddow, or a butterfly.
    How glorious then, my Lord, art thou to mee
    Seing to cleanse me, 's worke alone for thee.

The glory of all Types doth meet in thee.
    Thy glory doth their glory quite excell: 20
More than the Sun excells in its bright glee
    A nat, an Earewig, Weevill, Snaile, or Shell.
    Wonders in Crowds start up; your eyes may strut
    Viewing his Excellence, and's bleeding cut.

Oh! that I had but halfe an eye to view   25
    This excellence of thine, undazled: so
Therewith to give my heart a touch anew
    Untill I quickned am, and made to glow.
    All is too little for thee: but alass
    Most of my little all hath other pass.   30

1 *I*] orig: my   4 *thee,*] PW thee.   16 *To thine's*] orig: **Is but**
22 *nat,*] PW nat.

Then Pardon, Lord, my fault: and let thy beams
    Of Holiness pierce through this Heart of mine.
Ope to thy Blood a passage through my veans.
    Let thy pure blood my impure blood refine.
    Then with new blood and spirits I will dub   35
    My tunes upon thy Excellency good.

2. Meditation. Coll. 1.15. The First Born of Every Creature.

Undated.

Oh! Golden Rose! Oh. Glittering Lilly White
    Spic'd o're With heavens File divine, till Rayes
Fly forth whose Shine doth Wrack the strongest Sight
    That Wonders Eye is tent of, while't doth gaze
    On thee. Whose Swaddle Bonde's Eternity.   5
    And Sparkling Cradle is Rich Deity.

First Born of e'ry Being: hence a Son
    Begot o'th'First: Gods onely Son begot.
Hence Deity all ore. Gods nature run
    Into a Filiall Mould: Eternall knot.   10
    A Father then, and Son: persons distinct.
    Though them Sabellians contrar'ly inckt.

This mall of Steell falls hard upon those foes
    Of truth, who make the Holy Trinity
Into One Person: Arrians too and those   15
    Socinians calld, who do Christs Deity
    Bark out against. But Will they, nill they, they
    Shall finde this Mall to split their brains away.

Come shine, Deare Lord, out in my heart indeed
    First Born; in truth before thee there was none   20
First Born, as man, born of a Virgin's seed:
    Before or after thee such up ne'er sprung.

Hence Heir of all things lockt in natures Chest:
And in thy Fathers too: extreamly best.

Thou Object of Gods boundless brightest Love,   25
    Invested with all sparkling rayes of Light
Distill thou down, what hony falls above
    Bedew the Angells Copses, fill our Sight
    And hearts therewith within thy Father's joy.
    These are but Shreads under thy bench that ly.   30

Oh! that my Soul was all enamored
    With this First Born enough: a Lump of Love
Son of Eternall Father, Chambered
    Once in a Virgins Womb, dropt from above.
    All Humane royalty hereby Divin'de.   35
    The First Born's Antitype: in whom they're shrin'de.

Make mee thy Babe, and him my Elder Brother.
    A Right, Lord grant me in his Birth Right high.
His Grace, my Treasure make above all other:
    His Life my Sampler: My Life his joy.   40
    I'le hang my love then on his heart, and sing
    New Psalms on Davids Harpe to thee and him.

3. Meditation. Rom. 5.14. Who is the Figure of Him that was to come.

15. 8m [Oct.] *1693*. Pub. ETP, *W*.

Like to the Marigold, I blushing close
    My golden blossoms when thy sun goes down:
Moist'ning my leaves with Dewy Sighs, half frose
    By the nocturnall Cold, that hoares my Crown.
    Mine Apples ashes are in apple shells   5
    And dirty too: strange and bewitching spells!

28 *Copses,*] PW Copses.   29 *Father's*] PW Father

5: *Apples ashes.* The *apples* here are Apples of Sodom (Dead Sea Fruit)—of fair appearance but turning to smoke and ashes when plucked.

When Lord, mine Eye doth spie thy Grace to beame
    Thy Mediatoriall glory in the shine
Out Spouted so from Adams typick streame
    And Emblemiz'd in Noahs pollisht shrine   10
      Thine theirs outshines so far it makes their glory
      In brightest Colours, seem a smoaky story.

But when mine Eye full of these beams, doth cast
    Its rayes upon my dusty essence thin
Impregnate with a Sparke Divine, defacde,   15
    All Candid o're with Leprosie of Sin,
    Such Influences on my Spirits light,
    Which them as bitter gall, or Cold ice smite.

My brissled sins hence do so horrid peare,
    None but thyselfe, (and thou deckt up must bee   20
In thy Transcendent glory sparkling cleare)
    A Mediator unto God for mee.
    So high they rise, Faith scarce can toss a Sight
    Over their head upon thyselfe to light.

Is't possible such glory, Lord, ere should   25
    Center its Love on me Sins Dunghill else?
My Case up take? make it its own? Who would
    Wash with his blood my blots out? Crown his shelfe
    Or Dress his golden Cupboard with such ware?
    This makes my pale facde Hope almost despare.   30

Yet let my Titimouses Quill suck in
    Thy Graces milk Pails some small drop: or Cart
A Bit, or Splinter of some Ray, the wing
    Of Grace's sun sprindgd out, into my heart:
    To build there Wonders Chappell where thy Praise   35
    Shall be the Psalms sung forth in gracious layes.

9 *Out Spouted*] orig: Spouted out   11 *makes*] PW make
23 *high*] PW hugh

4. Meditation. Gal. 4.24. Which things are an Allegorie.

24. 10m [Dec.] *1693*. Pub. PET.

My Gracious Lord, I would thee glory doe:
　　But finde my Garden over grown with weeds:
My Soile is sandy; brambles o're it grow;
　　My Stock is stunted; branch no good Fruits breeds.
　　My Garden weed: Fatten my Soile, and prune　　　5
　　My Stock, and make it with thy glory bloome.

O Glorious One, the gloriou'st thought I thincke
　　Of thee falls black as Inck upon thy Glory.
The brightest Saints that rose, do Star like, pinck.
　　Nay, Abrams Shine to thee's an Allegory,　　　10
　　Or fleeting Sparke in th'Smoke, to typify
　　Thee, and thy Glorious Selfe in mystery.

Should all the Sparks in heaven, the Stars there dance
　　A Galliard, Round about the Sun, and stay
His Servants (while on Easter morn his prance　　　15
　　Is o're, which old wives prate of) O brave Play.
　　Thy glorious Saints thus boss thee round, which stand
　　Holding thy glorious Types out in their hand.

But can I thinck this Glory greate, its head
　　Thrust in a pitchy cloude, should strangled ly　　　20
Or tucking up its beams should go to bed
　　Within the Grave, darke me to glorify?
　　This Mighty thought my hearts too streight for, though
　　I hold it by the hand, and let not goe.

Then, my Blesst Lord, let not the Bondmaids type　　　25
　　Take place in mee. But thy blesst Promisd Seed.

25: Bondmaids. Cf. Gal. 4:22–24: "For it is written, that Abraham had two
sons, the one by a bondmaid, the other by a freewoman. But he who was of
the bondwoman was born after the flesh; but he of the freewoman was by
promise. Which things are an allegory."

Distill thy Spirit through thy royall Pipe
    Into my Soule, and so my Spirits feed,
    Then them, and me still into praises right
    Into thy Cup where I to swim delight.   30

Though I desire so much, I can't o're doe.
    All that my Can contains, to nothing comes
When summed up, it onely Cyphers grows
    Unless thou set thy Figures to my Sums.
    Lord set thy Figure 'fore them, greate, or small.   35
    To make them something, and I'l give thee all.

5. Meditation on Gal. 3.16. And to thy Seed Which is Christ.

4.1m [Mar.] *1693/4.*

Art thou, Lord, Abraham's Seed, and Isaac too?
    His Promisd Seed? That One and Only Seed?
How can this bee? Paul certainly saith true.
    But one Seed promisd. Sir this Riddle read.
    Christ is the Metall: Isaack is the Oar.   5
    Christ is the Pearle, in Abraham's tread therefore.

Christ's Antitype Isaac his Type up spires
    In many things, but Chiefly this because
This Isaac, and the Ram caught in the briars
    One Sacrifice, fore shew by typick laws   10
    Christs Person, all Divine, joynd whereto's made
    Unperson'd Manhood, on the Altar's laid.

The full grown Ram, provided none knows how,
    Typing Christ's Manhood, made by God alone
Caught in the brambles by the horns, must bow,   15
    Under the Knife: The manhoods Death, and Groan.

6 *tread*] Conj.   11 *joynd whereto's made*] orig: unto it tys
12 *on*] orig: and   *Altar's laid*] orig: Altar lys   14 *Christ's*] PW Christ

    Yet Isaac's leaping from the Altar's bed,
    Foretold its glorious rising from the Dead.

But why did things run thus? For Sin indeed,
    No lesser price than this could satisfy.   20
Oh costly Sin! this makes mine intraills bleed.
    What fills my Shell, did make my Saviour die.
    What Grace then's this of God, and Christ that stills
    Out of this Offering into our tills?

Lord with thine Altars Fire, mine Inward man   25
    Refine from dross: burn out my sinfull guise
And make my Soul thine Altars Drippen pan
    To Catch the Drippen of thy Sacrifice.
    This is the Unction thine receive; the which
    Doth teach them all things of an happy pitch.   30

Thy Altars Fire burns not to ashes down
    This Offering. But it doth roast it here.
This is thy Roastmeate cooked up sweet, brown,
    Upon thy table set for Souls good cheer.
    The Drippen, and the meate are royall fair   35
    That fatten Souls, that with it welcomd are.

My Trencher, Lord, with thy Roast Mutton dress:
    And my dry Bisket in thy Dripping Sap.
And feed my Soul with thy Choice Angell Mess:
    My heart thy Praise, Will, tweedling Larklike tap.   40
    My florid notes, like Tenderills of Vines
    Twine round thy Praise, plants sprung in true Love's Mines.

6. Meditation on Isai. 49.3. Thou art
my Servant, Oh, Israel.

27. 3m [May] *1694.*

I fain would praise thee, Lord, but finde black **Sin,**
    To stain my Tunes my Virginalls to spoile.
Fetch out the same with thy red blood and bring
    My Heart in kilter, and my Spirits oyle.
    My Theme is rich: my Skill is poore untill   5
    Thy Spirit makes my hand its holy quill.

I spy thyselfe, as Golden Bosses fixt
    On Bible Covers, shine in Types out bright,
Of Abraham, Isaac, Jacob, where's immixt
    Their streaming Beames of Christ displaying Light.   10
    Jacobs now jog my pen, whose golden rayes
    Do of thyselfe advance an holy blaze.

His Name as Jacob, saith there's stow'd in thee
    All Wisdom to mentain all Pious Skill
And that the Divells Heels should tript up bee   15
    By thee alone, thou dost his brains out spill.
    The Name of Israel in Scutcheons shows
    Thou art Gods Prince to batter down his Foes.

His Fathers blessing him, shews thou camest down
    Full of thy Fathers blessing: and his Griefe   20
That thou shouldst be a man of Grief: a Crown
    Of Thorns thou wer'st to purchase us reliefe.
    Isr'el by Joseph's had to Egypt, and
    Joseph thee thither, and from thence did hand.

Jacob doth from his Father go and seek   25
    A Spouse and purchasd by his service two.

21 *Grief:*] PW Grief

Thou from thy Father came'st thy Spouse most meek
    Of Jews, and Gentiles down to purchase, Wooe
    And gain, and as Twelve Stems did from him bud
    Thou twelve Apostles sentst, the Church to stud.   30

In all those Typick Lumps of Glory I
    Spy thee the Gem made up of all their shine
Which from them all in thickest glory fly
    And twist themselves into this Gem of thine.
    And as the Shine thereof doth touch my heart,   35
    Joy sincks my Soule seeing how rich thou art.

How rich art thou? How poore am I of Love
    To thee, when all this Glory at my Doore
Stands knocking for admission: and doth shove
    To ope't, and Cabbinet in't all her Store?   40
    Make Love inflamed rise, and all entwine
    About Thyselfe her Object all in Shine.

Lord pardon mee, my Sin, and all my trash:
    And bring my Soule in Surges of rich flame
Of love to thee. I truely Envie dash   45
    Upon my selfe, my hidebound selfe for shame,
    I fain would prize and praise thee, but do sende
    My Flame up smootherd by a Carnall minde.

Oh! blow my Coale with thy blesst Bellows till
    It Glow, and send Loves hottest Steams on thee.   50
I shall be warm; and thou mine arms shalt fill
    And mine Embraces shall thy Worship bee.
    I'le sacrifice to thee my Heart in praise,
    When thy Rich Grace shall be my hearty Phrase.

28 *down*] orig: camest   47 *thee,*] PW thee.   53 *praise,*] PW praise.

7. Meditation. Ps. 105.17. He sent a man
        before them, even Joseph, who
        was sold etc.

5. 6m [Aug.] *1694*. Pub. *W*.

All Dull, my Lord, my Spirits flat, and dead
        All water sockt and sapless to the skin.
Oh! Screw mee up and make my Spirits bed
        Thy quickening vertue For my inke is dim,
        My pensill blunt. Doth Joseph type out thee?   5
        Haraulds of Angells sing out, Bow the Knee.

Is Josephs glorious shine a Type of thee?
        How bright art thou? He Envi'de was as well.
And so was thou. He's stript, and pick't, poore hee,
        Into the pit. And so was thou. They shell   10
        Thee of thy Kirnell. He by Judah's sold
        For twenty Bits, thirty for thee he'd told.

Joseph was tempted by his Mistress vile.
        Thou by the Divell, but both shame the foe.
Joseph was cast into the jayle awhile.   15
        And so was thou. Sweet apples mellow so.
        Joseph did from his jayle to glory run.
        Thou from Death's pallot rose like morning sun.

Joseph layes in against the Famine, and
        Thou dost prepare the Bread of Life for thine.   20
He bought with Corn for Pharaoh th'men and Land.
        Thou with thy Bread mak'st such themselves Consign
        Over to thee, that eate it. Joseph makes
        His brethren bow before him. Thine too quake.

4 *dim*] orig: thin
10 *They*] PW they   *thee* at end of line canceled   14 *Divell*,] PW Divell.

Joseph constrains his Brethren till their sins   25
    Do gall their Souls. Repentance babbles fresh.
Thou treatest sinners till Repentance springs
      Then with him sendst a Benjamin like messe.
      Joseph doth Cheare his humble brethren. Thou
      Dost stud with Joy the mourning Saints that bow.   30

Josephs bright shine th'Eleven Tribes must preach.
    And thine Apostles now Eleven, thine.
They beare his presents to his Friends: thine reach
      Thine unto thine, thus now behold a shine.
      How hast thou pensild out, my Lord, most bright   35
      Thy glorious Image here, on Josephs Light.

This I bewaile in me under this shine
    To see so dull a Colour in my Skin.
Lord, lay thy brightsome Colours on me thine.
      Scoure thou my pipes then play thy tunes therein.   40
      I will not hang my Harp in Willows by.
      While thy sweet praise, my Tunes doth glorify.

8. Meditation. Rom. 5.8. God commends his Love
       unto us, in that while we were yet
       sinners, Christ died for us.

14. 8m [Oct.] *1694*. Pub. UPT.

Thou pry'st thou screw'st my sincking Soul up to,
    Lord th'Highest Vane amazements Summit Wears
Seeing thy Love ten thousand wonders do
    Breaking Sins Back that blockt it up: us snares.

40 *then play thy tunes therein*] orig: thy tunes then blow therein

   28: Benjamin like messe. The feast Joseph made for his brothers, at which
Benjamin's was five times as much as the others' (Gen. 43, esp. verse 34).

The Very Stars, and Sun themselves did scoule,   5
  Yea Angells too, till it shone out, did howle.

Poore sinfull man lay grovling on the ground.
  Thy wrath, and Curse to dust lay grinding him.
And Sin, that banisht Love out of these bounds
  Hath stufft the world with curses to the brim.   10
  Gods Love thus Caskt in Heaven, none can tap
  Or breake its truss hoops, or attain a Scrap.

Like as a flock of Doves with feathers washt,
  All o're with yellow gold, fly all away
At one Gun crack: so Lord thy Love Sin quasht   15
  And Chased hence to heaven (Darksom day).
  It nestles there: and Graces Bird did hatch
  Which in dim types we first Pen feather'd catch.

God takes his Son stows in him all his Love,
  (Oh Lovely One), him Lovely thus down sends   20
His rich Love Letter to us from above
  And chiefly in his Death his Love Commends,
  Writ all in Love from top to toe, and told
  Out Love more rich, and shining far than gold.

For e'ry Grain stands bellisht ore with Love,   25
  Each Letter, Syllable, Word, Action sounde
Gods Commendations to us from above,
  But yet Loves Emphasis most cleare is found
  Engrav'd upon his Grave Stone in his blood
  He shed for Sinners, Lord what Love? How good?   30

It rent the Heavens ope that seald up were
  Against poore Sinners: rend the very Skie
And rout the Curse, Sin, Divell, Hell (Oh Deare,)
  And brake Deaths jaw bones, and its Sting destroy.
  Will search its Coffers: fetch from thence the Dust   35
  Of Saints, and it attend to glory just.

My God! this thy Love Letter to mee send.
  Thy Love to mee spell out therein I will.

13 *with*] orig: whose **32** *Sinners:*] PW Sinners **33** *Deare*] conj.

And What choice Love thou dost mee there commend,
    I'le lay up safely in my Souls best till.   40
    I'le read, and read it; and With Angells soon
    My Mictams shall thy Hallelujahs tune.

9. Meditation. Deut. 18.[15] The Lord thy God
       will raise up unto thee a Prophet—like
       unto mee.

16. 10m [Dec.] *1694.* Unpublished.

Lord, let thy Dazzling Shine refracted fan'de
    In this bright Looking Glass, its favour lay
Upon mine Eyes that oculated stand
    And peep thereat, in button moulds of clay.
    Whose glory otherwise that Courts mine eye   5
    Will all its sparkling family destroy.

Yea let thy Beams, better ten thousand times
    Than brightest Eyebright, cherishing revive
The Houshold that possesseth all the Shrines
    In Visions Palace, that it well may thrive.   10
    Moses is made the Looking glass: in which
    Mine Eyes to spie thee in this Type I pitch.

Poor Parents bring him in, when bondage state
    On Israel lay: and so it was with thee.
He's persecuted. All male babes a late   15
    Are to be slain. Thy case was such we see.
    He's sav'de by miracle: and raisd up by
    A sire reputed. So thy matters ly.

Was he most Meeke, Courageous, Faithfull, Wise?
    These all shine bright in thee, out shine the Sun.   20
Did he his Father then in law suffice

15 *All*] PW all

With faithfull service? So thou well hast done.
Did he a gentile Wed? Thy Spouse so shines.
Was he a Mediator? This thee twines.

Did he Gods Israel from Egypt through   25
    The Red Sea lead, into the Wilderness?
Thou bringst Gods Israel from bondage too
    Of Sin into the World here through no less
    Than thy red blood: and in this Chace t'assoile
    The firy Serpents, whose black venoms boile.   30

He Fasted fourty days, and nights, did give
    Them Gods own Law: Thou didst the very same.
The Morall Law whereto we ought to live.
    The Gospell Law to laver out our Shame.
    Then Israel's Church-hood, Worship, Ministry   35
    He founded: which thou didst too gospelly.

He did confirm his Office Worke with Wonders,
    And to the Covenant annexed Seals.
Thou thine in miracles, and more in numbers.
    And Gospell Seals unto thy Church out dealst.   40
    He intercession made, and pardon gain'd
    Unto his people. Thou didst so, its fam'de.

He led them to the border of God's Land,
    Sang like a Swan his dying Song (Well known)
Laid down his hilts: and so discharg'd his hand.   45
    Dy'de, Buri'de, Rose, and went to glories throne.
    All which shine gloriously in thee that wee
    Do Moses finde a Well drawn Map of thee.

Good God! what grace is this takes place in thee?
    How dost thou make thy Son to shine, and prize   50
His glory thus? Thy Looking-glass give mee.
    And let thy Spirit wipe my Watry eyes.

24 *thee*] orig: 'bout thee   26 *Wilderness?*] PW Wilderness
30 *Serpents,*] PW Serpents.   31 *did give*] orig: then gave   34 *our*] orig: their
42 *so,*] PW so.

That I may see his flashing glory darte
Like Lightening quick till it infire my heart.

I long to see thy Sun upon mee shine,   55
    But feare I'st finde myselfe thereby shown worse.
Yet let his burning beams melt, and refine
    Me from my dross, yet not to singe my purse.
    Then of my metall make thy Warbling harp:
    That shall thy Praise deck't in sweet tunes out warp.   60

10. Meditation. Which our Fathers that Follow'd
       after, brought in with Jesus, into
       the Possession of the Gentiles.
       Acts. 7.45.

10. 12m [Feb.] *1694.*

Moses farewell. I with a mournfull teare
    Will wash thy Marble Vault, and leave thy Shine
To follow Josuah to Jordan where
    He weares a Type, of Jesus Christ, divine.
    Did by the Priests bearing the Arke off Cut   5
    Her Stream, that Isr'el through it drieshod foot.

58 *dross,*] PW dross.

    Cf. Josh. 4, describing the journey of the priests bearing the ark of the
covenant. They were permitted to pass over Jordan on dry ground; as a me-
morial of this event, Joshua ordered twelve stones, representing the twelve
tribes of Israel, to be placed in the midst of Jordan and twelve more to be
placed in Gilgal, site of the first encampment west of the Jordan. The place
was named Gilgal, according to Josh. 5:9, because the Israelites who had been
born during the march through the wilderness were circumcised there: "This
day I have rolled away [*galliothi*] the reproach of Egypt from off you. Where-
fore the name of the place is called Gilgal unto this day." Rahab (line 43)
was a harlot of Jericho who aided Joshua's spies on behalf of the Israelites
(Josh. 2).

Doth twelve men call who in the Channell raise
    Twelve Stones, and also other twelve up take
And Gilgal stud therewith, like pearles that blaze
    In Rings of Gold, this passage to relate.   10
    All speaking Types of Christ whose Ministry
    Doth Jordans Streams cut off, that 'fore them fly.

And brings the Church into the Promisd Coast
    And singles out his twelve Apostles who
Twelve flaming Carbuncles before his host   15
    Out of the Channell take, and them bestow
    As Monuments upon its banck most fair,
    Twelve Articles th'Apostles Creed doth bare.

Now Farewell Wilderness, with all thy Fare.
    The Water of the Rock, and Mannah too.   20
My Old-New Cloaths my Wildernesses Ware,
    The Cloud and Pillar bright, adjue adjue.
    You onely in the Wilderness did flower
    As flowring Types. With Angells now I bower.

Let Gilgal speake for mee, where Egypts Stain   25
    Lapt in my Foreskin up clipt off off took.
I feed on Can'ans Wheat, Mannah's plump grain.
    All Evangelicall our Bakers Cooke.
    I drink the Drink of Life and weare Christs Web
    And by the Sun of Righteousness am led.   30

Our Joshua doth draw his Troops out to
    The Lunar coast, this Jericho the World
And rounds it while the Gospell Levites blow
    Their Gospell Rams Horn Trumpets till down hurld
    Its walls lie flat, and it his sacrifice   35
    Doth burn in Zeale, whose Flame doth sindge the Skies.

As Joshuah doth fight Haile Stones smite down
    The Can'anites: so Christ with Haile Stones shall
Destroy his Enemies, and breake their Crown.
    The Sun and Moon shall stand to see them fall   40

The Heavens Chrystall Candlestick-like stand
    Holding for him their Candles in their hand.

Yet such as Rahab like come o're to him
    His Grace implanteth in his Golden Stock.
As Joshuah did each Tribe his lot out fling   45
    So Christ doth his in Glory portions lot.
    As Joshua fixt Gods Worship, and envest
    Them with the Promise. Christ thus his hath blest.

That blazing Star in Joshua's but a Beam
    Of thy bright Sun, my Lord, fix such in mee.   50
My Dish clout Soul Rence Wring, and make it clean.
    Then die it in that blood that fell from thee.
    And make the Waiting men within my heart
    Attend thy sweetest praise, in evry part.

11. Meditation. Jud. 13.3. The Angell of the Lord appeared to the Woman, etc.

19. 3m [May] *1695*. Pub. *W*.

Eternall Love burnisht in Glory thick,
    Doth butt, and Center in thee, Lord, my joy.
Thou portrai'd art in Colours bright, that stick
    Their Glory on the Choicest Saints, Whereby
    They are thy Pictures made. Samson Exceld   5
    Herein thy Type, as he thy foes once queld.

An Angell tells his mother of his birth.
    An Angell telleth thine of thine. Ye two
Both Males that ope the Womb in Wedlock Kerfe
    Both Nazarited from the Womb up grew.   10

49 *Beam*] orig: Ray   51 *clean*] Conj.   2 *butt*] PW but

He after pitchy night a Sunshine grows
And thou the Sun of Righteousness up rose.

His Love did Court a Gentile spouse, and thine
Espous'd a Gentile to bebride thyselfe.
His Gentile Bride apostatizd betime.   15
Apostasy in thine grew full of Wealth.
He sindgd the Authours of't with Foxes tails.
And foxy men by thee on thine prevaile.

The Fret now rose. Thousands upon him poure.
An asses Jaw his javling is, whereby   20
He slew a Thousand, heap by heap that hour.
Thou by weake means makest many thousands fly.
Thou ribbon like wast platted in his Locks
And hence he thus his Enemies did box.

He's by his Friend betray'd, for money sold,   25
Took, bound, blindfolded, made a May game Flout
Dies freely with great sinners, when they hold
A Sacred Feast. With arms stretcht greatly out,
Slew more by death, than in his Life he slew.
And all such things, my Lord, in thee are true.   30

Samson at Gaza went to bed to sleep.
The Gazites watch him and the Soldiers thee.
He Champion stout, at midnight rose full deep.
Took Gaza's Gate on's back away went hee.
Thou rose didst from thy Grave and also tookst   35
Deaths Doore away throwing it off o'th'hooks.

Thus all the shine that Samson wore is thine,
Thine in the Type. Oh. Glorious One, Rich glee.
Gods Love hath made thee thus. Hence thy bright shine
Commands our Love to bow thereto the Knee.   40
Thy Glory chargeth us in Sacrifice
To make our Hearts and Love to thee to rise.

11 *grows*] orig: rose
18 *on*] orig: do   22 *makest*] PW make'st   26 *made a May game Flout*]
orig: and made a may game   *May*] PW may   27 *hold*] orig: did hold
28 *greatly out*] orig: out to•••ain   32 *and*] orig: as   36 *o'th'*] PW oth
42 *thee*] orig: life

But woe is me! my heart doth run out to
    Poor bits of Clay: or dirty Gayes embrace.
Doth leave thy Lovely Selfe for loveless show: 45
    For lumps of Lust, nay sorrow and disgrace.
    Alas, poore Soule! a Pardon, Lord, I crave.
    I have dishonourd thee and all I have.

Be thou my Samson, Lord, a Rising Sun,
    Of Righteousness unto my Soule, I pray.   50
Conquour my Foes. Let Graces Spouts all run
    Upon my Soule O're which thy sunshine lay.
    And set me in thy Sunshine, make each flower
    Of Grace in me thy Praise perfum'd out poure.

12. Meditation. Ezek. 37.24. David my
Servant shall be their King.

7. 5m [July] *1695.*

Dull, Dull indeed! What shall it e're be thus?
    And why? Are not thy Promises, my Lord,
Rich, Quick'ning things? How should my full Cheeks blush
    To finde mee thus? And those a lifeless Word?
    My Heart is heedless: unconcernd hereat: 5
    I finde my Spirits Spiritless, and flat.

Thou Courtst mine Eyes in Sparkling Colours bright,
    Most bright indeed, and soul enamoring,
With the most Shining Sun, whose beames did smite
    Me with delightfull Smiles to make mee spring.   10
    Embellisht knots of Love assault my minde
    Which still is Dull, as if this Sun ne're shin'de.

David in all his gallantry now comes,
    Bringing to tende thy Shrine, his Royall Glory,

51 *run*] PW run.   4 *And*] PW and   13 *now*] orig: doth

Rich Prowess, Prudence, Victories, Sweet Songs,   15
    And Piety to Pensill out thy Story;
      To draw my Heart to thee in this brave shine
      Of typick Beams, most warm. But still I pine.

Shall not this Lovely Beauty, Lord, set out
    In Dazzling Shining Flashes 'fore mine Eye,   20
Enchant my heart, Love's golden mine, till't spout
      Out Streames of Love refin'd that on thee lie?
      Thy Glory's great: Thou Davids Kingdom shalt
      Enjoy for aye. I want and thats my fault.

Spare me, my Lord, spare me, I greatly pray,   25
    Let me thy Gold pass through thy Fire untill
Thy Fire refine, and take my filth away.
      That I may shine like Gold, and have my fill
      Of Love for thee; untill my Virginall
      Chime out in Changes sweet thy Praises shall.   30

Wipe off my Rust, Lord, with thy wisp me scoure,
    And make thy Beams pearch on my Strings their blaze.
My tunes Cloath with thy Shine, and Quavers poure
      My Cursing Strings on, loaded with thy Praise.
      My Fervent Love with Musick in her hand,   35
      Shall then attend thyselfe, and thy Command.

13. Meditation. Ps. 72. The title. A
Psalm for Solomon.

1.7m [Sept.] *1695.*

I fain would praise thee, Lord, but when I would,
    I finde my Sin my Praise dispraises bring.
I fain would lift my hands up as I should,
    But when I do, I finde them fould by Sin.

34 *My*] orig: Upon my

I strive to heave my heart to thee, but finde   5
    When striving, in my heart an heartless minde.

Oh! that my Love, and mine Affections rich
    Did spend themselves on thee and thou hadst them.
I strive to have thy Glory on them pitch
    And fetch thee them. Hence Solomon thy jem,   10
    And glorious Type thy Sparkling Beams out flings
    But in the same my Love but little springs.

Was He a bud of Davids stock? So thou.
    Was he a King? Thou art a King of Kings.
Was He a Make-peace King? Thy royall brow   15
    Doth weare a Crown which peace Eternall brings.
    Did He Excell in Wisdome? Thine doth flame.
    And thou art Wisdom's Storehouse whence his came.

I may aver he's of all fallen men
    The perfect'st piece that Nature ever bred.   20
Thy Human nature is the perfect'st jem
    That Adams offspring ever brudled.
    No spot nor Wrinckle did it ever smite.
    Adams in Paradise was ne're so bright.

Did He Gods Temple Build, in glory shown?   25
    Thou buildst Gods House, more gloriously bright.
Did he sit on a golden ivery Throne
    With Lions fenc'd? Thy Throne is far more White
    And glorious: garded with Angells strong.
    A Streame of fire doth with the Verdict come.   30

Did he his Spouse, a glorious Palace build?
    The Heavens are thy Palace for thy Spouse.
Gods house was by his pray're with Glory filld.
    God will for thine his Church in Glory house.
    Did Sheba's Queen faint viewing of his glory?   35
    Bright Angells stand amazed at thy Story.

13 *stock*] PW stok   20 *ever bred*] orig: bred
24 *ne're*] orig: not   25 *shown*] orig: bright   *shown?*] PW shown.
27 *Throne*] PW Thone   36 *amazed*] PW amaze'd   *at*] orig: stand at
The original version of this line was probably: Bright Angells then amaz'd
stand at thy Story

But hence griefe springs, finding these rayes of Light
    Scarce reach my heart, it is so ditcht with Sin.
I scarce can see I see it, or it smite
    Upon my Love that it doth run to him.   40
    Why so? my Lord! Why so? Shall Love up shrink?
    Or mine Affection to thee be a Shrimp?

Oh! feed me at thy Table, make Grace grow
    Knead in thy Bread, I eate, thy Love to mee,
And spice thy Cup I take, with rich grace so,   45
    That at thy Table I may honour thee.
    And if thy Banquet fill mee with thy Wealth,
    My growing Grace will glorify thyselfe.

14. Meditation. Col. 2.3. In whom are hid all
       the Treasures of Wisdom, and Knowledge.

3d. 9m [Nov.] *1695*. Pub. PET.

Halfe Dead: and rotten at the Coare: my Lord!
    I am Consumptive: and my Wasted lungs
Scarce draw a Breath of aire: my Silver Coard
    Is loose. My buckles almost have no tongues.
    My Heart is Fistulate: I am a Shell.   5
    In Guilt and Filth I wallow, Sent and Smell.

Shall not that Wisdom horded up in thee
    (One key whereof is Sacerdotall Types)
Provide a Cure for all this griefe in mee
    And in the Court of Justice save from Stripes,   10
    And purge away all Filth and Guilt, and bring
    A Cure to my Consumption as a King?

Shall not that Wisdom horded in thee (which
    Prophetick Types enucleate) forth shine

37 *springs,*] PW springs.   43 *Table,*] PW Table.
47 *Wealth,*] PW Wealth.   6 *wallow,*] PW wallow.   10 *Stripes,*] PW Stripes.

With Light enough a Saving Light to fix 15
    On my Poore Taper? And a Flame Divine?
    Making my Soule thy Candle and its Flame
    Thy Light to guide mee, till I Glory gain?

Shall not that Wisdom horded in thee up
    (Which Kingly Types do shine upon in thee) 20
Mee with its Chrystall Cupping Glasses cup
    And draine ill Humours wholy out of mee?
    Ore come my Sin? And mee adorn with Grace
    And fit me for thy Service, and thy Face?

How do these Pointers type thee out most right 25
    As Graces Officine of Wisdom pure
The fingers Salves and Medicines so right
    That never faile, when usd, to worke a Cure?
    Oh! that it would my Wasted lungs recrute.
    And make my feeble Spirits upward shute. 30

How Glorious art thou, Lord? Cloathd with the Glory
    Of Prophets, Priests, and Kings? Nay all Types come
To lay their Glory on thee. (Brightsome Story).
    Their Rayes attend thee, as Sun Beams the Sun.
    And shall my Ulcer'd Soule have such reliefe? 35
    Such glorious Cure? Lord strengthen my beliefe.

Why dost not love, my Soule? or Love grow strong?
    These glorious Beams of Wisdom on thee shine.
Will not this Sunshine make thy branch green long,
    And flowrish as it doth to heaven climbe? 40
    Oh! chide thyselfe out of thy Lethargie,
    And unto Christ on Angells wings up fly.

Draw out thy Wisdom, Lord, and make mee just.
    Draw out thy Wisdom. Wisdoms Crown give mee.
With shining Holiness Candy my Crust: 45
    And make mee to thy Scepter bow the knee.
    Let thy rich Grace mee save from Sin, and Death:
    And I will tune thy Praise with holy Breath.

25 *most*] orig: up   39 *green long*] orig: Green and Long

15. Meditation. Mat. 2.23. He shall bee
called a Nazarite.

Westfield 12. 10m [Dec.] *1695/6.*

A Nazarite indeed. Not such another.
    More rich than Jasper, finer far than Silke
More cleane than Heavens froth the Skies out pother:
    Purer than snow: and Whiter far than Milke.
    In Bodie ruddier than Rubies, nay   5
    Whose pollishing of Sapphire's brave, and gay.

Devoted by thy Father and thy selfe
    To all Examplary Holy Life.
Grace's Chiefe Flower pot on highest shelfe
    In all God's Hall. Here Holiness is rife.   10
    And higher Herbs of Grace can never grow
    In Bulk, or Brightness, than before us flow.

Thy Typick Holiness, more sweet than Muske,
    Ore tops the paltry Dainties of Strong Drinke:
Or Vines whose Fruite is Casked in an huske,   15
    And Kirnells with hard Stones: though from their Chink:
    Bleeds royall Wine: and grapes Sweet Raisens make
    The Wine will soure. Types may not of it take.

The letter of the Law of Nazarites
    Concerns thee not. The Spirit oft is meet   20
For thee alone. Thou art the Vine t'invite
    The Grape without Husk, Stone, The Raisen Sweet.
    Yea, thou thyselfe, the Wine, and Strong Drink art.
    E're sweet, nere Vinegar, or soureing sharp.

Thy Head that wares a Nazaritick Crown   25
    Of Holiness Deckt with its purple Hair

2 *Jasper,*] PW Jasper.   7 *selfe*] PW selfe.   18 *Types*] PW types
20 *The*] PW the   24 *sweet,*] PW sweet.   25 *that*] orig: doth
26 *Deckt*] orig: set

Dide in the Blood thy Grape shed when presst down
  Derides the Rasor. Saints there nestled are.
  And when thy Vow is o're, under the wing
  Of their Peace offering thy praise they'l sing.   30

Thou never wast defiled by the Dead.
  No Dead thing ever, yet disstained thee.
Life from thy Fingers ends runs, and ore spred
  Itselfe through all thy Works what e're they bee.
  Thy Thoughts, Words, Works are lively, frim, do still 35
  Out Spirituall Life. Thy Spirit doth them fill.

Pare off, my Lord, from mee I pray, my pelfe.
  Make mee thy Nazarite by imitation
Not of the Ceremony, but thy selfe,
  In Holiness of Heart, and Conversation.   40
  Then I shall weare thy Nazarite like Crown
  In Glory bright with Songs of thy Renown.

16. Meditation. Lu. 1.33. He shall reign
over the house of Jacob forever.

Westfield 9. 1m [Mar.] *1695/6.* Pub. UPT.

Thou art, my Lord, the King of Glory bright.
  A glory't is unto the Angells flame
To be thy Harauld publishing thy Light
  Unto the Sons of Men: and thy rich Name.
  They are thy Subjects. Yea thy realm is faire. 5
  Ore Jacobs House thou reignest: they declare.

Their brightest glory lies in thee their king.
  My Glory is that thou my king maist bee.
That I may be thy Subject thee to sing
  And thou may'st have thy kingdoms reign in mee. 10
  But when my Lips I make thy Scepter Kiss
  Unheartiness hatcht in my heart doth hiss.

Rich Reason, and Religion Good thus cry,
    Be Subject, Soule: of Jacobs house be one.
Here is a king for thee, Whom Angells fly   15
    To greet and honour sitting on his throne.
    Sins mutiny, and marr his intrest brave.
    My Pray'res grow Dead. Dead Corps laid in the grave.

The lowly Vine Grows fruitfull clusters, Rich.
    The Humble Olive fat with oyle abounds.   20
But I like to the fiery Bramble, Which
    Jumps at a Crown am but an empty Sound.
    A guilded Cask of tawny Pride, and Gall,
    With Veans of Venom o're my Spirits sprawle.

Like to the Daugh all glorious made when dresst   25
    In feathers borrowed of other birds
Must need be King of birds: but is distresst,
    When ery bird its feather hath, and Curbd
    Doth glout, and slouch her Wings. Pride acts this part.
    And base Hypocrisy. Oh! rotten heart!   30

Blesst Lord, my King, where is thy golden Sword?
    Oh! Sheath it in the bowells of my Sin.
Slay my Rebellion, make thy Law my Word.
    Against thine Enemies Without within.
    Implant mee as a branch in Gods true vine   35
    And then my grape will yield thy Cup rich wine.

Shall I now grafted in thy Olive tree
    The house of Jacob, bramble berries beare?
This burdens me to thinke of, much more thee.
    Breake off my black brire Claws: mee scrape, and pare.   40
    Lord make my Bramble bush thy rosie tree.
    And it will beare sweet Roses then for thee.

Kill my Hypocrisie, Pride Poison, Gall.
    And make my Daugh thy Turtle Dove ore laid
With golden feathers: and my fruites then shall   45

13 *cry,*] PW cry.   33 *Rebellion,*] PW Rebellion.   *my Word*] my Conj.
38 *beare?*] PW beare.

Flock Dovelike to thy Lockers, oh! Choice trade.
My Cooing then shall be thy Musick in,
The House of Jacob, tun'de to thee, my King.

17. Meditation. Eph. 5.2. And gave himselfe for
        us an offering, and a Sacrifice to God.

Westfield 16. 6[m] [Aug.] *1696.* Pub. UPT.

Thou Greate Supream, thou Infinite first One:
      Thy Being Being gave to all that be
Yea to the best of Beings thee alone
      To serve with Service best for best of fee.
      But man the best servd thee the Worst of all   5
      And so the Worst of incomes on him falls.

Hence I who'me Capable to serve thee best
      Of all the ranks of Beings here below
And best of Wages win, have been a pest
      And done the Worst, earn'd thus the Worst of Woe.   10
      Sin that imploys mee findes mee worke indeed
      Me qualifies, ill qualities doth breed.

This is an hell indeed thus to be held
      From that which nature holdst her chiefe delights
To that that is her horrour and refelld   15
      Ev'n by the Law God in her Essence writes.
      But for reliefe Grace in her tender would
      Massiah cast all Sacrifices told.

I sin'd. Christ, bailes. Grace takes him Surety,
      Translates my Sin upon his sinless Shine.   20
He's guilty thus, and Justice thus doth eye
      And sues the band, and brings on him the fine.
      All Sacrifices burn but yet their blood
      Can't quench the fire, When laid upon the Wood.

18 *Massiah cast*] orig: Did Cast Massiah

The type thy Veane phlebotomizd must bee   25
    To quench this Fire: no other blood nor thing
Can do't. Hence thou alone art made for mee
    Burnt, Meat, Peace Sin, and Trespass Offering.
    Thy blood must fall: thy life must go or I
    Under the Wrath of God must ever fry.   30

This fire upon thee burnt, and is allay'd
    For all of thine. Oh make mee thine I pray.
So shall this Wrath from mee be retrograde.
    No fire shall sindge my rags nor on them stay.
    New qualify mee. I shall then on go   35
    Anew about thy Service, and it do.

What Grace in God? What Love in Christ thus spring
    Up unto men, and to my poore poore heart?
That so thy burning fire no Sparke can fling
    Or sparkle on such Tinder, This impart   40
    Unto thy Servant. This will be my Health:
    And for a gift to thee I send myselfe.

Oh! that my Love, was rowld all ore and ore
    In thine, and Candi'd in't, and so refin'd
More bright than gold, and grown in bulke, far more   45
    Than tongue can tell of each best sort, and kind.
    All should be thine, and I thine own will be.
    Accept my gift, no better is with mee.

Then own thine own. Be thou my Sacrifice,
    Thy Father too, that he may father mee,   50
And I may be his Child, and thy blood prize,
    That thy attonement may my clearing bee.
    In hope of Which I in thy Service sing
    Unto thy Praise upon my Harp within.

25 *The*] PW They   50 *too*] PW to

18. Meditation. Heb. 13.10. Wee
have an Altar.

Westfield 18. 8m [Oct.] *1696*. Pub. *W*.

A Bran, a Chaff, a very Barly yawn,
    An Husk, a Shell, a Nothing, nay yet Worse,
A Thistle, Bryer prickle, pricking Thorn
      A Lump of Lewdeness, Pouch of Sin, a purse
      Of Naughtiness, I am, yea what not Lord?   5
      And wilt thou be mine Altar? and my bord?

Mine Heart's a Park or Chase of sins: Mine Head
    'S a Bowling Alley. Sins play Ninehole here.
Phansy's a Green: sin Barly breaks in't led.
      Judgment's a pingle. Blindeman's Buff's plaid there.   10
      Sin playes at Coursey Parke within my Minde.
      My Wills a Walke in which it aires what's blinde.

Sure then I lack Atonement. Lord me help.
    Thy Shittim Wood ore laid With Wealthy brass
Was an Atoning altar, and sweet smelt: 15
      But if ore laid with pure pure gold it was
      It was an Incense Altar, all perfum'd
      With Odours, wherein Lord thou thus was bloom'd.

Did this ere during Wood when thus orespread
    With these erelasting Metalls altarwise   20
Type thy Eternall Plank of Godhead, Wed
      Unto our Mortall Chip, its sacrifice?
      Thy Deity mine Altar. Manhood thine.
      Mine Offring on't for all men's Sins, and mine?

This Golden Altar puts such weight into   25
    The sacrifices offer'd on't, that it
Ore weighs the Weight of all the sins that flow

12 *it aires*] orig: they aire   24 *all men's Sins*] orig: Sins of all
26 *on't*] orig: up on't

In thine Elect. This Wedge, and beetle split
The knotty Logs of Vengeance too to shivers:
And from their Guilt and shame them cleare delivers.   30

This Holy Altar by its Heavenly fire
    Refines our Offerings: casts out their dross
And sanctifies their Gold by its rich 'tire
    And all their steams with Holy Odours boss.
    Pillars of Frankincense and rich Perfume   35
    They 'tone Gods nosthrills with, off from this Loom.

Good News, Good Sirs, more good than comes within
    The Canopy of Angells. Heavens Hall
Allows no better: this atones for sin,
    My Glorious God, Whose Grace here thickest falls.   40
    May I my Barly yawn, Bran, Bryer Claw,
    Lay on't a Sacrifice? or Chaff or Straw?

Shall I my sin Pouch lay, on thy Gold Bench
    My Offering, Lord, to thee? I've such alone
But have no better. For my sins do drench   45
    My very best unto their very bone.
    And shall mine Offering by thine Altars fire
    Refin'd, and sanctifi'd to God aspire?

Amen, ev'n so be it. I now will climb
    The stares up to thine Altar, and on't lay   50
Myselfe, and services, even for its shrine.
    My sacrifice brought thee accept I pray.
    My Morn, and Evning Offerings I'le bring
    And on this Golden Altar Incense fling.

Lord let thy Deity mine Altar bee   55
    And make thy Manhood, on't my sacrifice.
For mine Atonement: make them both for mee
    My Altar t'sanctify my gifts likewise

30 *shame*] Conj.   44 *thee?*] PW thee.
46 *bone.*] PW bone?   49 *Amen,*] PW Amen.   52 *brought thee*] orig: brought
to thee

That so myselfe and service on't may bring
Its worth along with them to thee my king.   60

The thoughts whereof, do make my tunes as fume,
From off this Altar rise to thee Most High
And all their steams stufft with thy Altars blooms,
My Sacrifice of Praise in Melody.
Let thy bright Angells catch my tune, and sing't.   65
That Equalls Davids Michtam which is in't.

19. Meditation. Can. 1.12. While the King
          sits at his Table, my Spicknard
          sends forth the Smell thereof.

Westfield 7. 10m [Dec.] *1696*. Pub. PET.

Lord dub my tongue with a new tier of Words
    More comprehensive far than my dull Speech
That I may dress thy Excellency Lord
    In Languague welted with Emphatick reech.
    Thou art my King: my Heart thy Table make   5
    And sit thereat untill my Spicknard wake.

My Garden Knot drawn out most curiously
    By thy brave hand set with the bravest Slips
Of Spicknard: Lavender that thence may fly
    Their Wealthy Spirits from their trunks and tips.   10
    That Spicknard Oyle, and Oyle of Spike most sweet
    May muskify thy Palace with their Reeke.

Then sit at thy round Table with delight
    And feast in mee, untill my Spicknard bloome,
And Crown thy head with Odour-Oyle rich bright   15
    And croud thy Chamber with her sweet perfume.

3 *Excellency*] PW Excelleny   4 *welted*] Conj.   *reech*] Conj.

The Spicknard in my knot then flourish will:
　　And frindge thy Locks with odour it doth still.

And when thou at thy Circuite Table sitst
　　Thine Ordinances, Lord, to greet poor hearts   20
Such Influences from thyselfe thou slipst
　　And make their Spicknard its sweet Smell impart.
　　So make my Lavender to spring, and sent.
　　In such attire her Spirits ever tent.

And as thou at thy Table sitst to feast   25
　　Thy Guests there at, Thy Supper, Lord, well drest,
Let my sweet Spicknard breath most sweet, at least
　　Those Odours that advance thy Glory best.
　　And make my heart thine Alabaster Box
　　Of my Rich Spicknard to perfume thy locks.   30

If this thou grant, (and grant thou this I pray)
　　And sit my King at thy rich table thus,
Then my Choice Spicknard shall its Smell display,
　　That sweetens mee and on thee sweet doth rush.
　　My Songs of Praise too sweeten'd with this fume   35
　　Shall scale thine Eares in Spicknardisick Tune.

20. Meditation. Heb. 9.11. By a Greater, and more Perfect Tabernacle.

7. 12m [Feb.] *1696.*

Didst thou, Lord, Cast mee in a Worship-mould
　　That I might Worship thee immediatly?
Hath Sin blurd all thy Print, that so I should
　　Be made in vain unto this End? and Why?
　　Lord print me ore again. Begon, begon,   5
　　Yee Fly blows all of hell: I'le harboùr none.

20 *Even* at beginning of line canceled   *Thine*] PW thine
26 *Guests*] PW Guess

That I might not receive this mould in vain
    Thy Son, my Lord, my Tabernacle he
Shall be: me run into thy mould again.
    Then in this Temple I will Worship thee.   10
    If he the Medium of my Worship stand
    Mee, and my Worship he will to thee hand.

I can't thee Worship now without an House.
    An house of Worship here will do no good,
Unless it type my Woe, in which I douse,   15
    And Remedy in deifyed Blood.
    Thy Tabernacle, and thy Temple they
    Such Types arose. Christ is their Sun, and Ray.

Thou wast their Authour: Art Christs too and his.
    They were of Choicest Matters. His's th'best blood.   20
Thy Spirits over shaddowing form'd them, This
    Did overshaddow Mary. Christ did bud.
    The Laver, Altar, Shew Bread, Table Gold
    And Golden Light and Oyle do Christs Shine hold.

The Efficacy that's lodgd in them all   25
    Came from thyselfe in influences, nay
Their Glory's but a painted Sun on th'Wall
    Compar'd to thine and that thou dost display.
    How glorious then art thou, when all their glory
    Is but a Paintery to thy bright Story.   30

Thou art the Laver to wash off my Sin:
    The Altars for atonement out of hand:
The Sweet Sweet Incense cast the fire within
    The Golden Table, where the Shew bread stand.
    The Golden Candlestick with holy Light   35
    Mentain'd by holy Oyle in Graces Pipe.

The flames whereof, enmixt with Grace assaile
    With Grace the heart in th'Light that takes the Eye
To light us in the way within the Vaile
    Unto the Arke in which the Angells prie   40

24 *Oyle*] PW Oyle.   26 *influences,*] PW influences.
37 *assaile*] orig: out throws   38 *With Grace the*] orig: Grace on the

Having the Law stand in't, up Coverd under
    The Mercy Seate, that Throne of Graces Wonder.

Thou art my Tabernacle, Temple right,
    My Cleansing, Holiness, Atonement, Food,
My Righteousness, My Guide of Temple Light   45
    In to the Holy Holies, (as is shewd)
        My Oracle, Arke, Mercy Seat: the place
        Of Cherubims amazde at such rich grace.

Thou art my Medium to God, thou art
    My Medium of Worship done to thee,   50
And of Divine Communion, Sweet heart!
        Oh Heavenly intercourse! Yee Angells see!
        Art thou my Temple, Lord? Then thou Most Choice
        Art Angells Play-House, and Saints Paradise.

Thy Temples Influences stick on mee,   55
    That I in Holy Love may stow my heart
Upon thyselfe, and on my God in thee,
        And with thy Holiness guild Every part
        Of me. And I will as I walke herein
        Thy Glory thee in Temple Musick bring.   60

21. Meditation. Col. 2.16.17. In respect of
            an Holy Day, of a New Moon, or a
            Sabbath. Which are figures.

    16.3m [May] *1697*. Unpublished.

Rich Temple Fair! Rich Festivalls my Lord,
    Thou makest to entertain thy Guests most dresst
In dishes up by SEVENS which afford
        Rich Mystery under their brims expresst.
        Which to discover clearly, make the brain   5
        Of most men wring, their kirnells to obtain.

44 *Atonement*] orig: my Atonement

Each Seventh Day a Sabbath Gracious Ware.
    A Seventh Week a yearly Festivall.
The Seventh Month a Feast nigh, all, rich fare.
    The Seventh Yeare a Feast Sabbaticall.   10
    And when seven years are seven times turnd about
    A Jubilee. Now turn their inside out.

What Secret Sweet Mysterie under the Wing
    Of this so much Elected number lies?
What Vean can e're Divine? Or Poet sing?   15
    Doubtless most Rich. For such shew God most Wise.
    I will adore the same although my quill
    Can't hit the String that's tun'd by such right Skill.

Sharpen my Sight my Lord that I may spie
    A lively Quickness in it jump for joy   20
And by the breaking of the Shell let fly
    Such pleasant Species as will folly stroy.
    Out of these Feasts, although the Number Seven
    I leave untill my Soul is housd in Heaven.

And here I beg thy aide Mine eyes refine   25
    Untill my Sight is strong enough to spy
Thyselfe my Lord deckt all in Sun Like Shine.
    And see myselfe cloathd in thy Beams that fly.
    My Sight is dim: With Spectacles mee suite
    Made of a pair of Stars it to recrute.   30

Make mee thy Lunar Body to be filld
    In full Conjunction, with thy Shining Selfe
The Sun of Righteousness: whose beams let guild
    My Face turnd up to heaven, on which high Shelfe
    I shall thy Glorys in my face that shine,   35
    Set in Reflected Rayes. Hence thou hast thine.

Moon-like I have no light here of mine own.
    My shining beams are borrowd of this Sun,
With which when 'ray'd its Rayes on mee are shown
    Unto this World as I it over run.   40

12 *Jubilee*] orig: Jubilee Steps in
23 *Out of these*] orig: These Feasts could   38 *Sun,*] PW Sun.

My black Side's Earthward Yet thy beams that flew
    Upon mee from thy face, are in its view.

Hence Angells will in heaven blow up aloud
    For joy thy Trumpet on my new Moon day
And in its Prime, the Golden Rayes that shroud   45
    Within thy Face will guild my Edges gay.
    Oh! Happy Change. The Sun of Righteousness
    With's healing Wings my moon doth richly dress.

And though this world doth eye thy brightness most
    When most in distance from thyselfe I'm backt,   50
Yet then I most am apt even from this Coast
    To be Ecclipsed, or by its fogs be blackt.
    My back at best, and dark side Godward bee,
    And pitchy clouds do hide thy face from mee.

Oh! let not Earth nor its thick fogs I pray   55
    E're slip between me, and thy lightsome Rayes
But let my Cloathing be thy Sunshine Ray.
    My New-Moon Trumpet then shall sound thy praise.
    I then in sweet Conjunction shall with thee
    The Sun of Righteousness abiding bee.   60

[*The following four stanzas appear after the conclusion of this poem in PW. They have been crossed out and appear, in slightly altered form, as the conclusion of Meditation 22.*]

But now I from the New Moon Feast do pass
    And pass the Passo're o're unto Gods Seales,
And come to Whitsuntide, and turn its glass
    To search for pearles amongst its sands and meals.
    For Israel had not fifty dayes been out   5
    Of Egypt, ere at Sinai Law did spout.

So Christ our Passover had not passt ore
    Full fifty days before in fiery wise
The Law of Spirit and of Life much more
    Went out from Zion. Gospell Law did rise.   10

9 *and*] orig: of

The Harvest of the former yeare is in'd.
    Injoy'd, and Consecrated Thanks for't pay'd.
All holding out the Right in things we sind
      Away restored is, and they all made
      Fit for our use, and that we thankfully   15
      Ourselves unto the using them should ply.

Then make me to this Penticost repare.
    Make mee thy Guest, Lord, at this feast, and live
Up to thy Gospell Law. And let my Fare
      Be of the two Wave Loaves this Feast doth give.   20
      If th'Prophets Seedtime spring my harvest I
      Will, as I reape't, sing thee my harvest joy.

22. Meditation. 1 Cor. 5.7. Christ our
        Passover is sacrificed for us.

Undated.

I from the New Moon of the first month high
    Unto its fourteenth day When she is Full
Of Light the Which the Shining Sun let fly
      And when the Sun's all black to see Sins pull
      The Sun of Righteousness from Heaven down   5
      Into the Grave and weare a Pascall Crown.

A Bond Slave in Egyptick Slavery
    This Noble Stem, Angellick Bud, this Seed
Of Heavenly Birth, my Soul, doth groaning ly.
      When shall its Passo're come? When shall't be Freed?   10

13 *the*] orig: hereby the   22 *sing*] orig: make sing
1 *month*] PW mon'th orig: pass   2 *Full*] PW Full,

    10: Passo're, Passover. Three feasts were enjoined by Mosaic law upon the
Hebrews: (1) the Passover, celebrated on the fourteenth day of Nisan, the
first month of the Hebraic year (corresponding to March–April), followed
by the Feast of Unleavened Bread, which began on the fifteenth day and
lasted for seven days; (2) the Feast of Weeks—also called Pentecost, or Harvest

The Lamb is slaine upon the fourteenth day
Of Month the first, my Doore posts do display.

Send out thy Slaughter Angell, Lord, and slay
    All my Enslaving 'Gypsies Sins, while I
Eate this rost Mutten, Paschall Lamb, Display   15
    Thy Grace herein, while I from Egypt high.
    I'le feed upon thy Roast meat here updresst,
    With Bitter hearbs, unleaven'd bread the best.

I'le banish Leaven from my very Soule
    And from its Leanetoe tent: and search out all   20
With Candles lest a Crum thereof should rowle
    Into its Corners or in mouseholes fall,
    Which when I finde I'le burn up, and will sweep
    From every Corner all, and all cleane keep.

My Bunch of Hyssop, Faith, dipt in thy blood   25
    My Paschall Lamb, held in thy Bason bright
Baptize my Doore Posts shall, make Crimson good.
    Let nothing off this Varnish from them wipe,
    And while they weare thy Crimson painted dy,
    No Slaughter Angell shall mine house annoy.   30

Lord, purge my Leaven out: my Tast make quick:
    My Souls strong Posts baptize with this rich blood

---

of First Fruits—held on the fiftieth day of the Passover season; and (3) the Feast of Tabernacles—or Feast of Booths, or Feast of the Ingathering (Sukkoth)—lasting seven days, held during the full moon of Tishri, the seventh month (September–October).

In this poem Taylor apparently has in mind all three feasts. According to biblical tradition, the first Passover was celebrated when the Lord commanded Moses and Aaron to prepare for departure from Egypt. A lamb in its first year was killed at sunset on the fourteenth day, and its blood was sprinkled on the side posts and lintel of the house of the family celebrating the Passover; the lamb was then roasted whole and eaten with unleavened bread and bitter herbs (Exod. 12). Killing a lamb in its first year symbolized God's determination to smite the first-born of the Egyptians; the blood was a sign to the Destroying Angel to pass over the house so marked.

The Feast of Tabernacles, or Feast of Booths, is referred to in detail in Meditation 24 (second series), p. 125.

21: lest a Crum thereof should rowle. Ritual cleanliness was essential in the celebration of the Passover.

By bunch of Hyssop, then I'le also lick
    Thy Dripping Pan: and eat thy Roast Lamb good,
    With Staff in hand, Loins Girt, and Feet well shod   35
    With Gospell ware as walking to my God.

I'le Goshen's Ramesis now leave apace.
    Thy Flag I'le follow to thy Succoth tent.
Thy sprinkled blood being my lintells grace
    Thy Flesh my Food With bitter herbs attent   40
    To minde me of my bitter bondage State
    And my Deliverance from all such fate.

I'le at this Feast my First Sheafe bring, and Wave
    Before thee, Lord, my Crop to sanctify
That in my first Fruits I my harvest have   45
    May blest unto my Cyckle Constantly.
    So at this Feast my harp shall Tunes advance
    Upon thy Lamb, and my Deliverance.

But now I from the Passover do pass.
    Easter farewell, rich jewells thou did shew,   50
And come to Whitsuntide; and turn the Glass
    To search her Sands for pearles therein anew.
    For Isra'l a fift'th day from Egypt broke,
    Gave Sinai's Law, and Crown'd the mount with Smoke.

And Christ oure Passover had not passt o're   55
    Full fifty dayes before in fiery guise
He gave Mount Zions Law from graces store.
    The Gospell Law of Spirit and Life out highs
    In fiery Tongues that did confound all those
    At Pentecost that Zions King oppose.   60

The Harvest of the year through Grace now inn'd,
    Enjoyd and Consecrated with Right praise,
All typefying that the right we sind
    Away's restor'd by Christ: and all things raisd

50 *farewell,*] PW farewell   *shew,*] PW shew
64 *raisd*] orig: made

    43: First Sheafe. The Omer, or first sheaf of the harvest, was offered to the
priest (Lev. 23:10–14).
    45–46: have / May blest, i.e. may have blessed.

Fit for our use, and that we thankfully   65
    Unto the use thereof ourselves should ply.

Lord make me to the Pentecost repare,
    Make me thy Guest too at this Feast, and live
Up to thy Gospell Law: and let my fare
    Be of the two white Loaves this feast doth give.   70
    If Prophets Seeding yield me harvest, I
    Will as I reap sing thee my harvest joy.

23. Meditation. 1 Joh. 2.2. He is the
Propitiation for our Sins.

17.7m [Sept.] *1697.*

Greate Lord, yea Greatest Lord of Lords thou art,
    And King of Kings, may my poor Creaking Pipe
Salute thine Eare; This thought doth sink my heart
    Ore burdened with over sweet Delight.
    An Ant bears more proportion to the World   5
    Than doth my piping to thine eare thus hurld.

It is a Sight amazing strange to see
    An Emperour picking an Emmets Egge.
More strange it's that Almighty should to mee
    E're lend his Eare. And yet this thing I beg.   10
    I'm small and Naught, thou mayst much less me spare
    Than I the Nit that hangeth on my hair.

But oh thy Grace! What glory on it hings,
    In that thou makest thy Son to bare away
The marrow of the matter choice that Clings   15
    Unto the Service of Atonment's day?
    This was his Type, He is its Treasure rich
    That Reconciles for Sin that doth us ditch.

4 This line is repeated at top of page in PW and canceled.

Sins thick and threefold at my threshold lay
    At Graces threshold I all gore in Sin.   20
Christ backt the Curtain, Grace made bright the day,
    As he did our Atonement full step in.
    So Glorious he. His Type is all unmeet
    To typify him till aton'd and sweet.

A'ron as he atonement made did ware   25
    His milke white linen Robes, to typify
Christ cloath'd in human flesh pure White, all fair,
    And undefild, atoneing God most High.
    Two Goates he took, and lots to know Gods will,
    Which he should send away: and Which, should kill.   30

Dear Christ, thy Natures two are typ't thereby
    Making one Sacrifice, Humane, Divine.
The Manhood is Gods Lot, and this must dy.
    The Godhead as the Scape Goate death declines.
    One Goat atones, one beares all Sin away.   35
    Thy natures do this work, each as they lay.

Aaron the blood must catch in's Vessell to hold.
    Lord let my Soule the Vessell be of thine.
Aaron must in a Censar all of Gold
    Sweet incense burn with Altars fire Divine   40
    To Typify the Incense of thy Prayer
    Perfuming of thy Service thou didst beare.

Aaron goes in unto the Holy place
    With blood of Sprinkling and sprinkles there
Atones the Tabernacle, Altars face   45
    And Congregation, for defild all were.
    Christ with his proper blood did enter in
    The Heavens bright, propitiates for Sin.

Aaron then burns the Goat without the Camp
    And Bullock too whose blood went in the Vaile.   50
Christ sufferd so without the Gate Deaths Cramp,
    And Cramped Hell thereby. The Divells quaile.

21 *day*,] PW day.   47 *proper blood*] PW proper, blood.

Thus done with God Aaron aside did lay
His Linen Robes, and put on's Golden Ray.

And in this Rich attire he doth apply   55
Himselfe before the peoples very eyes,
Unto the other Service, richly high
To typify the gracious properties
Wherewith Christs human nature was bedight
In which he mediates within Gods Sight.   60

What wonder's here? Shall such a sorry thing
As I have such rich Cost laid down for mee
Whose best at best as mine's not worth a Wing
Of one poore Fly, that I should have from thee
Such Influences of thy goodness smite mee   65
And make me mute as by delight envite mee?

Lord let thy Gracious hand me chafe, and rub
Till my numbd joynts be quickn'd and compleat,
With Heate and Spirits all divine, and good,
To make them nimble in thy Service Greate.   70
Oh! take my ALL thyselfe, all though I bee
All bad, I have no better gift for thee.

Although my gift is but a Wooden toole
If thou receive it, thou wilt it enrich
With Grace, thats better than Apollo's Stoole.   75
Thy Oracles 'twill utter out the which
Will make my Spirits thy bright golden Wyers,
ALTASCHAT Michtam tune in Angells Quires.

66 *mee?*] PW mee.   69 *good,*] PW good.

Meditation 24. Joh. 1.14. ἐσκήνωσε[ν] ἐν ἡμῖν Tabernacled amongst us.

25. 10m [Dec.] 1697.

My Soul would gazing all amazed stand,
    To see the burning Sun, with'ts golden locks
(An hundred sixty six times more than th'land)
    Ly buttond up in a Tobacco box.
    But this bright Wonder, Lord, that fore us playes   5
    May make bright Angells gasterd, at it gaze.

That thou, my Lord, that hast the Heavens bright
    Pav'd with the Sun, and Moon, with Stars o're pinckt,
Thy Tabernacle, yet shouldst take delight
    To make my flesh thy Tent, and tent with in't.   10
    Wonders themselves do seem to faint away
    To finde the Heavens Filler housd in Clay.

Thy Godhead Cabbin'd in a Myrtle bowre,
    A Palm branch tent, an Olive Tabernacle,
A Pine bough Booth, An Osier House or tower   15
    A mortall bitt of Manhood, where the Staple
    Doth fixt, uniting of thy natures, hold,
    And hold out marvels more than can be told.

Thy Tabernacles floore Celestiall
    Doth Canopie the Whole World. Lord; and wilt   20
Thou tabernacle in a tent so small?
    Have Tent, and Tent cloath of a Humane Quilt?
    Thy Person make a bit of flesh of mee
    Thy Tabernacle, and its Canopee?

Wonders! my Lord, Thy Nature all With Mine   25
    Doth by the Feast of Booths Conjoynd appeare

1 *would*] orig: doth   3 *more*] orig: bigger

26: *Feast of Booths*, one of the three Passover feasts: also called Sukkoth, also Feast of Tabernacles (see p. 120, note to line 10). During this festival

Together in thy Person all Divine
    Stand House, and House holder. What Wonder's here?
    Thy Person infinite, without compare
    Cloaths made of a Carnation leafe doth ware.   30

What Glory to my nature doth thy Grace
    Confer, that it is made a Booth for thine
To tabernacle in? Wonders take place.
    Thou low dost step aloft to lift up mine.
    Septembers fifteenth day did type the Birth   35
    Of this thy tabernacle here on earth.

And through this leafy Tent the glory cleare
    Of thy Rich Godhead shineth very much:
The Crowds of Sacrifices which swarm here
    Shew forth thy Efficacy now is such   40
    Flowing in from thy natures thus united
    As Clears off Sin, and Victims all benighted.

But yet the Wonder grows: and groweth much,
    For thou wilt Tabernacles change with mee.
Not onely Nature, but my person tuch.   45
    Thou wilst mee thy, and thee, my tent to bee.
    Thou wilt, if I my heart will to thee rent,
    My Tabernacle make thy Tenement.

Thou'lt tent in mee, I dwell in thee shall here.
    For housing thou wilt pay mee rent in bliss: 50
And I shall pay thee rent of Reverent fear
    For Quarters in thy house. Rent mutuall is.

42 *Sin,*] PW Sin.   46 *my*] PW my,

---

families lived in tents or booths made of boughs, in remembrance of the forty years' wandering of their nomadic ancestors. This celebration fell into abeyance among the Hebrews but was revived in the time of Ezra, as recounted in Neh. 8:13–18—a passage Taylor had in mind when he wrote the third stanza of Meditation 24. Taylor considered the Feast of Booths to be a type of Christ's incarnation: "if it [the Annunciation] be . . . just before the Conception it will Cast the birth of our Lord Christ into September a summer Month wherein the Jews kept the Feast of Tabernacles, a type of Christs Incarnation" (HG, 28).

Thy Tenent and thy Teniment I bee.
Thou Landlord art and Tenent too to mee.

Lord lease thyselfe to mee out: make mee give
    A Leafe unto thy Lordship of myselfe.
Thy Tenent, and thy Teniment I'le live.
    And give and take Rent of Celestiall Wealth.
    I'le be thy Tabernacle: thou shalt bee
    My Tabernacle. Lord thus mutuall wee.

The Feast of Tabernacles makes me sing
    Out thy Theanthropy, my Lord, I'le spare
No Musick here. Sweet Songs of praises in
    The Tabernacles of the Righteous are.
    My Palmifer'd Hosannah Songs I'le raise
    On my Shoshannims blossoming thy praise.

55

60

65

Meditation 25. Numb. 28.4.9. One Lamb shalt
    thou offer in the Morning, and the other
    at Even. And on the Sabbath day two
    Lambs etc.

6. 1m [Mar.] *1698.* Pub. PET.

Guilty, my Lord, What can I more declare?
    Thou knowst the Case, and Cases of my Soule.
A Box of tinder: Sparks that falling o're
    Set all on fire, and worke me all in Shoals.
    A Pouch of Passion is my Pericarde.
    Sparks fly when ere my Flint and Steele strike hard.

I am a Dish of Dumps: yea ponderous dross,
    Black blood all clotted, burdening my heart,
That Anger's anvill, and my bark bears moss.

5

60 *wee*] orig: bee   4 *fire,*] PW fire.

My Spirits soakt are drunke with blackish Art.   10
If any Vertue stir, it is but feeble.
Th'Earth Magnet is, my heart's the trembling needle.

My Mannah breedeth Worms: Thoughts fly blow'd are.
My heart's the Temple of the God of Flies.
My Tongue's an Altar of forbidden Weare   15
Fansy a foolish fire enflam'd by toys
Perfum'de with reeching Offerings of Sins
Whose steaming reechs delight hobgoblings.

My Lord, is there no help for this with thee?
Must I abuse, and be abused thus?   20
There Morn, and Even Sacrifices bee:
To cleans the Sins of Day, and Night from us.
Christ is the Lamb: my Pray're each morn and night
As Incense offer I up in thy Sight.

My morn, and evening Sacrifice I bring   25
With Incense sweet upon mine Altar Christ,
With Oyle and Wine two quarters of an Hin
With flower for a Meat Offering all well spic'dt,
On bended knees, with hands that tempt the Skies.
This is each day's atoning Sacrifice.   30

And thou the Sabbath settledst at the first
And wilt continue it till last. Wherefore,
Who strike down Gospell Sabbaths are accurst.
Two Lambs, a Meat, and Drinke offering God more
Conferd on it than any other Day   35
As types the Gospell Sabbaths to display.

Here is Atonement made: and Spirituall Wine
Pourd out to God: and Sanctified Bread
From Heaven's givn us: What! shall we decline
With God Communion, thus to be fed?   40
This Heavenly fare will make true Grace to thrive.
Such as deny this thing are not alive.

32 *till last*] orig: untill the last   **36** *As types*] orig: To typify

I'le tend thy Sabbaths: at thine Altar feed.
    And never make thy type a nullitie.
The Ceremonies cease, but yet the Creede   45
      Contained therein, continues gospelly,
      That make my feeble Spirits will grow frim.
      Hence I in Sabbath Service love to swim.

My Vespers, and my Mattins Ile attend:
    My Sabbath Service carry on I will.
Atoning Efficacy God doth send   50
      To Sinners in this path, and grace here stills.
      Still this on me untill I glory Gain.
      And then Ile sing thy praise in better Strain.

Meditation 26. Heb. 9.13.14. How much more shall the blood of Christ, etc.

26.4m [June] *1698*. Pub. UPT.

Unclean, Unclean: My Lord, Undone, all vile
    Yea all Defild: What shall thy Servant doe?
Unfit for thee: not fit for holy Soile,
    Nor for Communion of Saints below.
    A bag of botches, Lump of Loathsomeness: 5
    Defild by Touch, by Issue: Leproust flesh.

Thou wilt have all that enter do thy fold
    Pure, Cleane, and bright, Whiter than whitest Snow
Better refin'd than most refined Gold:
    I am not so: but fowle: What shall I doe?   10
    Shall thy Church Doors be shut, and shut out mee?
    Shall not Church fellowship my portion bee?

How can it be? Thy Churches do require
    Pure Holiness: I am all filth, alas!
Shall I defile them, tumbled thus in mire?   15

46 *gospelly,*] PW gospelly.
1 *Undone,*] PW Undone.   15 *them, tumbled*] orig: them entering, tumbled

Or they mee cleanse before I current pass?
If thus they do, Where is the Niter bright
And Sope they offer mee to wash me White?

The Brisk Red heifer's Ashes, when calcin'd,
    Mixt all in running Water, is too Weake   20
To wash away my Filth: The Dooves assign'd
    Burnt, and Sin Offerings neer do the feate
    But as they Emblemize the Fountain Spring
    Thy Blood, my Lord, set ope to wash off Sin.

Oh! richest Grace! Are thy Rich Veans then tapt   25
    To ope this Holy Fountain (boundless Sea)
For Sinners here to lavor off (all sapt
    With Sin) their Sins and Sinfulness away?
    In this bright Chrystall Crimson Fountain flows
    What washeth whiter, than the Swan or Rose.   30

Oh! wash mee, Lord, in this Choice Fountain, White
    That I may enter, and not sully here
Thy Church, whose floore is pav'de with Graces bright
    And hold Church fellowship with Saints most cleare.
    My Voice all sweet, with their melodious layes   35
    Shall make sweet Musick blossom'd with thy praise.

Meditation 27. Upon Heb. 9.13.14. How much more shall the Blood of Christ etc.

4.7m [Sept.] *1698*. Pub. UPT.

My mentall Eye, spying thy sparkling Fold
    Bedeckt, my Lord, with Glories shine alone,
That doth out do all Broideries of Gold:
    And Pavements of Rich Pearles, and Precious Stone

24 *off*] orig: away   *Upon Heb.*] PW upon Heb.   2 *shine*] orig: glittering
shine

Did double back its Beams to light my Sphere   5
    Making an inward Search, for what springs there.

And in my Search I finde myselfe defild:
    Issues and Leprosies all ore mee streame.
Such have not Enterance. I am beguild:
    My Seate, Bed, Saddle, Spittle too's uncleane.   10
    My Issue Running Leprosy doth spread:
    My upper Lip is Covered: not my Head.

Hence all ore ugly, Nature Poysond stands,
    Lungs all Corrupted, Skin all botch't and scabd
A Feeble Voice, a Stinking Breath out fand   15
    And with a Scurfy Skale I'me all ore clagd.
    Robes rent: Head bare, Lips Coverd too, I cry,
    Unclean, Unclean, and from thy Camp do fly.

Woe's mee. Undone! Undone! my Leprosy!
    Without a Miracle there is no Cure.   20
Worse than the Elephantick Mange I spie
    My Sickness is. And must I it endure?
    Dy of my Leprosy? Lord, say to't nay,
    I'le Cure thee in my wonder working way.

I see thy Gracious hand indeed hath caught   25
    Two Curious pritty pure Birds, types most sure
Of thy two Natures, and The one is brought
    To shed its blood in running waters pure
    Held in an Earthen Panchin which displays
    Thy Blood and Water preacht in Gospell dayes.   30

The slain Dove's buri'de: In whose Blood (in water)
    The Living Turtle, Ceder, Scarlet twine,
And Hysop dipted are (as an allator)
    Sprinkling the Leper with it Seven times
    That typify Christs Blood by Grace applide   35
    To Sinners vile, and then they're purifide.

Sprindge Lord mee With it. Wash me also in
    The Poole of Shiloam, and shave mee bare

34 *Sprinkling*] orig: And Sprinkled   38 *Shiloam,*] PW Shiloam.

With Gospells Razer. Though the Roots of Sin
    Bud up again, again shave off its hair.   40
    Thy Eighth dayes Bath, and Razer make more gay,
    Than th'Virgin Maries Purifying day.

My Tresspass, Sin, and my Burnt Sacrifices
    My Flowre and Oyle, for my meate Offering
My Lord, thou art. Whether Lambs or Doves up rise   45
    And with thy Holy Blood atonement bring,
    And put thy Blood upon my Right Eare fair
    Whose tip shall it, its Onely jewell, Ware.

And put it Gold-Ring-like on my Right Thumbe
    And on my Right Greate toe as a Rich Gem.   50
Thy Blood will not Head, Hand nor Foot benum,
    But satisfy and cleans all fault from them.
    Then put thy Holy Oyle upon the place
    Of th'Blood of my Right Eare, Thumb, Toe. Here's Grace.

Then Holiness shall Consecrate mine Eare.   55
    And sanctify my Fingers Ends, and Toes.
And in my hearing, Working, Walking here
    The Breath of Sanctifying Grace out goes.
    Perfuming all these Actions, and my life.
    Oh! Sweetest Sweet. Hence Holiness is rife.   60

Lord, Cleanse mee thus with thy Rich Bloods Sweet Shower
    My Issue stop: destroy my Leprosy.
Thy Holy Oyle upon my Head out poure
    And cloathe my heart and Life with Sanctity.
    My Head, my Hand and Foot shall strike thy praise,   65
    If thus besprinkled, and Encamp thy Wayes.

45 *art. Whether*] orig: art alone. Whether   51 *Thy*] Conj.
66 *besprinkled,*] PW besprinkled.

54: th'Blood of my Right Eare. Cf. Exod. 29:20: "Then shalt thou kill the ram, and take of his blood, and put it upon the tip of the right ear of Aaron, and upon the tip of the right ear of his sons, and upon the thumb of their right hand, and upon the great toe of their right foot, and sprinkle the blood upon the altar round about."

Meditation 28. Isai. 32.2. A man shall be
for a hiding place from the Winde.

11. 10m [Dec.] *1698*. Pub. UPT.

That Bowre, my Lord, which thou at first didst build
    Was pollished most gay, and every ranck
Of Creatures in't shone bright, each of them filld
    With dimpling Glory, Cield with golden planck
    Of smiling Beauty. Man then bore the Bell: 5
    Shone like a Carbuncle in Glories Shell!

How brave, and bright was I then, Lord, myselfe?
    But woe is mee! I have transgresst thy Law,
Undone, defild, Disgrac'd, destroy'd my Wealth,
    Persu'de by flaming Vengeance, as fire dry straw.   10
    All Ranks I broake, their Glory I benighted
    Their Beauty blasted, and their Bliss befrighted.

Hence Black-Blew, Purple Spots of Horrid guilt,
    Rise in my Soule. Mee Vengeance hath in Chase
To spill my blood, 'cause I her Glory spilt,   15
    And did the Creatures Glory all disgrace.
    Shall I fall by the Venger's hand, before
    I get within the Refuge Citie's doore?

Oh! give me Angells Wings to fly to thee,
    My Lord, all stumbling stones pick out of th'way.   20
Thou art my Refuge City, and shalt bee.
    Receive me in, let not th'Avenger slay.
    I do attempt to over run my Sin:
    And fly to thee, my Refuge. Let mee in.

Ive by my Sin a man, the Son of man   25
    Slain, and myselfe, Selfe Murderer, I slew.

2 *most*] orig: with most   14 *Chase*] PW Chrase

Yet on the Golden Wings of Faith which fan
    The Gospell Aire the Altars Horns I wooe,
    Renouncing all my Sins, and Vanity
    And am resolv'd before the same to dy.   30

Accept me, Lord, and give my Sailes thine Aire,
    That I may swiftly sayle unto thyselfe.
Be thou my Refuge and thy Blood my faire.
    Disgrace my Guilt, and grace me with thy Wealth.
    Be thou my Refuge City, take mee in.   35
    And I thy Praise will on Muth Labben sing.

Meditation 29. 1 Pet. 3.20. While the Ark was Building.

5. 12m [Feb.] *1698*. Pub. PET.

What shall I say, my Lord? with what begin?
    Immence Profaneness Wormholes ery part.
The World is saddlebackt with Loads of Sin.
    Sin Craks the Axle tree of this greate Cart.
    Floodgates of Firy Vengeance open fly   5
    And Smoakie Clouds of Wrath darken the Skie.

The Fountains of the Deep up broken are.
    The Cataracts of heaven do boile ore
With Wallowing Seas. Thunder, and Lightenings tare
    Spouts out of Heaven, Floods out from hell do roare.   10
    To overflow, and drownd the World all drownd
    And overflown with Sin, that doth abound.

Oh! for an Ark: an Ark of Gopher Wood.
    This Flood's too stately to be rode upon

36: Muth Labben. The phrase occurs in the title to the ninth Psalm: "To the chief Musician upon Muth-labben"; it may have been the opening words of a melody to which this Psalm was to be sung (*HBD*). Taylor probably considered it the name of a musical instrument.

By other boats, which are base swilling tubs.   15
    It gulps them up as gudgeons. And they're gone.
    But thou, my Lord, dost Antitype this Arke,
    And rod'st upon these Waves that toss and barke.

Thy Humane Nature, (oh Choice Timber Rich)
    Bituminated ore within, and out   20
With Dressing of the Holy Spirits pitch
    Propitiatory Grace parg'd round about.
    This Ark will ride upon the Flood, and live
    Nor passage to a drop through Chink holes give.

This Ark will swim upon the fiery flood:
    All Showrs of fire the heavens rain on't will   25
Slide off: though Hells and Heavens Spouts out stood
    And meet upon't to crush't to Shivers, still
    It neither sinks, breaks, Fires, nor Leaky prooves,
    But lives upon them all and upward mooves.   30

All that would not be drownded must be in't
    Be Arkd in Christ, or else the Cursed rout
Of Crimson Sins their Cargoe will them sinke
    And suffocate in Hell, because without.
    Then Ark me, Lord, thus in thyselfe that I   35
    May dance upon these drownding Waves with joye.

Sweet Ark, with Concord sweetend, in thee feed
    The Calfe, and Bare, Lamb, Lion at one Crib.
Here Rattlesnake and Squerrell jar not, breed.
    The Hawk and Dove, the Leopard, and the Kid   40
    Do live in Peace, the Child, and Cockatrice.
    As if Red Sin tantarrow'd in no vice.

Take me, my Lord, into thy golden Ark.
    Then when thy flood of fire shall come, I shall
Though Hell spews streams of Flames, and th'Heavens spark   45
    Out Storms of burning Coals, swim safe ore all.
    I'le make thy Curled flames my Citterns Wire
    To toss my Songs of Praise rung on them, higher.

17 *Arke,*] PW Arke.   21 *Spirits*] orig: Ghost's

Meditation 30. Math. 12.40. As Jonah was three Dayes, and three nights in the Whales belly. So must etc.

9. 2m [Apr.] *1699.* Pub. *W.*

Prest down with sorrow, Lord, not for my Sin
  But with Saint 'Tony Cross I crossed groane.
Thus my leane Muses garden thwarts the spring
  Instead of Anthems, breatheth her ahone.
  But duty raps upon her doore for Verse.   5
  That makes her bleed a poem through her searce.

When, Lord, man was the miror of thy Works
  In happy state, adorn'd with Glory's Wealth
What heedless thing was hee? The serpent lurks
  Under an apple paring, and by stealth   10
  Destroy'd her Glory. O poor keeper hee
  Was of himselfe: lost God, and lost his Glee.

Christ, as a Turtle Dove, puts out his Wing.
  Lay all on me, I will, saith hee, Convay
Away thy fault, and answer for thy sin.   15
  Thou'st be the Stowhouse of my Grace, and lay
  It and thyselfe out in my service pure
  And I will for thy sake the storm Endure.

Jonas did type this thing, who ran away
  From God and shipt for Tarsus, fell asleep.   20
A storm lies on the Ship. The Seamen they
  Bestir their stumps, and at wits end do weep.
  Wake, Jonas, who saith Heave me over deck.
  The Storm will Cease then, all lies on my neck.

They cast him overboard out of the ship.   25
  The tempest terrible, lies thereby still.
A Mighty Whale nam'd Neptunes Dog doth skip
  At such a Boon, Whose greedy gorge can't kill

12 *himselfe:*] PW himselfe. 21 *Ship. The*] PW Ship. the

Neither Concoct this gudgeon, but its Chest
Became the Prophets Coffin for the best.   30

He three dayes here lies trancifi'de and prayes.
    Prooves working Physick in the Fishes Crop.
Maybe in th'Euxine, or the Issick Bay
    She puking falls and he alive out drops.
    She vomits him alive out on the Land   35
    Whence he to Ninive receives command.

A sermon he unto the Gentiles preacht,
    Yet fortie dayes, and Ninus is destroy'd.
Space granted, this Repentance doth them teach
    God pardons them, and thus they ruine 'void.   40
    Oh! Sweet Sweet Providence, rich Grace hath spic'te
    This Overture to be a type of Christ.

Jonas our Turtle Dove, I Christ intend
    Is in the ship for Tarsus under saile.
A fiery storm tempestiously doth spend   45
    The Vessill, and its hands. All Spirits faile.
    The ship will sink or Wrack upon the rocks
    Unless the tempest cease the same to box.

None can it Charm but Jonas. Christ up posts
    Is heaved overboard into the sea.   50
The Dove must die. The storm gives up its Ghost
    And Neptune's Dogg leapes at him as a Prey.
    Whose stomach is his Grave where he doth sleep,
    Three Dayes sepulchred, Jonas in the Deep.

The Grave him swallow'd down as a rich Pill   55
    Of Working Physick full of Virtue which
Doth purge Death's Constitution of its ill.
    And womble-Crops her stomach where it sticks.
    It heaves her stomach till her hasps off fly.
    And out hee comes Cast up, rais'd up thereby.   60

36 *command*] orig: with command   40 *'void*] PW void   46 *All*] PW all
51 *The storm*] PW the storm

In glorious Grace he to the Heathen goes
    Envites them to Repentance, they accept.
Oh! Happy Message squandering Curst foes.
    Grace in her glorious Charriot here rides deckt.
    Wrath's Fire is quencht. And Graces sun out shines.   65
    Death on her deathbed lies, Consumes and pines.

Here is my rich Atonement in thy Death,
    My Lord, nought is so sweet, though sweat it cost.
This turns from me Gods wrath: Thy sweet sweet breath
    Revives my heart: thy Rising up o're bosst   70
    My Soule with Hope seeing acquittance in't.
    That all my sins are kill'd, that did mee sinke.

I thanke thee, Lord. Thy death hath deadned quite
    The Dreadfull Tempest. Let thy Dovy wings
Oreshadow me, and all my Faults benight   75
    And with Celestiall Dews my soule besprindge.
    In Angells Quires I'le then my Michtams sing,
    Upon my Jonath Elem Rechokim.

Meditation 33. Joh. 15.13. Greater Love hath no man than this, that a man lay down his Life for his Friend.

1. 8m [Oct.] *1699.* Pub. *W.*

Walking, my Lord, within thy Paradise
    I finde a Fruite whose Beauty smites mine Eye
And Taste my Tooth that had no Core nor Vice.
    An Hony Sweet, that's never rotting, ly

73 *Thy*] PW thy   74 *Let*] PW let   78 *Jonath*] PW Jonah

78: Jonath Elem Rechokim. The meaning of this phrase is obscure. It is found only once in the Bible—as heading of the fifty-sixth Psalm, where it may indicate the modulation of the Psalm. According to the *Biour* to Mendelssohn's Version of the Psalms, the phrase is the name of a musical instrument, and this seems to be Taylor's meaning.

Under a Tree, which view'd, I knew to bee   5
    The Tree of Life whose Bulk's Theanthropie.

And looking up, I saw its boughs all bow
    With Clusters of this Fruit that it doth bring,
Nam'de Greatest LOVE. And well, For bulk, and brow,
        Thereof, of th'sap of Godhood-Manhood spring.   10
        What Love is here for kinde? What sort? How much?
        None ever, but the Tree of Life, bore such.

Who is the Object of this Love? and in
    Whose mouth doth fall the Apple of this tree?
Is't Man? A Sinner? Such a Wormhol'de thing?   15
        Oh! matchless Love, Laid out on such as Hee!
        Should Gold Wed Dung, should Stars Wooe Lobster Claws,
        It would no wonder, like this Wonder, cause.

Is sinfull Man the Object of this Love?
    What then doth it for this its Object doe,   20
That doth require a purging far above
        The whiteness, Sope and Nitre can bestow,
        (Else Justice will its Object take away
        Out of its bosome, and to hell't convay?)

Hence in it steps, to justice saith, I'll make   25
    Thee satisfaction, and my Object shine.
I'l slay my Humane Nature for thy sake
        Fild with the Worthiness of thy Divine
        Make pay therewith. The Fruite doth sacrifice
        The tree that bore't. This for its object dies. 30

An Higher round upon this golden scale
    Love cannot Climbe, than to lay down the Life
Of him that loves, for him belov'd to bale,
        Thereby to satisfy, and end all strife.

15 *Is't*] PW Is   18 *It would*] PW 'Twould[?]   20 *doe,*] orig: doe?
21 *That*] orig: It   22 *bestow,*] orig: bestow?
27 *I'l slay my Humane Nature*] orig: The Humane Nature slayeth
34 *satisfy,*] PW satisfy.

Thou lay'st, my Lord, thy Life down for thy Friend   35
And greater Love than this none can out send.

Then make me, Lord, thy Friend, I humbly pray
Though I thereby should be deare bought by thee.
Not dearer yet than others, for the pay
Is but the same for others as for mee.   40
If I be in thy booke, my Life shall proove
My Love to thee, an Offering to thy Love.

34. Meditation. Rev. 1.5. Who loved us
and washed away our Sins in
his Blood.

26. 9m [Nov.] 1699.

Suppose this Earthy globe a Cocoe Nut
Whose Shell most bright, and hard out challenge should
The richest Carbunckle in gold ring put
How rich would proove the kirnell it should hold?
But be it so, who then could breake this Shell,   5
To pick the kirnell, walld within this Cell?

Should I, my Lord, call thee this nut, I should
Debase thy Worth, and of thee basely stut.
Thou dost its worth as far excell as would
Make it to thine worse than a worm eat nut.   10
Were all the World a sparkling pearle, 't would bee
Worse than a dot of Dung if weighd with thee.

What Elemented bit was that, thine eyes
Before the Elements were moulded, ey'd?
And it Encabbineting Jewell wise   15
Up in thy person, be'st nigh Deified?
It lay as pearle in dust in this wide world,
But thou it tookst, and in thy person firld.

To finde a Pearle in Oister Shells's not strange:
    For in such rugged bulwarks such abound.   20
But this Rich Gem in Humane Natures grange
    So bright could by none Eye but thine be found.
    Its mankind flowr'd, searst, kneaded up in Love
    To Manna in Gods moulding trough above.

This bit of Humane Flesh Divinizd in   25
    The Person of the Son of God; the Cell
Of Soule, and Blood, where Love Divine doth swim
    Through veans, through Arteries, Heart flesh, and fell,
    Doth with its Circkling Arms about entwinde
    A Portion of its kindred choice, Mankinde.   30

But these defild by Sin, Justice doth stave
    Off from the bliss Love them prepar'de, untill
She's satisfide, and sentence too she gave
    That thou should feel her vengeance and her will.
    Hence Love steps in, turns by the Conduit Cock: 35
    Her Veans full payment on the Counter drop.

Now Justice satisfi'de, Loves Milke white hand
    Them takes and brings unto her Ewer of blood
Doth make Free Grace her golden Wisp, and Sand
    With which she doth therein them Wash scoure, rub   40
    And Wrince them cleane untill their Beauty shows
    More pure, and white, than Lilly, Swan, or Rose.

What love, my Lord, dost thou lay out on thine
    When to the Court of Justice cald they're judg'd.
Thou with thy Blood and Life dost pay their fine   45
    Thy Life, for theirs, thy Blood for theirs must budge.
    Their Sin, Guilt, Curse upon thyselfe dost lay:
    Thy Grace, thy Justice, Life on them Convay.

Make such a Change, my Lord, with mee, I pray.
    I'le give thee then, my Heart, and Life to th'bargen.   50
Thy golden Scepter then my Soule shall sway
    Along my Path unto thy Palace garden.

21 *this*] orig: t' finde this

Wash off my filth, with thy rich blood, and I
Will stud thy praise with thankfull melody.

Meditation 35. Joh. 15.5. Without me
yee can do nothing.

3. 1m [Mar.] *1699/1700.*

My Blessed Lord, that Golden Linck that joyns
   My Soule, and thee, out blossoms on't this Spruice
Peart Pronown MY more spiritous than wines,
   Rooted in Rich Relation, Graces Sluce.
    This little Voice feasts mee with fatter Sweets   5
    Than all the Stars that pave the Heavens Streets.

It hands me All, my heart, and hand to thee
   And up doth lodge them in thy persons Lodge
And as a Golden bridg ore it to mee
   Thee, and thine All to me, and never dodge.   10
    In this small Ship a mutuall Intrest sayles
    From Heaven and Earth, by th'holy Spirits gales.

Thy Ware to me's so rich, should my Returns
   Be packt in sparkling Metaphors, out stilld
From Zion's garden flowers, by fire that burns   15
   Aright, of Saphire Battlements up filld
    And sent in Jasper Vialls it would bee
    A pack of guilded Non-Sense unto thee.

Such * * * * * Golden Palace Walled round
   With Walls made of transparent Silver bright   20
With Towers of Diamonds and in't is found
   A Throne of Sparkling Carbuncle like light
    Wherein sits Crownd one with the Sunn. The same
    Would be but Smoak compar'd to thy bright flame.

53 *with*] orig: and with   *and I*] orig: I   8 *up*] Conj.   10 *me, and*] orig: me
run, and   16 *Battlements*] Conj.   17 *sent*] Conj.   23 *one*] Conj.

Thy Humane frame's a Curious Palace, raisd   25
    Of th'Creame of Natures top Perfection here
Where Grace sits Sovereign that ere ore blazd
    The splendent beams of precious Stones most clear.
    Whose Mace, and Scepter richer Matter shine,
    Than Berill, Amathyst or Smaregdine.   30

Here is a Living Spring of power which tapt
    All-doing influences hence do flow.
What we have done undone us hath, (sad hapt)
    That we without thee now can nothing do.
    We cannot do what do we should, (in Summ)   35
    Nor undo what undoes us, by us done.

We have our Souls undone, Can't undo this.
    We have Undone the Law, this can't undo:
We have undone the World, when did amiss,
    We can't undoe the Curse that brings in Woe.   40
    Our Undo-Doing can't undo, its true.
    Wee can't our Souls, and things undone, renew.

Without thee wee can nothing do, its sure.
    Thou saidst the same. We finde thy Saying true.
Thou canst do all things: all amiss canst cure,   45
    Undo our Undo-doing, make all new.
    Thou madst this World: dost it thy play-house keep
    Wherein the Stars themselves play Hide-and-Seek.

It is thy Green, where all thy Creatures play
    At Barly-Breake and often lose their fleece.   50
But we poore wee our Soules a wager lay
    At Nine-Mens Morrice, and at Fox and Geese.
    Let me not play myselfe away, nor Grace.
    Nor lose my Soule, My Lord, at prison base.

Reclaim thy Claim: finde me refinde; I'm thine.   55
    Without thee I can nothing do, Dispense,
Thyselfe to me, and all things thine are mine,

33 *sad*] Conj.   41 *undo,*] PW undo.   48 *play*] orig: do play
50 *fleece*] Conj.   51 *wager lay*] Conj.   57 *all*] orig: when all

I'le not account of what thou countst offence.
Give me thy Power to work, and thou shalt finde
Thy Work attended with my hand, and minde. 60

36. [Meditation.] Col. 1.18. He is the Head of the Body.

19. 3m [May] *1700.*

An Head, my Lord, an honourable piece;
    Nature's high tower, and wealthy Jewelry;
A box of Brains, furld up in reasons fleece:
    Casement of Senses: Reason's Chancery:
    Religions Chancell pia-mater'd ore 5
    With Damask Roses that Sweet wisdom bore.

This is, my Lord, the rosie Emblem sweet,
    Blazing thyselfe out, on my mudd wall, fair,
And in thy Palace, where the rosy feet
    Of thy Deare Spouse doth thee her head thus ware. 10
    Her Head thou art: Head glory of her Knot.
    Thou art her Flower, and she thy flower pot.

The Metall Kingdoms had a Golden head,
    Yet had't no brains, or had its brains out dasht.
But Zions Kingdome fram'd hath better sped, 15
    Through which the Rayes of thy rich head are lasht.
    She wares thee Head, thou art her strong defence
    Head of Priority, and Excellence.

Hence art an head of Arguments so strong
    To argue all unto thyselfe, when bent 20
And quickly tongue ty, or pluck out the tongue
    Of all Contrary pleas or arguments.
    It makes them weake as water, for the tide
    Of Truth and Excellence rise on this Side.

23 *water,*] PW water.

Lord, let these barbed Arrows from thy bow   25
    Fly through mine Eyes, and Eares to strike my heart.
And force my Will, and Reason to thee so
    And stifle pleas made for the other part
    That so my Soule, rid of their Sophistry
    In rapid flames of Love to thee may fly.   30

My Metaphors are but dull Tacklings tag'd
    With ragged Non-Sense. Can such draw to thee
My stund affections all with Cinders clag'd,
    If thy bright beaming headship touch not mee?
    If that thy headship shines not in mine eyes,   35
    My heart will fuddled ly with wordly toyes.

Lord play thy Excellency on this pin
    To tongue ty other pleas my gadding heart
Is tooke withall. Chime my affections in
    To serve thy Sacred selfe with Sacred art.   40
    Oh! let thy Head stretch ore my heart its wing
    And then my Heart thy Headships praise shall sing.

37. Meditation. Col. 1.18. He is the Head, etc.

14. 5m [July] *1700*. Pub. PET.

It grieves mee, Lord, to thinke thy famous Name
    Should not be guilded ore with my bright Love.
Yet griev'd I am to thinke thy splendid fame
    Should be bedotcht by such poore Stuff I moove,
    That thy Bright Pearle, impald in gold, My Theme,   5
    Should by my addle brains, finde a dull veane.

Thou art an Head, the richest, that e're wore
    A Crown of Glory, where the Kirnell lies
Of deepest Wisdom, boxt in Brains, that sore

32 *thee*] PW the   35 *eyes,*] PW eyes.   39 *my*] orig: all my

In highest Notions, of the richest Sise   10
    Compar'd whereto man's Wisdom up doth rise
    Like Childrens catching speckled Butterflies.

Thou art the Head of Causes to thy Church:
    Its Cause of Reconciliation art,
Thou it Redeemdst, and hast gi'n hell the lurch.   15
    Thou Sanctifiest it in Life, and Heart.
    Thou dost it Form, Inform, Reform, and Try
    Conform to thee, marre her Deformity.

A Glorious Heade of Choicest influence
    More rich than Rubies, golden rivlets lie   20
Convaying Grace along these channells thence
    To heart, hand, foot, head, tongue, to eare, and eye.
    That man, as th'golden Tree, golde blossoms shoots.
    And glorifieth God with golden fruites.

A Royall Head of Majesty to make   25
    Heade of thy foes thy footstoole Stepping Stone.
Thou giv'st forth Holy Laws, and up dost take
    The Ruling Scepter over every one.
    The Golden Rule is ever in thy hand
    By which thine walk unto the golden Strand.   30

Be thou my Head: and of thy Body make mee
    Thy Influences in my Cue distill.
Guild thou my Chamber with thy Grace, and take mee
    Under thy Rule, and rule mee by thy Will.
    Be thou my head, and act my tongue whereby   35
    Its tittle-tattle may thee glorify.

32 *Cue*] orig: Cew

38. Meditation. Col. 1.18. He is the Head of the Body, the Church, who is the Beginning.

22. 7m [Sept.] *1700.*

If that my Power was answerable to
    My minde, my Lord, my little mite would rise
With something in its hand of Worth to 'stow
    And send to thee through the bright azure Skies.
    For next unto Infinity, I finde   5
    Its Love unto thyselfe of boundless kinde.

Its Love, Desire, Esteem of thee all scorn
    Confining limits, whose Dimensions stand
Immeasurable, but my Power's down born,
    Its impotency; Cannot heave a Sand   10
    Over a Straw, that all the fruites my Will
    Can e're produce can't * * * or one Sin kill.

This Wracks my heart, and low my person layes
    And rowles mee in the dust at thoughts hereon.
That thou, who dost deserve all glorious praise   15
    Should with an Empty Will, whose power is **none**
    Be paid, indeed; But yet, (O pardon mee)
    I want a power, not will to honour thee.

Thou Wisdom art, Wisdom's the heads Chiefe thing,
    Thou the Beginning art of Gods Creation.   20
And therefore art of Excellence the Spring
    And the Beginning of all Holy Station.
    First born from th'Dead: Sun like thy Excellence
    All Good things doth like Sunbeames forth dispense.

All Love, and Praise, all Service, Honour bright   25
    From all the Sons of men is but thy due.

9 *Immeasurable,*] PW Immeasurable.   13 *low*] orig: layes

Thou their beginning art: they and their might
    Should sing thy glory out and it forth show.
    But, oh my Shame, I have no Power nor Skill
    To do the Same, onely an Empty Will.   30

But, O my Lord, thou the Beginning art,
    Begin to draw afresh thine Image out
In Shining Colours, on my Life, and Heart
    Begin anew thy foes in mee to route.
    Begin again to breize upon my Soule   35
    Breize after brieze untill I touch the goale.

Thou the Beginning art of Order, and
    Art Head of Principalities and Power
Archont of Kings, Archangell to the Band
    Of Angells, and Archangells in their flower.   40
    Thou art, Lord, Principall: whose Beings run
    And all best things, like Sun beames from the Sun.

Be ever, Lord beginning till I end,
    At carrying on thine Intrest in my Soule.
For thy beginning will my marrd minde mende   45
    And make it pray Lord, take mee for thy tole.
    If mee as Wheate thy Tole-Dish doth once greet
    My tune's to thee Al-tashcheth Mictam Sweet.

39. Meditation. Col. 1.18. The First
Born from the Dead.

10m [Dec.] *1700.*

Poor wither'd Crickling, My lord, am I
    Whose shrunke up Skin hidebounds my kirnell so
That Love its Vitall Sparke's so squeezd thereby
    'T must breake the prisons Walls ere it can go

41 *whose*] Conj.   42 *things, like*] orig: things hence, like

Unto thyselfe. Hence let thy warm beams just   5
Make it to grow that it may breake its husk.

Love like to hunger'll breake through stone strong Walls.
    Nay brazen Walls cannot imprison it
Up from its object, when its object calls
    In Beams attractive falling on it thick.   10
    My Chilly Love sick of the Ague lies.
    Lord touch it with thy Sun shine, make it rise.

Death shall not deaden it, while thy Sun shines.
    The keyes of Hell, and Death are at thy Side.
Thy Conquoring Powre draws ore the grave thy lines,   15
    Whose darksom Dungeon thy dead body tri'de.
    Thou hast Death's Shady Region Conquoured
    Rose, as the Sun, up First born from the Dead.

First Fruits of them that sleep to sanctify
    The Harvest all, thou art. Thou art therefore   20
The First born from the Dead in Dignity
    In kinde, Cause, Order, to dy, and rise no more,
    As those raisd up before must, whose Erection
    Rather Reduction was than Resurrection.

Thy Humane Nature in the Cock-Pit dread,   25
    Like as the morning birds when day peeps, strout
Stands Crowing ore the Grave, laid Death there dead,
    And ore its Carkass neckt, doth Crow about,
    Throws down the Prison doors, comes out, and lay
    Them ope that th'Prisoners may come away.   30

But Lord strike down the iron Gate also
    Of Spirituall Death. Unprison thus my Soule.
Breath in the Realm of Life on it bestow,
    And in thy Heavenly Records me enrowle.
    And then my bird shall Crow thus roosted high   35
    Death, where's thy Sting? Grave, where's thy Victory?

7 *hunger'll*] orig: hunger will   18 *Rose*] orig: And Rose   20 *Thou*] PW thou
therefore] orig: still therefore   26 *Like as the*] orig: And like the
Like] PW like   34 *Heavenly Records*] orig: Records   36 *Victory?*] PW Victory.

The Golden Twist of Unity Divine
    Lord make the Ligaments to ty mee fast
Unto thyselfe, a Member with this twine
    Binde me to thee, For this will ever last.   40
    My Tunes shall rap thy prayses then good Store
    In Death upon the Resurrection Doore.

40. Meditation. Col. 1.18. That in all things he might have the Preheminence.

1701. Pub. ETG.

Under thy Rod, my God, thy smarting Rod,
    That hath off broke my James, that Primrose, Why?
Is't for my sin? Or Triall? Dost thou nod
    At me, to teach mee? or mee sanctify?
    I needed have this hand, that broke off hath   5
    This Bud of Civill, and of Sacred Faith.

But doth my sickness want such remedies,
    As Mummy draind out of that Body spun
Out of my bowells first? Must th'Cure arise
    Out of the Coffin of a pious son?   10
    Well: so be it. I'le kiss the Rod, and shun
    To quarrell at the Stroake. Thy Will be done.

Yet let the Rose of Sharon spring up cleare,
    Out of my James his ashes unto mee,
In radient sweet and shining Beames to cheer   15
    My sorrowfull Soule, and light my way to thee.
    Let thy Preheminence which, Lord, indeed
    Ore all things is, me help in time of need.

8 *draind out*] orig: draind of out

    This poem was written upon the death of Taylor's son James, who died in the West Indies on January 30, 1701.

Thy Humane nature so divinely ti'de
    Unto thy Person all Divine's a Spring   20
So high advanc'd, that in it doth reside
    Preheminence large over ev'ry thing.
    Thy Humane flesh with its Perfections shine
    So 'bove all others Beauties in their prime.

The like ne're seen in Heaven, nor Earth so broad.   25
    Adorn'd with Graces all, grown ripe in glory.
Thy Person with all Excellency stowd
    Perfections shine is lodgd in ev'ry story.
    Here all Created, all Creating faire,
    And Increated Eminences are.   30

Here all Preheminence of Offices
    Priest, Prophet-King-Hood too, their glorys rise
Conferrd on thee, my Lord, and all their Keyes
    That open us thy shining Mysteries
    Which do enflame our hearts their heads to run   35
    Under the shining Wings of this bright Sun.

Lord lead my sight to thy Preheminence.
    Raise thou in mee right feare of thee thereby.
My Love to thee advance till it Commence
    In all Degrees of Love, a Graduate high.   40
    When thy Preheminence doth ply this pin,
    My Musick shall thy Praises sweetly bring.

41. Meditation. Heb. 5.8. He learned by the things which he suffered.

6.5m [July] *1701*. Pub. PET.

That Wisdom bright whose vastness for extent
    Commensurates Dimension infinite
A Palace built with Saphir-Battlement
    Bepinkt with Sun, Moon, Starrs, all gold-fire bright,

Plac'de man his Pupill here, and ev'ry thing,   5
With loads of Learning, came to tutor him.

But he (alas) did at the threashould trip
    Fell, Crackt the glass through which the Sun should shine
That darkness gross his noble Soule doth tip.
    Each twig is bow'd with loads of follies Rhime.   10
    That ev'ry thing in tutoring, is a toole
    To whip the Scholler that did play the foole.

The Case thus stands: Hence matters up arose
    More sweet than Roses, and out-shine the Sun:
That Living Wisdom put on dying Cloaths: 15
    In mortal roabs to Sorrows Schoole house run.
    The Vessell full can hold no more, doth goe
    To Schoole to learn, whose learning cannot grow.

Christ, where all Wisdom's Treasures hidden are,
    Is Schollar, Suffering's his Tutor-Master: 20
Obedience, is his Lesson, which (as fair
    As Light in th' Sun) flows from him, yea and faster.
    But how should he learn any learning more
    In whom all Learning's ever lodg'd before?

Surely it must be said, the Humane Hall,   25
    Though furnished with all Ripe Grace, yet was
Not all ore Window, that no beame at all
    Of further light could have into it pass.
    He grew in Wisdom, Wisdom grew in him
    As in's, though's Godhead other wayes did't bring.   30

Though Grace in Christ forever perfect was
    And he e're perfectly was free from Sin
His progress yet in Knowledg needs must pass
    The Passes, humane modes, admit the thing.
    Hence learnd Obedience in his Suff'ring-Schoole.   35
    Experience taught him (though a Feeble toole).

12 *whip*] orig: whipte   18 *learn,*] PW learn.   27 *Not all*] orig: Not o're all
36 *taught*] PW teaght *him (though*] orig: him th' Mistress of

O Condescention! Shall the Heavens do
    Low Conjues to the Earth? or Sun array
Itselfe with Clouds, and to a Glow worm go
    For Light to make all o're the World light day?   40
    That thou should learn in Sorrows Schoole, in whom
    All learning is, and whence all learnings come?

Wonder, my Soule, at this great Wonder bright
    And in this frame, Lord, let my heart to thee
On Angells Wings fly, out of Earths Eyesight.   45
    Obedience learn in Sorrows Schoole of thee
    Till right Obedience me hath handed in
    Among thy Palace Songs thy praise to sing.

42. Meditation. Heb. 10.5. A Body hast thou prepared mee. σῶμα δὲ κατηρτίσω μοι

31. 6m [Aug.] *1701*. Pub. PET.

I fain would prize thee, Lord, but finde the price
    Of Earthy things to rise so high in mee
That I no pretious matter in my choice
    Can finde within my heart to offer thee.
    The price of worldly toyes is grown so deare,   5
    They pick my purse. Thy Gaine is little there.

But oh! if thou one Sparke of heavenly fire
    Wilt but drop on my hearth; its holy flame
Will burn my trash up. And refin'de desire
    Will rise to thee in th'Curlings of the same,   10
    As Pillars of Perfumeing incense rise,
    And Surges bright of Glory, 'bove the Skies.

6 *Thy*] PW thy

Oh! that my Soul was Walled round about
    With Orient Pearle fetcht out of holy Mine
And made a Castle, where thy Graces stoute   15
    Keep garison against my foes and thine.
    Then they each peeping thought sent Scout of Sin
    Would quickly take, and gibbit up therein.

But oh! the Swarms of enemies to thee
    (Bold Sawceboxes) make in these quarters spoile,   20
Make insurrection 'gainst the motions free
    Of thy good Spirit: Lord, come, scoure the Ile
    Of these and quarter here each flourishing grace.
    The Whole will then be in a Wealthy Case.

Thou for this end, a Body hadst preparde,   25
    Where Sin ne'er set a foot, nor shewd its head
But ev'ry grace was in it, and Well far'de.
    Whose fruite, Lord, let into my heart be shed.
    Then grace shall grace my Soule, my Soule shall thee
    Begrace, and shall thy gracefull Palace bee.   30

Thy Body is a Building all like mine,
    In Matter, Form, in Essence, Properties.
Yet Sin ne'er toucht it, Grace ne'er ceast in't'shine.
    It, though not Godded, next to th'Godhead lies.
    This honour have I, more than th'Angells bright.   35
    Thy Person, and my Nature do Unite.

Oh! Thanks, my Lord, accept this dusty thing:
    If I had better, thou should better have.
I blush, because I can no better bring:
    The best I do possess, I for thee save.
    Wash in thy blood, my gift till white it bee: 40
    And made acceptable to God by thee.

In humble wise I thee implore to make
    Me, what thou, and thy Father ever love.
Empt me of Sin: Fill mee with Grace: and take   45

20 *make in these quarters spoile*] orig: *these quarters spoile* changed to *these
quarters all do spoile* changed to *do all these quarters spoile*   27 *it,*] PW it.

Up while I'me here, my heart to thee above.
My Soule shall sing Thanksgiving unto thee,
If thou wilt tune it to thy praise in mee.

Meditation 43. Rom. 9.5. God blessed
   forever.

26. 8m [Oct.] *1701*. Pub. PET.

When, Lord, I seeke to shew thy praises, then
     Thy shining Majesty doth stund my minde,
Encramps my tongue and tongue ties fast my Pen,
     That all my doings, do not what's designd.
          My Speeche's Organs are so trancifide   5
          My words stand startld, can't thy praises stride.

Nay Speeches Bloomery can't from the Ore
     Of Reasons mine, melt words for to define
Thy Deity, nor t'deck the reechs that sore
     From Loves rich Vales, sweeter than hony rhimes.   10
          Words though the finest twine of reason, are
          Too Course a web for Deity to ware.

Words Mentall are syllabicated thoughts:
     Words Orall but thoughts Whiffld in the Winde.
Words Writ, are incky, Goose quill-slabbred draughts,   15
     Although the fairest blossoms of the minde.
          Then can such glasses cleare enough descry
          My Love to thee, or thy rich Deity?

Words are befould, Thoughts filthy fumes that smoake,
     From Smutty Huts, like Will-a-Wisps that rise   20
From Quaugmires, run ore bogs where frogs do Croake,
     Lead all astray led by them by the eyes.
          My muddy Words so dark thy Deity,
          And cloude thy Sun-Shine, and its Shining Sky.

47 *thee,*] PW thee.   **8** *melt*] orig: smelt[?]

Yet spare mee, Lord, to use this hurden ware.   25
　　I have no finer Stuff to use, and I
Will use it now my Creed but to declare
　　And not thy Glorious Selfe to beautify.
　　Thou art all-God: all Godhead then is thine
　　Although the manhood there unto doth joyne.   30

Thou art all Godhead bright, although there bee
　　Something beside the Godhead in thee bright.
Thou art all Infinite although in thee
　　There is a nature pure, not infinite.
　　Thou art Almighty, though thy Humane tent   35
　　Of Humane frailty upon earth did sent.

He needs must be the Deity most High,
　　To whom all properties essensiall to
The Godhead do belong Essentially
　　And not to others: nor from Godhead go   40
　　And thou art thus, my Lord, to Godhead joynd.
　　We finde thee thus in Holy Writ definde.

Thou art Eternall; Infinite thou art;
　　Omnipotent, Omniscient, Erywhere,
All Holy, Just, Good, Gracious, True, in heart,   45
　　Immortal, though with mortall nature here.
　　Religious worship hence belongs to thee
　　From men and angells: all, of each degree.

Be thou my God, and make mee thine Elect
　　To kiss thy feet, and worship give to thee: 50
Accept of mee, and make mee thee accept.
　　So I'st be safe, and thou shalt served bee.
　　I'le bring thee praise, buskt up in Songs perfum'de,
　　When thou with grace my Soule hast sweetly tun'de.

27 *now*] orig: onely now   33 *in*] orig: there b[e] in   41 *thou*] orig: thus thou
44 *Erywhere*] orig: Ubitary   46 *here*] orig: weary[?] wary[?]
48 *all*] orig: from men and all

Meditation 44. Joh. 1.14. The word was made Flesh.

28. 10m [Dec.] *1701.*

The Orator from Rhetorick gardens picks
    His Spangled Flowers of sweet-breathd Eloquence
Wherewith his Oratory brisk he tricks
    Whose Spicy Charms Eare jewells do commence.
    Shall bits of Brains be candid thus for eares?   5
    My Theme claims Sugar Candid far more cleare.

Things styld Transcendent, do transcende the Stile
    Of Reason, reason's stares neere reach so high.
But Jacob's golden Ladder rounds do foile
    All reasons Strides, wrought of THEANTHROPIE.   10
    Two Natures distance-standing, infinite,
    Are Onifide, in person, and Unite.

In Essence two, in Properties each are
    Unlike, as unlike can be. One All-Might
A Mite the other; One Immortall fair.   15
    One mortall, this all Glory, that all night.
    One Infinite, One finite. So for ever:
    Yet ONED are in Person, part'd never.

The Godhead personated in Gods Son
    Assum'd the Manhood to its Person known,   20
When that the Manhoods essence first begun
    That it did never Humane person own.
    Each natures Essence e're abides the same.
    In person joynd, one person each do claim.

Oh! Dignifide Humanity indeed: 25
    Divinely person'd: almost Deifide.
Nameing one Godhead person, in our Creed,

11 *infinite,*] PW infinite.   18 *Person,*] PW Person.   25 *Oh!*] PW Oh.

The Word-made-Flesh. Here's Grace's 'maizing stride.
    The vilst design, that villany e're hatcht
Hath tap't such Grace in God, that can't be matcht.   30

Our Nature spoild: under all Curses groans
    Is purg'd, tooke, grac'd with grace, united to
A Godhead person, Godhead-person owns
    Its onely person. Angells, Lord its so.
    This Union ever lasts, if not relate   35
    Which Cov'nant claims Christs Manhood, separate.

You Holy Angells, Morning-Stars, bright Sparks,
    Give place: and lower your top gallants. Shew
Your top-saile Conjues to our slender barkes:
    The highest honour to our nature's due.   40
    Its neerer Godhead by the Godhead made
    Than yours in you that never from God stray'd.

Here is good anchor hold: and argument
    To anchor here, Lord, make my Anchor stronge
And Cable, both of holy geer, out sent   45
    And in this anch'ring dropt and let at length.
    My bark shall safely ride then though there fall
    On't th'strongest tempests hell can raise of all.

Unite my Soule, Lord, to thyselfe, and stamp
    Thy holy print on my unholy heart.   50
I'st nimble be when thou destroyst my cramp
    And take thy paths when thou dost take my part.
    If thou wilt blow this Oaten Straw of mine,
    The sweetest piped praises shall be thine.

32 *purg'd, tooke, grac'd*] orig: tooke, washt, grac'd
34 *Angells*] orig: Lord of Angells   37 *Angells*] PW Angell
45 *out*] orig: to hold fast and out   53 *mine,*] PW mine.

45. Meditation. Col. 2.3. In whom are hid
        all the Treasures of Wisdom.

15.12m [Feb.] *1701.*

My head, my Lord, that ivory Cabinet
    'S a nest of Brains dust, dry, ne're yet could Ware
The Velvet locks of Vertue for its deck
    Or golden Fleece of Wisdoms virdent hair.
    The Scull without, not fring'd with Wisdom fleece.   5
    The pan within a goose pen full of geese.

There Reason's wick yarn-like ore twisted Snarles
    Chandled with Sensuall tallow out doth blaze
A smoaky flame upon its hurden harles
    That Wil-a-Wisps it into boggy wayes.   10
    Melt off this fat, my Reason make thy Candle
    And light it with thy Wisdom's flames that spangle.

Thy Person's Wisdoms Sparkling Treasury:
    Consisting of two natures: One of which
Runs parallell with blest infinity   15
    All treasures here of Wisdom ever pitch.
    Wise Counsills all, of everlasting date,
    And Wisdom them t'effect, here sits in state.

Th'other's a Locker of a Humane frame
    With richer than Corinthian Amber tills   20
And Shelves of Emralds. Here to deck the same
    All Wisdom that's Created comes, and fills.
    Created Wisdom all and all its Wealths
    Of Grace are treasur'de in these Tills and Shelfes.

Like to a Sparkling Carbuncle up Caskt   25
    Within a Globe of Chrystall glass most cleare
Fills 't all with Shine which through its sides are flasht

Col. 2.3.] PW Col. 23.
2 *dust,*] PW dust.   5 *fring'd*] orig: ruff   18 *t'effect*] orig: to effect

And makes all glorious Shine: so much more here
These treasures of thy Wisdom shine out bright
In thee. My Candle With thy Flame, Lord, Light.   30

Or as the Sun within its Azure bowre
    That guilds its Chrystall Walls with golden rayes
It from its bowl like body, light out poures
        Exiling darkness, making glorious dayes
        All Wisdom so, and Wisdoms Treasures all   35
        Are shining out in thee, their Arcinall.

Unlock thy Locker, make my faith Key here
    To back the Wards. Lord ope the Wicket gate
And from thine Emrald Shelves, and Pinchase there
        A beame of every sort of Wisdom take   40
        And set it in the Socket of my Soule
        To make all day within, and night controle.

And from these tills, and drawers take a grain
    Of evry sort of Sanctifying grace
Wherewith impregnate thou the former beame.   45
        Set in my Soule a lamp to light that place
        That so these beames let in, may generate
        Grace in my Soule, and so an Holy State.

If wisdom in the Socket of my heart
    And Grace within its Cradle rockt do shine   50
My head shall ware a frindg of Wisdoms art.
        Thy grace shall guild this pilgrim life of mine.
        Thy Wisdom's Treasure thus Conferrd on mee
        Will have my glory all Conferrd on thee.

31 *Azure*] orig: Chr[ystall?]   39 *Shelves*] PW Slelves
48 *Soule,*] PW Soule.   50 *Grace within its Cradle rockt do*] orig:
in its Cradle Grace rockt there do

46. Meditation. Col. 2.9. The Fulness of the Godhead dwelleth in him bodily.

10.3m [May] *1702*. Pub. PET.

I drown, my Lord. What though the Streame I'm in
    Rosewater bee, Or Ocean to its brinkes
Of Aqua Vitae where the Ship doth swim?
    The Surges drown the Soul, oreflowd, that sinks.
    A Sea of Liquid gold with rocks of pearle   5
    May drownd as well as Neptune's Fishy Well.

Thy Fulness, Lord, my Filberd cannot hold.
    How should an acorn bowle the Sea lade dry?
A Red rose leafe the Suns bright bulk up fold?
    Or halfe an Ants egge Canopy the Sky?   10
    The world play in a Sneale horn Hide, and Seek
    May, ere my thimble can thy fulness meete.

All fulness is in thee my Lord, and Christ.
    The fulness of all Excellence is thine.
All's palac'de in thy person, and bespic'de.   15
    All Kinds, and Quantities of't in thee shine.
    The Fulness of the Godhead in respect
    Unto the Manhood's in thy person kept.

Hence all the Properties, that Godhead hath,
    And all their Godhead Operations brave,   20
Which are the Fulness Godhead forth display'th,
    Thy person for their Temple ever have.
    All always as transcendent Stones bright, set,
    Encabin'd are in thee their Cabbinet.

Oh! what a Lord and Lordship's here my Lord?   25
    How doth thy Fulness, fill thy Hall with Shine?

Col. 2.9.] PW Col. 3.9   *The Fulness*] PW The the Fulness
5 *A Sea*] orig: Will drown A Sea
6 *Neptune's*] PW Neptune   23 *always*] PW alwaye

Some Rayes thereof my Cottage now afford
    And let these golden rayes its inside line.
    Thy Fulness all, or none at all, Will goe
    Together, and in part will never flow.   30

All, Lord, or None at all! this makes mee dread.
    All is so Good, and None at all so bad.
All puts faith to't: but none at all strikes dead.
    I'le hope for all, lest none at all makes sad.
    Hold up this hope. Lord, then this hope shall sing   35
    Thy praises sweetly, spite of feares Sad Sting.

47. Meditation. Joh. 5.26. The Son hath
        life in himselfe.

12. 5m [July] *1702.*

Noe mervaile if my mite amaized bee
    Musing upon Almighties Mighty ALL
In all its Fulness socketed in thee
    As furniture, my Lord, to grace thy Hall.
    Thy Work requires that so the Case should goe.   5
    But oh! what Grace doth hence to Sinners flow?

I strike mine oare not in the golden Sea
    Of Godhead Fulness, thine essentially.
But in the Silver Ocean make my way
    Of All Created Fulness, thine Most high.   10
    Thy Humane Glass, God wondrously did build:
    And Grace oreflowing, with All fulness Filld.

Thou dost all Fulness of all Life possess.
    Thy Life all varnisht is with virdent flowers
'Bove Sense and Reason in their brightest dress.
    Lifes best top gallant ever in thee towers.   15
    The Life of Grace that Life of Life within
    Thy knot in heavenly Sparks is flourishing.

Besides thy proper Lifes tall fulness-Wealth,
  There's Life in thee, like golden Spirits, stills,   20
To ery member of thy Mystick Selfe,
  Through secret Chases into th'vitall tills
  Or like the Light embodi'd in the Sun
  That to each living thing with life doth run.

A Well of Living Water: Tree of Life   25
  From whom Life comes to every thing alive:
Some Eate and Drink Eternall Life most rife.
  Some life have for a while by a reprive.
  Who in this well do let their bucket down
  Shall never in the lake of Lethe drown.   30

Lord, bath mee in this Well of Life. This Dew
  Of Vitall Fruite will make mee ever live.
My branch make green: my Rose ware vivid hew
  An Holy and a fragrant sent out give.
  My kirnell ripe shall rattle out thy praise   35
  And Orient blush shall on my actions blaze.

48. Meditation. Rev. 1.8. The Almighty.

13.7m [Sept.] *1702.*

O! What a thing is Might right mannag'd? 'Twill
  That Proverb brain, whose face doth ware this paint.
(Might ore goe's Right) for might doth Right fulfill
  Will Right revive when wrong makes Right to faint.
  Might hatches Right: Right hatches Might, they are 5
  Each Dam, and Chick, to each: a Lovely paire.

Then Might well mannag'd riseth mighty: yet
  Doth never rise up to Almightiness.
Almightiness nere's in a mortall bit.

24 *each living thing*] orig: each thing alive

But, Lord, thou dost Almightiness possess.   10
    Might in it's fulness: all mights Fulness bee
Of ery Sort and Sise stow'd up in thee.

But what am I, poor Mite, all mightless thing!
    That cannot rive a rush, that I should e're
Adventure t'dress Almighty up, or bring   15
    Almightiness deckt in its mighty geere?
    Then spare my Stutting Stamring, inky Quill,
    If it its bowells on thy Power distill.

My Mite (if I such Solicisms might
    But use) would spend its mitie Strength for thee   20
Of Mightless might, of feeble stronge delight.
    Its little ALL thy Sacrifice showld bee.
    For thee't would mock at all the Might and Power
    That Earth, and Hell possess: and on thee shower.

A Fig for Foes, for Divells, Hell, and all   25
    The powres of darkness, thou now on my Side
Their Might's a little mite, Powers powerless fall.
    My Mite Almighty will not let down slide.
    I will not trust unto this Might of mine:
    Nor in my Mite distrust, while I am thine.   30

Thy Love Almighty is, to Love mee deare,
    Thy Grace Almighty mee to save: thy Truth
Almighty to depend on. Justice cleare
    Almighty t'justify, and judge. Grace shewth.
    Thy Wisdom too's Almighty all to eye,   35
    And Holiness is such to sanctify.

If thy Almightiness, and all my Mite
    United be in sacred Marriage knot,
My Mite is thine: Mine thine Almighty Might.
    Then thine Almightiness my Mite hath got.   40

12 *stow'd*] orig: stored   15 *up,*] PW up.
24 *shower*] orig: pow[er]   30 *Mite*] orig: Migh[t]   35 *eye,*] PW eye.

My Quill makes thine Almightiness a String
Of Pearls to grace the tune my Mite doth sing.

49. [Meditation.] Joh. 1.14. Full of Grace.

8. 9m [Nov.] *1702.* Pub. PET.

Gold in its Ore, must melted be, to bring
    It midwift from its mother womb: requires
To make it shine and a rich market thing,
    A fining Pot, and Test, and melting fire.
    So do I, Lord, before thy grace do shine   5
    In mee, require, thy fire may mee refine.

My Flame hath left its Coale, my fire's gone t'bed:
    Like Embers in their ashie lodgen gray.
Lord let the Influences of thy head
    Most graciously remoove this rug away.   10
    If with the Bellows of thy grace thou blow
    My ashes off, thy Coale will shine, and glow.

Thy Clay, and Mine, out of one pit are dug:
    Although with Spades of vastest differing kinde.
Thine all bright Godhead; mine of mortall Wood.   15
    Thine shod with Glory; Mine with Sin all rin'de.
    Thy Soule, and Mine made of one minerall
    And each made regent o're their Clayie Hall.

But oh! alas! mine's Wall is worm-hold, and
    My House and Household sogd with noisom Sin   20
And no reliefe can have in Creature's hand
    While thine all Sparkling Shines without, and in,
    Fild with all Grace, and Graces Fullness all
    Adorning of thy Household and thy Hall.

41 *makes thine Almightiness a String*] orig: shall thine Almightiness forth
sing   **6** *may mee refine*] orig: mee to refine   **9** *of thy*] orig: of kick thy
15 *of*] orig: all

But woe is mee. Unclean I am: my Slips!   25
    Lord, let a Seraphim a live Coale take
Off of thine Altar, with it touch my lips.
        And purge away my Sins for mercys sake.
        I thus do pray finding thy Cask within
        With Grace, and graces fulness fild to th'brim.   30

I empty, thou top full, of Grace! Lord, take
    A Gracious Cluster of thy glorious grace
And busk it in my bosom, Sweet to make
        It, and my life: and gracious, in thy face.
        If thou with gracious Sweetness sweeten mee   35
        My Life with Grace sweetly perfum'de shall bee.

Can I a graceless member be of thee,
    While that thy hand's a Spring of Grace? and Heart
All gracious is to give? Then influence mee
        With thy free Grace. Thou art my lovely marke.   40
        When thy rich Grace doth tune my Song, sung high
        Thy Glory then shall rise its melody.

50. Meditation. Joh. 1.14. Full of Truth.

27. 10m [Dec.] *1702.*

The Artists Hand more gloriously bright,
    Than is the Sun itselfe, in'ts shining glory
Wrought with a stone axe made of Pearle, as light
        As light itselfe, out of a Rock all flory
        Of Precious Pearle, a Box most lively made   5
        More rich than gold Brimfull of Truth enlaid.

Which Box should forth a race of boxes send
    Teemd from its Womb such as itselfe, to run
Down from the Worlds beginning to its end.
        But, o! this box of Pearle Fell, Broke, undone.   10
10 *Broke,*] PW Broke.

Truth from it flew: It lost Smaragdine Glory:
Was filld with Falshood: Boxes teemd of Sory.

The Artist puts his glorious hand again
    Out to the Worke: His Skill out flames more bright
Now than before. The worke he goes to gain,   15
    He did portray in flaming Rayes of light.
        A Box of Pearle shall from this Sory, pass
        More rich than that Smaragdine Truth-Box was.

Which Box, four thousand yeares, o'r ere 'twas made,
    In golden Scutchons lay'd in inke Divine   20
Of Promises, of a Prophetick Shade,
    And in embellishments of Types that shine.
        Whose Beames in this Choice pearle-made-Box all meet
        And bedded in't their glorious Truth to keep.

But now, my Lord, thy Humane Nature, I   25
    Doe by the Rayes this Scutcheon sends out, finde
Is this Smaragdine Box where Truth doth ly
    Of Types, and Promises, that thee out lin'de.
        Their Truth they finde in thee: this makes them shine.
        Their Shine on thee makes thee appeare Divine.   30

Thou givst thy Truth to them, thus true they bee.
    They bring their Witness out for thee. Hereby
Their Truth appeares emboxt indeed in thee:
    And thou the true Messiah shin'st thereby.
        Hence Thou, and They make One another true   35
        And They, and Thou each others Glory shew.

Hence thou art full of Truth, and full dost stand,
    Of Promises, of Prophesies, and Types.
But that's not all: All truth is in thy hand,
    Thy lips drop onely Truth, give Falshood gripes.   40
        Leade through the World to glory, that ne'er ends
        By Truth's bright Hand all such as Grace befriends.

19 *o'r ere*] PW o'rere
22 *embellishments*] PW embellisments   24 *to*] orig: do
25 *Lord*] orig: Glorious Lord   28 *Promises,*] PW Promises.
31 *thus true they*] orig: this true is   40 *Truth,*] PW Truth.

O! Box of Truth! tenent my Credence in
　　　The mortase of thy Truth: and Thou in Mee.
These Mortases, and Tenents make so trim,　　　　　　　　45
　　　That They and Thou, and I ne'er severd bee.
　　　Embox my Faith, Lord, in thy Truth a part
　　　And I'st by Faith embox thee in my heart.

51. Meditation. Eph. 1.23. Which is his body,
　　　　the fulness of him that filleth
　　　　all in all.

　　　14.12m [Feb.] *1702.*

My Heart, my Lord, 's a naughty thing all o're:
　　　Yet if renew'd, the best in mee, 't would fain
Find Words to waft thy praises in, ashore,
　　　Suited unto the Excellence in thee.
　　　But easier 't is to hide the Sun up under　　　　5
　　　Th'black of my naile, than words to weald this Wonder.

Had I Corinthian Brass: nay Amber here
　　　Nay Ophir Gold transparently refinde.
Nay, th'heavenly Orbs all Quintessenced clear,
　　　To do the deed, 't would quite deceive my minde:　　　10
　　　Words all run wast, so these a nit may Weigh:
　　　The World in scale, ere I thy wealth display.

Then what doe I, but as the Lady Bee
　　　Doth tune her Musick in her mudd wall Cell:
My Humming so, no musick makes to thee:　　　　15
　　　Nor can my bagpipes play thy glory well.

8 *transparently*] PW trasparently　　　9 *Nay, th'*] PW Nay 'th'
11 *wast,*] PW wast.　　*a*] orig: too a

　　43 ff.: O! Box of Truth! etc. Taylor, like Herbert, showed an interest in
joinery. Cf. Herbert's "Ungratefulness," lines 28–29, and "Confession," lines
1–6.

Amaizd I stand to see thee all Compleate:
Compleated by a body, thou makst neate.

Thy Church, (what though its matter of it here
    Be brightest Saints, and Angells, all Compact   20
With Spirituall Glow, with grace out shining cleare
    And brimfull full of what the World ere lackt)
    Whom thou hast filld with all her fulness, shee
    Thy fulness is, and so she filleth thee.

Oh! wondrous strange. Angells and Men here are   25
    Incorporated in one body tite.
Two kinds are gain'd into one mortase, fair.
    Me tenent in thyselfe my Lord, my Light.
    These are thy body: thou their head, we see
    Thou fillst them first, then they do fill up thee.   30

This gracious fulness thus runs to and fro
    From thee to them: from them to thee again:
Not as the tides that Ebbe, as well as flow.
    The Banks are ever Full, and so remain.
    What mystery's here. Thou canst not wanty bee.   35
    Yet wantest them, as sure as they want thee.

Necessity doth in the middle stand
    Layes hands on both: constrains the body to
The head and head unto the body's band.
    The Head, and Body both together goe.   40
    The Head Compleats the body as its such:
    The Body doth Compleate the Head, as much.

Am I a bit, Lord, of thy Body? Oh!
    Then I do claim thy Head to be mine own.
Thy Heads sweet Influence let to mee flow,   45
    That I may be thy fulness, full up grown.
    Then in thy Churches fullness thou shalt be
    Compleated in a Sense, and sung by mee.

21 *Glow*] PW Glew[?]   34 *Full,*] PW Full.   42 *as*] orig: and

52. Meditation. Mat. 28.18. All Power in
Heaven, and Earth is given mee.

11. 2m [Apr.] *1703.*

What Power is this? What all Authoritie
    In Earth and Heaven too? What Lord is here?
And given All to thee! Here's Majisty.
    All Worldly Power hence slinks away for feare.
    Then blush, my Soule that thou dost frozen ly: 5
    Under the beams of such bright Majesty.

What flying Flakes of Rapid flames of Love
    Scal'de from my heart by those bright beams that bed
Do in thy selfe, up mount to thee above
    Oretoping golden mountains with their head.   10
    But Why, my heart? O! why so drossy now;
    When such Authority doth to thee bow?

One Sprig of this Authority doth beare
    The Tree of Life, that spreads ore heaven quite
And Sinners sprinkles with its Sap t'make faire.   15
    And with its juyce doth quench Gods wrath out right.
    With God it maketh Reconciliation
    By offering, and Holy Intercession.

Within whose Shade my sin scorcht Soule doth bathe
    In Gods bright Sun shine, smiling heart-sweet beams.   20
Whose Rosie sents reviv'de my Spirits have.
    Whose Spirits wash away my guilt and Stains.
    Amongst whose leaves my heart doth shroude its head
    And in whose buds my grounded hopes do bed.

O that I could once frown away my sloath: 25
    And dart my dulness through with glouts that stroy!
That mine Affections, (O! their sluggish growth)

15 *Sap t'make*] orig: juice on

Might with Seraphick Wings, Lord, swiftly fly,
Unto thine Altar for an Holy Cure
Produced by a Coale thence took most pure. 30

When this is gain'd, a Golden Trumpet I,
All full of Grace shall be, wherein, in rayse
Of thy bright Priesthoods sweet Authority
My spirit trumpet shall, tun'd to thy praise
Till when let this unskilfull ditty still 35
Tunes in thine Eares, pipd through my sorry quill.

53. Meditation. Mat. 28.18. All Power is given me in Heaven, and in earth.

13th. 4m [June] 1703.

Were not my fancy stagnate, and the Lake
Of mine affections frozen ore with ice
And Spirits Crampt, or else Catochizate
The sweet breath'd smells the briezes of the Spice
My Theme doth vent, would raise such waves upon 5
The Sea of Eloquence, they'd skip thereon.

Shall I be lumpish when such lightsom showers
Of livning influences still on mee?
Shall I be lowring, when such lovely flowers
Spring smiling up, and Court mee too for thee? 10
When such heart liv'ning glances breake and fly
Out through the Sides of thy Authority?

Oh! that this, Thine Authority was made
A Golden Anvill: and my Contemplation
A Smiting Hammer: and my heart was laid 15
Thereon, and hammerd up for emendation.

34 *My*] orig: The   3–4 *or else Catochizate / The sweet breath'd smells*]
written in margin of PW with sign to insert after *Crampt*
4 *breath'd*] Conj.

And anvilld stoutly to a better frame
To entertain thy rayes that round the same.

Thou hast the golden key, that doth unlock,
    The heart of God: Wisdoms bright Counsills Tower   20
All Power Prophetick This the boundless Stock
    Of Gods Designs displayes in Gospell Shower.
    These gleames may liven our dead Spirits then,
    File bright our rusty brains, and sharpen them.

Thou nothing but the Will of God declarst.   25
    And nothing less: For thine Authority
Should be abusd; if not improov'd, or spar'd.
    If't more or less than Gods good Will descry.
    This cannot be abusd: We therefore must
    The Lesson learn then setst, and therein trust.   30

But here is still another gleame out breakes,
    All Royall Power in heaven, and earth do lodge
In thee, my Lord, this thou wilt not out leake
    Nor smoother up: it will not hast nor dodge.
    A right to mannage all things: therefore thou   35
    Wilt thine secure, and make thy foes down bow.

Thou Law deliverst: Thine Authority
    Cannot be idle; nor exceed the right.
Hence such as will not with thy rule Comply,
    Thou with thy iron Scepter down wilt smite.   40
    This Power will raise the dead, and judge all too.
    His own will Crown with Life. To hell foes throw.

Lord let thy Doctrine melt my Soule anew:
    And let thy Scepter drill my heart in mee:
And let thy Spirits Cotters pierce it through   45
    Like golden rivits, Clencht, mee hold to thee.
    Then thou and I shall ne'er be separate.
    Thy Praise shall be my Glory sung in state.

22 *Designs displayes*] orig: Designs do displayes   *Shower*] PW Showers[?]
36 *secure,*] PW secure.   41 *dead,*] PW dead.

54. Meditation. Matt. 28.18. All Power is given mee In Heaven, and in earth.

22th. 6m [Aug.] *1703.*

Untun'de, my Lord. My Cankard brassy wire
    'S unfit to harp thee Musick. Angells pipes
Are squeaking things: soon out of breath. Desires
    Exceed them; yet screwd highst up are but mites
    To meddle with the Musicking thy glory.   5
    What then's my jews trump meet to tune thy Story?

File off the rust: forgive my Sin, and make
    My Heart thy Harp: and mine Affections brac'de
With gracious Grace thy Golden Strings to shake
    With Quavers of thy glory well begrac'de.   10
    Though small's my mite, its dusty Wings e're will
    Sprindg out thy fame tun'de by thy Spirits Skill.

Three Shining Suns rise in the Chrystall Skies
    Of Mankinde Orbs, and Orbs Angelicall.
Whose Rayes out Shine all pimping Stars that rise   15
    Within these Spheres and Circuite through them all.
    These do evigorate all Action done
    By men and angells right, wherein they run.

The Shine of these three Suns is all the Same,
    Yet sparkling differently according to   20
The Matter form'd therewith, and beares the Name
    Authority, and by the Same doth goe,
    Into a trine of Offices. Hence springs
    Good warrant, for just Prophets, Priests and Kings.

These three are brightest Suns, held in the Skies   25
    Or shining Orb of Man, or Angell kinde.

1 *Cankard*] orig: rusty   7 *off*] PW of   *Sin,*] PW Sin.   11 *mite,*] PW mite.
14 *Orbs,*] PW Orbs.   21 *therewith,*] PW therewith.   22 *Authority,*] PW
Authority.   *goe,*] PW goe.   23 *Offices.*] PW Offices

    17: evigorate. For envigorate.

And all attain unto a Sovereign Sise
    Of Shine, that hitherto ascend, we finde.
    The brightest brightness, and the mighti'st Might
    Is lodg'd in each one of these Balls of Light.   30

He that hath any one of these, doth weare
    A Supreme Shine. But all these three Suns came
To no man; but alone unto thy Share,
    My Lord, they fall. Thou hast the Sovereign name.
    And all the glorious Sunshine of these three   35
    Bright Suns, shines bright and powerfull out in thee.

Here's three fold glory, Prophet's, Priest's and King's
    Trible Authority bestud thy Crown.
As Mediatour all that Pow're within
    The Heaven, and Earth is thine. O bright Renown.   40
    To view those glories in thy Crown that vapor,
    Would make bright Angells eyes to run a-water.

O! plant mee in thy Priestly Sunshine, I
    Shall then be reconcild to God. In mee
A beame of thy Propheticke Sun imploy.   45
    'Twill fill my Spirits Eye with light to see.
    Make in my heart thy Kingly Sunshine flame.
    'Twill burn my Sin up, sanctify my frame.

My Gracious-Glorious Lord, shall I be thine?
    Wilt thou be mine? Then happy, happy mee!   50
I shall then cloath'd be with the Sun, and shine,
    Crown'd with tweeve Starrs, Moon under foot too see.
    Lord, so be it. My rusty Wires then shall
    Bee fined gold, to tune thee praise with all.

33 *no man*] PW noman

37: *Prophet's, Priest's and King's.* Cf. The Westminster Shorter Catechism: "Christ, as our Redeemer, executeth the offices of a Prophet, of a Priest, and of a King, both in his estate of humiliation and exaltation." As quoted in Philip Schaff, *The Creeds of Christendom* (3 vols. New York, Harper, 1877), *3*, 680–81.

56. Meditation. Joh. 15.24. Had I not done amongst
        them the works, that none other man hath
        done, etc.

10. 8m [Oct.] *1703.* Pub. *W.*

Should I with silver tooles delve through the Hill
        Of Cordilera for rich thoughts, that I
My Lord, might weave with an angelick skill
        A Damask Web of Velvet Verse thereby
        To deck thy Works up, all my Web would run   5
        To rags, and jags: so snicksnarld to the thrum.

Thine are so rich: Within, Without. Refin'd.
        No workes like thine. No Fruits so sweete that grow
On th'trees of righteousness, of Angell kinde
        And Saints, whose limbs reev'd with them bow down low.   10
        Should I search ore the Nutmeg Gardens shine
        Its fruits in flourish are but skegs to thine.

The Clove, when in its White-green'd blossoms shoots,
        Some Call the pleasentst sent the World doth show.
None Eye e're saw, nor nose e're smelt such Fruits   15
        My Lord, as thine, Thou Tree of Life in'ts blow.
        Thou Rose of Sharon, Vallies Lilly true
        Thy Fruits most sweet and Glorious ever grew.

Thou art a Tree of Perfect nature trim
        Whose golden lining is of perfect Grace   20
Perfum'de with Deity unto the brim,
        Whose fruits, of the perfection, grow, of Grace.
        Thy Buds, thy Blossoms, and thy fruits adorne
        Thyselfe, and Works, more shining than the morn.

Art, natures Ape, hath many brave things done   25
        As th'Pyramids, the Lake of Meris vast

2 *rich*] orig: Wealthiest   4 *Verse*] PW Velse   14 *show*] orig: know
20 *golden*] orig: glowing

The Pensile Orchards built in Babylon,
    Psammitich's Labyrinth. (arts Cramping task)
    Archimedes his Engins made for war.
    Romes Golden House. Titus his Theater.   30

The Clock at Strasburgh, Dresdens Table-Sight
    Regiamonts Fly of Steele about that flew.
Turrian's Wooden Sparrows in a flight.
    And th'Artificiall man Aquinas slew.
    Mark Scaliota's Lock, and Key and Chain   35
    Drawn by a Flea, in our Queen Betties reign.

Might but my pen in natures Inventory
    Its progress make, 't might make such things to jump

32 *Regiamonts*] orig: Regsamonts

29: Archimedes his Engins. Archimedes, during the siege of Syracuse by Marcellus, postponed its fall with the military engines he invented (*Cent. Dict.*).

30: Romes Golden House, palace built by Nero containing porticoes 2800 feet long (*Cent. Dict.*).

30: Titus his Theater, the Colosseum; it was finished by Titus Vespasianus (40–81 A.D.) (*Cent. Dict.*).

31: Clock at Strasburgh, clock built by mathematician Conrad Dasypodius in 1574 (*W*).

31: Dresdens Table-Sight. Possibly a reference to a collection of Chinese porcelains belonging to Augustus II, elector of Saxony (1670–1733) (*W*).

32: Regiamonts Fly of Steele. Taylor has mentioned this fly, as well as other marvels, elsewhere in his writings: "If Albertus Magnus could make an Artificiall man that by artificiall Engins did walk and speak; If Regiomontanus made a Wooden Eagle which when the Emperor Maximilian came to Nuremberg flew a quarter of a mile out of the City to meet him and then accompanied him to his lodgen and also an Iron fly which at a feast flew out of his hand and about the room and then returned and lighted on his hand again, surely the Angels much more can make not by a creating but by an Artificiall hand Visible Bodies" (HG, 17). Taylor took his information on Regiomontanus from Peter Heylyn, *Cosmographie* (London, 1657), p. 399; he copied into CP a number of passages from this work, including a description of Psammitich's Labyrinth (mentioned in line 28).

34: th'Artificiall man Aquinas slew. A talking head or artificial woman constructed by Albertus Magnus, teacher of Thomas Aquinas. Thomas destroyed the contrivance because it disturbed him in his studies—or perhaps because he thought it was a diabolic illusion. See Robert R. Hodges, "Edward Taylor's 'Artificiall Man,'" *American Literature, 31* (1959), 76–77.

All which are but Inventions Vents or glory
    Wits Wantonings, and Fancies frollicks plump.   40
    Within whose maws lies buried Times, and Treasures
    Embalmed up in thick dawbd sinfull pleasures.

Nature doth better work than Art: yet thine
    Out vie both works of nature and of Art.
Natures Perfection and the perfect shine   45
    Of Grace attend thy deed in ev'ry part.
    A Thought, a Word, and Worke of thine, will kill
    Sin, Satan, and the Curse: and Law fulfill.

Thou art the Tree of Life in Paradise,
    Whose lively branches are with Clusters hung   50
Of Lovely fruits, and Flowers more sweet than spice
    Bende down to us: and doe out shine the sun,
    Delightfull unto God, doe man rejoyce
    The pleasentst fruits in all Gods Paradise.

Lord feed mine eyes then with thy Doings rare,   55
    And fat my heart with these ripe fruites thou bearst.
Adorn my Life well with thy works, make faire
    My Person with apparrell thou prepar'st.
    My Boughs shall loaded bee with fruits that spring
    Up from thy Works, while to thy praise I sing.   60

40 *Wantonings,*] PW Wantonings.

59. Meditation. 1 Cor. 10.2. Baptized in the Cloud.

6. 12m [Feb.] *1703.*

Wilt thou enoculate within mine Eye
    Thy Image bright, My Lord, that bright doth shine
Forth in the Cloudy-Firy Pillar high
    Thy Tabernacles Looking-Glass Divine?
    What glorious Rooms are then mine Eyeholes made.   5
    Thine Image on my windows Glass portrai'd?

Oh! Pillar strange, made of a Cloude, and Fire.
    Whose Stoole is Israels Camp, it sits upon.
Whose Skirts doe Canopy that Camp: Whose Spire
    Doth kiss the Heavens, leading Israel on.   10
    Sure't is Christ's Charret drawn by Angells high.
    The Humane jacket, typ'te, of's Deity.

A Sun by night, to Dayify the dark.
    A Shade by Day, Sunbeames to mollify.
The Churches Pilot out her way to mark: 15
    Her Quarter Master quarters to descry.
    Its Christ's Watch tower over his Churches Host,
    With Angells kept. Tent of the Holy Ghost.

Christs Looking Glass that on his Camp gives Shine.
    Whose backside's pitchy darkness to his foes.   20
A Wall of Fire about his Israel twines
    To burn up all that offer to oppose:
    The Mediatory Province in a Map.
    The Feather in the Tabernacle's Cap.

Christ in this Pillar, Godhead-Man'd doth rise   25
    The Churches King, to guid, support, Defend.
Her Priest to Cleanse her: in the Cloud to baptize.

6 *Image*] PW Images   7 *strange,*] PW strange.   15 *mark*] orig: pry

And Reconcile with Incense that ascends.
Her Prophet too that Lights her in her way
By Night With Lanthorn Fire. With Cloud by day.   30

Then lead me, Lord, through all this Wilderness
    By this Choice shining Pillar Cloud and Fire.
By Day, and Night I shall not then digress.
    If thou wilt lead, I shall not lag nor tire
    But as to Cana'n I am journeying   35
    I shall thy praise under this Shadow sing.

60[A]. Meditation. Joh. 6.51. I am the
                 Living Bread, that came down
                 from Heaven.

16. 2m [Apr.] *1704.*

Count me not liquorish if my Soule do pine
    And long for Angells bread of Heavens wheate
Ground in thy Quorns, Searcde in the Laws Lawn fine
    And bakt in Heavens backhouse for our meate.
    Ist die of Famine, Lord, My Stomach's weak.   5
    And if I live, Manna must be my meate.

I'm sick; my sickness is mortality
    And Sin both Complicate (the worst of all).
No cure is found under the Chrystall Sky
    Save Manna, that from heaven down doth fall.   10
    My Queasy Stomach this alone doth Crave.
    Nought but a bit of manna can mee save.

This Bread came down from heaven in a Dew
    In which it bedded was, untill the Sun
Remoov'd its Cover lid: and did it shew   15
    Disht dayly food, while fourty years do run.

34 *lead,*] PW lead.   7 *sick;*] PW sick.   11 *this*] PW thus[?]

For Isra'ls Camp to feast upon their fill
Thy Emblem, Lord, in print by perfect Skill.

Thou in thy word as in a bed of Dewes
Like Manna on thy Camp dost fall and light   20
Hid Manna, till the Sun Shine bright remooves
The Rug, and doth display its beauty bright
Like pearly Bdellium White and Cleare to set
The Sight, and Appetite the same to get.

This is a Shining Glass, wherein thy face   25
My Lord, as Bread of Life, is clearly seen.
The Bread of Life, and Life of lively Grace
Of such as live upon't do flowrish Green.
That makes their lives that on it live ascend
In heav'nly rayes to heaven that have none end.   30

Refresh my Sight, Lord, with thy Manna's eye.
Delight my tast with this sweet Honied Cake.
Enrich my Stomach with this Cake bread high.
And with this Angells bread me recreate.
Lord, make my Soule thy Manna's Golden Pot   35
Within thine Arke: and never more forgot.

Here's food for ery day, and th'Seventh too:
(Though't never fell upon the Seventh day
But on the first, and ery week day new)
And now is on the Camp shour'd ery way.   40
Yet where it is not rightly usd it turns
To nauseous sent, and doth occasion worms.

It's first daye's Mess Disht up in Heavenly Dew.
Lord feede mee all wayes with't: it will enable
Mee much to live up to thy praise anew.   45
Angells delight, attending on this table.
If on this Angell fare I'm fed, I shall
Sing forth thy glory with bright Angells all.

18 *print*] PW prent

60[B]. Meditation. Cor. 10.4. And all drunk
the same spirituall drinke.

30. 5m [July] *1704*. Pub. *W*.

Ye Angells bright, pluck from your Wings a Quill.
    Make me a pen thereof that best will write.
Lende me your fancy, and Angellick skill
      To treate this Theme, more rich than Rubies bright.
      My muddy Inke, and Cloudy fancy dark,   5
      Will dull its glory, lacking highest Art.

An Eye at Centre righter may describe
    The Worlds Circumferentiall glory vast
As in its nutshell bed it snugs fast tide,
      Than any angells pen can glory Cast   10
      Upon this Drink Drawn from the Rock, tapt by
      The Rod of God, in Horeb, typickly.

Sea water straind through Mineralls, Rocks, and Sands
    Well Clarifi'de by Sunbeams, Dulcifi'de,
Insipid, Sordid, Swill, Dishwater stands.   15
      But here's a Rock of Aqua-Vitae tride.
      When once God broacht it, out a River came
      To bath and bibble in, for Israels train.

Some Rocks have sweat. Some Pillars bled out tears.
    But here's a River in a Rock up tun'd   20
Not of Sea Water nor of Swill. Its beere.
      No Nectar like it. Yet it once Unbund
      A River down out runs through ages all.
      A Fountain opte, to wash off Sin and Fall.

19 *Pillars*] PW Pillar   22 *it once*] orig: being

21: Its beere. Taylor's daily familiarity with beer, while he was butler at
Harvard College, did not decrease his respect for this beverage.

Christ is this Horebs Rock, the streames that slide   25
    A River is of Aqua Vitae Deare
Yet costs us nothing, gushing from his side.
    Celestiall Wine our Sinsunk souls to cheare.
    This Rock and Water, Sacramentall Cup
    Are made, Lords Supper Wine for us to sup.   30

This Rock's the Grape that Zions Vineyard bore
    Which Moses Rod did smiting pound, and press
Untill its blood, the brooke of Life, run ore.
    All Glorious Grace, and Gracious Righteousness.
    We in this brook must bath: and with faiths quill   35
    Suck Grace, and Life out of this Rock our fill.

Lord, oynt me with this Petro oyle. I'm sick.
    Make mee drinke Water of the Rock. I'm dry.
Me in this fountain wash. My filth is thick.
    I'm faint, give Aqua Vitae or I dy.   40
    If in this stream thou cleanse and Chearish mee
    My Heart thy Hallelujahs Pipe shall bee.

61. Meditation. Joh. 3.14. As Moses lift up
the Serpent in the Wilderness
so must the Son of man be lift up.

17.7m [Sept.] *1704.*

My Mights too mean, lend your Angelick might
    Ye mighty Angells, brightly to define.
A piece of burnisht brass, formd Serpent like
    To Countermand all poison Serpentine.
    No Remedie could cure the Serpents Bite   5
    But One: to wit, The brazen Serpent's Sight.

2 *brightly*] orig: to brightly   **6** *wit*] Conj.

Shall brass the bosoms poison in't Contain
 A Counter poison, better than what beds
In Creatures bosoms? Nay, But its vertue came
 Through that brass Shapt from God that healing sheds. 10
 Its Vertue rode in th'golden Coach of th'eyes
 Into the Soule, and Serpents Sting defies.

So that a Sight of the brazen Serpent hung
 Up in the Banner Standard of the Camp
Was made a Charet wherein rode and run 15
 A Healing vertue to the Serpents Cramp.
 But that's not all. Christ in this Snake shapt brass
 Raist on the Standard, Crucified was.

As in this Serpent lay the onely Cure
 Unto the fiery Serpents burning bite, 20
Not by its Physick Vertue, (that is sure)
 But by a Beam Divine of Grace's might
 Whose Vertue onely is the plaster 'plide
 Unto the Wound, by Faith in Christs blood di'de.

A Sight of th'Artificiall Serpent heales 25
 The venom wound the naturall Serpent made.
A Spirituall Sight of Christ, from Christ down steals.
 A Cure against the Hellish Serpents trade.
 Not that the Springhead of the Cure was found
 In Christs humanity with sharp thorns Crownd. 30

This Brazen Serpent is a Doctors Shop.
 On ev'ry Shelfe's a Sovereign remedy.
The Serpents Flesh the Sovereign Salve is got
 Against the Serpents bite, gaind by the eye.
 The Eyebeames agents are that forth do bring 35
 The Sovereign Counter poison, and let't in.

I by the fiery Serpent bitt be here.
 Be thou my brazen Serpent me to Cure.
My Sight, Lord, make thy golden Charet cleare
 To bring thy remedy unto my Sore. 40

9 bosoms?] PW bosoms,

If this thou dost I shall be heald: My wound
Shall sing thy praises: and thy glory sound.

62. Meditation. Can. 1.12. While the King
        sitteth at his table, my Spicknard
        sendeth forth the smell thereof.

18. 9m [Nov.] *1704.* Pub. *W.*

Oh! thou, my Lord, thou king of Saints, here mak'st
        A royal Banquet thine to entertain.
With rich, and royall fare, Celestiall Cates,
        And sittest at the Table rich of fame.
        Am I bid to this Feast? Sure Angells stare,   5
        Such Rugged looks, and Ragged robes I ware.

I'le surely come, Lord fit mee for this feast:
        Purge me with Palma Christi from my Sin.
With Plastrum Gratiae Dei, or at least
        Unguent Apostolorum healing bring.   10
        Give me thy Sage, and Savory: me dub
        With Golden Rod, and with Saints Johns Wort good.

Root up my Henbain, Fawnbain, Divells bit.
        My Dragons, Chokewort, Crosswort, Ragwort, vice,
And set my knot with Honysuckles, stick   15
        Rich Herb-a-Grace, and Grains of Paradise
        Angelica, yea Sharons Rose the best
        And Herba Trinitatis in my breast.

Then let thy Sweetspike sweat its liquid Dew
        Into my Crystall Viall: and there swim.   20
And as thou at thy Table in Rich Shew
        With royal Dainties, sweet discourse as King
        Dost Welcome thine. My Spiknard with its Smell
        Shall vapour out perfumed Spirits Well.

Whether I at thy Table Guest do sit,   25
    And feed my tast: or Wait, and fat mine Eye
And Eare with Sights and Sounds, Heart Raptures fit,
    My Spicknard breaths its sweet perfumes with joy.
    My heart thy Viall with this spicknard fill.
    Perfumed praise to thee then breath it will.   30

63. Meditation. Cant. 6.11. I went down
          into the Garden of Nuts, to see
          the fruits etc.

4. 12m [Feb.] *1704.*

Oh that I was the Bird of Paradise!
    Then in thy Nutmeg Garden, Lord, thy Bower
Celestiall Musick blossom should my voice
    Enchanted with thy gardens aire and flower.
    This Aromatick aire would so enspire   5
    My ravisht Soule to sing with angells Quire.

What is thy Church, my Lord, thy Garden which
    Doth gain the best of Soils? Such Spots indeed
Are Choicest Plots empalde with Palings rich
    And set with slips, herbs best, and best of seed.   10
    As th' Hanging Gardens rare of Babylon
    And Palace Garden of King Solomon.

But that which doth excell all gardens here
    Was Edens Garden: Adams Palace bright.
The Tree of Life, and knowledge too were there   15
    Sweet herbs and sweetest flowers all sweet Delight
    A Paradise indeed of all Perfume
    That to the Nose, the Eyes and Eares doth tune.

But all these Artificiall Gardens bright
    Enameled with bravest knots of Pincks   20
27 *fit,*] PW fit.

And flowers enspangld with black, red and White
    Compar'd with this are truely stincking sincks.
    As Dunghills reech with stinking sents that dish
    Us out, so these, when balanced with this.

For Zions Paradise, Christs Garden Deare   25
    His Church, enwalld, with Heavenly Crystall fine
Hath every Bed beset with Pearle all Cleare
    And Allies Opald with Gold, and Silver Shrine.
    The shining Angells are its Centinalls
    With flaming Swords Chaunting out Madrigalls.   30

The Sparkling Plants, Sweet Spices, Herbs and Trees,
    The glorious Shews of aromatick Flowers,
The pleasing beauties soakt in sweet breath lees
    Of Christs rich garden ever upward towers.
    For Christ Sweet Showers of Grace makes on it fall.   35
    It therefore bears the bell away from all.

The Nut of evry kinde is found to grow big,
    With food, and Physick, lodgd within a tower
A Wooden Wall with Husky Coverlid,
    Or Shell flesht ore, or in an Arching bower   40
    Beech, Hazle, Wallnut, Cocho, Almond brave
    Pistick or Chestnut in its prickly Cave.

These all as meate, and med'cine, emblems choice
    Of Spirituall Food, and Physike are which sport
Up in Christs Garden. Yet the Nutmeg's Spice   45
    A leathern Coate wares, and a Macie Shirt,
    Doth far excell them all. Aromatize
    My Soule therewith, my Lord, and spirituall wise.

Oh! Sweet Sweet Paradise, Whose Spiced Spring
    Will make the lips of him asleep to tune   50

30 *Madrigalls*] PW Macridalls
35 *Christ*] PW Christs   41 *Hazle, Wallnut*] PW Hazle Wall, nut
43 *med'cine,*] PW med'cine   44 *are which sport*] orig: which do sport
48 *and*] orig: in

    36: bears the bell (see also Glossary). The phrase also occurs in Herbert's
"The Church-Porch," line 187, and "The Search," line 59.

Heart ravishing tunes, sweet Musick for our king
    In Aromatick aire of blesst perfume
    Open thy garden doore: mee entrance give
    And in thy Nut tree garden make me live.

If, Lord, thou opst, and in thy garden bring   55
    Mee, then thy little Linet sweetly Will
Upon thy Nut tree sit and sweetly sing
    Will Crack a Nut and eat the kirnell still.
    Thou wilt mine Eyes, my Nose, and Palate greet
    With Curious Flowers, Sweet Odors, Viands Sweet.   60

Thy Gardens Odorif'rous aire mee make
    Suck in, and out t'aromatize my lungs.
That I thy garden, and its Spicie State
    May breath upon with such ensweetned Songs.
    My Lungs and Breath ensweetend thus shall raise   65
    The Glory of thy garden in its praise.

64. Meditation. Can. 6.11. To see—if the Vine Flowrisht, and the Pomegranate bud.

   2. 2m [Apr.] *1705.* Pub. PET.

Oh! that my Chilly Fancy, fluttering soe,
    Was Elevated with a dram of Wine
The Grapes and Pomegranates do yield, that grow
    Upon thy Gardens Appletrees and Vines.
    It shouldst have liquour with a flavour fraight   5
    To pensil out thy Vines and Pomgranates.

But I, as dry, as is a Chip, scarce get
    A peep hole through thy garden pales at these,
Thy garden plants. How should I then ere set
    The glory out of its brave Cherry trees?   10

56 *Will*] orig: sing   1 *soe*] orig: low   6 orig: Thy Vine to
paint out and thy Pomgranates

Then make my fancy, Lord, thy pen t'unfold
    Thy Vines and Pomegranates in liquid gold.

Whence come thy garden plants? So brave? So Choice?
    They Almugs be'nt from Ophirs golden land:
But Vines and Pomegranates of Paradise   15
    Spicknard, Sweet Cane, and Cynamon plants here stand.
    What heavenly aire is breezing in this Coast?
    Here blows the Trade winde of the Holy Ghost.

Thy Pomegranates that blushy freckles ware
    Under their pleasant jackets spirituall frize,   20
And Vines, though Feeble, fine, and flowrishing are
    Not Sibmahs, but mount Zions here arise.
    Here best of Vines, and Pomegranates up hight,
    Yea Sharons Rose, and Carmels Lillies White.

These trees are reev'd with Gilliads balm each one   25
    Myrrh trees, and Lign Aloes: Frankincense,
Here planted grow; heres Saffron Cynamon
    Spicknard and Calamus with Spice Ensenc'd.
    Oh fairest garden: evry bed doth beare
    All brave blown flowers whose breath is heavenly aire.   30

Make me thy Vine and Pomegranate to be
    And in thy garden flowrish fruitfully
And in their branches bowre, there then to thee
    In sweetend breath shall come sweet melody.
    My Spirit then engrapd and pomegranat'de   35
    Shall sweetly sing thee o're thy garden gated.

65. Meditation. Can. 6.11. To see the Fruits of the Vally.

10.4m [June] 1705. Pub. PET.

The Vines of Lebanon that briskly grew
    Roses of Sharon in their flowrish fair,

27 grow;] PW grow.   2 Roses] orig: The Roses

The Lillies of the Vallies Beauteous shew
    And Carmels Glorious Flowery Robes most rare
    In all their lively looks blusht brisk, appeare   5
    Dull Wan lookt things, Lord, to thy Gardens geere.

Engedi's Vineyard, that brave Camphire bower,
    The Cypress Banks and Beds of bravery
And Eshcol's Grapes that royall juyce out shower,
    And Wine of Hesbon in its flavor high   10
    With Elevating Sparks stand shrinking, blush
    To see the flowrish of thy Garden flush.

Mount Olivet with Olive Trees full green,
    The flowrishing Almonds in their smiling ray
And Sibma's vaporing Wines that frolick seem   15
    Are all unmand as tipsy, slink away
    As blushing at their manners to behold
    Thy Nut trees Gardens buds and flowers unfold.

Whose Buds not Gracious but pure Grace do shine.
    Whose blossoms are not sweet but sweetness 'brace   20
Whose Grapes are not Vine berries, but rich Wine:
    Whose Olives Oyle Springs be'n't, but Oyle of Grace.
    When pound and presst, they Cordiall juyce bleed all
    And Spirits Unction. Oh! Sweet Hony fall.

These Buds are better than blown Roses fair: 25
    These Blossoms fairer bee than Carmels hew:
These Vines beare Grapes sweeter than Raisens are.
    These Nuts are better than ere Nutmegs grew.
    Olivets Olive's but a grease pots mate
    To thy Nut Gardens Vine and Pomegranate.   30

In thy Nut Garden make my heart a Bed
    And set therein thy Spicknard, Cypress, Vine
Rose, Olive, Almonds, Pares, Plumbs White, and Red,
    Pomegranats, Spices, Frankincense divine.

5 *blusht*] PW blust   15 *that*] orig: and   20 *'brace*] PW brace
22 *Olives Oyle*] orig: Olives are not   24 *Spirits Unction. Oh!*] orig: Unction
of the Spirits   33 *Olive,*] PW Olive   34 *Spices*] orig: Spicknard

If thou dost stud my heart with graces thus   35
    My heart shall beare thee fruits perfumed flush.

Make thou my Soule, Lord, thy mount Olivet
    And plant it with thy Olive Trees fair Green,
Adornd with Holy blossoms, thence beset
    With Heavens Olives, Happy to be seen.   40
    Thy Sacred Oyle will then make bright to shine
    My Soul its face, and all the works of mine.

Set thou therein thy Pomegranate of State
    Thy Spice Trees, Cloves and Mace, thy Cynamon.
Thy Lemons, Orenges, Nuts, Almonds, Dates,   45
    Thy Nutmeg trees and Vines of Lebanon
    With Lillies Violets Carnations rare.
    My heart thy Spice box then shall breath sweet aire.

My Vine shall then beare Raisens of the Sun,
    My Grapes will rain May Shower of Sacred Wine.   50
The Smiling Dimples on my Fruits Cheeks hung
    Will as rich jewells adde unto their Shine.
    Then plant my heart with thy rich fruit trees sweet
    And it shall beare thee Fruits stew'd in sweet reech.

66. Meditation. Joh. 15.13. Greater Love
       hath no man than this That a man
       lay down his Life for his Friends.

19. 6m [Aug.] *1705.*

O! what a thing is Love? who can define
    Or liniament it out? Its strange to tell.
A Sparke of Spirit empearld pill like and fine
    In't shugard pargings, crusted, and doth dwell

45 *Almonds,*] PW Almonds   *Life*] PW Live   4 *doth dwell*] orig: filld well

Within the heart, where thron'd, without Controle   5
It ruleth all the Inmates of the Soule.

It makes a poother in its Secret Sell
    Mongst the affections: oh! it swells, its paind,
Like kirnells soked untill it breaks its Shell
    Unless its object be obtained and gain'd.   10
    Like Caskd wines jumbled breake the Caske, this Sparke
    Oft swells when crusht: untill it breakes the Heart.

O! Strange Strange Love! 'Stroy Life and't selfe thereby.
    Hence lose its Object, lay down all't can moove.
For nothing rather choose indeed to dy,   15
    And nothing be, than be without its love.
    Not t'be, than be without its fanci'de bliss!
    Is this Love's nature? What a thing is this?

Love thus ascending to its highest twig,
    May sit and Cherp such ditties. Sing and dy.   20
This highest Note is but a Black-Cap's jig
    Compar'd to thine my Lord, all Heavenly.
    A greater love than such man ne'er mentain'd.
    A greater Love than such thou yet hast gain'd.

Thy Love laid down thy Life hath for thy Sheep: 25
    Thy friends by grace: thy foes by Nature's Crimes.
And yet thy Life more precious is and sweet
    More worth than all the World ten thousand times.
    And yet thy Love did give bright Wisdoms Shine
    In laying down thy precious life for thine.   30

This Love was ne'er adulterate: e're pure.
    Noe Whiffe of Fancy: But rich Wisdomes Beams,
No Huff of Hot affection men endure.
    But sweetend Chimings of Celestiall gleams
    Play'd and Display'd upon the golden Wyer   35
    That doth thy Human Cymball brave, attire.

5 *heart,*] PW heart.   *where*] PW whre
8 *swells, its*] orig: swells also its   11 *Caskd wines*] PW Caskdwines
13 *'Stroy*] PW Stroy   *Life*] PW Live   14 *Object,*] PW Object.

Thy Love that laid thy life all down for thine
    Did not thereby destroy itselfe at all.
It was preserved in thy Selfe Divine
    When it did make thy Humane Selfe down fall.   40
    And when thy body as the Sun up rose
    It did itselfe like flaming beames disclose.

Lord, let thy Love shine on my Soule! Mee bath
    In this Celestiall Gleame of this pure Love.
O! gain my heart and thou my Love shalt have   45
    Clime up thy golden Stares to thee above.
    And in thy upper Chamber sit and sing
    The glory of thy Love when Entred in.

67[A]. Meditation. Mal. 4.2. But unto you that
             Feare my name, shall the Sun of
             Righteousness arise.

21. 8m [Oct.] *1705.*

My China Ware or Amber Casket bright,
    Filld with Ambrosian Spirits soakt and Bindg'd,
Made all a Mass of Quicken'd metall right,
    Transparent Silver Bowles with flowers Enfringd
    Sent to the Temple by king Ptolemy   5
    Compard thereto are but vile Trumpery.

These Spirits, drawn by heavens Chymistry
    And Casked up, with Cask Conspire into
A Lump of Sacred Fire that actively
    About thy Sacred Selfe entwine and grow   10
    So that this Cask bindgd with these Spirits rise
    A fearer of Jehovah, holy wise.

40 *thy Humane*] orig: thyselfe

In acting of the same with Holy Skill
    And Sanctifying Sight as Shining Eyes
Some soure, and muddy Humors soon do still   15
    When that the Glass is jumbled up arise
    Or in its China ware some spot or Dimple,
    Or Amber Cask unhoopt hath Crack or Wrinkle.

The Spirits and the Vial both are sick.
    The Lump Consisting of them both so trim   20
Is out of trim, sore wounded to the quick
    Distemperd by ill Humors bred therein.
    Some poyson's in the golden Cup of wine,
    That treason works against the king Divine.

I fain would purge the poison out, and Cleare   25
    The liquor from the musty dregs therein.
The Bottle free from Crack, Dint, and bad geer,
    The China Ware from Spot or Wrinkling
    And all the Quickend Lump I fain would Cure
    Of all ill Humors, Sickness, wound, or Sore.   30

But cannot do the same, yet this I finde,
    To them that feare thy Name Lord, there doth rise
The Sun of Righteousness, (this Cheers my minde)
    With healing in his Wings Physicianwise.
    This yields reliefe. Some things in such as do   35
    The Fear is bad: in them diseases grow.

Mine argument let winde into thine heart,
    That hence I do assume seing its sure
None that do feare thee, perfect bee, each part.
    I'm one of them or none of them I'm sure.   40
    If one of them, my bad Distempers shall
    Not it disproove. I don't excell them all.

They want a Cure: and so do I: I'm not
    Pleasd with my mud: Sin doth not tickle mee.
The Wrinkles Crest, or Dints my ware hath got   45

36 *Fear is*] orig: Fear thee are   38 *assume seing*] orig: assume by pious art
39 *perfect*] orig: right perfect   41 *Distempers*] PW Distembers

My Sores and Sicknesses my Sorrows bee.
I'l strive against them till I'st strive no more.
While healing Wings abide, Ile not give o're.

The Objects of the Sun of Righteousness
    Doth with its healing wing rise Cleare upon   50
Have need of healing. I do need no less.
    Our wants for kinde are equall hereupon.
    We both are of our sickness sick. Hence shown
    We both are by the argument proovd one.

Hence this I pray, and pray no less than this.   55
    Grant, Lord, mine Eyes with acute Sight not dim,
Thy Shining Sun of Righteousness may kiss
    And broodled bee under its Healing Wing.
    My Bird like to a Nighting gaile in th'Spring
    With breast on sharpest thorn, thy praise shall sing.   60

68[A]. Meditation. Mal. 4.2. The Sun of Righteousness, etc.

16. 10m [Dec.] *1705.*

Methinks I spy Almighty holding in
    His hand the Crystall Sky and Sun in't bright:
As Candle and bright Lanthorn lightening,
    The World with this bright lanthorns flaming light
    Endungeoning all Darkness underground,   5
    Making all Sunshine Day Heavenward abound.

The Spirituall World, this world doth, Lord out vie:
    Its Skie this Crystall Lanthorn doth orematch.
Its Sun, thou Art, that in'ts bright Canopy
    Outshines that Candle, Darkness doth dispatch.   10

50 *Cleare*] orig: up Cleare   55 *pray,*] PW pray.   58 *bee*] orig: up bee
59 *gaile*] orig: Gaile

Thy Crystall Globe of Glorious Sunshine furld
Light, Life and heate in't Sundayeth the World.

The World without the Sun,'s as dungeon, darke.
   The Sun without its Light would Dungeon spring.
The Moon and Stars are but as Chilly Sparks
   Of Dying fire. The Sun Cheeres ery thing.   15
   But oh thy Light, Lightsom, delightsom falls
   Upon the Soul above all Cordialls.

All Light delights. Yet Dozde wood light is cold.
   Some light hath heate yet Darkness doth it bound   20
As Lamp and Glowworm light. The Stars do hold
   A twinkling lifeless Light. The Sun is found
   A Ball of Light, of Life, Warmth to natures race.
   But thou'rt that Sun, that shines out Saving Grace.

Doz'de wood-light is but glimmer, with no Smoke.
   And Candle Light's a smoaky lifeless thing.   25
The light lodgd in the glowworm's peticoate
   Is but a Shew. Star light's nights twinkling.
   Moonlight is nightish, Sun makes day: these all
   Without our Visive Organs lightless fall.   30

But thou, my Lord no Dozed Wood Shine art.
   No Smoky Candle Light rose from thy Wick.
Thy Light ne'er linde the glowworms velvet part.
   Thy Shine makes Stars, Moons, Sunlight darkness thick.
   Thou art the Sun of Heavens bright light rose in
   The Heavenly Orbs. And Heavens blesst glories spring.   35

Were all the trees on earth fir'de Torches made,
   And all her Grass Wax Candles set on flame
This Light could not make day, this lightsom trade
   Would be a darksom Smoke when Sun shines plaine.   40
   But thy Shine, Lord, darkens this Sunshine bright,
   And makes the Seing Organ, and its Light.

Within the Horizontall Hemisphere
   Of this Blesst Sun, Lord, let mee Mansion have.

22 *Sun is*] orig: Sunlight   34 *Stars,*] PW Stars

Make Day, thou Shining Sun, unto mee cleare   45
    Thy Sorry Servant earnestly doth crave.
    Let not the Moon ere intervene or fix
    Between me and this Sun to make Ecclipse.

O! bright, bright Day. Lord let this Sun Shine flow.
    Drive hence my Sin and Darkness greate profound   50
And up them Coffin in Earths Shade below
    In darkness gross, on th'other side the ground.
    Neer let the Soyle spew fogs to foile the Light
    Of this Sweet Aire pregnant with Sunbeams bright.

How shall my Soule (Such thoughts Enravish mee)   55
    Under the Canopy of this bright Day
Imparadisde, Lightend and Livend bee
    Bathd in this Sun Shine 'mong bright Angells play
    And with them strive in sweetest tunes expresst
    Which can thy glorious praises sing out best.   60

67[B]. Meditation. Mal. 4.2. With Healing in His Wings.

10. 12m [Feb.] *1705.*

Doe Fables say, the Rising Sun doth Dance
    On Easter Day for joy, thou didst ascende.
O Sun of Righteousness; tho't be a glance
    Of Falshoods Spectacles on Rome's nose end?
    And shall not I, furled in thy glorious beams,   5
    Ev'n jump for joy, Enjoying such sweet gleams?

What doth the rising Sun with its Curld Locks
    And golden wings soon make the Chilly world
Shook with an Ague Fit by night shade drops,
    Revive, grow brisk, Suns Eyebright on it hurld?   10

10 *brisk,*] PW brisk.

How should my Soule then sick of th'Scurvy spring
When thy sweet medicating rayes come in?

Alas! Sweet Sun of Righteousness, Dost shine
    Upon such Dunghills, as I am? Methinks
My Soule sends out such putrid sents, and rhimes   15
    That with thy beams would Choke the aire with Stincks.
    And Nasty vapors ery where, whereby
    Thy rayes should venom'd be that from thee fly.

The Fiery Darts of Satan stob my heart.
    His Punyards Thrusts are deep, and venom'd too.   20
His Arrows wound my thoughts, Words, Works, each part
    They all a bleeding ly by th' Stobs, and rue.
    His Aire I breath in, poison doth my Lungs.
    Hence come Consumptions, Fevers, Head pains: Turns.

Yea, Lythargy, the Apoplectick Stroke: 25
    The Catochee, Soul Blindness, Surdity,
Ill Tongue, Mouth Ulcers, Frog, the Quinsie Throate
    The Palate Fallen, Wheezings, Pleurisy.
    Heart Ach, the Syncopee, bad stomach tricks
    Gaul Tumors, Liver grown; spleen evills Cricks.   30

The Kidny toucht, The Iliak, Colick Griefe
    The Ricats, Dropsy, Gout, the Scurvy, Sore
The Miserere Mei. O Reliefe
    I want and would, and beg it at thy doore.
    O! Sun of Righteousness Thy Beams bright, Hot   35
    Rafter a Doctors, and a Surgeons Shop.

I ope my Case to thee, my Lord: mee in
    Thy glorious Bath, of Sun Shine, Bathe, and Sweate.
So rout Ill Humors: And thy purges bring.
    Administer in Sunbeame Light, and Heate.   40

20 *deep,*] PW deep.   21 *thoughts*] PW thougts
27 orig: Ill Tongue, Mouth ulcers, the Frog, Angina Throate—canceled and
revised as here   29 *Syncopee,*] PW Syncopee.   30 *Cricks*] orig: thick
32 *Scurvy, Sore*] orig: Scurvy e're Sore

Pound some for Cordiall powders very small
    To Cure my Kidnies, Spleen, My Liver, Gaul.

And with the same refresh my Heart, and Lungs
    From Wasts, and Weakness. Free from Pleurisy
Bad Stomach, Iliak, Colick Fever, turns,   45
    From Scurvy, Dropsy, Gout, and Leprosy
    From Itch, Botch Scab. And purify my Blood
    From all Ill Humors: So make all things good.

Weave, Lord, these golden Locks into a web
    Of Spiritual Taffity; make of the same   50
A sweet perfumed Rheum-Cap for my head
    To free from Lythargy, the Turn, and Pain,
    From Waking-Sleep, Sin-Falling Mallady
    From Whimsy, Melancholy Frenzy-dy.

Thy Curled Rayes, Lord, make mine Eare Picker   55
    To Cure my Deafeness: Light, Ophthalmicks pure
To heate my Eyes and make the Sight the Quicker.
    That I may use Sins Spectacles no more.
    O still some Beams. And with the Spirits fresh
    My Palate Ulcerd Mouth, and Ill Tongue dress.   60

And ply my wounds with Pledgets dipt therein.
    And wash therewith my Scabs and Boils so sore,
And all my Stobs, and Arrow wounds come, bring
    And syrrindge with the Same. It will them Cure.
    With tents made of these Beams well tent them all.   65
    They Fistula'es and Gangrenes Conquour shall.

Lord plaster mee herewith to bring soon down
    My Swellings. Stick a Feather of thy Wing
Within my Cap to Cure my Aching Crown.
    And with these beams Heale mee of all my Sin.   70
    When with these Wings thou dost mee medicine
    I'st weare the Cure, thou th'glory of this Shine.

41 orig: Pound for Cordiall powders some rayes very small   67 *soon*] orig: all
72 *thou*] orig: then, thou

68[B]. Meditation. Mal. 4.2. Ye shall go forth
          and grow as Calves of the Stall.

28. 2m [Apr.] *1706.*

My megre Soule, when wilt thou fleshed bee,
 With Spirituall plumpness? Serpents flesh dost eat
Which maketh leane? Thy bones stick out in thee.
 Art thou Consumptive? And Concoctst not meat?
 Art not a Chick of th'Sun of Righteousness?   5
 Do not its healing Wings thy ailes redress?

Hast not Chang'd place with Mercury? And made
 Thy robes of Broadcloath of the Golden Fleece
Of Wooly Sun beams? (O! Warm Shining trade!)
 Souls freshen sure in Cloaths of such a piece   10
 And gloriously dance on these golden Cords.
 Yet till a Cure is got, Griefe o're them Lords.

And if thou bruddled liest, (though Qualms arise)
 Under the healing wings of this bright Sun
Of Righteousness, as Chicken Chearping wise   15
 Under its Dam, the Cure is surely Done.
 Some healing Beam a Certain med'cine brings
 To all Distemper'd Souls under these wings.

This is the Heavenly Alkahest that brings
 Lean Souls t'ore thrive all Pharao's fattest Ware. 20
Grow like the Stalled Oxe, or Fattlings
 Plump, Fleshy, Fat, Slick, brisk, and rightly fair.
 A spirituall fat of Collops, gracious greate
 Shall Cloath the Whole and make it grace-Compleat.

Though th'Wicker bird Cage is of rusty Wyer: 25
 This Sunshine will imbellish it and bright.
Though th'bird in't of immortall breed, much tire

18 *Distemper'd*] PW Distemer'd

These healing wings will make it fully ripe.
    My little Pipkin Soule of heavenly Clay
    Shall fatted to the brim with grace grow gay.   30

My Heade, O Sun, hide in thy healing Wing.
    Thy Warmth will to my megre Soule flesh give.
My growth shall Beauty to thine Eyesight bring.
    Thy Sight shall make me plump and pleasant live,
    And all my Growth to thee shall bud with blooms   35
    Of Praises Whistling in Angelick Tunes.

69. Meditation. Cant. 2.2. The Lillie of the Vallies.

30. 4m [June] *1706*. Pub. PET.

Dull! Dull! my Lord, as if I eaten had
    A Peck of Melancholy: or my Soule
Was lockt up by a Poppy key, black, sad:
    Or had been fuddled with an Hen bane bowle.
    Oh, Leaden temper! my Rich Thesis Would   5
    Try metall to the back, sharp, it t'unfold.

Alas! my Soule, Thy Sunburnt Skin looks dun:
    Thy Elementall jacket's Snake like pi'de.
I am Deform'd, and Uggly all become.
    Soule Sicknesses do nest in mee: and Pride.   10
    I nauseous am: and mine iniquites
    Like Crawling Worms doe worm eat on my joys.

All black though plac'de in a White lilly Grove:
    Not sweet, though in a bed of Lillies rowle,
Though in Physicians shop I dwell, a Drove   15
    Of Hellish Vermin range all ore my Soul.
    All Spirituall Maladies play rex in mee,
    Though Christ should Lilly of my Vally bee.

35 *to thee shall*] orig: shall to thee
Cant. 2.2.] For King James version the text should read Cant. 2.1.

But, Oh! the Wonder! Christ alone the Sun
    Of Righteousness, that he might do the Cure   20
The Lilly of the Vallies is become
    Whose Lillie properties do health restore.
    It's glory shews I'm filthy: yet must spring
    Up innocent, and beautifull by him.

Its Vally State and Bowing Head declare   25
    I'm Haughty but must have a Humble minde.
Its Healing Virtue shew I'm sick: yet rare
    Rich Remedies I'st in this Lilly finde.
    Yea Christ the Lilly of the Vallies shall
    Be to mee Glory, Med'cine, Sweetness, all.   30

The Lillies Beautie, and its Fragrancy
    Shews my ill-favourdness, and Nauseous Stinck:
And that I must be beautifull, fully,
    And breath a Sweetness that the aire must drink.
    This Beauty, Odour, Med'cin, Humble Case   35
    This Vallys Lilly shall my Soul begrace.

Lord, make me th'Vally where this Lilly grows.
    Then I am thine, and thou art mine indeed.
Propriety is mutuall: Glorious shows
    And Oderif'rous breath shall in me breed,   40
    Which twisted in my Tunes, thy praise shall ring
    On my Shoshannim's sweetest Well tun'de string.

33 *beautifull,*] PW beautifull.   36 *begrace*] orig: with grace

71. Meditation. 1 Cor. 5.8. Let us keep
the Feast, not with old Leven.

20. 8m [Oct.] *1706.*

Oh! What a Cookroom's here? all Deity
    Thick blancht all ore with Properties Divine
Varnisht with grace that shineth gloriously.
    Pollisht with glorious folds of brightest Shine
    Enricht with Heavens Cookery the best   5
    The Turtle Dove, and Paschall Lamb's here drest.

Oh! Dove most innocent. O Lamb, most White.
    A spotless Male in prime. Whose blood's the Dier
That dies the Doore posts of the Soule most bright.
    Whose body all is rost at justice's fire   10
    And yet no bone is broken, though the Spit
    Whereon its rost runs speare like, thorow it.

This Choicest Cookery is made the Feast
    Where glories king doth entertain his Guests.
Where Pastie past is Godhead, filld at least   15
    With Venison, of Paschall Lamb the best.
    All spic'd and Plumb'd with Grace and disht up right
    Upon Gods Table Plate Divinely bright.

This Spirituall Fare in Ordinances, and
    The Wine bled from the Holy Grape, and Vine,   20
Thats on the Table orderd by God's hand
    The Supper of the Lord, the feast Divine
    God's Gospel Priests this to that Table beare
    Where Saints are Guests and Angells waiters are.

13 *Choicest*] PW Coicest   18 *Plate*] orig: Gods Plate

   7: *Oh! Dove most innocent.* The first-born males of men and beasts be-
longed to God, according to Hebraic law (Exod. 13:2). First-born men were
redeemed with an offering—perhaps a lamb or a pair of turtle doves.

The Wedden garment of Christs Righteousness   25
  And Holy Cloathes of Sanctity most pure,
Are their atire, their Festivall rich dress:
  Faith feeds upon the Paschall Lamb its sure
  That on God's Porslain Dish is disht for them
  And drinks the Cup studded with graces Gem.   30

Let at this Table, Lord, thy Servant sit,
  And load my trencher with thy Paschall Lamb.
My Doore posts dy with the red blood of it.
  The stroying angells weapon therewith sham
  And let my Faith on thy rost mutton feed   35
  And Drinke the Wine thy holy grape doth bleed.

Lord make my Faith feed on it heartily.
  Let holy Charity my heart Cement
Unto thy Saints: and for a Cordiall high
  Make mee partaker of thy Sacrament.   40
  When with this Paschall bread and Wine I'm brisk
  I in sweet Tunes thy sweetest praise will twist.

72. Meditation. Mar. 16.19. Sat down on the right hand of God.

15. 10m [Dec.] *1706.*

Enoculate into my mentall Eye
  The Visive Spirits of the Holy Ghost
My Lord, that I may see the Dignity
  Of thy bright Honour in thy heavenly Coast
  Thou art deckt with as Sunshine bright displaid   5
  That makes bright Angells in it, cast a Shade.

Enrich my Phansy with Seraphick Life,
  Enquicknd nimbly to catch the Beams

26 *pure,*] PW pure. 27 *atire,*] PW atire. 3 *the Dignity*] orig: the ●●●ght

Thy Honour flurs abroad: in joyous Strife
    To make sweet Musick on such Happy Themes.   10
    That in such Raptures, and Transports of joy,
    To Honour kings I may my Phansy 'ploy.

At God's Right Hand! Doth God mans parts enjoy?
    This with Infinity can never stande.
Yet so God sayes, His Son to Dignify   15
    In manhood, said, sit at my right hand.
    The manhood thus a brighter Honour bears
    By Deity than Deity ere wares.

The Splendor of the matter of each Story
    Of th'Heavenly Palace Hall all brightend cleare,   20
The Presence Chamber of the King of Glory
    Common with thee, to Saints and Angells there.
    They share with thee in this Celestiall Shine.
    Although their Share is lesser far than thine.

Yet they in all this glorious Splendor bright,   25
    So many Suns like, shining on each other,
Encreasing each's glory, fall down right
    To kiss thy feet, whose Shine this glorie Covers.
    Their brightest Shine, in Glory's highest Story,
    Is t'stand before thee in thy bright-bright glory.   30

Thy Honour brightens theirs, as't on theirs falls.
    Its Royall Honour thou inheritst, Cleare,
A Throne of Glory in bright glories Hall:
    At Gods right Hand thou sits enthroned there.
    The Highest Throne in brightest glory thou   35
    Enjoyest. Saints, and Angels 'fore thee bow.

Come down, bright Angells, Now I claim my place.
    My nature hath more Honour due, than yours:
Mine is Enthron'de at Gods Right-Hand, through Grace.
    This Grace for mine and not for yours, endures.   40
    Yours is not there, unless in part of mine,
    As Species in their Genus do combine.

22 *Common*] orig: ***s Common   24 *their*] Conj.   41 *is*] orig: makes

Hence make my Life, Lord, keep thine Honour bright.
    And let thine Honour brighten mee by grace.
And make thy Grace in mee, thee honour right.
      And let not mee thy Honour ere deface.   45
      Grant me the Honour then to honour thee
      And on my Bells thine Honour chimed shall bee.

73. Meditation. 1 Tim. 3.16. Received into Glory.

9. 12m [Feb.] *1706.*

Glory! oh Glory! Wonderfull, and more.
    How dost thou Croude with all thy Ranks most bright?
Thou never playdst such Glorious Cast, before
    Nor ever wor'st such flourishing delight.
      Thy heart doth leape for joy, to have the gain   5
      When thou Receivdst my Lord in Glories Flame.

Who can the Ranks of Glory ere relate,
    As they stand up in Honours Palace Hall?
They sparkle Flashing spangles, golden flakes
    Of burnisht shines, with lowly Conjues all   10
      To kisse thy hand, my Lord, and hande thee in
      To tend thee and attend thee, her head spring.

Glory was never glorifide so much,
    She ne're receiv'd such glory heretofore.
As that that doth Embrace her, (it is such,)
      As she unto my Lord, doth ope her doore.   15
      When he receivd was into glory's Sphere
      Glory then found her glory brightest were.

When unto Angell's Glory opens doore,
    Or unto Saints, all to be glorifi'de,   20

47 *honour*] PW **hornour**

She well bestows herselfe, t'enriche her Store:
    Yet blushes much to eye thy Glories tide.
    When she doth make herselfe thy Cloaths to bee,
    She's cloathd with brighter glory far by thee.

The greatest glory glory doth enjoy,   25
    Lies in her hanging upon thee Wherein
Glory that glorifies thee mightily,
    Is far more glorifide. Hence Glories spring.
    Now Graces Glory, Heavens Glory, and
    Gloryes of Saints, and Angells, guild thy hand.   30

A Glorious Palace, a Bright Crown of Glory
    A glorious train of Saints, and Angells Shine
And glorious exercise as sweetest posy,
    Do sacrifice themselves unto thy Shrine.
    They give their all to thee. And so receive   35
    Therein from thee a much more brighter Wreath.

Let some, my Lord, of thy bright Glories beams,
    Flash quickening Flames of Glory in mine eye
T'enquicken my dull Spirits, drunke with dreams
    Of Melancholy juyce that stupify.   40
    A Coale from thy bright Altars Glory sure
    Kissing my lips, my Lethargy will Cure.

If Envy ere by Sanctifying Skill
    Could gracious be, or be a Grace, I would
I could it on my Spirits Cold and Chill   45
    Well Exercise, that Love thus ever should
    Ly lockt by Melancholy's key up in my Heart.
    And hardly smile when Glories beautyes dart.

Lord make thy beams my frost bit heart to warm.
    Ride on these Rayes into my bosom's chill   50
And make thy Glory mine affections Charm.
    Thy rapid flames my Love enquicken will.
    Then I in Glories Tower thy Praise will sing
    On my Shoshanims tun'd on ev'ry String.

25 *enjoy,*] PW enjoy.   46 *ever*] orig: should ever

74. Meditation. Phi. 3.21. His Glorious
          Body. τῷ σώματι τῆς
          δόξης αυτοῦ

6. 2m [Apr.] *1707.*

I fain would have a rich, fine Phansy ripe
    That Curious pollishings elaborate
Should lay, Lord, on thy glorious Body bright
    The more my lumpish-heart to animate.
    But searching ore the Workhouse of my minde,   5
    I but one there; and dull and meger finde.

Hence, Lord, my Search hand thou from this dark Shop
    (Its foule, and wanteth Sweeping) up unto
Thy Glorious Body whose bright beames let drop
    Upon my heart: and Chant it with the Show.   10
    Because the Shine that from thy body flows,
    More glorious is than is the brightest Rose.

Sun Shine is to this Glory but a Smoke.
    Saints in their brightest Shines are clouds therein.
Bright Angells are like motes i'th'Sun unto't.   15
    Its Beames gild heavens bright Hall, that's sparkling.
    Of all Created Glory, that doth shine
    Thy Bodies Glory is most bright and fine.

The Beauty of Humanity Compleate,
    Where ery organ is adepted right,   20
Wherein such Spirits brisk, do act full neate
    Make Natures operations fully ripe.
    All Harmonizing in their actions done
    That ery twig's with glorious blossoms hung.

And still more sweet: thou'rt with more glory deckt.   25
    The Glory of ripe Grace of brightest kinde

6 *but*] orig: see one but
15 *i'th'*] PW ith'   19 *Compleate,*] PW Compleate.   20 *right,*] PW right.

Like lumps of living Fire, by nothing Checkt
    Thrumping the Stars, as pinking things half blinde.
    This makes thy Bodies glory Choice and fine,
    A spirituall light in Corporall Lanthorn shine.   30

Yea, still more Glory. Oh! thy Humane Frame
    Is th'brightst Temple of the Holy Ghost.
Whose Rayes run through the Whole in brightest flame.
    Hence on thy body campeth Glories Hoast.
    What more can still be said? I add but this.   35
    That Glory bright thy Bodies Tilt-Clothe is.

Oh! Glorious Body! Pull my eye lids ope:
    Make my quick Eye, Lord, thy brisk Glory greet,
Whose rapid flames when they my heart revoke
    From other Beauties, make't for thee more sweet.   40
    If such blest Sight shall twist my heart with thine,
    Thy Glory make the Web, thy Praise the Twine.

75. Meditation. Phil. 3. ult. Our Vile Bodie
τὸ σῶμα τῆς ταπεινώσεως ἡμῶν

1.4m [June] *1707.* Pub. UPT.

Oh! Strang, my Lord. Here's reason at a set.
    Run out of 'ts Wits, construing Grace's Style.
Nay Shining Angells in an holy fret
    Confounded are, to see our Bodies Vile
    Made Cabinets of Sparkling Gems that far   5
    Out shine the brightest shining heavenly Star.

Mudd made with Muscadine int' mortar Rich,
    Dirt wrought with Aqua-Vitae for a Wall
Built all of Precious Stones laid in it, Which
    Is with leafe gold bespangled, 'maizes all.   10

41 *thine,*] PW thine.   42 *Web,*] PW Web.   2 *Wits,*] PW Wits.

Yet this Amaizment's scarce a minutes Sise
Compar'd unto the matter 'fore our eyes.

Here is a Mudwall tent, whose Matters are
    Dead Elements, which mixt make dirty trade:
Which with Life Animall are wrought up faire   15
    A Living mudwall by Gods holy Spade.
        Yet though a Wall alive all spruice, and crouce
        Its Base, and Vile. And baseness keeps its House.

Nature's Alembick 't is, Its true: that stills
    The Noblest Spirits terrene fruits possess,   20
Yet, oh! the Relicks in the Caldron will
    Proove all things else, Guts, Garbage, Rotteness.
        And all its pipes but Sincks of nasty ware
        That foule Earths face, and do defile the aire.

A varnisht pot of putrid excrements,   25
    And quickly turns to excrements itselfe,
By natures Law: but, oh! there therein tents
    A sparke immortall and no mortall elfe.
        An Angell bright here in a Swine Sty dwell!
        What Lodge of Wonders's this? What tongue can tell?   30

But, oh! how doth this Wonder still encrease?
    The Soule Creeps in't. And by it's too defil'd.
Are both made base, and vile, can have no peace
    Without, nor in: and's of its Shine beguil'd.
        And though this Spirit in it dwells yet here   35
        Its glory will not dwell with such sad geere.

Both grac'd together, and disgrac'd. Sad Case.
    What now becomes of Gods Electing Love?
This now doth raise the Miracle apace,
    Christ doth step in, and Graces Art improove.   40
        He kills the Leprosy that taints the Walls:
        And sanctifies the house before it falls.

And nature here, though mean and base beside,
    With marks and Stains of Sin, and Sin not dead,
14 *dirty*] PW dusty[?]   33 *vile,*] PW vile.

Though mortifi'de and dying, in't reside,   45
     With Graces precious Pearls its flourished.
     And in our bodies very vile and base
     Christ hath enthron'de all sanctifying Grace.

That these dark Cells, and Mudwalld Tents defild,
     With nastiness should Cabinets be made   50
For th'Choicest Pearls in Glories ring enfoild
     Out shining all the shining starry trade.
     Its glorious Wonders, wrought by Graces hand,
     Whereat bright Angells all amaized stand.

Oh! make my Body, Lord, Although its vile,   55
     Thy Warehouse where Grace doth her treasures lay.
And Cleanse the house and ery Room from Soile.
     Deck all my Rooms with thy rich Grace I pray.
     If thy free Grace doth my low tent, perfume,
     I'll sing thy Glorious praise in ery room.   60

76. Meditation. Phi. 3.21. Who shall change
          our vile body, that it may be fashioned
          like his Glorious body.

27.5m [July] *1707.* Pub. *W.*

Will yee be neighbourly, ye Angells bright?
     Then lend mee your Admiring Facultie:
Wonders presented stand, above my might.
     That call from mee the highest Extasie.
     If you deny mee this: my pimping Soule,   5
     These Wonders pins up in an Auger hole.

If my Rush Candle on its wick ware flame,
     Of Ignis lambens. Oh! bright garb indeed:
What then, when Flakes of flaming Glory train
     From thy bright glorious bulk to 'ray my weed.   10

What my vile Body like thy Glorious, Formd?
What Wonder here? My body thus adornd!

What shall mine hempen harle wove in thy Loome
    Into a web (an hurden web indeed)
Be made its Makers Tent Cloth? I presume.   15
    Within these Curtains Grace keeps Hall, and breeds:
    But shall my hurden-hangings ever ware
    A bright bright Glory like thy body faire?

Meethinks thy smile doth make thy Footstoole so
    Spread its green Carpet 'fore thy feet for joy.   20
And Bryers climb in t'bright Rose that flows
    Out in sweet reechs to meet thee in the sky:
    And makes the sportive Starrs play Hide-and-Seek
    And on thy bodies Glory peeping keep.

And shall not I (whose form transformd shall bee   25
    To be shap'te like thy glorious body, Lord.
That Angells bright, as Gasterd, gaze at mee
    To see such Glory on my dresser board),
    Transported be hereat for very joy,
    Whose intrest lies herein, and gloriously?   30

What shall the frosty Rhime upon my locks,
    Congeale my brains with Chilly dews, whereby
My Phansie is benumbd: and put in Stocks,

21 *And Bryers climb in t'bright Rose that flows*] PW Line heavily corrected.
Last six words of line in text written in margin. An interlinear version of the
marginal words appears to read: *Climb there up in t'bright Rose that Flow*.
Original version of these words illegible. *W* and Bryers: climb thereup, bright
roses blow

   13: mine hempen harle. The comparison of the body to coarse cloth occurs
in Herbert's "Mans medley," lines 13–18:

        In soul he mounts and flies,
           In flesh he dies.
     He wears a stuffe whose thread is course and round,
        But trimm'd with curious lace,
          And should take place
    After the trimming, not the stuffe and ground.

And thaws not into Steams of reeching joy?
Oh! strange Ingratitude! Let not this Frame   35
Abide, Lord, in mee. Fire mee with thy flame.

Lord, let thy glorious Body send such rayes
    Into my Soule, as ravish shall my heart,
That Thoughts how thy bright Glory out shall blaze
    Upon my body, may such Rayes thee dart.   40
    My Tunes shall dance then on these Rayes and Caper
    Unto thy Praise. When Glory lights my Taper.

77. Meditation. Zech. 9.11. The Pit
       wherein is no water.

5. 8m [Oct.] *1707*. Pub. *W*.

A State, a State, Oh! Dungeon State indeed.
    In which mee headlong, long agoe Sin pitcht:
As dark as Pitch, where Nastiness doth breed:
    And Filth defiles: and I am with it ditcht.
    A Sinfull State: This Pit no Water's in't.   5
    A Bugbare State: as black as any inke.

I once sat singing on the Summit high
    'Mong the Celestiall Coire in Musick Sweet
On highest bough of Paradisall joy,
    Glory and Innocence did in mee meet.   10
    I, as a Gold-Fincht Nighting Gale, tun'd ore
    Melodious Songs 'fore Glorie's Palace Doore.

But on this bough I tuning Pearcht not long:
    Th'Infernall Foe shot out a Shaft from Hell,
A Fiery Dart pilde with Sins poison strong: 15
    That struck my heart, and down I headlong fell.
    And from the Highest Pinicle of Light
    Into this Lowest pit more darke than night.

15 *pilde*] Conj.

A Pit indeed of Sin: No water's here:
    Whose bottom's furthest off from Heaven bright,   20
And is next doore to Hell Gate, to it neer:
    And here I dwell in sad and solemn night,
    My Gold-Fincht Angell Feathers dapled in
    Hells Scarlet Dy fat, blood red grown with Sin.

I in this Pit all Destitute of Light   25
    Cram'd full of Horrid Darkness, here do Crawle
Up over head, and Eares, in Nauseous plight:
    And Swinelike Wallow in this mire, and Gall:
    No Heavenly Dews nor Holy Waters drill:
    Nor Sweet Aire Brieze, nor Comfort here distill.   30

Here for Companions, are Fears, Heart-Achs, Grief
    Frogs, Toads, Newts, Bats, Horrid Hob-Goblins, Ghosts:
Ill Spirits haunt this Pit: and no reliefe:
    Nor Coard can fetch me hence in Creatures Coasts.
    I who once lodgd at Heavens Palace Gate   35
    With full Fledgd Angells, now possess this fate.

But yet, my Lord, thy golden Chain of Grace
    Thou canst let down, and draw mee up into
Thy Holy Aire, and Glory's Happy Place.
    Out from these Hellish damps and pit so low.   40
    And if thy Grace shall do't, My Harp I'le raise,
    Whose Strings toucht by this Grace, Will twang thy praise.

21 *Gate,*] PW Gate.   22 *night*] Conj.   30 *Sweet*] orig: briezes of Sweet
39 *Glory's*] orig: happy

78. Meditation. Zech. 9.11. By the Blood
          of thy Covenant I have sent forth
          thy Prisoners out of the Pit wherein
          is no water.

14. 10m [Dec.] *1707*. Pub. UPT.

Mine Eyes, that at the Beautious Sight of Fruite
    On th'Tree of, Knowledge, drew black venom in
That did bemegerim my brains at root
    That they turnd round, and tippled me int' Sin.
    I thus then in t'Barath'rick pit down fell.   5
    Thats Waterless and next doore is to Hell:

No water's here: It is a Springless Well.
    Like Josephs Pit, all dry of Comforts Spring.
Oh! Hopeless, Helpless Case: In such I fell.
    The Creatures buckets dry, no help can bring: 10
    Oh, here's a Spring: Indeed its Lethe Lake
    Of Aqua-Infernales: don't mistake.

This Pit indeed's Sins Filthy Dungeon State,
    No water's in't, but filth, and mire, Sins juyce.
Wherein I sinke ore Head, and Eares: sad fate,   15
    And ever shall, if Grace hath here no Sluce.
    Its Well Coards whip Coards are: not Coards to draw
    (Like Pully Coards) out of this Dungeons maw.

Yet in the upper room of Paradise
    An Artist anvill'd out Reliefe sure, Good,   20
A Golden Coarde, and bucket of Grace Choice
    Let down top full of Covenantall blood.
    Which when it touches, oh! the happy Cry!
    The doores fly ope. Now's jayle's Deliverie.

2 *Knowledge*] PW Knowled   5 *then in t'Barath'rick*] orig: into th' **Barath'rick**
14 *in't,*] PW in't.   23 *Cry*] orig: Conj. Life[?] Saile[?]

This is a Spring of Liquour, heavenly, Cleare.   25
    Its Streams oreflow these banks. Its boundless Grace
Whose Spring head's Godhead, and its Channells where
        It runs, is Manhood veans that Christ keeps Chase
        For it, and when it makes a Springtide Flood
        This Pit is drown'd with Covenantall blood.   30

And now the Prisoners sent out, do come
    Padling in their Canooes apace with joyes
Along this blood red Sea, Where joyes do throng,
        And sayling in the Arke of Grace that flies
        Drove sweetly by Gailes of the Holy Ghost   35
        Who sweetly briezes all along this Coast.

Here's Covenant blood, indeed: and 't down the banks
    Of this dry Pit breakes: Also 'tis a key
T'unlock the Shackles Sin hung on their Shanks
        And wash the durt off: send them cleane away.   40
        The Pris'ners freed, do on this Red Sea swim
        In Zions Barke: and in their Cabbins sing.

Lord let this Covenantall blood send mee
    Poore Prisner, out of Sins dry Dungeon pound.
And on this Red Sea saile mee safe to thee   45
        In which none Israelite was ever drown'd.
        My Sayles shall tune thee praise along this coast
        If waft with Gailes breath'd by the Holy Ghost.

79. Meditation. Can. 2.16. My Beloved is mine and I am his.

8. 12m [Feb.] 1707. Pub. UPT.

Had I Promethius' filching Ferula
    Filld with its sacred theft the stoln Fire:
To animate my Fancy lodg'd in clay,
      Pandora's Box would peps the theft with ire.
      But if thy Love, My Lord, shall animate   5
      My Clay with holy fire, 'twill flame in State.

Fables fain'd Wonders do relate so strange
    That do amuse when heard. But oh! thy Fame
Pend by the Holy Ghost, (and ne'er shall Change
      Nor vary from the truth) is wonders flame   10
      Glazde o're with Heavens Embelishments, and fan'd
      From evry Chaff, Dust, Weedy Seed, or Sand.

What wilt thou change thyselfe for me, and take
    In lew thereof my sorry selfe; whereby,
I am no more mine own, but thine, probate,   15
      Thou not so thine, as not mine too thereby?
      Dost purchase me to be thine own, thyselfe
      And be'st exchange for mee, thyselfe, and wealth?

I'm Thine, Thou Mine! Mutuall propriety:
    Thou giv'st thyselfe. And for this gift takst mee   20
To be thine own. I give myselfe (poore toy)
      And take thee for myne own, and so to bee.
      Thou giv'st thyselfe, yet dost thyselfe possess,
      I give and keep myselfe too neretheless.

1 *Promethius'*] PW Promethiu's   2 With its *** canceled at beginning of line   *Filld*] PW filld   6 *Clay*] orig: Fan[cy]

1–2: Promethius' . . . Fire. Prometheus stole from the gods enough fire to make the pitch of a stalk of giant fennel smoulder; from this, men once again obtained fire (*Oxford Classical Dictionary*).

Both gi'n away and yet retain'd aright.   25
    Oh! Strange! I have thee mine, who hast thyselfe,
Yet in possession Thou hast mee as tite,
      Who still enjoy myselfe, and thee my wealth.
      What strang appropriations hence arise?
      Thy Person mine, Mine thine, even weddenwise?   30

Thine mine, mine Thine, a mutuall claim is made.
    Mine, thine are Predicates unto us both.
But oh! the Odds in th'purchase price down laid:
      Thyselfe's thy Price, myselfe my mony go'th.
      Thy Purchase mony's infinitly high;   35
      Of Value for me: mine for thee, 's a toy.

Thou'rt Heir of Glory, dost Bright image stand
    Ev'n of the God of Glory. Ownest all.
Hast all Wealth Wisdom Glory, Might at hand
      And all what e're can to mans Glory fall.
      And yet thou givst thyselfe to purchase mee   40
      Ev'n of myselfe, to give myselfe to thee.

And what am I? a little bit of Clay.
    Not more, nor better thing at all I give.
(Though give myselfe) to thee as Purchase pay.
      For thee, and for thy all, that I may live.   45
      What hard terms art thou held unto by me.
      Both in thy Sale, and Purchase, laid on thee?

But yet this thing doth not impov'rish thee
    Although thou payest down thy glorious selfe.
And my down laying of myselfe I see   50
      For thee,'s the way for mee to blessed wealth.
      Thou freely givst what I buy Cheape of thee.
      I freely give what thou buyst deare of mee.

The Purchasd Gift, and Given Purchase here   55
    (For they're both Gifts, and Purchases) by each

31 *is made*] orig: runs thus
32 *are*] orig: is   *unto*] orig: to   39 *Might at hand*] orig: Might and Power at
hand   40 *to*] orig: unto   49 *thing*] orig: bargain   56 *Purchases*] *too* has been
inserted after this word and repeated in the margin. The marginal *too* appears
to have been canceled.

For each, make each to one anothers deare,
>   And each delight t'heare one anothers Speech.
>   Oh! Happy Purchase. And oh! Happy Sale:
>   Making each others joye in joyous gales.   60

Let this dash out the snarling teeth that grin,
>   Of that Damnd Heresy, calld SHERLOSISM,
That mocks, and scoffs the UNION (that blesst thing)
>   To Christs Blesst Person, Happy Enkentrism.
>   For if thats true, Christs Spouse spake false in this   65
>   Saying My Beloved's Mine, and I am his.

Hence, Oh! my Lord, make thou mee thine that so
>   I may be bed wherein thy Love shall ly,
And be thou mine that thou mayst ever show
>   Thyselfe the Bed my Love its lodge may spy.   70
>   Then this shall be the burden of my Song
>   My Well belov'de is mine: I'm his become.

57 *one*] PW on   66 *Beloved's*] orig: Beloved is

62: SHERLOSISM, the doctrines of Dr. William Sherlock (1641?–1707), Dean of
St. Paul's—doctrines which Taylor attacked in his sermons as well as in this
Meditation. Sherlock's concept of the Trinity as being composed of three in-
finite distinct minds and substances was condemned at Oxford as heretical.
Sherlock objected to that form of Christianity which made the person of
Christ almost the sole object of Christian religion; he also objected to the
notion of the mystical union between Christ and the members of the
church, and it is this latter objection that Taylor is condemning here.
Taylor's position is the same as that of Edward Polhill, whose *An Answer
to the Discourse of William Sherlock Touching the Knowledge of Christ*
was in Taylor's library. DNB notes that Polhill's writings were strongly
Calvinistic.

92. Meditation. Math. 24.27. So also shall
           the Coming of the Son of Man be.

27.9m [Nov.] *1709.*

It grieves mee, Lord, my Fancy's rusty: rub
      And brighten't on an Angells Rubston sharp.
Furbish it with thy Spirits File: and dub
      It with a live Coale of thine Altars Spark.
      Yea, with thy holly Oyle make thou it slick   5
      Till like a Flash of Lightning, it grow Quick.

My Heart may ake to finde so bright a Theme
      Which brighten might even Angels wits, to bee,
By my thick, Rusty Fancy and dull Veane
      Barbd of its brightsom sparkling Shine by mee.   10
      Quicken my Fancy Lord; and mend my Pen:
      To Flowerish up the same, as brightest Gem.

What is thy Humane Coach thy Soule rides in,
      Bathing in Bright, Heart ravishing glory all
In Gods Celestiall splendent Palace trim,   15
      Full of it's Fulgient Glory of that hall?
      And wilt thou from this glorious Palace come
      Again to us on earth, where Sinners throng?

Methinks I see, when thou appearest thus,
      The Clouds to rend, and Skies their Crystall Doore   20
Open like thunder for thy pass to us
      And thy Bright Body deckt with Shine all Ore
      Flash through the Same like rapid Lightening Waver
      That gilds the Clouds, and makes the Heavens Quaver.

Proud Sinners now that ore Gods Children crow   25
      Would if they could creep into Augur holes,

3 *Furbish*] PW Furbush   9 *and dull Veane*] orig: and Dull **Fancy**
20 orig: Thy Glorious body Deckt with Shine all o'er:
Canceled and rewritten as l.22.

Thy Lightening Flashing in their faces so,
 Melts down their Courage, terrifies their Souls.
 Thy Rapid Lightning Flashes pierce like darts
 Of Red hot fiery arrows through their hearts. 30

Now Glory to the Righteous is the Song.
 Their dusty Frame drops off its drossiness
Puts on bright robes, doth jump for joy, doth run
 To meet thee in the Clouds in lightning Dress.
 Whose nimble Flashes dancing on each thing 35
 While Angells trumpet-musick makes them sing.

Make Sanctifying Grace, my tapestry,
 My person make thy Lookinglass Lord, clear
And in my Looking Glass cast thou thine Eye.
 Thy Image view that standeth shining there. 40
 Then as thou com'st like Light'ning, I shall rise
 In Glories Dress to meet thee in the Skies.

93. Meditation. Joh. 14.2. In my Fathers
   house are many Mansions.

 22.11m [Jan.] *1709.*

Could but a Glance of that bright City fair,
 Whose walls are sparkling, Pretious Stones, whose Gates
Bright pollisht Splendent Pearls, Whose Porters are
 Swash Flaming Angells, and Whose Streets rich Plates
 Of pure transparent Gold, mine Eyes enjoy, 5
 My Ravisht heart on Raptures Wings would fly.

My Lumpish Soule, enfir'd with such bright flame
 And Quick'ning influences of this Sight
Darting themselves throughout my drossy frame
 Would jump for joy, and sing with greate delight 10

38 *My person make*] orig: And make my person
5 *Gold,*] PW Gold. 8 *Quick'ning influences*] PW Quick'ming infuences

To thee, my Lord, who deckst thy Royall Hall,
With glorious Mansions for thy Saints even all.

Thy Lower House, this World well garnished
        With richest Furniture of Ev'ry kinde
Of Creatures of each Colours varnished   15
        Most glorious, a Silver Box of Winde.
        The Crystall Skies pinkt with Sun, Moon, and Stars
        Are made its Battlements on azure Spars.

But on these Battlements above, thoust placdst
        Thy Upper House, that Royall Palace town,   20
In which these Mansions are, that made thou hast
        For Saints and Angells Dwellings of renown.
        Should we suppose these mansions, Chambers neate
        Like ours, 't would sordid be, not fit this Seate.

But if these Mansions, built so very bright   25
        Beyond the worlds Bright Battlements, yet should
Be of materialls Celestiall right
        Streets of such Houses, of transparent gold
        For Saints and Angells to possess in Glory's
        Would they unfit thy Upper House as Stories.   30

Though we can't ken these Mansions, now, yet this
        Our Faith doth dwell upon while on this Shore
That there are Mansions, in Celestiall Bliss
        For Saints and Angells t'dwell in evermore.
        Then cheer up, Soule, and take the Kings path brave   35
        Unto these Mansions promises do pave.

Bright Jasper Hall Walld with translucid gold,
        Floors pav'd with Pearls, to these are durty Sells.
Then what bright lives ought all men here uphold
        That hope within these mansions ere to dwell?   40
        Adorne my Soule, Lord, with thy Graces here
        Till by their Shine, I'm fitted to dwell there.

24 *'t would sordid be*] orig: 't would be sordid and
28 *transparent*] PW tranparent   31 *now,*] PW now.   40 *mansions*] PW
mansion

Let as I bring thy Glory home, in mee
    Grace shine, and me thy paths tread pav'de with jems,
Unto thy house, wherein these Mansions bee,   45
    And let mee dwell within their Curtain Hems.
    Thy Praise shall then my Virginalls inspire
    To play a Michtam on her golden wyer.

94. Meditation. Joh. 14.2. In my Fathers House are Many Mansions.

19. 1m [Mar.] *1709/10.*

Celestiall Mansions! Wonder, oh my Soul!
    Angells Pavillions surely: and no Halls
For Mud walld Matter, wherein Vermins rowle,
    Worm eaten'd ore with Sin, like wormhold Walls.
    Shall Earthen Pitchers set be on the Shelfe   5
    Of such blesst Mansions Heavenly Plate of Wealth?

May I presume to screw a single thought
    Well splic'de with Saving Faith, into my Heart,
That my poore Potshread, all o're good for nought
    May ever in these Lodgens have a part   10
    The influences of the Same would fly
    With rapid flashes through my heart of joy.

Oh! that thy Spirit would my Soule Inlay
    With such rich lining, Graces Web, that would
While in my Loom, me in these Tents convay,   15
    And that thy Sovereign Love might ever hold
    Me in the paths that to these Mansions bring,
    That I might ever dwell with thee therein.

44 *Grace*] orig: Thy Grace   10 *Lodgens have a part*] orig: Rest a
part   11 *would fly*] orig: that fly   15 *Tents convay*] orig: Lodgens gay

  9: Potshread (i.e. potsherd). Cf. Isa. 45:9.

Oh! that my Meditations all were frindg'd
    With Sanctifying Gifts: and all my wayes   20
Borderd were with Obedience rightly hindg'd
        Lord on thy word thy Honour bright to raise.
        Oh! that my Paths were pavde with Holiness
        And that thy Glory were their shining dress.

Array me, Lord, with such rich robes all ore   25
    As for their Matter, and their modes usd are
Within these Mansions. Dye them all therefore
        Deep in thy blood: to make them gracious Ware.
        If with thy precious robes will't dress me here
        My present tunes shall sing thy praise when there.   30

95. Meditation. Joh. 14.2. I go to prepare a place for you.

14. 3m [May] *1710.* Pub. UPT.

What shall a Mote up to a Monarch rise?
    An Emmet match an Emperor in might?
If Princes make their personall Exercise
        Betriming mouse holes, painting with delight!
        Or hanging Hornets nests with rich attire   5
        All that pretende to Wisdome would admire.

The Highest Office and Highst Officer
    Expende on lowest intrest in the world
The greatest Cost and wealthiest treasure far
        Twould shew mans wisdom's up in folly furld.   10
        That Humane Wisdom's hatcht within the nest
        Of addle brains which wisdom ne'er possesst.

But blush, poor Soule, at th'thought of such a thought
    Touching my Lord, the King of Kings most bright
As acting thus, for us all over nought,   15

29 Entire line Conj.   2 *might?*] PW might   5 *nests*] PW **nest**

Worse than poor Ants, or Spider catchers mite
Who goes away t'prepare's a place most cleare
Whose Shine o're shines the shining Sunshine here.

Ye Heavens wonder, shall your maker come
　　To Crumbs of Clay, bing'd all and drencht in Sin　　　　20
To stop the gap with Graces boughs, defray
　　The Cost the Law transgresst, doth on us bring?
　　Thy head layst down under the axe on th'block
　　That for our Sins did off the same there lop:

But that's not all. Thou now didst sweep Death's Cave　　　　25
　　Clean with thy hand: and leavest not a dust
Of Flesh, or Bone that there th'Elect dropt have,
　　But bringst out all, new buildst the Fabrick just,
　　(Having the Scrowle of Gods Displeasure clear'd)
　　Bringst back the Soule putst in its tent new rear'd.　　　　30

But thats not all: Now from Deaths realm, erect,
　　Thou gloriously gost to thy Fathers Hall:
And pleadst their Case preparst them place well dect
　　All with thy Merits hung. Blesst Mansions all.
　　Dost ope the Doore lockt fast 'gainst Sins that so　　　　35
　　These Holy Rooms admit them may thereto.

But thats not all. Leaving these dolefull roomes
　　Thou com'st and takst them by the hands, Most High,
Dost them translate out from their Death bed toombs,
　　To th'rooms prepar'd filld with Eternall joy.　　　　40
　　Them Crownst and thronst there, there their lips be shall
　　Pearld with Eternall Praises that's but all.

Lord Let me bee one of these Crumbs of thine.
　　And though Im dust adorn me with thy graces
That though all flect with Sin, thy Grace may shine　　　　45
　　As thou Conductst me to these furnisht places.
　　Make mee, thy Golden trumpet, sounded bee,
　　By thy Good Spirits melody to thee.

22 *bring?*] PW b̆ring　　27 *that there th'Elect dropt have*] orig: the Elect dropt
there have　　40 *th'rooms*] PW th rooms

96. Meditation. Cant. 1.2. Let him kiss
        me with the Kisse of his mouth.

9. 5m [July] *1710.*

What placed in the Sun: and yet my ware,
    A Cloud upon my head? an Hoodwinke blinde?
In middst of Love thou layst on mee, despare?
    And not a blinke of Sunshine in my minde?
    Shall Christ bestow his lovely Love on his,   5
    And mask his face? allowing not a kiss?

Shall ardent love to Christ enfire the Heart?
    Shall hearty love in Christ embrace the Soule?
And shall the Spirituall Eye be wholy dark,
    In th'heart of Love, as not belov'd, Condole?   10
    In th'midst of Loves bright Sun, and yet not see
    A Beame of Love allow'd to lighten thee?

Lord! read the Riddle: Shall a gracious heart
    The object of thy love be sick of Love?
And beg a kiss under the piercing Smart,   15
    Of want thereof? Lord pitty from above.
    What wear the Sun, without a ray of light?
    In midst of Sunshine, meet a pitchy night?

Thy foes, whose Souls Sins bowling alley's grown
    With Cankering Envy rusty made, stand out   20
Without all Sense of thy Sweet Love ere shown
    Is no great wonder. Thou lov'st not this rout.
    But wonder't is that such that grudge their hearts
    Hold love too little for thee, should thus smart.

Nay, nay, stand Sir: here's wisdom very cleare.   25
    None sensibly can have thy love decline:
That never had a drop thereof: nor ere

5 *Love*] orig: pure Love   22 *Thou*] PW thou   23 *their*] PW there

Did tast thereof. This is the right of thine.
Such as enjoy thy Love, may lack the Sense
May have thy love and not loves evidence.   30

Maybe thy measures are above thy might.
    Desires Crave more than thou canst hold by far:
If thou shouldst have but what thou would, if right,
    Thy pipkin soon would run ore, breake, or jar.
    Wisdom allows enough: none t'wast is known.   35
    Because thou hast not all, say not, thoust none.

Christ loves to lay thy Love under Constraint.
    He therefore lets not's Love her Candle light,
To see her Lovely arms that never faint
    Circle thyself about, with greate Delight.   40
    The prayers of Love ascend in gracious tune
    To him as Musick, and as heart perfume.

But listen, Soule, here seest thou not a Cheate.
    Earth is not heaven: Faith not Vision. No.
To see the Love of Christ on thee Compleate   45
    Would make heavens Rivers of joy, earth overflow.
    This is the Vale of tears, not mount of joyes.
    Some Crystal drops while here may well suffice.

But, oh my Lord! let mee lodge in thy Love.
    Although thy Love play bow-peep with me here.   50
Though I be dark: want Spectacles to prove
    Thou lovest mee: I shall at last see Clear.
    And though not now, I then shall sing thy praise.
    In that thy love did tende me all my dayes.

28 *This*] PW this

97. Meditation. Can. 1.2. Let him kiss me
with the Kisses of his mouth.

3. 7m [Sept.] *1710.* Unpublished.

My onely Lord, when with no muddy Sight,
    Mine Eyes behold that ardent Flame of Love,
Thy Spouse, when that her day Light seemed night
    In passionate affection seemd to move.
    When thou to her didst onely Cease to show   5
    Thy sweet love token: makes me cry out, Oh!

Although in trying, I through grace can finde
    My heart holds such Conclusions in't, that I
Account this World, Silver, and Gold, refinde
    Pearles, Pretious Stones, Riches, and Friends a toy.   10
    Methinks I could part with them all for thee
    Yet know not what I should if tri'de should bee.

I dare not say, such ardent flames would rise
    Of true Loves passion, in its Blinks or Blisses,
As in thy Holy Spouse's heart that cries   15
    Oh! let him kiss mee with his orall kisses.
    Should he but stop such acts of love and grace
    Making dark Clouds mask up his brightsom face.

If such strong Flame of Love, be made the mark
    And Cata Pantos of true Love, then who   20
Can prove his marriage knot to Christ in's heart

6 *makes me cry out*] orig: she makes me cry   12 *if tri'de should bee*] orig:
should I tride bee

20: *Cata Pantos,* i.e. *kata pantos,* first of the three Aristotelian laws of
method adopted by Peter Ramus: *lex de omni* or *lex kata pantos* 'law of
universal application'; the others were *lex per se* or *lex kath' hauto* 'law of
essential application' and *lex de universali* or *lex kath' holou* 'law of total
application.' Ramist logic was strongly influential in shaping 16th- and 17th-
century New England thought. Walter J. Ong, *Ramus* (Cambridge, Harvard
University Press, 1958), pp. 258–59.

That doth not finde such ardent flames oreflow?
When thy bright Sun-Shine Face doth weare a Cloude
Methinks my Soule in Sorrows thicket shroudes.

Yet pardon, Lord, give me this word again: 25
    I feare to wrong myselfe, or Gracious thee.
This I can say, and can this say mentain,
    If thou withdrawst, my heart soon sinks in mee.
    Though oftentimes my Spirits dulled, grow,
    If so I am, I am not alwayes soe: 30

When thou dost shine, a Sunshine day I have:
    When I am cloudy then I finde not thee:
When thou dost cloud thy face, thy Face I crave.
    The Shining of thy face enlivens mee.
    I live and dy as Smiles and Frowns take place: 35
    The Life, and Death of Joy Lodge in thy face.

But yet methinks my pipkin is too small.
    It holds too little of Loves liquour in't.
All that it holds for thee seems none at all.
    Thou art so dear, it is too cheape a Drink.   40
    If I had more thou shouldst have more of mee
    If Better, better too. I all give thee.

If thou, my Lord, didst not accept a mite
    More than a mountain, if the mite doth hold
More than a mountain of the heart Love right   45
    I should be blankt, my heart would grow so cold.
    A Quarter of a Farthen halfe a mite
    Of Love thou likest well, its heart delight.

Then let thy Loveliness, Lord touch my heart.
    And let my heart imbrace thy loveliness: 50
That my small mite of Love might on thee dart,
    And thy great selfe might my poor love possess.

44 *mountain*,] PW mountain   48 *well*,] PW well.

My little mite of Love shall musick sweet
Tune forth on thee, its harp, that heaven shall greet.

101. Meditation. Isai. 24.23. Then shall the
            Moon be Confounded, and the Sun
            ashamed when the Lord of host shall
            rain in Mount Zion—Gloriously.

15. 2m [Apr.] *1711.*

Glory, thou Shine of Shining things made fine
    To fill the Fancy peeping through the Eyes
At thee that wantons with thy glittering Shine
        That onely dances on the Outside guise
        Yet art the brightest blossom fine things bring   5
        To please our Fancies with and make them sing.

But spare me, Lord, if I while thou dost use
    This Metaphor to make thyselfe appeare
In taking Colours, fancy it to Choose
        To blandish mine affections with and Cheare   10
        Them with thy glory, ever shining best.
        Thus brought to thee so takingly up dresst.

May I but Eye thy Excellency's guise
    From which thy glory flows, all sparkling bright
Th'Property of all thy Properties   15
        Being both inside, and their Outside Light
        The flowing flakes of brightest glories flame
        Would my affections set on fire amain.

Thy Holy Essence, and its Properties
    Divine and Human all this Glory ware.   20

53 *mite*] orig: might   6 *Fancies*] PW Fances
11 *ever shining*] orig: shining ever   17 *brightest*] PW brighest
18 *set on fire*] orig: all enfire

Thou art Bright Sun Glorie the Beams our Eyes
    Are gilded with which from its body are.
    Magnetick vertue raising Exhalation
    Out of the humble soule unto thy Station.

My blissful Lord, thou and thy properties   25
    And all thy Adjuncts that upon thee throng
Enbedded altogether up arise
    And moulded up into a Splenderous Sun
    And in thy Kingly Glory out do shine
    In Zions mount, outshineing Glories line.   30

Created Glory dangling on all things
    Of brightest sweet breathd flowers and Fields and glaze
The spurred starry Tribes whose sparkling wings
    Flur glory down in Shining Beames and Rayes
    Do blush and are asham'd of all their grace   35
    Beholding that bright Glory of thy Face.

The Silver Candlesticks of th'heaven bright,
    Bearing the Blazing torches round about
The Moon and Sun the Worlds bright Candle's light
    These Candles flames thy Glory blows all out.   40
    These Candle flames lighting the World as tapers,
    Set in thy Sunshine seem like smokie vapors.

The Glory bright of Glorified Saints
    And brightest Glory sparkling out with grace
Comparde with thine my Lord is but as Paint   45
    But glances on them of thy glorious Face.
    Its weak reflection of thy glories Shine,
    Painting their Walls not to compare with thine.

But, Lord, art thou deckt up in glory thus?
    And dost thou in this Glory come and Wooe   50
To bring our hearts to thee compelling us
    With such bright arguments of Glories hew?
    Oh! Adamantine Hearts if we withstand
    Such taking Charming pleas in Glories hand.

22 *are*] orig: run[?]   26 *all*] Conj.   30 *mount*] orig: mont   52 *hew?*] PW hew

Thy splendid glory lapt in Graces mantle   55
    Confer on mee Lord, with thy gracious hand.
Let not my feet upon such glory trample
      But make me for thee and thy Glory stand.
      If that thy Gracious Glory win my Heart
      Thy Glory's Grace I'le on Shoshannims harp.   60

102. Meditation. Mat. 26.26. While they
        were Eating, he took Bread
        and Blessed etc.

   10.4m [June] *1711*.

What Grace is here? Looke ery way and see
    How Grace's Splendor like the bright Sun, shines
Out on my head, and I encentred bee
      Within the Center of its radien lines,
      Thou glories King send out thy Kingly Glory   5
      In shining Institutions laid before mee.

The Basis of thy gracious functions stands
    Ensocketted in thy Essentiall Grace
As its foundation, Rock (not loose loose Sands)
      Bearing the Splendor of this shining face   10
      Th'New Covenant, Whose Articles Divine
      Do far surmount lines wrote in Gold for Shine.

And as the King of Zion thou putst out
    Thy Institutions, Zions Statutes, th'Laws
Of thy New Covenant, which all through out   15
      Thy bright Prophetick trumpet sounds, its Cause.
      To this New Covenant, thou sets thy hand
      And Royall Seale eternally to stand.

59 *Glory win*] orig: Glory doth win   14 *Zions*] orig: these
16 *sounds*,] PW sounds.

A Counterpane indented right with this
  Thou giv'st indeed a Deed of Gift to all   20
That Give to thee their Hearts, a Deed for bliss.
  Which with their hands and Seales they sign too shall.
  One seale they at the Articling embrace:
  The other oft must be renew'd, through grace.

Unto the Articles of this Contract   25
  Our Lord did institute even at the Grave
Of the Last Passover, when off its packt.
  This Seale for our attendance oft to have.
  This Seal made of New Cov'nant wax, red di'de,
  In Cov'nant blood, by faith to be appli'de.   30

Oh! this Broad Seale, of Grace's Covenant
  Bears, Lord, thy Flesh set in its rim aright.
All Crucifide and blood, (Grace hath no want)
  As shed for us, and on us us to White.
  Let's not neglect this gracious law nor breake   35
  But on this Flesh and blood both drinke and Eate.

Seing thou, Lord, thy Cov'nant writst in blood
  My blood red Sins to blot out quite from me
Bathe thou my Soule in this sweet gracious flood,
  Give me thy Grace that I may live to thee.   40
  My heart, thy harp, make, and thy Grace my string.
  Thy Glory then shall be my Song I'l sing.

103. Meditation. Mat. 26.26. As they were
    eating he tooke bread etc.

12. 6m [Aug.] *1711.*

The Deity did call a Parliament
  Of all the Properties Divine to sit

20 *of Gift*] orig: to all 22 *too*] orig: it

About mankinde. Justice her Law out went.
    All Vote man's life to stand or fall by it,
    But Grace gave band securing Gods Elect.   5
    Justice, if Wisdom tended Grace, accepts.

Man out doth come, and soon this Law disgrac't.
    Justice offended, Grace to worke doth Fall
And in the way of Purest wisdom, traced
    New Covenants man and to return him calls.   10
    Erects New Cov'nant worship suited to
    His present State to save him from all Woe.

And in this Course Glory to offer bright
    Through Graces Hand unto Almighty God
Her Credits Good. Justice therein delights.   15
    Rests in her Bill yet Grace prepares a Rod
    That if her subjects her sweet rules neglect,
    She with her golden rod may them Correct.

New Covenant worship Wisdom first proclaims
    Deckt up in Types and Ceremonies gay.   20
Rich Metaphors the first Edition gains.
    A Divine key unlocks these trunks to lay
    All spirituall treasures in them open Cleare.
    The Ark and Mannah, in't, Christ and Good Cheere.

This first Edition did the Cov'nant tend   25
    With Typick Seales and Rites and Ceremonie
That till the Typick Dispensations end
    Should ratify it as Gods Testimony.
    'Mong which the Passover (whose Kirnell's Christ)
    Tooke place with all its Rites, graciously spic't.   30

But when the Pay day came their kirnells Pickt.
    The Shell is cast out hence. Cloudes flew away.
Now Types good night, with Ceremonies strict,
    The Glorious Sun is risen, its broad day.
    Now Passover farewell, and leave thy Place.   35
    Lords Supper seales the Covenant of Grace.

33 *night,*] PW night.

But though the Passover is passt away.
    And Ceremonies that belong'd to it,
Yet doth its kirnell and their Kirnell stay
    Attending on the Seale succeeding it.   40
    The Ceremony parting leaves behinde
    Its Spirit to attend this Seale designd.

As it passt off, it passt its place o're to
    The Supper of the Lord (Choice Feast) to seale
The Covenant of Grace thus, even so   45
    The Ceremoniall Cleaness did reveale
    A Spirituall Cleaness qualifying all
    That have a Right to tend this Festivall.

All must grant Ceremonies must have Sense.
    Or Ceremonies are but senseless things.   50
Had God no reason when, for to dispense
    His Grace, he ope'd all Ceremoniall Springs?
    The reason why God deckt his sacred Shine
    With Senseless Ceremonies, here Divine.

A Typick Ceremony well attends   55
    A Typick Ordinance, these harmonize.
A Spirituall Ordinance the Type suspendes
    And Onely owneth Spirituall Qualities
    To have a right thereto. And this the Will
    The dying Ceremony made, stands still.   60

Morall, and Ceremoniall cleaness, which
    The Pascall Lamb requir'd Foreshow the Guests
Must at the Supper Seale with Spoiles be rich
    Of Sin and be with Saving Grace up dresst.
    God Chose no Ceremonies for their sake   65
    But for Signification did them take.

Give me true Grace that I may grace thy Feast.
    My Gracious Lord, and so sit at thy Table.

51 *Had*] orig: Did
53 *deckt*] PW deck   61 *Ceremoniall*] PW Ceremiall   62 *requir'd*] orig:
requires   67 *Feast*] orig: Table

Thy Spirituall Dainties this Rich Dress at least
    Will have the Guests have. Nothing less is able   70
    To prove their right to't. This therefore bestow.
    Then as I eate, my lips with Grace shall flow.

104. Meditation. Matth. 26.26.27. He tooke
Bread.—And he also tooke the Cup:

30.7m [Sept.] *1711.* Pub. SMT.

What? Bread, and Wine, My Lord! Art thou thus made?
    And made thus unto thine in th'Sacrament?
These are both Cordiall: and both displai'd
    Food for the Living. Spirituall Nourishment.
    Thou hence art food, and Physick rightly 'pli'de   5
    To Living Souls. Such none for dead provide.

Stir up thy Appetite, my Soule, afresh,
    Here's Bread, and Wine as Signs, to signify
The richest Dainties Cookery can Dress
    Thy Table with, filld with felicity.   10
    Purge out and Vomit by Repentance all
    Ill Humours which thy Spirituall Tast forestall.

Bread, Yea substantiall Bread dresst daintily
    Gods White bread made of th'kidnie of Wheate
Ground in his Mill to finest Flowre, we spy,   15
    Searc'de through his strict right Bolter, all compleate
    Moulded up by Gods hand and baked tite
    In Justices hot oven, Gods Cake-bread white.

It is Gods Temple bread; the fine Flower Cake.
    The pure Shew Bread on th'golden Table set,   20
Before the Mercy-Seate in golden Plate,
    Thy Palate for this Zions Simnill whet.

71 *This*] PW this orig: Give this
10 *with,*] PW with.   12 *Spirituall Tast forestall*] orig: Tast do quite

If in this oyled Wafer thou dost eate
Celestiall Mannah, Oh! the Happy meate.

But that's not all. Here's wine too of brave State.   25
    The Blood, the pure red blood of Zions Grape
Grounde in the Mill of Righteousness to 'bate
    Gods firy wrath and presst into the Shape
    Of Royall Wine in Zion's Sacred bowles
    That Purges Cleanse and Chearish doth poore Soules.   30

This Bread, and Wine hold forth the selfe same thing
    As they from their first Wheat and Vine made flow
Successively into their Beings, bring
    The manner of Christs Manhood and forth show
    It was derived from th'head Humanity   35
    Through Generations all successively.

And as this Bread and Wine receive their forms
    Not fram'd by natures acting, but by Art.
So Christs Humanity was not ere born
    By natures Vertue which she did impart.   40
    But by Almighty power which acted so
    Transendently, did nature overdoe.

These two are of all food most Choice indeed
    Do Emblemise Christ's Elementall frame
Most Excellent and fine, of refinde Seed,   45
    With Sparkling Grace deckt, and their Works in flame
    As grafted in and flowing from his Nature
    And here is food of which his are partaker.

Bread must be broke and Eate Wine pourd out too
    And drunke and so they feed and do delight.   50
Christ broken was upon Gods wheele (its true)
    And so is spirituall bread that feeds aright
    And his Choice blood shead for our Sins is made
    Drinke for our Souls: a Spirituall Drinke displaid.

Food though its ne're so rich, doth not beget   55
    Nor make its Eaters; but their Lives mentain.

44 *Christ's*] PW Christ

This Bread and Wine begets not Souls; but's set
    'Fore spirituall life to feed upon the Same.
    This Feast is no Regenerating fare.
    But food for those Regenerate that are.   60

Spit out thy Fur, my Tongue; renew thy Tast.
    Oh! whet thine Appetite, and cleanly brush
Thy Cloaths and trim thy Soule. Here food thou hast
    Of Royall Dainties, that requires thee thus
    That thou adorned be in Spirituall State: 65
    This Bread ne're moulds, nor wine entoxicate.

They both are Food, and Physick, purge out Sin
    From right Receivers. Filth, and Faults away:
They both are Cordialls rich, do Comfort bring.
    Make Sanctifying Grace thrive ery day,   70
    Making the spirituall man hate spirituall sloath
    And to abound in things of Holy growth.

Lord, feed me with th'Bread of thy Sacrament:
    And make me drinke thy Sacramentall Wine:
That I may Grow by Graces nourishment   75
    Wash't in thy Vinall liquour till I shine,
    And rai'd in Sparkling Grace unto thy Glory,
    That so my Life may be a gracious story.

105. Meditation. Matt. 26.26. Jesus tooke
        Bread and blessed it, and
        brake it.

23. 10m [Dec.] *1711.* Pub. SMT.

If I was all well melted down, refinde
    In graces Furnace and run in the mould

76 *Wash't*] PW wash't orig: And washt
1 *well melted*] orig: melted well   2 *in*] orig: into

Of bright bright Glory, that with Glory shinde
    More bright than glory doth, my Lord I would
    Crown thee therewith thou shouldst have all, except   5
    The dross I in refining did eject.

Hast thou unto thy Godhead nature tooke
    My nature and unto that nature joyn'de
Making a Union thereby, whose root
    Too deep's for reasons delving toole to finde,   10
    Which is held out thus by thy Taking Bread,
    In this sweet Feast in which our Souls are fed?

This Union, that it is, wee clearely see
    But se not How, or What it is; although
We stande and gaze on't, at't amazed bee.   15
    But Why it is Grace graciously doth show.
    These natures thus United have (as't shown)
    Each done by each, what neither could alone.

The Reason of it Grace declares, whose hand
    This Union made; its made (and thinke hereon)   20
That so our Nature Cansell might that Bande.
    She'd forfeited, and Justice sude upon.
    For natures Purse could not the Fine defray.
    Hence she had Gold from Godheads Mint to pay.

This Mystery more rich than massy gold   25
    Our Lord lapt up in a Choice napkin fine
Of Heavenly trade an Ordinance that hold
    The same out doth to us all sweet, Divine,
    That this might live, he in his Dying night
    Portraide it on his Supper last, as light.   30

To shew that he our nature took, he then
    Tooke breade, and wine best Elementall trade,
Designed as the Sign thereof. Which when
    He had his blessing over it display'de
    To shew his Consecration, then it brake,   35
    To signify his Sufferings for our sake.

4 *glory*] PW gloly   12 *Souls*] PW Soals   20 *made;*] PW made.,
35 *brake,*] PW brake.

Hence in this Bread, and Wine thou dost present
    Thyselfe, my Lord, Celestiall Food indeed,
Rich spirituall fare Soul-Food, Faiths nourishment,
    And such as doth all Saving Graces feed.
    For which an Heavenfull of thanks, all free,   40
    Is not too much my Lord to render thee.

Yet my poore Pipe can hardly stut a tune
    Above an hungry thanks unto thy name
For all this grace, My Lord, My heart perfume   45
    With greater measures, till thy Grace out flame
    And leade mee on in Graces path along
    To Glory, then I'l sing a brighter song.

106. Meditation. Matth. 26.26.27—take
      Eate—Drinke yee.

17. 12m [Feb.] *1711.* Pub. SMT.

I fain would Prize, and Praise thee, Lord, but finde
    My Prizing Faculty imprison'd lyes.
That its Appreciation is confinde
    Within its prison walls and small doth rise.
    Its Prizing Act it would mount up so high   5
    That might oremount its possibility.

I fain would praise thee, but want words to do't:
    And searching ore the realm of thoughts finde none
Significant enough and therefore vote
    For a new set of Words and thoughts hereon   10
    And leap beyond the line such words to gain
    In other Realms, to praise thee: but in vain.

Me pitty, parden mee and Lord accept
    My Penny Prize, and penny worth of Praise.
Words and their Sense within thy bounds are kept   15
    And richer Fruits my Vintage cannot raise.

42 *too*] PW to   5 *Act*] Conj.   11 *leap*] orig: leaping

I can no better bring, do what I can:
    Accept thereof and make me better man.

With Consecrated Bread and Wine indeed
    Of Zions Floore, and Wine press me sustain.   20
These fruits thy Boddy, and thy blood doth breed
    Thy Pay and Purchase for mee mee to gain.
    Lord make thy Vitall Principall in mee
    In Gospellwise to eate and drink on thee.

These acts of mine that from thy Vitall Spark   25
    In mee being to thyself, my Lord, my Deare,
As formative in touching thee their marke
    Of this thy Sacrament, my Spirituall Cheere.
    Life first doth Act and Faith that's lifes First-born
    Receiving gives the Sacramentall form.   30

Hence its as needfull as the forme unto
    This Choice formation Hypocrites beg on.
Elfes Vizzarded, and Lambskinde Woolves hence goe.
    Your Counterfeted Coine is worse than none.
    Your gilding though it may the Schoole beguile   35
    The Court will Cast and all your gilt off file.

Morality is here no market ware,
    Although it in the Outward Court is free.
A State of Sin this Banquet cannot beare.
    Old and New Cov'nant Guests here don't agree.   40
    The Wedden Robe is Welcome, but the back
    This Supper cloaths not with, that doth it lack.

32 *formation*] PW formatum[?]   38 *is free*] orig: may bee

   40: Old and New Cov'nant Guests. Old and new covenant is defined by
Perkins as follows: "The Covenant [of Grace], albeit it be one in substance,
yet is distinguished into the olde and new testament. The old testament or
covenant is that which in types and shadowes prefigured Christ to come,
and to be exhibited. The new testament declareth Christ already come in
the flesh, and is apparently sheewed in the Gospell" (*The Workes of . . .
William Perkins,* 3 vols. London, 1612–13, *1,* 70). See also Glossary, OLD AND
NEW COVENANT

Food is for living Limbs, not Wooden legs:
    Life's necessary, unto nourishment.
Dead limbs must be cut off: the Addle Eggs   45
    Rot by the heat the dam upon them spent.
    A State of Sin that takes this bread and Wine
    From the Signatum tareth off the Signe.

A Principle of life, to eate implies,
    And of such life that sutes the Foods desire.   50
Food naturall doth naturall Life supply.
    And spirituall food doth spirituall life require.
    The Dead don't eate. Though Folly childish dotes
    In th'Child that gives his Hobby horses oates.

To Eat's an Act of life that life out sent   55
    Employing Food. Life's property alive
Yet acts uniting with foods nourishment
    Which spreads o're nature quite to make it thrive.
    Life Naturall and Spirituall Life renewd
    Precedes their Acts, their Acts precede their food.   60

Then form mee Lord, a former here to bee
    Of this thy Sacrament receiving here
And let me in this Bread and Wine take thee:
    And entertain me with thy Spirituall Cheer.
    Which well Concocted will make joy up start,   65
    That makes thy praises leape up from my heart.

107. Meditation. Lu. 22.19. This do in
        remembrance of Mee.

13. 2m [Apr.] *1712.* Pub. SMT.

Oh! what a Lord is mine? There's none like him.
    Born heir of th'Vastest Realms, and not Confinde,

66 *That*] orig: To   *leape*] orig: to leape

Within, nor o're the Canopy or rim
    Of th'Starry Region, and as vastly kinde.
    But's bright'st Dominion gloriously lies   5
    In th'Realm of Angells above the Starry Skies.

When man had sin'd he saw that nothing could
    In all's Dominnion Satisfaction make
To milke white Justice, but himselfe, who should
    Then Drinke Deaths health, he did the matter take   10
    Upon himselfe by Compact, new and good
    On such Conditions that requir'd his blood.

Yet entred he in Cov'nant with God,
    The Father for to do the thing himselfe
Which to perform he took a Humane Clod   15
    In union to his Godhead, it enwealth,
    That he might in it fully pay the Score
    Of's fallen friends, and them from death restore.

And having in our nature well sufficde
    The hungry law, with active Righteousness   20
His life did pay our debt. Death him surprizde.
    His blood he made the Law's sufficing mess.
    With Active and with Passive duties hee
    Balanc't th'accounts, and set the Captives free.

But drawing nigh upon Death's Coasts indeed   25
    He made his Will bequeathing legacies
To all his Children, a Choice Holy seed
    As they did up in Covenant new arise.
    He his last Night them feasts and at that meale
    His Supper institutes his Cov'nant Seale.   30

Four Causes do each thing produc'd attend:
    The End, Efficient, Matter and the Form.
These last th'Efficient passt through to the End,
    And so obtains the same the babe is born.
    So in this Supper causes foure attend   35
    Th'Efficient, Matter, Form, and now the End.

25 *Coasts*] PW Costs

The Primall End whereof is Obsignation
    Unto the Covenant of Grace most sweet.
Another is a right Commemoration
    Of Christs Rich Death upon our hearts to keep   40
    And to declare his own till he again
    Shall come. This Ordinance doth at these aim.

And Secondary Ends were in Christ's Eye
    In instituting of this Sacrament,
As Union, and Communion Sanctity   45
    Held with himselfe by these usd Elements
    In Union and Comunion which are fit,
    Of Saints Compacted in Church Fellowship.

But lest this Covenant of Grace should ere
    Be held by doubting Saints all Violate   50
By their infirmities as Adams were
    By one transgression and be so vacate
    Its Seale is food and's often to be usd,
    To seale new pardons freshening faith, misusd.

Then make me, Lord, at thy Sweet Supper spy   55
    Thy graces all well flourishing in mee.
And seale me pardon up and ratify
    Thy Covenant with mee, thus gracious bee.
    My Faculties all deckt with grace shall Chime
    Thy praise, with Angells and my grace shall shine.   60

108. Meditation. Matt. 26.26.27. Jesus took bread—and he took the Cup:

8. 4m [June] *1712.* Pub. SMT.

What Royall Feast Magnificent is this,
    I am invited to, where all the fare

41–2 *again / Shall come*] orig: shall come / Again   43 *Christ's*] PW Christ
54 *faith*] orig: the faith   57 *up*] Conj.   58 *mee,*] PW mee.
60 *praise*] PW paise

Is spic'd with Adjuncts, (ornamentall bliss)
    Which are its robes it ever more doth ware?
    These Robes of Adjuncts shining round about   5
    Christs golden Sheers did cut exactly out.

The Bread and Wine true Doctrine teach for faith
    (True Consequence from Truth will never ly)
Their Adjuncts teach Christs humane nature hath
    A Certain place and not Ubiquity.   10
    Hence this Condemns Ubiquitarians
    And whom deny Christs Manhood too it damns.

It Consubstantiation too Confounds.
    Bread still is bread, Wine still is wine its sure.
It Transubstantiation deadly wounds.   15
    Your touch, Tast, Sight say true. The Pope's a whore.
    Can Bread and Wine by words be Carnifide?
    And manifestly bread and Wine abide?

What monsterous thing doth Transubstantiation
    And Consubstantiation also make   20
Christs Body, having a Ubique-Station,
    When thousands Sacraments men Celebrate
    Upon a day, if th'Bread and wine should e're
    Be Con—, or Trans-Substantiated there?

If in Christs Doctrine taught us in this Feast,   25
    There lies No ly. (And Christ can never ly)
The Christian Faith cannot abide at least
    To dash out reasons brains, or blinde its eye.
    Faith never blindeth reasons Eye but cleares
    Its Sight to see things quite above its Sphere.   30

These Adjuncts shew this feast is ray'd in ware
    Of Holiness enlin'de with honours Shine.
Its Sabbath Entertainment, spirituall fare.
    It's Churches banquet, Spirituall Bread and Wine.
    It is the Signet of the Kings right hande,   35
    Seale to the Covenant of Grace Gods bande.

19 *monsterous thing*] orig: monster then
20 *also*] orig: too   31 *in ware*] orig: robes

The Sign, bread, made of th'kidnies of Wheate
    That grew in Zions field: And th'juyce we sup
Presst from the grape of Zions Vine sweet, great
    Doth make the Signall Wine within the Cup.   40
    Those Signals Bread and Wine are food that bear
    Christ in them Crucified, as spirituall fare.

Here is a feast indeed! in ev'ry Dish
    A Whole Redeemer, Cookt up bravely, Good,
Is served up in holy Sauce that is,   45
    A mess of Delicates made of his blood,
    Adornd with graces Sippits: rich Sweet-Meats.
    Comfort and Comforts sweeten whom them eats.

Lord, Make thou me at this rich feast thy Guest
    And let my food a whole redeemer bee.   50
Let Grace Carve him for mee in ev'ry mess:
    And rowle her Cuttings in this Sawce for mee.
    If thou me fatten with this Faire While here.
    Here after shall thy praise be my good Cheere.

109. Meditation. Mat. 26.26.27: And gave
      it to his Disciples.

3. 6m [Aug.] *1712.* Pub. SMT.

A Feast is said to be for Laughter made.
    Belshazzars Feast was made for Luxury.
Ahashueru's feast for pomp's displayde.
    George Nevill's Feast at Yorks, for gluttony.

2: Belshazzars Feast, the feast climaxed by Daniel's interpretation of the hand writing on the wall (Dan. 5).
3: Ahashueru's feast, the feast described in Esther 1:1–8. Ahasuerus was a Persian king—perhaps Xerxes—described as reigning over a hundred and twenty-seven provinces from India to Ethiopia.
4: George Nevill's Feast at Yorks, the feast celebrating the installment of George Nevill (ca. 1432–76) as the Archbishop of York in 1470. Taylor's

But thou my Lord a Spirituall Feast hast dresst   5
Whereat the Angells gaze. And Saints are Guests.

Suppose a Feast in such a Room is kept
    Thats deckt in flaming Guildings every where,
And richest Fare in China Chargers deckt
    And set on golden Tables. Waiters there   10
    In flaming robes waite pouring Royall wine
    In Jasper Cups out. Oh! what glories shine?

But all this Glorious Feast seems but a Cloud,
    My Lord, unto the Feast thou makst for thine.
Although the matters thou hast thine allowd,   15
    Plain as a pike Staffe bee, as Bread and Wine,
    This feast doth fall below thine, Lord, as far
    As the bright Sun excells a painted Star.

Thine is a Feast, the Funerall feast to prize
    The Death, Oh! my Redeemer, of the Son   20
Of God Almighty King of Heaven and'ts joys,
    Where spirituall food disht on thy Table comes.
    All Heavenly Bread and Spirituall Wine, rich rare,
    Almighty gives, here's Mannah, Angells Fare.

This Feast indeed yields gracious Laughing ripe   25
    Wherein its Authour laugheth Hell to Scorn:
Lifts up the Soule that drowns in tears, a wipe
    To give th'old Serpent. Now his head piece's torn.
    Thou art, my Lord, the Authour, and beside
    The Good Cheer of this Feast, as Crucifide.   30

The Palace where thou this dost Celebrate
    Is New Jerusalem with Precious Stones
Walld in: all pavde with Gold: and Every Gate,
    A precious pearle: An Angell keeps each one.
    And at the Table head, more rich than gold,   35
    Dost sit thyselfe, and thy rich fare unfold.

9 *Chargers*] PW Charges
16 *bee,*] PW bee.   28 *Now*] PW now   33 *Gate,*] PW Gate.

---

description of the feast (CP) lists the amounts of food and liquor consumed:
300 tuns of ale, 80 fat oxen, etc.

Thy Table's set with fare that doth Excell
    The richest Bread, and Wine that ever were
Squeezd out of Corn or Vines: and Cookt up well.
        Its Mannah, Angells food. Yea, Heavens Good Cheer.   40
        Thou art the Authour, and the Feast itselfe.
        Thy Table Feast hence doth excell all wealth.

Thou sittest at the table head in Glory,
    With thy brave guests With grace adornd and drest.
No Table e're was set like thine, in Story,   45
        Or with such guests as thine was ever blesst,
        That linings have embroider'd as with gold,
        And upper robes all glorious to behold.

They'r Gods Elect, and thy Selected Ones,
    Whose Inward man doth ware rich robes of Grace,   50
Tongues tipt with Zion Languague, Precious Stones.
        Their Robes are quilted ore with graces lace.
        Their Lives are Checker work of th'Holy Ghost.
        Their 'ffections journy unto Heavens Coast.

The Subjects that at first sat at this feast   55
    With Christ himselfe, faithfull Disciples were
Whose gracious frames 'fore this time so increast
        Into Apostleship that brought them here.
        Who when Christ comes in Glory, saith, they shall
        Sit with him on twelve thrones in's Judgment hall.   60

These sample out the Subjects and the Guests
    That Welcome are unto this Table bright,
As Qualifide Disciples up well drest
        In Spiritual apparell whitend white
        Else Spot there's in this feast. They cannot thrive   65
        For none can eate, or ere he be alive.

Thou satst in flaming Grace at table head.
    Thy flaming Grace falling upon the rest
That with thee sat, did make their graces shed
        Their Odours out most sweet which they possesst.   70

54 *Coast.*] PW Coast,   65 *They*] PW they   67 *in*] orig: at th'Table in

Judas that graceless wretch packt hence before.
That onely gracious ones enjoyd this Store.

Lord Deck my Soule with thy bright Grace I pray:
    That I may at thy Table Welcome bee,
Thy hand Let take my heart its Captive prey   75
    In Chains of Grace that it ne're slip from thee.
    When that thy Grace hath set my heart in trim
    My Heart shall end thy Supper with an Hymn.

110. Meditation. Matt. 26.30. When they
            had sung an Hymn.

    5. 8m [Oct.] 1712. Pub. W.

The Angells sung a Carole at thy Birth,
    My Lord, and thou thyselfe didst sweetly sing
An Epinicioum at thy Death, on Earth
    And order'st thine, in memory of this thing
    Thy Holy Supper, closing it at last   5
    Up with an Hymn, and Choakst the foe thou hast.

This Feast thou madst in memory of thy death
    Which is disht up most graciously: and towers
Of reeching vapours from thy Grave (Sweet breath)
    Aromatize the Skies. That sweetest Showers   10
    Richly perfumed by the Holy Ghost,
    Are rained thence upon the Churches Coast.

Thy Grave beares flowers to dress thy Church withall.
    In which thou dost thy Table dress for thine.
With Gospell Carpet, Chargers, Festivall   15
    And Spirituall Venison, White Bread and Wine
    Being the Fruits thy Grave brings forth and hands
    Upon thy Table where thou waiting standst.

75 *Thy hand Let*] orig: Let grace too   3 *at*] orig: ore

Dainties most rich, all spiced o're with Grace,
    That grow out of thy Grave do deck thy Table   20
To entertain thy Guests, thou callst, and place
      Allowst, with welcome, (and this is no Fable)
      And with these Guests I am invited to't
      And this rich banquet makes me thus a Poet.

Thy Cross planted within thy Coffin beares   25
    Sweet Blossoms and rich Fruits, Whose steams do rise
Out of thy Sepulcher and purge the aire
      Of all Sins damps and fogs that Choake the Skies.
      This Fume perfumes Saints hearts as it out peeps
      Ascending up to bury thee in th'reechs.   30

Joy stands on tiptoes all the while thy Guests
    Sit at thy Table, ready forth to sing
Its Hallilujuhs in sweet musicks dress
      Waiting for Organs to imploy herein.
      Here matter is allowd to all, rich, high,   35
      My Lord, to tune thee Hymns melodiously.

Oh! make my heart thy Pipe: the Holy Ghost
    The Breath that fills the same and Spiritually.
Then play on mee thy pipe that is almost
      Worn out with piping tunes of Vanity.   40
      Winde musick is the best if thou delight
      To play the same thyselfe, upon my pipe.

Hence make me, Lord, thy Golden Trumpet Choice
    And trumpet thou thyselfe upon the same
Thy heart enravishing Hymns with Sweetest Voice.   45
      When thou thy Trumpet soundst, thy tunes will flame.
      My heart shall then sing forth thy praises sweet
      When sounded thus with thy Sepulcher reech.

Make too my Soul thy Cittern, and its wyers
    Make my affections: and rub off their rust   50
With thy bright Grace. And screw my Strings up higher

23 *to't*] PW to'te   29 *it out peeps*] orig: they out peepe.   46 *thy*] orig: this

And tune the same to tune thy praise most Just.
Ile close thy Supper then with Hymns, most sweet
Burr'ing thy Grave in thy Sepulcher's reech.

111. Meditation. 1. Cor. 10.16. The Cup of
           blessing which wee bless, is it
           not the Comunion of the body of
           Christ? etc.

7. 10m [**Dec.**] *1712.* Pub. SMT.

Oh! Gracious Grace! whither soarst thou? How high
     Even from thy root to thy top branch dost tower?
Thou springst from th'essence of blesst Deity
     And grow'st to th'top of Heavens all blissfull flower.
     Thou art not blackt but brightend by the Sin   5
     Of Gods Elect, whom thou from filth dost bring.

Thou Graces Egg layst in their very hearts
     Hatchest and brudl'st in this nest Divine
Its Chickin, that it fledge. And still impartsts
     It influences, through their lives that shine.   10
     Them takest by the hand, and handst them o're
     The Worlds wild waves to the Celestiall Shoare.

And as thou leadst them 'long the way to glory
     Thou hast the Wells of Aqua Vitae cleare.
For them to take good drachms of (Oh! blesst Story)   15
     And Inns to entertain them with good Cheere.
     That so they may not faint, but upward grow
     Unto their ripeness, and to glory Soe.

6 *thou from filth*] orig: from out filth   8 *brudl'st in this nest*] orig: brudlest
up in nest   9 *it*] PW its   12 *to*] orig: unto   15 *good*] orig: their good
17 *faint,*] PW faint.

They take a drachm of Heavenly Spirits in,
　　From every Duty. Here is blessed Ware.　　　20
Thou hast them draughts of Spiritual Liquour gi'n
　　And ev'ry Sabbath tenders us good fare,
　　　But Oh! the Supper of our Lord! What joy?
　　　This Feast doth fat the Soul most graceously.

Theandrick Blood, and Body With Compleate　　25
　　Full Satisfaction and rich Purchase made
Disht on this golden Table, spirituall meate
　　Stands. And Gods Saints are Welcm'd with this trade
　　　The Satisfaction, and the Purchase which
　　　Thy Blood and Body made, how Good,? how rich?　　30

Oh! blesst effects flow from this table then.
　　The feeding on this fare and Spiritually
Must needs produce a Spirituall Crop for them
　　That rightly do this table fare enjoy
　　　Whatever other Ordinances doe!　　　35
　　　This addeth Seale, and Sealing wax thereto.

This is a Common that consists of all
　　That Christ ere had to give. And oh! how much!
Of Grace and Glory here? These ripe fruits fall
　　Into Saints baskets: they up gather Such.　　40
　　　All fruits that other ordinances which
　　　Are Edifying, Do this Feast enrich.

But still besides these there are properly
　　Its own effects which it doth beare and hath.
Its Spirituall Food that nourisheth spiritualy.　　45
　　The new born babe to thrive in using Faith
　　　The Soule it quiets: Conscience doth not sting.
　　　It seales fresh pardon to the Soul of Sin.

It maketh Charity's sweet rosy breath
　　Streach o're the Whole Society of Saints.　　50
It huggeth them. That nothing of the Earth

30 *Thy*] orig: The　　*made,*] PW made.
42 *Do*] orig: too　　49 *breath*] orig: Wings

Or its infection its affections taints.
Grace now grow strong, Faith sturdy. Joy, and Peace
And other Vertues in the Soule encrease.

Gods Love shines brighter now upon the heart: 55
    In that he seals Christ Dying with a Feast
Wherein he smiles doth on the Soul impart:
    With all Christs Righteousness: Joy now's increast.
    The Soul grows valient and resists the foe.
    The Spirituall Vigour vigorous doth grow.   60

Lord, on thy Commons let my Spirits feed
    So nourish thou thy new Born babe in mee.
At thy Communion Table up mee breed
    Communicate thy Blood and Body free.
    Thy Table yielding Spirituall Bread, and Wine   65
    Will make my Soul grow brisk, thy praise to Chime.

112. Meditation. 2 Cor. 5.14. If one died for
all then are all Dead.

15. 12m [Feb.] 1712. Pub. ETP, W.

Oh! Good, Good, Good, my Lord. What more Love yet.
    Thou dy for mee! What, am I dead in thee?
What did Deaths arrow shot at me thee hit?
    Didst slip between that flying shaft and mee?
    Didst make thyselfe Deaths marke shot at for mee?   5
    So that her Shaft shall fly no far than thee?

Di'dst dy for mee indeed, and in thy Death
    Take in thy Dying thus my death the Cause?
And lay I dying in thy Dying breath,
    According to Graces Redemption Laws?   10
    If one did dy for all, it needs must bee
    That all did dy in one, and from death free.

58 *Righteousness*] orig: Satisfaction   59 *resists*] PW resist   10 *to*] orig: unto

Infinities fierce firy arrow red
    Shot from the splendid Bow of Justice bright
Did smite thee down, for thine. Thou art their head.   15
    They di'de in thee. Their death did on thee light.
    They di'de their Death in thee, thy Death is theirs.
    Hence thine is mine, thy death my trespass clears.

How sweet is this: my Death lies buried
    Within thy Grave, my Lord, deep under ground,   20
It is unskin'd, as Carrion rotten Dead.
    For Grace's hand gave Death its deadly wound.
    Deaths no such terrour on th'Saints blesst Coast.
    Its but a harmless Shade: No walking Ghost.

The Painter lies: the Bellfrey Pillars weare   25
    A false Effigies now of Death, alas!
With empty Eyeholes, Butter teeth, bones bare
    And spraggling arms, having an Hour Glass
    In one grim paw. Th'other a Spade doth hold
    To shew deaths frightfull region under mould.   30

Whereas its Sting is gone: its life is lost.
    Though unto Christless ones it is most Grim
Its but a Shade to Saints whose path it Crosst,
    Or Shell or Washen face, in which she sings
    Their Bodies in her lap a Lollaboy   35
    And sends their Souls to sing their Masters joy.

Lord let me finde Sin, Curse and Death that doe
    Belong to me ly slain too in thy Grave.
And let thy law my clearing hence bestow
    And from these things let me acquittance have.   40
    The Law suffic'de: and I discharg'd, Hence sing
    Thy praise I will over Deaths Death, and Sin.

21 *unskin'd,*] PW unskin'd.   23 *on*] orig: in   24 *harmless*] orig: Shade
29 *Th'*] PW th'   34 *sings*] PW sing   38 *to me*] orig: in you   *ly slain too*]
PW ly slain to

113. Meditation. Rev. 22.16. I am the
              Root and Offspring of David.

12. 2m [Apr.] 1713.

Help, oh! my Lord, anoint mine Eyes to see
    How thou art Wonderfull thyselfe all ore,
A Common Wealth of Wonders: Rich Vine tree
    Whose Boughs are reevd with miracles good Store.
    Let thy Sweet Clew lead me thy Servant right   5
    Throughout this Labyrinth of Wonders bright.

Here I attempt thy rich delightfull Vine
    Whose bowing boughs buncht with sweet clusters, ripe
Amongst the which I take as Cordiall wine
    This Bunch doth bleed into my Cup delight.   10
    It Cramps my thoughts. What Root, and Offspring too
    Of David: Oh! how can this thing be true?

What top and bottom, Root and Branch unto
    The selfe same tree how can this be? oh-fiddle!
It cannot be. This thing may surely goe   15
    As harder far to read than Sampsons Riddle.
    A Father and a Son to th'selfe same man!
    This wond'rous is indeed: read it who can.

The Root the tree, the Tree the branch doth beare.
    The tree doth run between the branch, and Root.   20
The root and branch are too distinct a pair
    To be the same: Cause and Effect they sute.
    How then is Christ the Root, and Offspring bright
    Of David, Shew, come, read this riddle right.

Lend me thy key, holy Eliakim,   25
    T'unlock the doore untill thy glory shine.

7 *attempt*] PW attemp   9 *as Cordiall wine*] orig: this one most fine
15 *This*] PW this   18 *who*] orig: read

    25: *Eliakim,* steward of King Hezekiah's palace, who Isaiah prophesied
would displace Shebna in the house of the king. The reference here is to

And by thy Clew me thorow lead and bring
 Cleare through this Labyrinth by this rich twine.
 Posamnitick's Labyrinth now doth appeare
 An Easy thing unto the passage here.   30

But this doth seem the key unto the Lock.
 Thy Deity, my Lord, is Davids root:
It sprang from it: its rooted on this rock.
 Thy Humane nature is its Offspring-Sute.
 Thy Deity gave David Being, though   35
 Thy Humane Being did from David flow.

Hence thou both Lord, and Son of David art,
 Him Being gav'st, and Being tookst of him.
This doth unbolt the Doore, and light impart
 To shew the nature of this wondrous thing.   40
 Hence two best natures do appeare to stand
 United in thy Person hand in hand.

My blessed Lord, thou art like none indeed.
 Godhead, and Manhood harmonize in thee.
Hence thou alone wee mediator read,   45
 'Tween God, and Man, and setst Gods Children free
 From all Gods wrath, and wholy them restore
 Into that Favour, which they lost before.

Hence give thou me true Faith in thee to have:
 Make me thy branch, be thou my root thyselfe, 50
And let thy Grace root in my heart, I Crave
 And let thy purchase be my proper Wealth:
 And when this Sweet hath in my heart full Sway
 My sweetest musick shall thy praise display.

38 *gav'st*] orig: giv'st 48 *that*] orig: this

Isa. 22:22: "And the key of the house of David will I lay upon his shoulder;
so he shall open, and none shall shut; and he shall shut, and none shall open."
 27–28: And by thy Clew . . . twine. Cf. Herbert's "The Pearl," lines 37–40:

  Yet through these labyrinths, not my groveling wit,
  But thy silk twist let down from heav'n to me,
  Did both conduct and teach me, how by it
   To climbe to thee.

114. Meditation. Rev: 22.16. The bright and morning Star.

9. 6m [Aug.] 1713. Pub. ETG.

A Star, Bright Morning Star, the shining Sun
    Of Righteousness, in Heaven Lord thou art.
Thou pilotst us by night, which being run
    Away, thou bidst all darkness to depart.
    The Morning Star peeps up an usher gay   5
    'Fore th'Sun of Righteousness to grace the day.

All men benighted are by fall, and Sin:
    Thou Graces pole star art to pilote's from it:
The night of Sorrow and Desertion spring,
    Thou morning Starr dost rise, and not a Comet.   10
    This night expired now, is dead and gone:
    The Day Spring of sweet Comfort cometh on.

The Morning Star doth rise, Dews gracious fall:
    And spirituall Herbs, and sweet Celestiall flowers
Sprinkled therewith most fragrantly do call   15
    The Day Star up, with golden Curls, and Towers
    Put back the Curtains of the azure skies
    And gilde the aire while that the Sun doth rise.

The night of Persecution up arose.
    Not Even, but the morning star there to   20
Soon riseth: vant ill looks: the last Cock Crows
    The Morning Star up: out the Sun doth go.
    Farewell darke night, Welcome bright gracious day.
    As Joy Divine comes on, Griefe goes away.

This world's a night-shade, or a pitchy night,   25
    All Canopi'de with storms and Cloudes all darke.
Sending out thunders, Lightnings and with might,

16 *Towers*] orig: Showers

But thou our Pole star art, which we must marke.
While th'morning Star hands dawning light along:
Let Grace sing now, Birds singing time is come.   30

Whilst thou, my Pole-star shinst my Lord, on mee
    Let my poore pinnace saile thereby aright,
Through this darke night untill its harbor bee
    The Daystars bay, the spring of dayly light,
    The Usher bidding of the night, good night   35
    And Day, Good morrow lightend with delight.

If I by thee, my Pole star, steere aright
    Through this dark night of foule hard weather here
My Vessell safely to the harbour bright
    Of thee, my Morning Star, ere shining clear.   40
    I then shall soon Eternal Day possess
    Wherever shines the Sun of Righteousness.

Grant me, my Lord, by thee, my Star to steere.
    Through this darke vale of tears untill I meet,
Thee here my morning Star outshining cleare,   45
    Shewing my night is past, and day doth peep.
    When thou my Sun of Righteousness makst day.
    My Harp shall thy Eternall praise then play.

Thou Jacobs Star, in's Horizon didst rise.
    And fix't in Heaven, Heavens Steeridge Star.   50
To steer poor sinners out from Enemies
    Coasts unto Graces Realm, (Best State by far).
    Thou sentst a star in th'East to lead Wise men
    Thence to thyselfe, when born in Bethlehem.

The golden locks of this bright star, I pray,   55
    Make leade us from sins quarters to the Coast
Of Graces tillage: darkness from, to th'Bay
    Of Consolation and the Holy Ghost.
    And from this Vale of tears to Glory bright
    Where our tunde breath shall ne're be Choakt by th'night.

29 *th'morning*] PW th morning   31 *shinst*] orig: shineth   57 *darkness
from*] orig: from affection

146. Meditation. Cant. 6.13. Return, oh Shulamite, return return.

11. 11m [Jan.] *1718.*

My Deare Deare Lord, I know not what to say:
 Speech is too Course a web for me to cloath
My Love to thee in or it to array,
 Or make a mantle. Wouldst thou not such loath?
 Thy Love to mee's too great, for mee to shape   5
 A Vesture for the Same at any rate.

When as thy Love doth Touch my Heart down tost
 It tremblingly runs, seeking thee its all,
And as a Child when it his nurse hath lost
 Runs seeking her, and after her doth Call.   10
 So when thou hidst from me, I seek and sigh.
 Thou saist return return Oh Shulamite.

Rent out on Use thy Love thy Love I pray.
 My Love to thee shall be thy Rent and I
Thee Use on Use, Intrest on intrest pay.   15
 There's none Extortion in such Usury.

I'le pay thee Use on Use for't and therefore
 Thou shalt become the greatest Usurer.
But yet the principall I'le neer restore.
 The Same is thine and mine. We shall not Jar.   20
 And so this blessed Usury shall be
 Most profitable both to thee and mee.

And shouldst thou hide thy shining face most fair
 Away from me. And in a sinking wise

146. Meditation] PW 137. Meditation   2 *too*] PW to   3 *or it to array*]
orig: Such stuff I loath, or thee   4 *Wouldst*] PW wouldst
loath?] PW loath   9 *lost*] Conj.   13–16 a four line stanza
13 *thy Love I*] orig: my Lord I   14 *and*] orig: I pay and

My trembling beating heart brought nigh t'dispare   25
      Should cry to thee and in a trembling guise
      Lord quicken it. Drop in its Eares delight
      Saying Return, Return my Shulamite.

27 *Drop*] PW drop

Gods Determinations touch-

ing his Elect: and

The Elects Combat in their

Conversion, and

Coming up to God in Christ

together with the

Comfortable Effects thereof.

The Preface.

Undated. On the title page:
"This a MS of the Revd. Edward Taylor of Westfield, who died there A.D. 1728, or 1729. Aetat. circa 88, velsupra. Attest Ezra Stiles D.D. His Grandson 1786." Below these lines, in another hand: "Henry W. Taylor his Great Grandson 1868."

Infinity, when all things it beheld
In Nothing, and of Nothing all did build,
Upon what Base was fixt the Lath, wherein
He turn'd this Globe, and riggalld it so trim?
Who blew the Bellows of his Furnace Vast?   5
Or held the Mould wherein the world was Cast?
Who laid its Corner Stone? Or whose Command?
Where stand the Pillars upon which it stands?
Who Lac'de and Fillitted the earth so fine,
With Rivers like green Ribbons Smaragdine?   10
Who made the Sea's its Selvedge, and it locks
Like a Quilt Ball within a Silver Box?
Who Spread its Canopy? Or Curtains Spun?
Who in this Bowling Alley bowld the Sun?
Who made it always when it rises set   15
To go at once both down, and up to get?
Who th'Curtain rods made for this Tapistry?
Who hung the twinckling Lanthorns in the Sky?
Who? who did this? or who is he? Why, know
Its Onely Might Almighty this did doe.   20
His hand hath made this noble worke which Stands
His Glorious Handywork not made by hands.
Who spake all things from nothing; and with ease
Can speake all things to nothing, if he please.
Whose Little finger at his pleasure Can   25
Out mete ten thousand worlds with halfe a Span:
Whose Might Almighty can by half a looks
Root up the rocks and rock the hills by th'roots.
Can take this mighty World up in his hande,
And shake it like a Squitchen or a Wand.   30

15 *always*] PW alway 16 *down, and up*] orig: a going and up

7 *ff.:* See Job 38:4–8.

Whose single Frown will make the Heavens shake
Like as an aspen leafe the Winde makes quake.
Oh! what a might is this Whose single frown
Doth shake the world as it would shake it down?
Which All from Nothing fet, from Nothing, All: 35
Hath All on Nothing set, lets Nothing fall.
Gave All to nothing Man indeed, whereby
Through nothing man all might him Glorify.
In Nothing then imbosst the brightest Gem
More pretious than all pretiousness in them.   40
But Nothing man did throw down all by Sin:
And darkened that lightsom Gem in him.
            That now his Brightest Diamond is grown
            Darker by far than any Coalpit Stone.

The Effects of Mans Apostacy.

            While man unmarr'd abode his Spirits all
In Vivid hue were active in their hall,
This Spotless Body, here and there mentain
Their traffick for the Universall gain.
Till Sin Beat up for Volunteers. Whence came   5
A thousand Griefs attending on the same.
Which march in ranck, and file, proceed to make
A Battery, and the fort of Life to take.
Which when the Centinalls did spy, the Heart
Did beate alarum up in every part.   10
The Vitall Spirits apprehend thereby
Exposde to danger great the suburbs ly,
The which they do desert, and speedily
The Fort of Life the Heart, they Fortify.
The Heart beats up still by her Pulse to Call   15

11: Vitall Spirits. The vital spirits in 17th-century psychology were com-
posed of airy and fiery matter, which resided in the heart and were dis-
persed by the arteries; they helped carry out the decisions of the sensible soul.

Out of the outworks her train Souldiers all
Which quickly come hence: now the Looks grow pale
Limbs feeble too: the Enemies prevaile.
Do scale the Outworks where there's Scarce a Scoute
That can be Spi'de sent from the Castle out.   20

    Man at a muze, and in a maze doth stand,
While Feare the Generall of all the Band
Makes inroads on him: then he Searches why,
And quickly Findes God stand as Enemy.
Whom he would fain subdue, yet Fears affright   25
In Varnishing their Weapons in his Sight.
Troops after troops, Bands after Bands do high,
Armies of armed terrours drawing nigh:
He lookes within, and sad amazement's there,
Without, and all things fly about his Eares.   30
Above, and sees Heaven falling on his pate,
Below and spies th'Infernall burning lake,
Before and sees God storming in his Face,
Behinde, and spies Vengeance persues his trace.
To stay he dares not, go he knows not where   35
From God he can't, to God he dreads for Feare.
To Dy he Dreads; For Vengeance's due to him;
To Live he must not, Death persues his Sin:
He Knows not what to have, nor what to loose
Nor what to do, nor what to take or Choose: 40
Thus over Stretcht upon the Wrack of Woe,
Bereav'd of Reason, he proceeds now so,
Betakes himself unto his Heels in hast,
Runs like a Madman till his Spirits wast,
Then like a Child that fears the Poker Clapp   45
Him on his face doth on his Mothers lap
Doth hold his breath, lies still for fear least hee
Should by his breathing lowd discover'd bee.
Thus on his face doth see no outward thing
But still his heart for Feare doth pant within.   50
Doth make its Drummer beate so loud it makes

17 *hence:*] PW hence   27 *troops,*] PW troops.

The Very Bulworks of the City Quake:
Yet gets no aide: Wherefore the Spirits they
Are ready all to leave, and run away.
For Nature in this Pannick feare scarce gives   55
Him life enough, to let him feel he lives.
Yet this he easily feels, he liveth in
A Dying Life, and Living Death by Sin,
Yet in this Lifeless life wherein he lies,
Some Figments of Excuses doth devise   60
That he may Something say, when rain'd, although
His Say seems nothing, and for nought will go.
But while he Sculking on his face close lies
Espying nought, the Eye Divine him spies.
Justice and Mercy then fall to debate   65
Concerning this poore fallen mans estate,
Before the Bench of the Almighties Breast
Th' ensuing Dialogues hint their Contest.

66 *fallen mans*] orig: mans fallen

A Dialogue between Justice and Mercy.

Offended Justice comes in fiery Rage,
    Like to a Rampant Lyon new assaild,
Array'd in Flaming fire now to engage,
    With red hot burning Wrath poore man unbaild.
    In whose Dread Vissage sinfull man may spy   5
    Confounding, Rending, Flaming Majesty.

Out Rebell, out (saith Justice) to the Wrack,
    Which every joynt unjoynts, doth streatch, and strain,
Where Sinews tortur'de are untill they Crack
    And Flesh is torn asunder grain by grain.   10
    What Spit thy Venom in my Face! Come out
    To handy gripes seing thou art so stoute.

Mercy takes up the Challenge, Comes as meeke
    As any Lamb, on mans behalfe, she speakes
Like new blown pincks, breaths out perfumed reech   15
    And doth revive the heart before it breaks.
    Justice (saith Mercy) if thou Storm so fast,
    Man is but dust that flies before thy blast.

JUSTICE

My Essence is ingag'de, I cannot bate,
    Justice not done no Justice is; and hence   20
I cannot hold off of the Rebells pate
    The Vengeance he halls down with Violence.
    If Justice wronged be she must revenge:
    Unless a way be found to make all friends.

MERCY

My Essence is engag'de pitty to show.   25
    Mercy not done no Mercy is. And hence
I'le put my shoulders to the burden so
    Halld on his head with hands of Violence.
    As Justice justice evermore must doe:
    So Mercy Mercy evermore must show.   30

JUSTICE

I'le take thy Bond: But know thou this must doe.
    Thou from thy Fathers bosom must depart:

8 *unjoynts*] orig: doth unjoynts   11 *Face!*] PW Face

And be incarnate like a slave below
> Must pay mans Debts unto the utmost marke.
> Thou must sustain that burden, that will make   35
> The Angells sink into th' Infernall lake.

Nay on thy shoulders bare must beare the smart
> Which makes the Stoutest Angell buckling cry
Nay makes thy Soule to Cry through griefe of heart,
> ELI, ELI, LAMA SABACHTANI.   40
> If this thou wilt, come then, and do not spare.
> Beare up the Burden on thy Shoulders bare.

MERCY

All this I'le do, and do it o're and o're,
> Before my Clients Case shall ever faile.
I'le pay his Debt, and wipe out all his Score   45
> And till the pay day Come I'le be his baile.
> I Heaven, and Earth do on my shoulders beare,
> Yet down I'le throw them all rather than Spare.

JUSTICE

Yet notwithstanding still this is too Small,
> Although there was a thousand times more done.   50
If sinless man did, sinfull man will fall:
> If out of debt, will on a new score run.
> Then stand away, and let me strike at first:
> For better now, than when he's at the Worst.

MERCY

If more a thousand times too little bee   55
> Ten thousand times yet more than this I'le do:
I'le free him from his Sin, and Set him free
> From all those faults the which he's subject to.
> Then Stand away, and strike not at the first.
> He'l better grow when he is at the worst.   60

JUSTICE

Nay, this ten thousand times as much can still
> Confer no hony to the Sinners hive.

34 *unto the utmost*] PW unto utmost

40: ELI, ELI, LAMA SABACHTANI. Cf. Matt. 27:46.

For man though shrived throughly from all ill
   His Righteousness is merely negative.
The Though none be damnd but such as sin imbrace: 65
   Yet none are sav'd without Inherent Grace.

MERCY

What, though ten thousand times, too little bee?
   I will ten thousand thousand times more do.
I will not onely from his sin him free,
   But fill him with Inherent grace also.   70
   Though none are Sav'd that wickedness imbrace.
   Yet none are Damn'd that have Inherent Grace.

JUSTICE

Yet this ten thousand thousand times more shall,
   Though Doubled o're, and o're for little stands.
The Righteousness of God should be his all   75
   The which he cannot have for want of hands.
   Then though he's spar'de at first, at last he'l fall
   For want of hands to hold himselfe withall.

MERCY

Though this ten thousand thousand times much more
   Though doubled o're and o're for little go,   80
I'le double still its double o're and ore
   And trible that untill I make it do.

66, 72: *Inherent Grace*, grace which sanctifies the inner man. "There is a
double state of grace, one adherent, (which some not unfitly call federall
grace) sanctifying to the purifying of the flesh, Hebr. 9:13, another inherent,
sanctifying the inner man. And of this latter there be two sorts, one wherein
persons in Covenant are sanctified by common graces which make them
serviceable and useful in their callings, as Saul, Jehu, Judas, and Demas, and
such like hypocrites. Another whereby Persons in Covenant are sanctified
unto union and communion with Christ and his members in a way of re-
generation and salvation." From John Cotton's "The Grounds and Ends of
the Baptisme of the Children of the Faithful," p. 43, as quoted in Peter Y.
De Jong, *The Covenant Idea in New England Theology, 1620–1847* (Grand
Rapids, Mich., Erdmans, 1945), pp. 88–89. It is clear from the context that
Taylor is using *inherent grace* to mean 'saving grace' and not 'common grace.'

I'le make him hands of Faith to hold full fast.
Spare him at first, then he'l not fall at last.

For by these hands he'l lay his Sins Upon   85
    The Scape Goats head, o're whom he shall **Confess**
And with these hands he rightly shall put on
    My milkwhite Robe of Lovely Righteousness.
    Now Justice on, thy Will fulfilled bee.
    Thou dost no wrong: the Sinner's just like thee.   90

JUSTICE

If so, its so: then I'l his Quittance seale:
    Or shall accuse myselfe as well as him:
If so, I Justice shall of Justice faile
    Which if I do, Justice herselfe should sin.
    Justice unspotted is, and therefore must,   95
    * * * * * * * * * * *

MERCY

I do foresee Proud man will me abuse,
    He'th broke his Legs, yets Legs his stilts must bee:
And I may stand untill the Chilly Dews
    Do pearle my Locks before he'l stand on mee.   100
    For set a Beggar upon horseback, see
    He'll ride as if no man so good as hee.

JUSTICE

And I foresee Proude man will me abuse.
    Judging his Shekel is the Sanctuaries:
He on his durty stilts to walk will Choose: 105
    Yea is as Clean as I, and nothing Varies
    Although his Shekel is not Silver good
    And's tilting stilts do stick within the mudd.

MERCY

But most he'l me abuse, I feare, for still
    Some will have Farms to farm, some wives to wed: 110

97 In PW this stanza begins a new page at the top of which is written: *A*
Dialogue between $\begin{cases} \textit{Mercy } \textit{\&} \\ \textit{Justice} \end{cases}$

   83: hands of Faith. The phrase occurs in Herbert's "The Sacrifice," lines
45–46.   101 *see*] orig: hee

Some beasts to buy; and I must waite their Will.
> Though while they scrape their naile, or scratch their head
> Nay though with Cap in hand I Wooe them long
> They'l whistle out their Whistle e're they'l come.

JUSTICE

I see I'st be abus'de by greate, and small:
> And most will count me blinde, or will not see:
Me leaden heel'd, with iron hands they'l Call:
> Or am unjust, or they more just than mee.
> And while they while away their Mercy so,
> They set their bristles up at Justice do.

MERCY

I feare the Humble Soul will be too shie;
> Judging my Mercy lesser than his Sin.
Inlarging this, but lessening that thereby.
> 'S if Mercy would not Mercy be to him.
> Alas! poore Heart! how art thou damnifide,
> By Proud Humility, and Humble Pride?

JUSTICE

The Humble Soul deales worse with me, doth Cry
> If I be just, I'le on him Vengeance take
As if I su'de Debtor, and Surety
> And double Debt and intrest too would rake.
> If Justice sue the Bonds that Cancelld are
> Sue Justice then before a juster bar.

MERCY

But in this Case alas, what must be done
> That haughty souls may humble be, and low?
That Humble souls may suck the Hony Comb?
> And thou for Justice, I for Mercy go?
> This Query weighty is, Lets therefore shew
> What must be done herein by me, and you.

JUSTICE

Lest that the Soule in Sin securely ly,
> And do neglect Free Grace, I'le steping in

115

120

125

130

135

140

130 *rake*] orig: scrape

Convince him by the Morall Law, whereby
    Ile'st se in what a pickle he is in.
For all he hath, for nothing stand it shall
    If of the Law one hair breadth short it fall.

MERCY

And lest the Soule should quite discourag'de stand   145
    I will step in, and smile him in the face,
Nay I to him will hold out in my hand
    The golden scepter of my Rich-Rich Grace.
    Intreating him with smiling lips most cleare
    At Court of Justice in my robes t'appeare.   150

JUSTICE

If any after Satans Pipes do Caper
    Red burning Coales from hell in Wrath I gripe,
And make them in his face with Vengeance Vaper,
    Untill he dance after the Gospell Pipe.
    Whose Sun is Sin, when Sin in Sorrows shrow'd,   155
    Their Sun of Joy sets in a grievous Cloud.

MERCY

When any such are startled from ill,
    And cry help, help, with tears, I will advance
The Musick of the Gospell Minsterill,
    Whose strokes they strike, and tunes exactly dance.   160
    Who mourn when Justice frowns, when Mercie playes
    Will to her sounding Viall Chant out Praise.

JUSTICE

The Works of Merit-Mongers I will weigh
    Within the Ballance of the sanctuary:
Their Matter, and their Manner I will lay   165
    Unto the Standard-Rule t'see how they Vary.
    Whosever trust doth to his golden deed
    Doth rob a barren Garden for a Weed.

MERCY

Yet if they'l onely on my Merits trust
    They'st in Gods Paradise themselves solace,   170

156 *sets*] PW set orig: laid[?]

Their beauteous garden knot I'le also thrust
 With Royall Slips, Sweet Flowers, and Herbs of Grace.
 Their Knots I'le weed, to give a spangling show
 In Order: and perfumes shall from them flow.

JUSTICE

Those that are ignorant, and do not know   175
 What meaneth Sin, nor what means Sanctity,
I will Convince that all save Saints must go
 Into hot fire, and brimston there to fry.
 Whose Pains hot scalding boyling Lead transcends,
 But evermore adds more and never Ends.   180

MERCY

Though simple, learn of mee. I will you teach,
 True Wisdom for your Souls Felicity,
Wisdom Extending to the Endless reach
 And blissfull end of all Eternity.
 Wisdom that doth all else transcend as far   185
 As Sol's bright Glory doth a painted Star.

JUSTICE

You that Extenuate your sins, come see
 Them in Gods multiplying Glass: for here
Your little sins will just like mountains bee,
 And as they are just so they Will appeare.   190
 Who doth a little sin Extenuate
 Extends the same, and two thereof doth make.

MERCY

A little sin is sin: and is Sin Small?
 Excuse it not, but aggrivate it more.
Lest that your little Sin asunder fall   195
 And two become, each bigger than before.
 Who scants his sin will scarce get grace to save.
 For little Sins, but little pardons have.

JUSTICE

Unto the Humble Humble Soule I say,
 Cheer up, poor Heart, for satisfi'de am I.   200
178 *brimston*] PW brinston

For Justice nothing to thy Charge can lay,
    Thou hast Acquittance in thy surety.
    The Court of Justice thee acquits: therefore
    Thou to the Court of Mercy are bound o're.

MERCY

My Dove, come hither linger not, nor stay.   205
    Though thou among the pots hast lain, behold
Thy Wings with Silver Colours I'le o're lay:
    And lay thy feathers o're with yellow gold.
    Justice in Justice must adjudge thee just:
    If thou in Mercies Mercy put thy trust.   210

Mans Perplexity when calld to an account.

    Justice, and Mercy ending their Contest,
In such a sort, now thrust away the Desk.
And other titles come in Majesty,
All to attend Almighty royally.
Which sparkle out, call man to come and tell   5
How he his Cloath defild and how he fell?

    He on his skirts with Guilt, and Filth out peeps
With Pallid Pannick Fear upon his Cheeks,
With Trembling joynts, and Quiverring Lips, doth quake
As if each Word he was about to make,   10
Should hackt a sunder be, and Chopt as small
As Pot herbs for the pot before they Call
Upon the Understanding to draw neer,
By tabbering on the Drum within the eare.
His Spirits are so low they'l scarce afford   15
Him Winde enough to wast a single word
Over the Tongue unto one's eare: yet loe,
This tale at last with sobs, and sighs lets goe,
Saying, my Mate procurde me all this hurt,
Who threw me in my best Cloaths in the Dirt.   20

Thus man hath lost his Freehold by his ill:
Now to his Land Lord tenent is at Will.
And must the Tenement keep in repare
Whate're the ruins, and the Charges are.
Nay, and must mannage war against his Foes. 25
Although ten thousand strong, he must oppose.
Some seeming Friends prove secret foes, which will
Thrust Fire i'th'thatch, nay stob, Cut throate and kill.
Some undermine the Walls: Some knock them down,
And make them tumble on the Tenents Crown. 30

He's then turnd out of Doors, and so must stay,
Till's house be rais'd against the Reckoning day.

Gods Selecting Love in the Decree.

Man in this Lapst Estate at very best,
A Cripple is and footsore, sore opprest,
Can't track Gods Trace but Pains, and pritches prick
Like poyson'd splinters sticking in the Quick.
Yet jims in th'Downy path with pleasures spread 5
As 'twas below him on the Earth to tread.
Can prance, and trip within the way of Sin,
Yet in Gods path moves not a little wing.

Almighty this foreseing, and withall
That all this stately worke of his would fall 10
Tumble, and Dash to pieces Did in lay
Before it was too late for it a Stay.
Doth with his hands hold, and uphold the same.
Hence his Eternall Purpose doth proclaim.
Whereby transcendently he makes to shine
Transplendent Glory in his Grace Divine. 15
Almighty makes a mighty sumptuous feast:
Doth make the Sinfull Sons of men his guests.
But yet in speciall Grace he hath to some,

(Because they Cripples are, and Cannot come)   20
He sends a Royall Coach forth for the same,
To fetch them in, and names them name by name.
A Royall Coach whose scarlet Canopy
O're silver Pillars, doth expanded ly:
All bottomed with purest gold refin'de,   25
And inside o're with lovely Love all linde.
Which Coach indeed you may exactly spy
All mankinde splits in a Dicotomy.
  For all ride to the feast that favour finde.
  The rest do slite the Call and stay behind.   30

  O! Honour! Honour! Honours! Oh! the Gain!
And all such Honours all the saints obtain.
It is the Chariot of the King of Kings:
That all who Glory gain, to glory brings.
Whose Glory makes the rest, (when spi'de) beg in.   35
Some gaze and stare. Some stranging at the thing.
Some peep therein; some rage thereat, but all,
Like market people seing on a stall,
Some rare Commodity Clap hands thereon
And Cheapen't hastily, but soon are gone.   40
For hearing of the price, and wanting pay
Do pish thereat, and Coily pass away.
So hearing of the terms, whist, they'le abide
At home before they'l pay so much to ride.
But they to whom its sent had rather all,   45
Dy in this Coach, than let their journey fall.
They up therefore do get, and in it ride
Unto Eternal bliss, while down the tide
The other scull unto eternall woe;
By letting slip their former journey so.   50
For when they finde the Silver Pillars fair
The Golden bottom pav'de with Love as rare,
To be the Spirits sumptuous building cleare,
When in the Soul his Temple he doth reare
And Purple Canopy to bee (they spy)   55
All Graces Needlework and Huswifry;

Their stomachs rise: these graces will not down.
They think them Slobber Sawces: therefore frown.
They loath the same, wamble keck, heave they do:
Their Spleen thereat out at their mouths they throw,　　　60
Which while they do, the Coach away doth high
Wheeling the Saints in't to eternall joy.
　　　These therefore and their journey now do come
　　　For to be treated on, and Coacht along.

The Frowardness of the Elect in the Work of Conversion.

　　　Those upon whom Almighty doth intend
His all Eternall Glory to expend,
Lulld in the lap of sinfull Nature snugg,
Like Pearls in Puddles cover'd ore with mudd:
Whom, if you search, perhaps some few you'l finde,　　　5
That to notorious Sins were ne're inclinde.
Some shunning some, some most, some greate, some small.
Some this, that or the other, some none at all.
But all, or almost all you'st easly finde,
To all, or almost all Defects inclinde　　　10
To Revell with the Rabble rout who say
Let's hiss this Piety out of our Day.
And those whose frame is made of finer twine
Stand further off from Grace than Wash from Wine.
Those who suck Grace from th'breast, are nigh as rare　　　15
As Black Swans that in milkwhite Rivers are.
Grace therefore calls them all, and sweetly wooes.
Some won come in, the rest as yet refuse,
And run away: Mercy persues apace,
Then some Cast down their arms, Cry Quarter, Grace.　　　20
Some Chased out of breath drop down with feare

Perceiving the persuer drawing neer.
The rest persude, divide into two rancks
And this way one, and that the other prancks.

    Then in comes Justice with her forces by her,   25
And doth persue as hot as sparkling fire.
The right wing then begins to fly away.
But in the streights strong Baracadoes lay.
They're therefore forc'd to face about, and have
Their spirits Queld, and therefore Quarter Crave.   30
These Captivde thus: justice persues the Game
With all her troops to take the other train.
Which being Chast in a Peninsula
And followd close, they finde no other way
To make escape, but t'rally round about: 35
Which if it faile them that they get not out,
They're forct into the Infernall Gulfe alive
Or hackt in pieces are or took Captive.
But spying Mercy stand with Justice, they
Cast down their Weapons, and for Quarter pray.   40
Their lives are therefore spar'de, yet they are ta'ne
As th'other band: and prisoners must remain.
And so they must now Justice's Captives bee
On Mercies Quarrell: Mercy sets not free.

    Their former Captain is their Deadly foe.   45
    And now, poor souls, they know not what to do.

Satans Rage at them in their Conversion.

    Grace by the Aide of Justice wins the day.
And Satans Captives Captives leads away,
Who finding of their former Captains Cheates,

24 *other*] PW othe   37 *They're forct into*] orig:
They forct are into   41 *Their*] PW There

To be Rebellion, him a Rebell Greate,
Against his Rightfull Sovereign, by whom   5
He shortly shall to Execution Come,
They sue for Pardon do at Mercies Doore
Bewailing of that war they wag'd before.

    Then Satan in a red-hot firy rage
Comes belling, roaring ready to ingage   10
To rend, and tare in pieces small all those,
Whom in the former Quarrell he did lose.
But's boyling Poyson'd madness, being by
A shield Divine repelld, he thus lets fly.
You Rebells all, I Will you gripe, and fist.   15
I'le make my Jaws a Mill to grin'de such Grists.
Look not for Mercy, Mercy well doth see
You'l be more false to her than Unto mee.
You're the first Van that fell; you're Traitors, Foes,
And Unto such Grace will no trust repose.   20
You Second Ranck are Cowards, if Christ Come
With you to fight his field, you'l from him run.
You third are feeble-hearted; if Christs Crown
Must stand or fall by you, you'l fling it down.
You last did last the longest: but being ta'ne   25
Are Prisoners made, and Jayle Birds must remain.
It had been better on the Turff to dy
Then in such Deadly slavery to ly.
Nay, at the best you all are Captive Foes.
Will Wisdom have no better aid than those?   30
Trust to a forced Faith? To hearts well known
To be (like yours) to all black Treason Prone?
For when I shall let fly at you, you'l fall:
And so fall foule Upon your Generall.
Hee'l Hang you up alive then; by and by.   35
And I'le you wrack too for your treachery.
He will become your foe, you then shall bee

7 *sue*] PW shew
15 *all, I*] orig: all all, I I   19 *fell;*] PW fell   20 *Grace*] orig: Grace Grace

Flanckt of by him before, behinde by mee.
You'st stand between us two our spears to dunce.
Can you Offend and Fence both wayes at once?   40
You'l then have sharper service than the Whale,
Between the Sword fish, and the Threshers taile.
You'l then be mawld worse than the hand thats right
Between the heads of Wheelhorn'd Rams that fight.
        What will you do when you shall squezed bee   45
        Between such Monstrous Gyants Jaws as Wee?

The Souls Address to Christ against these Assaults.

Thou Gracious Lord, Our Honour'd Generall
        May't suite thy Pleasure never to impute,
It our Presumption, when presume we shall
        To line thy Noble Ears with our Greate suite?
        With ropes about our necks we come and lie,   5
        Before thy pleasure's Will, and Clemency.

When we unto the height of Sin were grown,
        We sought thy Throne to overthrow; but were
In this our seeking Quickly overthrown:
        A Mass of Mercy in thy face shone cleare.   10
        We quarter had: though if we'de had our share
        We had been quarter'd up as Rebells are.

Didst thou thy Grace on Treators arch expend?
        And force thy Favour on thy stubborn Foe?
And hast no Favour for a failing Friend,   15
        That in thy Quarrell trippeth with his toe?
        If thus it be, thy Foes Speed better far,
        Than do thy Friends, that go to fight thy War.

39 *You'st*] PW You st   46 *Wee?*] PW Wee.

    42 Cf. Donne, *Progresse of the Soule*, line 351: "The flaile-finn'd Thresher,
and steel-beak'd Sword-fish"

But is it as the Adversary said?
    Dost thou not hear his murdering Canons roare?   20
What Vollies fly? What Ambushments are laid?
    And still his stratagems grow more, and more.
      Lord, fright this frightfull Enemy away.
      A Trip makes not a Traitor: Spare we pray.

And if thou still suspect us come, and search: 25
    Pluck out our hearts and search them narrowly.
If Sin allow'd in any Corner learch,
      We beg a Pardon, and a Remedy.
      Lord Gybbit up such Rebells Arch Who do
      Set ope the back doore to thy Cursed foe.   30

Christs Reply.

    I am a Captain to your Will.
    You found me Gracious, so shall still,
Whilst that my Will is your Design.
    If that you stick unto my Cause
    Opposing whom oppose my Laws   5
I am your own, and you are mine.

    The weary Soule I will refresh
    And Ease him of his heaviness.
Who'le slay a Friend? And save a Foe?
    Who in my War do take delight,   10
    Fight not for prey, but Pray, and Fight
Although they slip, I'le mercy show.

    Then Credit not your Enemy
    Whose Chiefest daintie is a lie.
I will you comfort sweet extend.   15
    Behold I am a sun and shield

4 *If that you stick*] PW If you that stick orig: If you that stick stick **Close**

And a sharp sword to win the field.
I'l surely Crown you in the End.

His murdering Canons which do roare
And Engins though as many more   20
Shoot onely aire: no Bullets fly.
Unless you dare him with your Crest,
And ope to him the naked breast,
Small Execution's done thereby.

To him that smiteth hip, and thigh,   25
My foes as his: Walks warily,
I'le give him Grace: he'st give me praise.
Let him whose foot doth hit a Stone
Through weakeness, not rebellion
Not faint, but think on former dayes.   30

The Effect of this Reply with a fresh Assault from Satan.

Like as the Shining Sun, we do behold,
Is hot, and Light, when th'Weather waxeth Cold:
Like as brave Valour in a Captain steels
His Armies Courage, when their spirit reels.
As Aqua Vitae when the Vitalls faile:
So doth this speech the Drooping Soul availe.
How doth this Answer Mercies Captives Cheer?
Yet those whom Justice took still Drooping were,
And in this nick of time the Foe through spite
Doth like a glorious Angell seem of Light.   10
Yet though he painteth o're his Velvet smut.
He Cannot yet Conceal his Cloven foot.
Hence in their joy he straweth poyson on,
Those Objects that their senses feed upon.

20 *Engins*] PW Engims

By some odde straggling thought up poyson flies   15
Into the heart: and through the Eares, and Eyes.
Which sick, lies gasping: Other thoughts then high
To hold its head; and Venom'd are thereby.
Hence they are influenc't to selfe Ends: these darts
Strike secret swelling Pride up in their hearts.   20
    The which he fosters till the bladder flies
    In pieces; then joy lies agast and dies.

    Now Satan counts the Cast his own thus thrown:
Off goes the Angels Coate, on goes his own.
With Griping Paws, and Goggling Eyes draws nigher,   25
Like some fierce Shagg'd Red Lion, belching fire:
Doth stoutly Charge them home that they did fall
And breake the Laws of their Choice Admirall.
And his attend: and so were his. For they
Must needs be his whom ever they obey.   30
Thus he in frightfull wise assaults them all,
Then one by one doth singly on them fall,
    Doth winnow them with all his wiles, he can,
    As Wheate is winnow'd with the Sieve, and Fan.

First Satans Assault against those that first Came up to Mercys terms.

SATAN

Soon ripe, soon rot. Young Saint, Old Divell. Loe
Why to an Empty Whistle did you goe?
What Come Uncalld? And Run unsent for? Stay
Its Childrens Bread: Hands off: out, Dogs, away.

SOUL

It's not an Empty Whistle: yet withall,   5
And if it be a Whistle, then a Call:
A Call to Childrens Bread, which take we may.
Thou onely art the Dog whipt hence away.

SATAN

If I then you: for by Apostasy
You are the Imps of Death as much as I.   10
And Death doth reign o're you through Sin: you see,
As well as Sin doth reign to Death in mee.

SOUL

It is deni'd: Gods Mercy taking place,
Prepared Grace for us, and us for Grace.
And Graces Coach in Grace hath fetcht us in,   15
Unto her Feast. We shall not dy in Sin.

SATAN

If it be so, your sins are Crucifide:
Which if they be, they struggl'd when they di'de.
It is not so with you: you judge before
You felt them gird, you'de got them out of Doore.   20

SOUL

Mercy the Quartermaster speedily,
Did stifle Sin, and still its hidious Cry,
Whose Knife at first stuck in its heart to th'head:
That sin, before it hard did sprunt, fell dead.

SATAN

A mere Delusion! Nature shows that Life   25
Will strugle most upon the bloody Knife
And so will Sin. Nay Christ doth onely Call,
And offer ease to such as are in thrall.

SOUL

He offer'd unto mee, and I receiv'd
Of what hee wrought, I am not yet bereav'd.   30
Though Justice set Amercement on mee
Mercy hath took it off, and set me free.

SATAN

Is Mercy impudent? or Justice blinde?
I am to make distraint on thee Designd.

10 *much as I*] PW much I

34: distraint (see Glossary). Taylor, like Calvin, is fond of using legal terms
in defining God's relation to man.

The North must wake before the South proves Kind.   35
The Law must breake before the Gospell binde.

SOUL

But Giliads Balm, like Balsom heald my wound
Makes not the Patient sore, yet leaves him sound.
The Gospell did the Law prevent: my heart
Is therefore dresst from Sin: and did not smart.   40

SATAN

A likely thing! Oh shame! presume on Grace!
Here's Sin in Grain: it hath a Double Face.
Come, Come with mee I'le shew your Outs, and Inns,
Your Inside, and your out: your Holy things.
    For these I will anatomize then see,   45
    Believe your very Eyes, believe not mee.

The Accusation of the Inward Man.

    You want Cleare Spectacles: your eyes are dim:
Turn inside out: and turn your Eyes within.
Your sins like motes in th'sun do swim: nay see
Your Mites are Molehills, Molehills Mountains bee.
Your Mountain Sins do magnitude transcend: 5
Whose number's numberless, and do want end.
The Understandings dark, and therefore Will
Account of Ill for Good, and Good for ill.
As to a Purblinde man men oft appeare
Like Walking Trees within the Hemisphere.   10
So in the judgment Carnall things Excell:
Pleasures and Profits beare away the Bell.
The Will is hereupon perverted so,
It laquyes after ill, doth good foregoe.
The Reasonable Soule doth much delight   15
A Pickpack t'ride o'th'Sensuall Appitite.

5 do] orig: doth   6 do] orig: doth

And hence the heart is hardened and toyes,
With Love, Delight, and Joy, yea Vanities.

    Make but a thorow search, and you may spy
Your soul a trudging hard, though secretly
Upon the feet of your Affections mute.   20
And hankering after all forbidden fruite.
Ask but yourselfe in secret laying neer
Thy head thereto: 'twill Whisper in thine eare
That it is tickled much, though secretly.   25
And greatly itches after Vilany.
'Twill fleere thee in thy face, and though it say,
It must not tell, it scorns to tell thee nay.
But Slack the rains, and Come a Loophole lower:
You'l finde it was but Pen-coop't up before.
Nay, muster up your thoughts, and take the Pole   30
Of what walk in the Entry of your Soule
Which if you do, you certainly will finde
With Robbers, Cut-throats, Theives its mostly linde.
And hundred Roagues you'l finde, ly gaming there.   35
For one true man, that in that path appears.
Your True man too's oft footsore, sildom is,
Sound Winde, and Limb: and still to add to this,
He's but a Traviller within that Way:
Whereas the rest there pitch their Tents, and stay.   40
Nay, nay, what thoughts Unclean? Lacivious?
Blasphemous? Murderous? and Malicious?
Tyranick? Wrathfull? Atheistick rise
Of Evills New, and Old, of e'ry Sise?
These bed, and board here, make the heart a sty   45
Of all Abominable Brothlery.

      Then is it pure? is this the fruite of Grace?
      If so, how do yee: You and I Embrace.

The Outward Man accused.

Turn o're thy Outward man, and judge aright.
Doth not a Pagans Life out Shine thy Light?
Thy fleering Looks, thy Wanton Eyes, each part
Are Painted Sign-Post of a Wanton heart.
If thou art weigh'd in Golden Scales; Dost do   5
To others as thou wouldst be done unto?
Weigh weigh thy Words: thy Untruths, all which came
Out of thy mouth, and thou Confest the same.
Why did thy Tongue detract from any one,
Whisper such tales thou wouldst not have be known?   10
When thou was got in such a merry veane
How far didst thou exceed the golden mean?
When that thou wast at such a Boon, or Feast
Why didst thou rather ly, than lose thy jeast?
How wast thou tickled when thy droughty Eares   15
Allay'de their Thirst with filthy squibs, and jears?
Why didst thou glaver men of place? And why,
Scowle, Glout, and Frown, on honest Poverty?
Why did'st thou spend thy State in foolish prancks?
And Peacock up thyselfe above thy rancks?   20
Why thoughtst thyselfe out of the World as shut,
When not with others in the Cony Cut?
Hold up thy head, is't thus or no? if yea,
How then is all thy folly purgd away?
   If no, thy tongue belies itselfe, for loe   25
   Thou saidst thy heart was dresst from sin also.

The Soul accused in its Serving God.

When thou dost go to serve thy God, behold
What greate Distractions do thy Soule infold?
How thy Religious Worship's much abusde?
And with Confusion greate thy Soul's amus'de?
What thoughts to God on Errand dost thou send   5
That have not Sin therein, or in the End?
In Holy-Waters I delight to fish
For then I mudd them, or attain a Dish,
Of Holy things. I oft have Chiefest part,
And Cutting: nay do Carve the fat, and heart.   10
For in Gods worship still thy heart doth cling
Unto and follows toyish Earthly things.
And what thou offer'st God his Holy Eye
Sees, is an Offering of Hypocrisy.
And if thou saw'st no hell, nor heaven; I see,   15
My Soule for thine, thy Soule and mine agree.
What then's thy Love to God, and Piety?
Is it not selfish? And Comes in by th'by?
For selfe is all thine aim; not God thine end:
And what Delight hath he in such a friend?   20
Lip Love is little else, but such a ly,
As makes the matter but Hypocrisy.

What's thy Repentance? Can'st thou come and show
By those salt Rivers which do Ebb, and Flow
By th'motion of that Ocean Vast within,   25
Of pickled sorrow rising for thy Sin?
For Sin prooves very Costly unto all.
It Cost Saint Peter bitter tears, and Paul.
Thy joy is groundless, Faith is false, thy Hope
Presumption, and Desire is almost broke.   30
Zeale Wildfire is, thy Pray'res are sapless most,
Or like the Whistling of some Dead mans Ghost:

Thy Holy Conference is onely like
An Empty Voice that tooteth through a pipe.
Thy Soule doth peep out at thine Eares, and Eyes   35
To bless those bawbles that are earthly toyes.
But when Gods Words in at those Windows peepe
To kiss thy Soul, thy Soul lies dead asleep.
Examine but thy Conscience, her reply,
Will suite hereto: For Conscience dare not ly.   40
When did thine Eyes run down for sin as sin,
That thus thy heart runs up with joy to sing?
     Thy sins do sculk under a flowrisht paint.
     Hence thou a Sinner art, or I a Saint.

SOUL

Well, Satan, well: with thee I'le parle no more.   45
But do adjure thee hence: begone therefore.
If I as yet was thine, I thus do say
I from thy flag would quickly flag away.
     Begone therefore; to him I'le send a groane
     Against thee drawn, who makes my heart his Throne.   50

The Souls Groan to Christ for Succour.

Good Lord, behold this Dreadfull Enemy
     Who makes me tremble with his fierce assaults,
I dare not trust, yet feare to give the ly,
     For in my soul, my soul finds many faults.
     And though I justify myselfe to's face: 5
     I do Condemn myselfe before thy Grace.

He strives to mount my sins, and them advance
     Above thy Merits, Pardons, or Good Will
Thy Grace to lessen, and thy Wrath t'inhance
     As if thou couldst not pay the sinners bill.   10
     He Chiefly injures thy rich Grace, I finde
     Though I confess my heart to sin inclin'de.

Those Graces which thy Grace enwrought in mee,
    He makes as nothing but a pack of Sins.
He maketh Grace no grace, but Crueltie,
    Is Graces Honey Comb, a Comb of Stings?   15
      This makes me ready leave thy Grace and run.
      Which if I do, I finde I am undone.

I know he is thy Cur, therefore I bee
    Perplexed lest I from thy Pasture stray.
He bayghs, and barks so veh'mently at mee.   20
      Come rate this Cur, Lord, breake his teeth I pray.
      Remember me I humbly pray thee first.
      Then halter up this Cur that is so Curst.

Christs Reply.

Peace, Peace, my Hony, do not Cry,
My Little Darling, wipe thine eye,
    Oh Cheer, Cheer up, come see.
Is anything too deare, my Dove,
Is anything too good, my Love
    To get or give for thee?   5

If in the severall thou art
This Yelper fierce will at thee bark:
    That thou art mine this shows.
As Spot barks back the sheep again
Before they to the Pound are ta'ne,   10
    So he and hence 'way goes.

But yet this Cur that bayghs so sore
Is broken tootht, and muzzled sure,
    Fear not, my Pritty Heart.
His barking is to make thee Cling   15

5 *Is anything*] orig: I thinke   *too*] PW to

Close underneath thy Saviours Wing.
    Why did my sweeten start?

And if he run an inch too far,
I'le Check his Chain, and rate the Cur.   20
    My Chick, keep clost to mee.
The Poles shall sooner kiss, and greet
And Paralells shall sooner meet
    Than thou shalt harmed bee.

He seeks to aggrivate thy sin   25
And screw them to the highest pin,
    To make thy faith to quaile.
Yet mountain Sins like mites should show
And then these mites for naught should goe
    Could he but once prevaile.   30

I smote thy sins upon the Head.
They Dead'ned are, though not quite dead:
    And shall not rise again.
I'l put away the Guilt thereof,
And purge its Filthiness cleare off: 35
    My Blood doth out the stain.

And though thy judgment was remiss
Thy Headstrong Will too Wilfull is.
    I will Renew the same.
And though thou do too frequently   40
Offend as heretofore hereby
    I'l not severly blaim.

And though thy senses do inveagle
Thy Noble Soul to tend the Beagle,
    That t'hunt her games forth go.   45

45 *t'hunt*] PW t'hunts

    22–24: The Poles . . . harmed bee. Cf. Herbert's "The Search," lines 41–44:

    Thy will such a strange distance is,
        As that to it
    East and West touch, and poles do kisse,
        And parallels meet.

I'le Lure her back to me, and Change
Those fond Affections that do range
  As yelping beagles doe.

Although thy sins increase their race,
And though when thou hast sought for Grace,   50
  Thou fallst more than before
If thou by true Repentence Rise,
And Faith makes me thy Sacrifice,
  I'l pardon all, though more.

Though Satan strive to block thy way
By all his Stratagems he may: 55
  Come, come though through the fire.
For Hell that Gulph of fire for sins,
Is not so hot as t'burn thy Shins.
  Then Credit not the Lyar.   60

Those Cursed Vermin Sins that Crawle
All ore thy Soul, both Greate, and small
  Are onely Satans own:
Which he in his Malignity
Unto thy Souls true Sanctity   65
  In at the doors hath thrown.

And though they be Rebellion high,
Ath'ism or Apostacy:
  Though blasphemy it bee:
Unto what Quality, or Sise
Excepting one, so e're it rise.   70
  Repent, I'le pardon thee.

Although thy Soule was once a Stall
Rich hung with Satans nicknacks all;
  If thou Repent thy Sin,
A Tabernacle in't I'le place   75
Fild with Gods Spirit, and his Grace.
  Oh Comfortable thing!

77 *Gods*] PW God

I dare the World therefore to show
A God like me, to anger slow: 80
    Whose wrath is full of Grace.
Doth hate all Sins both Greate, and small:
Yet when Repented, pardons all.
    Frowns with a Smiling Face.

As for thy outward Postures each, 85
Thy Gestures, Actions, and thy Speech,
    I Eye and Eying spare,
If thou repent. My Grace is more
Ten thousand times still tribled ore
    Than thou canst want, or ware. 90

As for the Wicked Charge he makes,
That he of Every Dish first takes
    Of all thy holy things.
Its false, deny the same, and say,
That which he had he stool away 95
    Out of thy Offerings.

Though to thy Griefe, poor Heart, thou finde
In Pray're too oft a wandring minde,
    In Sermons Spirits dull.
Though faith in firy furnace flags, 100
And Zeale in Chilly Seasons lags.
    Temptations powerfull.

These faults are his, and none of thine
So far as thou dost them decline.
    Come then receive my Grace. 105
And when he buffits thee therefore
If thou my aid, and Grace implore
    I'le shew a pleasant face.

But still look for Temptations Deep,
Whilst that thy Noble Sparke doth keep 110
    Within a Mudwald Cote.
These White Frosts and the Showers that fall

Are but to whiten thee withall.
    Not rot the Web they smote.

If in the fire where Gold is tride
Thy Soule is put, and purifide   115
    Wilt thou lament thy loss?
If silver-like this fire refine
Thy Soul and make it brighter shine:
    Wilt thou bewaile the Dross?
                                                                  120

Oh! fight my Field: no Colours fear:
I'l be thy Front, I'l be thy reare.
    Fail not: my Battells fight.
Defy the Tempter, and his Mock.
Anchor thy heart on mee thy Rock.
    I do in thee Delight.   125

An Extasy of Joy let in by this Reply
returnd in Admiration.

My Sweet Deare Lord, for thee I'le Live, Dy, Fight.
    Gracious indeed! My Front! my Rear!
    Almighty magnify a Mite:
        O! What a Wonder's here?

Had I ten thousand times ten thousand hearts: 5
    And Every Heart ten thousand Tongues;
    To praise, I should but stut odd parts
        Of what to thee belongs.

If all the world did in Alimbeck ly,
    Bleeding its Spirits out in Sweat;
    It could not halfe enlife a Fly   10
        To Hum thy Praises greate.

If all can't halfe enlife a Fly to hum,
    (Which scarce an Animall we call)

118 *silver-like*] PW silver like   *refine*] orig: refine refine

Thy Praises then which from me come,   15
    Come next to none at all.

For I have made myselfe ten thousand times
    More naught than nought itselfe, by Sin.
    Yet thou extendst thy Gracious Shines
        For me to bath therein.   20

Oh! Stand amaizd yee Angells Bright, come run
    Yee Glorious Heavens and Saints, to sing:
    Place yee your praises in the sun,
        Ore all the world to ring.

Nay stand agast, ye sparkling Spirits bright!   25
    Shall little Clods of Dust you peere?
    Shall they toote Praises on your pipe?
        Oh! that we had it here.

What can a Crumb of Dust sally such praise
    Which do from Earth all heaven o're ring   30
    Who swaddle up the suns bright rayes
        Can in a Flesh Flie's Wing?

Can any Ant stand on the Earth and spit
    Another out to peer with this?
    Or Drink the Ocean up, and yet   35
        Its belly empty is?

Thou may'st this World as easily up hide
    Under the Blackness of thy naile:
    As scape Sins Gulph without a Guide:
        Or Hell without a bale.   40

If all the Earthy Mass were rambd in Sacks
    And saddled on an Emmet small,
    Its Load were light unto those packs
        Which Sins do bring on all.

But sure this burden'd Emmet moves no wing.   45
    Nay, nay, Compar'd with thee, it flies.

27 *pipe?*] PW pipe.   42 *Emmet*] PW Emmets

Yet man is easd his weight of Sin.
    From hell to Heav'n doth rise.

When that the World was new, its Chiefe Delight,
    One Paradise alone Contain'de: 50
    The Bridle of Mans Appetite
        The Appletree refrain'de.

The which he robbing, eat the fruit as good,
    Whose Coare hath Chokd him and his race.
    And juyce hath poyson'd all their blood,   55
        He's in a Dismall Case.

None can this Coare remove, Poyson expell:
    He, if his Blood ben't Clarifi'de
    Within Christs veans, must fry in Hell,
        Till God be satisfi'de.   60

Christ to his Father saith, Incarnate make
    Mee, Mee thy Son; and I will doe't:
    I'le purify his Blood, and take
        The Coare out of his Throate.

All this he did, and did for us, vile Clay: 65
    Oh! let our Praise his Grace assaile.
    To free us from Sins Gulph each way,
        He's both our Bridge, and Raile.

Although we fall and Fall, and Fall and Fall
    And Satan fall on us as fast.
    He purgeth us and doth us call   70
        Our trust on him to Cast.

My Lumpish Soule why art thou hamper'd thus
    Within a Crumb of Dust? Arise,
    Trumpet out Praises. Christ for us   75
        Hath slain our Enemies.

Screw up, Deare Lord, upon the highest pin:
    My soul thy ample Praise to sound.

66 *assaile*] PW assai'le

O tune it right, that every string
     May make thy praise rebound.   80

But oh! how slack, slow, dull? with what delay,
    Do I this Musick to, repare,
    While tabernacled in Clay
     My Organs Cottag'de are?

Yet Lord accept this Pittance of thy praise   85
    Which as a Traveller I bring,
    While travelling along thy wayes
     In broken notes I sing.

And at my journies end in endless joyes
    I'l make amends where Angells meet   90
    And sing their flaming Melodies
     In Ravishing tunes most sweet.

The Second Ranke Accused.

   You that are branded for Rebellion
What whimsy Crotchets do you feed upon?
Under my Flag you fighting did Defie
And Vend much Venom spit at God most high:
You dar'de him as a Coward, out, and Went   5
Flinging your Poyson'd darts against his tent.
When Grace did sound her parle, you stopt the Eare:
You backward drew as she to you drew neere.
But whats this Grace, which you, forsooth, so prize,
For which you stand your own Sworn Enemies?   10
Whoever saw smelt, tasted felt the same?
Its but an airy notion, or a name.
Fine food for fools, or shallow brains, who know
No better fair and therefore let all go.
Did mercy better Cain, or make him thrive   15

90 *Angells*] PW Angell   11 *smelt*] PW smest

When he pronounc'd himselfe a Fugitive?
What Benefit had Esau who did weep
And in Repenting teares did scald his Cheek?
Or what King Ahab, that he softly went?
Or what poore Judas that he did repent?   20
Grace doom'd them down to hellish flames, although
To Court the same they steep't their Souls in woe.
To whom she yields a smile, she doth expect
That with a smile, her smile they soon accept
But you have hitherto like sturdy Clowns   25
Affronted Grace and paid her Smiles with Frowns.
Nay Mercy lookes before she Gives, to see
That those to whom she gives true Christians bee.
That all the Graces of the Spirit do
Like Clouds of sweet perfume from such forth flow.   30
And that their Souls be to the spirits feet
An Aromatick Spicery most sweet.
Is't so with you? You from her scepter fly,
As judging it a grace graceless to dy.
Your Faith's a Phancy: Fear a Slavery.   35
Your Hope is Vain, Patience Stupidity.
Your Love is Carnall, selfish, set on toyes:
Your Pray'res are Prattle, or Tautologies.
Your Hearts are full of sins both small, and Greate.
They are as full as is an Egge of meate.   40
Your Holy Conference and talkings do
But for a Broken Piece of Non-Sense go.
If so, you are accurst; God doth impart
His Blessings onely on the broken heart.
But search your peace turnd o're, and view each side   45
Graces Magnetick touch will it abide?
Doth Mercys Sun through Peaces lattice clear
Shine in thy Soule? Then what's that Uproare there?
Look well about you, try before you trust.
Though Grace is Gracious; Justice still is just.   50

16 *Fugitive?*] PW Figitive.

19: Ahab. See I Kings 21, 22.

If so it be with you, say what you can
You are not Saints, or I no Sinner am.

The Third Rank accused.

What thou art too for Christ, it seems? Yet fain
Thou wouldst the World with all her Pomps mentain.
But such as share of Christ, fall short of these.
And have but faint affections to such fees.
Go Coach thy Eyes about the world, and eye   5
Those Rich inchanting Braveries there Cry
Give us your heart? Wherefore thy heart doth ake
That it such Amorous Objects must forsake.
The Love whereto so stuffs thy heart; no place
Is left therein for any Saving Grace.   10
Its folly then to think that Grace was shown,
When in persute thy heart was overthrown.
It was not Grace in Grace that made thee fall:
For unto Grace thou hast no heart at all.
Thou thoughtst these Objects of thy Love would faile.   15
The thoughts of which do make thy Spirits faile.
And this is easely prov'd: for thou didst goe
Into the field with God, as with a foe.
And bravely didst outbrave the Notion Grace.
And Chose to flee rather than it imbrace.   20
And well thou mightst, A Bird in hand doth far
Transcend the Quires that in the Hedges are.
And so its still: turn o're thy heart, thou'lt finde
As formerly so still thou art inclinde.
In sin thou hadst delight, didst grace defy: 25
And dost so still: For still thou dost reply.
Whoever went to Hell, and Came again
To shew to anyone, what is that pain?

1 *Yet*] PW yet   5 *Eyes*] orig: World

Did ever any slip to Heaven to see
Whether there's there a God? and who is hee?   30
What is that fancide God rowld o're the tongue?
Oh! Brainsick Notion, or an Oldwifes Song!
That He should wholy be in e'ry place
At once all here, and there, yet in no space.
That all should be in any part though small: 35
That any part of him should be him all.
And that he hath no parts though Head, and Heart.
Hands, Ears, and Eyes he hath, he hath no part.
That he is all in all, yea all in thee,
That he is also all that time in mee.   40
That he should be all in each Atom small:
And yet the whole cannot contain him all.
That he doth all things in a moment see,
At once, of things to Come, Past, and now bee.
That He no Elder, he no Younger is,   45
Than when the World began: (What wonders this?)
That time that flies from all with him remains,
These are Chamaera's Coin'd in Wanton brains.
Among which Fopperies mans Soul may go,
Concerning which thou mak'st so much ado.   50
Nay; what? or where is Hell Can any show?
This Bugbare in the Darke, 's a mere Scar-Crow.
But say its true, there is an Hell: a God.
A Soul Immortall in a mortall Clod:
Did God such principles infuse as egge   55
The Soul from him into Eternall plague?
Thou dost Confess that God doth not Command
Such things of us as had are of no hand.
Which sure he doth, if he deny to save
Whom live by Natures Law: which Law he Gave.   60
Yet grant this tenet which thy heart denies,
Christ saveth none but whom he sanctifies.
Thou art not sanctifide in any part:
For sins keepe Centinall within thy heart
And there they train, therein they Rentdevouz.   65

34 *there,*] PW there.   53 *true,*] PW true.   57 *Command*] orig: Demand

Her troops therein do quarter: and do house.
And hence as from a fountain Head there streams
Through ev'ry part Pollution in the Veans.
Hence sprouts Presumption making much too bold
To catch such Shaddows which no hand can hold.   70
Hence Harebrain'd Rashness rushes in the Brain:
Hence Madbrain'd Anger which no man can tame.
Hence Crackbrain'd folly, or a shatter'd Wit
That none Can Plaster: none can med'cine it.
Hence a stiff, stubborn, and Rebellious Will   75
That sooner breakes than buckles to fulfill
Gods Laws: and so for other sins thou'lt find
A Forward Will joyn'd with a froward minde.
Thy Heart doth lip such Languague, though thy Lip
Is loath to let such Languague open slip.   80
I see thy secret thoughts: and such they bee,
That Wish there was no God, or I was Hee.
Or that there was no Holiness, unless
Those sins thou'rt given to, were Holiness.
Or that there was no Hell, except for those   85
Who stand for Holiness, and sin oppose.
Or that there was no heaven t'enter in,
Except for those Who pass their Lives in Sin.
Though thou the Languague of thy heart outface
Dost, yet thou huggest sin, dost hiss out Grace.   90
Set Heaven, and Hell aside its clearly shown,
Thou lov'st mee more than God thou seem'st to own.
Hence was it not for these, it plainly 'pears
Thy God for servants might go shake his ears.
For thou to keep within my booke dost still   95
Ungod thy God not walking by his Will.
     This Languague of thy heart doth this impart
     I am a Saint, if thou no Sinner art.

81 *secret*] orig: secret secret
87 *t'enter*] orig: to enter   90 *dost*] orig: and   97 *impart*] orig: declare

A Threnodiall Dialogue between The
Second and Third Ranks.

SECOND

Oh you! How do you? Alas! how do things go
With you, and with your Souls? For once we know
You did as we, Welt, Wallow, Soake in Sin;
For which Gods ire infires our hearts within.

THIRD

Ne're worse, though when secure in sin much worse.   5
Though curst by sin, we did not feele the Curse.
Now seing we no help can see, we, rue.
Would God it was with us as't is with you.

SECOND

With us! alas! a Flint would melt to see
A Deadly foe, in such a Case as wee.   10
God seems our Foe, repent we Can't: but finde
To ill Goodwill, to Good, a wayward minde.

THIRD

This is in you your Grace, we easely spie
The Love of God within your looks to ly.
But oh! our Souls set in sins Cramp stand bent   15
To Badness, and no Grace we have t'Repent.

SECOND

This is your Charity. But if you saw
Those ugly Crawling Sins that do us knaw
You'd Change your minde. You mourn, and pray we see:
We would not for a World, you were as wee.   20

THIRD

Repent! and Pray! Aye, so the Traytor Cast,
Cries, *Good my Lord!* yea, when his Doom is past.

9 *Flint*] PW Flent   10 *such a Case*] PW such Case   16 *no*] orig: we've not
22 *Good my Lord!*] PW These words written in large lower-case letters with
G and L capitalized

You erre through your Abundant Charity.
We dare not wish, as we, our Enemy.

SECOND

Your Low esteemings of yourselves enlarge   25
Ours of you much. But oh, that Dismall Charge!
We don't Repent, Believe, we nothing do:
No Grace we have though something Gracelike show.

THIRD

Is't so with you who do so much out do
Poor nothings us? Oh! whither shall we go?   30
Our Grace a Mockgrace is: of Ulcerous Boiles.
We are as full, as Satan is of Wiles.

SECOND

There's not a Sin that is not in our Heart.
And if Occasion were, it would out start.
There's not a Precept that we have not broke.   35
Hence not a Promise unto us is spoke.

THIRD

Its worse with us: The Preacher speaks no word.
The Word of God no sentence doth afford;
But fall like burning Coals of Hell new blown
Upon our Souls: and on our Heads are thrown.   40

SECOND

Its worse with us. Behold Gods threatonings all;
Nay Law, and Gospell, on our Heads do fall.
Both Hell, and Heaven, God and Divell Do
With Wracking Terrours Consummate our Woe.

THIRD

We'le ne're believe that you are worse than wee,   45
For Worse than us wee judge no Soul can bee.
We know not where to run, nor what to doe.
Would God it was no worse with us than you.

38 *sentence*] orig: Comfort   40 *on*] orig: it on
43 *God*] orig: both God

SECOND

Than us, alas! What, would you fain aspire
Out of the Frying Pan into the Fire?   50
Change States with you with all our hearts we would
Nay, and give boot therewith, if that we could.

THIRD

Say what you can, we can't but thinke this true
That Grace's Ambush hath surprized you.
But Judgment layes an Ambush strong to take   55
* * * * * * * * * * * * * * * * * * * *

SECOND

What Charity have you for us? When thus
You judge amiss both of yourselves and us?
What pitty is't? Yet God will you repay.
Although we perish, and be cast away.   60

THIRD

The Lord forbid the last, and grant we may
Deceived be wherein we be, you say.
We Cannot wish a Toade as wee, but Crave,
Your prayers for us, that we may pardon have.

SECOND

Our Pray'res, are pray'reless: Oh! to what we bee   65
An ugly Toad's an Angell bright we see.
Oh pray, pray you, oh pray, for us that so
The Lord of Mercy Mercy on's may show.

THIRD

O would we could! but oh Hells Gripes do grinde
Yea writh our Souls with Cramps of e'ry kinde.   70
If Grace begrace us not, we go to Hell.
The Good Lord help us both, thus fare you Well.

53 *but*] orig: believe but   54 *Ambush*] orig: tender
Ambush   56 This line is worn away at the bottom of the page in PW.
63 *wee,*] PW wee.

Their Call in this Sad State for Mercy.

We humbly beg, oh Lord, to know our Crime.
That we thus tortur'de are before our time.
Before our Time? Lord give's this Word again.
For we have long ago deserv'de Hells flame.
If Mercy wrought not Miracles none could   5
Us monuments of mercy now behold.
But oh! while Mercy waits we slaves to sin,
Heap up sins Epha far above the brim.
What shall we do when to account we're Calld?
How will abused Mercy burn, and scald?   10
We know not How, nor Where to stay or goe.
We know not whom, nor What to trust or doe.
Should we run hence from Mercy, Justice will
Run hotly after us our blood to spill.
But should we run to Mercy, Justice may   15
Hold Mercies hands while Vengeance doth us slay.
And if we trust to Grace, necessity
Binds us by force at Grace's Grace to ly.
But if we run from Grace, we headlong cast
Ourselves upon the Spiles of Ruine Vast.   20
And if we claim her ours, she'l surely smite
Us, for presuming on an others right.

Who'le with a Leaking, old Crack't Hulk assay,
To brave the raging Waves of Adria?
Or who can Cross the Main Pacifick o're?   25
Without a Vessell Wade from Shore to Shore?
What wade the mighty main from brim to brim,
As if it would not reach above the Chin?
But, oh! poor wee, must wade from brinck to brinck
With such a Weight as would bright Angells sink.   30
Or venture angry Adria, or drown

21 *ours,*] PW ours.   31 *angry*] PW **argry**

When Vengeance's sea doth break her floodgates down.
If stay, or Go to sea we drown. Then see
In what a wofull Pickle, Lord, we bee.
Rather than tarry, or the rough sea trust,   35
On the Pacificke Ocean forth we thrust.
Necessity lies on's: we dare not stay:
If drown we must, we'l drown in Mercy's Sea.
Impute it not presumption if we high
To Cast ourselves on Mercies Clemency.   40
Is't not as great Presumption, Lord, to stand
And gaze on ruine, but refuse the hand
Which offers help? Or on such Courses fall
Which fall to ruin, ruinating all?
Lord, pitty, pitty us, Lord pitty send: 45
A thousand pitties tis we should offend.
But oh! we did, and are thereto propence:
And what we count off, oft thou Countst offence.
We've none to trust: but on thy Grace we ly,
If dy we must, in mercy's arms wee'l dy.   50
    Then pardon, Lord, and put away our guilt.
    So we be thine, deale with us as thou wilt.

The Soule Bemoning Sorrow rowling upon a resolution to seek Advice of Gods people.

    Alas! my Soule, product of Breath Divine,
For to illuminate a Lump of Slime.
Sad Providence! Must thou below thus tent,
In such a Cote as strangles with ill sent?
Or in such sensuall Organs make thy stay   5
Which from thy noble end do make thee stray?
My nobler part, why dost thou laquy to
The Carnall Whynings of my senses so?
What? thou become a Page, a Peasant, nay,

A Slave unto a Durty Clod of Clay!   10
Why should the Kirnell bring such Cankers forth
To please the shell, as will devour them both?
Why didst thou thus thy Milkwhite Robes defile
With Crimson spots of scarlet sins most vile?

   My Muddy Tent, Why hast thou done so ill   15
To Court, and kiss my Soule, yet kissing kill?
Why didst thou Whyning, egg her thus away
Thy sensuall Appetite to satisfy?
Art thou so safe, and firm a Cabinet
As though thou soaking lie in nasty wet,   20
And in all filthy Puddles: yet though thin
Can ne're drench through to stain the Pearle within?
Its no such thing: Thou'rt but a Cawle-wrought Case.
And when thou fallst, thou foulst its shining face.
Or but her mudwalld Lid which, wet by sin   25
Diffuseth all in her that it shuts in.
One stain stains both, when both in one Combine.
A Musty Cask doth marre rich Malmsy Wine.

   Woe's mee! my mouldring Heart! What must I do?
When is my moulting time to shed my woe?   30
Oh! Woefull fall! what fall from Heavenly bliss
To th'bottom of the bottomless Abyss?
Above an angry God! Below, black-blew
Brimstony flames of hell where Sinners rue!
Behinde, a Traile of Sins! Before appeare   35
An Host of Mercies that abused were!
Without a Raging Divell! and Within
A Wracking Conscience Galling home for Sin!
What Canst not finde one Remedy, my Soule,
On Mercies File for mee? Oh! Search the Rowle.   40
What freeze to death under such melting means,
Of Grace's Golden, Life Enliv'ning Beams?
What? not one Hope? Alas! I hope there's some.
Although I know not in what way it come.
Although there is no hope within my minde   45

21 *though*] PW the

I'le force Hope's Faculty, till Hope I finde.
Some glimmerings of Hope, I hope to spy
In Mercies Golden Stacks, or Remedy.
I therefore am Resolv'd a search to make,
And of the Pious Wise some Counsill take.   50
Ile then in Pensiveness myselfe apply
To them in hope, but yet halfe hopelessly.
Perhaps these thoughts are blessed motions, though
From whence they are, as yet I do not know.
      And if from Christ, Oh! then thrice Happy mee.   55
      If not, I'st not be worser than I bee.

48 *Stacks,*] PW Stacks.   **55** *Christ,*] PW Christ.

The Preface.

SOUL

Long lookt for Sir! Happy, right Happy Saint.
I long to lay before you my Complaint:
And gain your Counsill: but you're strange: and I
Through backwardness lost opportunity.

SAINT

How is't good Sir: methinks I finde there dart 5
Some pleasant Hopes of you within my heart.
What is your Rantery declinde, foregone?
Your looks are like the Earth you Tread upon.

SOUL

Its true: I do, and well may look so, too
For worse than mee the world did never show. 10
My sins are dide in grain: all Grace I lack.
This doth my Soul on tenterhooks enwrack.
Wherefore I Counsill Crave touching my sin
My Want of Grace. Temptations too within.

SOUL] PW omits this first stanza heading   9 *so,*] PW so.

The Souls Doubts touching its Sins Answerd.

SAINT

Is this thy Case, Poor Soul, Come then begin:
Make known thy griefe: anatomize thy sin.
Although thy sins as Mountains vast do show,
Yet Grace's fountain doth these mountains flow.

SOUL

True, true indeed, where Mountains sinke but where   5
They swim, their Heads above these mountains peare.
Mine swim in Mercies boundless Ocean do:
Therefore their Heads above these waters goe.

SAINT

I thought as you, but loe the Lyon hee
Is not so fierce as he is feign'd to bee.   10
But grant they swim, they'l then swim quite away
On Mercies main, if you Repenting stay.

SOUL

I swim in Mercy: but my sins are sayles
That waft my barke to Hell by Graces Gales.
Is't possible for such as Grace outbrave   15
(Which is my Case) true Saving Grace to have?

SAINT

That's not thy Sin: thou didst not thus transgress,
Thy Grace-outbraveing sin is bashfulness.
Thou art too backward. Satan strives to hold
Thee fast hereby, and saith, thou art too bold.   20

SOUL

Alas! How are you out in mee, behold
My best is poison in a Box of Gold.
If with mine Eyes you saw my hearts black stain,
You'de judge my Sins were double dide in grain.

SAINT

Deluded Soul, Satan beguiles thee so   25
Thou judgst the bend the back side of the bow

6 *They*] PW The   24 *judge*] orig: my judge

Dost press thyselfe too hard: Straite Wands appeare
Crook't in, and out, in running rivlets Clear.

SOUL

You raise the fabrick of your pious hope
Upon such water Bells, as rots denote.   30
For my Profession doth but cloake my sin.
A guilded Maukin's stufft with Chaff within.

SAINT

I love not thus to row in such a Stream:
And if I did, I should so touch my Theme.
But muster up your Sins, though more or few: 35
Grace hath an Edge to Cut their bonds atwo.

SOUL

This is my Sin, My Sin I love, but hate
God and his Grace. And who's in such a state?
My Love, and Hatred do according rise
Unto Sins height, and unto Grace's sise.   40

SAINT

I thought as you when first to make me see
God powred out his Spirit sweet on mee.
But oh strange Fetch! What Love, yet hate to have?
And hate in heart what heartily you Crave?

SOUL

Sometimes meethinks I wish. Oh! that there were   45
No Heaven nor Hell. For then I need not feare.
I'm pestred with black thoughts of Blasphemy,
And after thoughts do with these thoughts Comply.

SAINT

See Satans Wiles: while thou in sin didst dwell
Thou Calledst not in Question Heaven, or Hell.   50
But now thou'rt out with sin he makes thee Call
In Question both, that thou in Hell mightst fall.

SOUL

But, oh! methinks, I finde I sometimes wish
There was no God, or that there was not this.

Or that his wayes were other than they bee.   55
Oh! Horrid, horrid, Hellish thoughts in mee!

SAINT

'Twas thus, or worse with me. I often thought,
Oh! that there was no God: or God was Naught.
Or that his Wayes were other Wayes. Yet hee
In mighty mercy hath bemerci'de mee.   60

SOUL

My Heart is full of thoughts, and ev'ry thought
Full of Sad, Hellish, Drugstery enwrought.
Methinks it strange to Faith that God should bee
Thus All in All, yet all in Each part. See.

SAINT

'Twas so with me. Then let your Faith abound   65
For Faith will stand where Reason hath no ground.
This proves that God is Onely God: for hee
Surpasseth the superlative degree.

SOUL

Methinks I am a Frigot fully fraught,
And stoughed full with each Ath'istick thought.
Methinks I hate to think on God: anone   70
Methinks there is no God to thinke upon.

SAINT

I thought as much at first: my thoughts, so vain,
Were thus that God was but stampt i'th'brain.
But God disperst these Wicked thoughts. Behold   75
The Various methods of the serpent old!

SOUL

All arguments against mee argue still:
I see not one bespeaks me ought, but ill.
Whatse're I use I do abuse: Oh! shew,
Whether the Case was ever thus with you.   80

74 *i'th'brain*] PW ith'brain

SAINT

It was: But see how Satan acts, for his
He troubles not with such a thought as this.
But Wicked thoughts he in the Saints doth fling,
And saith they're theirs, accusing them of Sin.

SOUL

Methinks my heart is harder than a flint,   85
My Will is Wilfull, frowardness is in't,
And mine Affections do my Soule betray,
Sedaning of it from the blessed way.

SAINT

Loe, Satan hath thy thoughts inchanted quite,
And Carries them a pickpack from the right.   90
Thou art too Credulous: For Satan lies.
It is not as you deem: deem otherwise.

SOUL

But I allow of sin: I like it Well,
And Chiefly grieve, because it goes to hell.
And Were it ever so with you, I see   95
Grace hath prevented you which doth not mee.

SAINT

I thought as you: but now I clearly spy,
These Satans brats will like their Curst Sire ly.
He squibd these thoughts in you, you know not how.
And tempts you then to deem you them allow.   100

SOUL

And so I do: would I could Sins disown:
But if I do, thy'l own me for their own.
I have no Grace to do't: this prooves me in
A Lamentable State, a State of Sin.

SAINT

What ambling work within a Ring is here?   105
What Circular Disputes of Satans Geer?

86 *is in't*] Conj.   95 *Were*] orig: if Were   105 *within a Ring is here*] orig:
is here within a Ring

To proove thee Graceless he thy sins persues:
To proove thee sinfull, doth thy Grace accuse.
    Why dost thou then believe the Tempter so?
    He seeks by helping thee thy Overthrow.   110

Doubts from the Want of Grace Answerd.

SOUL

Such as are Gracious grow in Grace therefore
Such as have Grace, are Gracious evermore.
Who sin Commit are sinfull: and thereby
They grow Ungodly. So I feare do I.

SAINT

Such as are Gracious, Graces have therefore   5
They evermore desire to have more.
But such as never knew this dainty fare
Do never wish them 'cause they dainties are.

SOUL

Alas! alas! this still doth me benight.
I've no desire, or no Desire aright.   10
And this is Clear: my Hopes do witherd ly,
Before their buds breake out, their blossoms dy.

SAINT

When fruits do thrive, the blossom falls off quite.
No need of blossoms when the seed is ripe.
The Apple plainly prooves the blossoms were.   15
Thy withred Hopes hold out Desires as Cleare.

SOUL

Alas! my Hopes seem but like blasted fruit.
Dead on the Stoole before it leaves its root.

15 *blossoms*] PW blossom

For if it lively were a growth it hath,
And would be grown e're this to Saving Faith.   20

SAINT
* * * * * * * * * * * I'le make most plain
* * * * * * * * * * * * * * * * * * * *
Which lively is, layes hold on Christ too, though
Thou deemst it doth like blasted blossoms show.

SOUL
If it was so, then Certainly I should,   25
With Faith Repentance have. But, oh! behold,
This Grace leaves not in mee a single print.
Mine Eyes are Adamant, my Heart is Flint.

SAINT
Repentance is not argued so from Tears.
As from the Change that in the Soul appears.   30
And Faith Ruld by the Word. Hence ever spare
To mete Repentance out by Satans square.

SOUL
I fear Repentance is not Genuine.
Its Feare that makes me from my sins decline.
And if it was, I should delight much more,   35
To bathe in all Gods Ordinances pure.

SAINT
And dost thou not? Poore Soule, thou dost I know.
Why else dost thou Relent, and sorrow so?
But Satan doth molest thee much to fling
Thee from thy Dutie into e'ry Sin.   40

SOUL
If these were my Delight, I should Embrace
The royall Retinue of Saving Grace,
Peace, Patience Pray're, Meekness, Humility,
Love, Temp'rance, Feare, Syncerety, and Joy.

SAINT

You do: though not alike at all times sure,   45
And you do much desire to have more.
I wonder that you judge them worth the having,
Or Crave them, if they are not got by Craving.

SOUL

My measure is so small, I doubt, alas!
Its next to none, and will for nothing pass.   50
But if I had but this or that Degree,
Of all these Graces, then thrice Happy mee!

SAINT

You have not what you Would, and therefore will
Not own you have at all. What Sullen still?
If God should fill you, and not work your bane,   55
You would not be Content, but would Complain.

SOUL

What must my vessell voide of Grace be thrust
By you in Glory thus among the Just
As Gracious though the Dose of Grace I finde
Is scarce a Grain? Can this Content your minde?   60

SAINT

God, and His All, 's the Object of the Will:
All God alone can onely it up fill.
He'd kill the Willer, if his Will he should
Fill to the brim, while Cabbined in mould.
What Mortall can contain immortall bliss;   65
If it be poured on him as it is?
A single Beam thus touching him Would make
The stoutest mortall man to ashes shake.
Will nothing give Content unless you have
While here a mortall, all your Will can Crave?   70
If so, the Promise which is made to those
That hunger after Righteousness you'l lose.
For being full, you could not hunger still
Nor Wish for more you having once your Will.

You cant contain Halfe, what in truth you would   75
Or do not Wish for Halfe of what you should.
Can't all the sea o'refill an Acorn bole?
Can't God orefill a little Whimpring Soul?
What Can a Nutshell all the World Enfold?
Or can thy Heart all Heavens Glory Hold?   80
And never break? What! Canst thou here below
Weld Heavens bliss while mortall thus? Oh! No.
God Loves you better than to grant your Cry,
When you do Cry for that which will destroy.
Give but a Child a Knife to still his Din: 85
He'l cut his Fingers with it ere he blin.

SOUL

Had I but any Sparke of Grace, I might
Have much more than I have with much delight.
How can I trust to you? You do not know
Whether I have a Grain of Grace, or no.   90

SAINT

You think you might have more: you shall have so,
But if you'd all at once, you could not grow.
And if you could not grow, you'd grieving fall.
All would not then Content you, had you all.
Should Graces Floodgate thus at once breake down   95
You most would lose, or else it would you drown.
He'l fill you but by drops that so he may
Not drown you in't, nor Cast a Drop away.

Doubts from Satans Temptations Answered.

SOUL

But oh the Tempter harries me so fast
And on me falls to make me fall at last.

86 *He'l*] PW Hel

Had I but Grace surely I might repell
His firy Darts that dart on fire from hell.

SAINT

If you had none, he never would bestow   5
Such darts upon you Grace to overthrow.
The Bullets shot are blinde, the fowlers eye
Aims at the marke before he lets them fly.

SOUL

But he bewilders me: I scarce can finde
But lose myselfe again within my minde.   10
My thoughts are Laberryntht, I can't enjoyn
Any thereof the rest to discipline.

SAINT

I once was thus. The Crooked Serpent old
Doth strive to hinder what he can't withhold.
And where he cannot keep from Grace, he's loath,   15
To keep from keeping Saving Grace from Growth.

SOUL

But if a Pious thought appeare, I finde
It's brambled in the briers of my minde.
Or in those brambles lost, or slinks away:
But Viprous thoughts do in these thickets stay.   20
With these I pest'red am in Duty so,
I doubt I undo all thereby I do.

SAINT

First Satan envies each Choice thought: then hee
To murder it, or make't short winded bee
Doth raise a Fog, or fude of thoughts most vile   25
Within the soul; and darkens all that ile.
And when he cannot hinder pray're he'le strive
To spoil the same, but still hold on, and thrive.

19 *those*] PW thoses   20 *thoughts*] PW thought

SOUL

But yet I feare there oft lurks secretly
Under each Duty done Hypocrisy.   30
I finde no heart unto the Wayes of Grace.
It's but their End my heart would fain imbrace.

SAINT

Why give you Credit to your deadly foe?
He turns ore ery stone Grace t'overthrow.
He'l fight on both sides Grace, Grace to destroy.   35
To ruinate your Souls Eternally.
He makes some thus red mad on mischiefe grow
And not to matter what they say, or do.
He makes Civility to pass for Grace,
With such as hunt riches hot senting trace.   40
To such as God doth Call, he doth reply
That all their Grace is but Hypocrisy.

    Contrarily, a Refuge strong to make
For e'ry sin, he doth this method take.
He tells the Doubting soul, this is no Sin,   45
Until he Diveth over head therein.
But then to breake his Heart he doth reply:
That done is Sin, He sinned willingly.
He to the Sinner saith, Great Sins are small,
Small Sins he telleth him, are none at all.   50
And so to such there is no sin: for why
Great sins are small, Small None. But oh but eye
If God awakes a Soul, he doth begin
To make him count indifferent things as Sin,
Nay Lawfull things wanting a Circumstance   55
Or having one too much although by Chance.
And thus he doth involve the doubting soule
In dismall doubts and makes it fear to rowle,
Himselfe on Christ for fear it should presume.
But if he doth he quickly turns his tune   60

33 *foe?*] PW foe   50 *Sins*] orig: thing

And doth accuse, because he did not take
As soon as mercy did an offer make.
Oh! see the Craft the Serpent old doth use
To hopple souls in Sin, and Sin to Choose.
One while he terms true Grace a morall thing.   65
One while morality a splendid Sin.

SOUL

You shew the matter as the matter is
But shew me how in such a Case as this,
T'repell the Tempter, and the field t'obtain,
To Chaff away the Chaff and Choose the grain.   70

SAINT

Perform the Duty, leave th'event unto
His Grace that doth both in, and outside know.
Beg pardon for your Sins: bad thoughts defy,
That are Cast in you by the Enemy.
Approove yourselfe to God, and unto his   75
And beg a pardon where you do amiss.
If wronged go to God for right, and pray
Hard thoughted Saints black thoughted thoughts away.
Renew your acts of Faith: believe in him,
Who died on the Cross to Cross out Sin.   80
Allow not any Sin: and if you sin
Through frailty, Faith will a new pardon bring.
Do all Good Works, work all good things you know
As if you should be sav'd for doing so.
Then undo all you've done, and it deny   85
And on a naked Christ alone rely.
Believe not Satan, Unbelieve his tales
Lest you should misbelieve the Gospell bales.
        Do what is right, and for the right Contend.
        Make Grace your way, and Glory'l be your End.   90

Yet as a further Caution still I'le shew
You other Wiles of Satan to eschue.
And that a Saint may of a Saint account
Not as a Saint though once with God in th'mount.

Some of Satans Sophestry.

The Tempter greatly seeks, though secretly,
    With an Ath'istick Hoodwinke man to blinde,
That so the Footsteps of the Deity
    Might stand no longer stampt upon his minde.
    Which when he can't blot out, by blinding quite,   5
    He strives to turn him from the Purer Light.

With Wiles enough, he on his thoughts intrudes,
    That God's a Heape of Contradictions high,
But when these thoughts man from his thoughts excludes
    Thou knowst not then (saith he) this Mystery.   10
    And when the first String breaks, he strives to bring
    Into sins brambles by the other string.

When God Calls out a Soule, he subtilly
    Saith God is kinde: you need not yet forsake
Your Sins: but if he doth, he doth reply,   15
    Thou'st outstood Grace. Justice will vengeance take.
    He'l tell you you Presume on Grace, to fright
    You to despare, beholding Justice bright.

Though just before mans mountain sins were mites,
    His mites were nothing. Now the scales are turn'd.   20
His mites are mountains now, of mighty height
    And must with Vengeance-Lightening be burn'd.
    Greate Sins are Small, till men repent of Sin:
    Then Small are far too big to be forgi'n.

While man thinks slightly, that he will repent,   25
    There's time enough (saith he), it's easly done.
But when repent he doth, the time is spent,
    Saith he, it is too late to be begun.
    To keep man from't, it's easly done, saith he,
    To dant him in't, he saith, it Cannot bee.   30

So Faith is easy till the Soule resolves
    To Live to Christ, and upon Christ rely.
Then Saving Faith he bold presumption Calls.
    Hast thou (saith he) in Christ propriety?
    The Faithfulls Faith, he stiles Presumption great,   35
    But the Presumptuous, theirs is Faith Compleat.

Nay though the Faith be true he acts so sly,
    As to raise doubts: and then it must not do:
Unless Assurance do it Certify:
    Which if it do, it douts of it also.   40
    Faith is without Assurance shuffled out,
    And if Assurance be, that's still a Doubt.

But should the Soule assured once, once Doubt,
    Then his Assurance no Assurance is:
Assurance doth assure the Soul right out   45
    Leave not a single Doubt to do amiss.
    But Satan still will seeke to Pick an hole
    In thy Assurance to unsure thy Soul.

Should any Soule once an Assurance get,
    Into his hands, soon Satans Pick-Lock key   50
With Sinfull Wards Unlocks his Cabinet
    To Steal the Jewell in it thence away.
    The Soul thus pillag'de, droops unto the grave.
    It's greater grief to lose than not to have.

He doth molest the Soule, it cannot see   55
    Without Assurance Extraordinary
Which should it have, it would soon take to bee
    A Mere Delusion of the Adversary.
    Assurance would not serve, should God Convay
    It in an Usuall or Unusuall way.   60

Thus I might search, Poor Soul, the Magazeen
    Of Gospell Graces over: I might paint
Out Satan sculking each side each unseen
    To Hoodwinck Sinners, and to hopple Saints.
    For he to dim their Grace, and slick up sin   65
    Calls Brass bright Gold, bright Golde but brass or tin.

57 *would*] orig: quickly up would

He tempts to bring the soul too low or high,
    To have it e're in this or that extream:
To see no want or want alone to eye:
    To keep on either side the golden mean.   70
    If it was in't to get it out he'l 'ledge,
    Thou on the wrong side art the Pale or Hedge.

When God awakes a Soule he'l seeke to thrust
    It on Despare for want of Grace or get
And puff't with Pride, or in Securety hush't   75
    Or Couzen it with Graces Counterfet.
    Which if he can't he'l Carp at Grace, and raile
    And say, this is not Grace, it thus doth faile.

And thus he strives with Spite, Spleen, bitter Gall
    That Sinners might Dishonour God Most high: 80
That Saints might never honour God at all.
    That those in Sin, Those not in Grace might dy.
    And that the Righteous, Gracious, Pious, Grave,
    Might have no Comfort of the Grace they have.

Lest you be foild herewith, watch well unto   85
    Your Soul, that thrice Ennobled noble Gem:
For Sins are flaws therein, and double woe
    Belongs thereto if it be found in them.
    Are Flaws in Venice Glasses bad? What in
    Bright Diamonds? What then in man is Sin?   90

Difficulties arising from Uncharitable Cariages of Christians.

When these assaults proove vain, the Enemy
    One Saint upon another oft doth set,
To make each fret like to Gum'd Taffity,
    And fire out Grace thus by a Chafe or Fret.

89 *Glasses*] PW Grasses   4 *fire*] orig: enfire

Uncharitable Christians inj'rous are: 5
Two Freestons rubd together each do ware.

When Satan jogs the Elbow of the one
   To Spleenish Passions which too oft doth rise,
For want of Charity, or hereupon
      From some Uncharitable harsh Surmise,   10
      Then the Poore Doubting Soul is oft oppresst,
      By hard Reflections from an harder breast.

Th' Uncharitable Soul oft thus reflects,
   After each Birth a second birth doth Come.
Your Second Birth no Second Birth ejects.   15
      The Babe of Grace then's strangld in the Womb.
      There's no new Birth born in thy Soul thou'lt find
      If that the after Birth abide behinde.

The Babe of Grace, thinks he, 's not born its sure.
   Sins Secundine is not as yet out Cast.   20
The Soul no Bracelet of Graces pure
      Doth ware, while wrapt in nature's slough so fast.
      And thus he doth for want of Charity,
      The wounded wound Uncharitably.

And thus some Child of God, when led awry   25
   By Satan, doth with Satan take a part,
Against some Child of God, whom frowardly
      He by Reflections harsh wounds thus in heart.
      Pough! Here's Religion! Strange indeed! Quoth hee.
      Grace makes a Conscience of things here that bee.   30

Grace Conscious makes one how to spend ones time
   How to perform the Duties of one's place
Not onely in the things which are Divine;
      But in the things which ware a Sublime Face.
      Do you do so? And order good persue?   35
      Don't Earth and Heaven interfer in you?

Will God accept the service if the time
   Is stolen from our Calling him to pay?

13 *oft*] orig: doth oft   24 *wound*] orig: uncharitably wound

What will he yield that Sacrifice his shine,
    That from anothers Altar's stole away?   40
God and our Callings Call: and th' Sacrifice
    Stole from our Callings Altar he defies.

Yet if it falls on worldly things intense
    Its soon scourgd then with whips of Worldliness:
It gives to many, nay to all, offence   45
    And gathers to itselfe great penciveness.
    Intense on God, or on the world, all's one.
    The Harmless Soule is hardly thought upon.

Such Traps, and Wilds as these are, Satan sets,
    For to intrap the Innocent therein: 50
These are his Wyers, Snares, and tangling Nets,
    To hanck, and hopple harmless souls in Sin.
    If in such briars thou enbrambled light
    Call on the Mighty God with all thy might.

On God in Christ Call hard: For in him hee   55
    Hath Bowells melting, and Expanded arms:
Hath sweet imbraces, Tender mercy free
    Hath Might Almighty too to save from harms.
    Into his Dove streakt Downy bosom fly,
    In Spite of Spite, or Spiters Enmity.   60

These are Gods Way-Marks thus inscrib'd; this hand
    Points you the way unto the Land Divine,
The Land of Promise, Good Immanuels Land.
    To New Jerusalem above the line.
    Ten thousand times thrice tribled blesst he is,   65
    That walketh in the suburbs here of bliss.

His Wildred state will wane away, and hence
    These Crooked Passages will soon appeare
The Curious needlework of Providence,
    Embrodered with golden Spangles Cleare.   70
    Judge not this Web while in the Loom, but stay
    From judging it untill the judgment day.

60 *In Spite*] PW In Spit

For while its foiled up the best Can see
    But little of it, and that little too
Shews weather beaten but when it shall bee   75
      Hung open all at once, Oh beautious shew!
      Though thrids run in, and out, Cross snarld and twinde
      The Web will even be enwrought you'l finde.

If in the golden Meshes of this Net
    (The Checkerwork of Providence) you're Caught   80
And Carride hence to Heaven, never fret:
    Your Barke shall to an Happy Bay be brought.
    You'l se both Good and Bad drawn up hereby,
    These to Hells Horrour, those to Heavens Joy.

Fear not Presumption then, when God invites: 85
    Invite not Fear, when that he doth thee Call:
Call not in Question whether he delights
    In thee, but make him thy Delight, and all.
    Presumption lies in Backward Bashfulness,
    When one is backward though a bidden Guest.   90

The Effect of this Discourse upon the second,
and third Rancks.

RANK TWO

Whence Come these Spicy Gales? Shall we abuse
    Such sweet Perfumes with putrid noses?
Who did in this Diffusive Aire Diffuse
    Such Aromatick fumes or Posies?
These Spirits are with Graces sweetly splic'te;   5
What Good Comes in them? Oh! they Come from Christ!

79 *Meshes*] PW Mashes[?]
88 *thee,*] PW thee.   *TWO*] PW 2 Numbers designating the ranks in this
poem are indicated by numerals in PW

RANK THREE

Whence Come these Cloudy Pillars of Perfume?
    Sure Christ doth on his Garden blow
Or open Graces Spice Box, I presume
    From whence these Reechs do flow: 10
For oh! heart Ravishing steams do scale my Soule,
And do in Heavenly Raptures it enrowle.

RANK TWO

Sure Grace a progress in her Coach doth ride,
    Lapt up in all Perfumes, whose sent,
Hath suffocated sin, and nullifi'de   15
    Sad Griefe, as in our Souls it went.
Sin sincks the Soul to Hell: but here is Love
Sincks Sin to Hell; and soars the Soul above.

RANK THREE

I strove to soar on high. But oh! methought
    Like to a Lump of Lead my sin   20
Prest down my Soul; But now it's off, she's Caught
    In holy Raptures up to him.
Oh! let us then sing Praise: methinks I soar
Above the stars, and stand at Heavens Doore.

Our Insufficiency to Praise God
suitably, for his Mercy.

Should all the World so wide to atoms fall
    Should th'Aire be shred to motes, should we
    Se all the Earth hackt here so small
        That none Could smaller bee?
Should Heaven, and Earth be Atomizd, we guess   5
The Number of these Motes were numberless.

18 *Sincks*] PW Sinck

But should we then a World each Atom deem,
    Where dwell as many pious men
      As all these Motes the world Could teem
        Were it shred into them?   10
Each Atom would the World surmount wee guess
Whose men in number would be numberless.

But had each pious man, as many Tongues
    At singing all together then
      The Praise that to the Lord belongs   15
        As all these Atoms men?
Each man would sing a World of Praise, we guess,
Whose Tongues in number would be numberless.

And had each Tongue, as many Songs of Praise
    To sing to the Almighty ALL   20
      As all these men have Tongues to raise
        To him their Holy Call?
Each Tongue would tune a World of Praise, we guess
Whose songs in number would be numberless.

Nay, had each song as many Tunes most sweet   25
    Or one intwisting in't as many,
      As all these Tongues have songs most meet
        Unparallelld by any?
Each song a world of Musick makes we guess
Whose Tunes in number would be numberless.   30

Now should all these Conspire in us that we
    Could breath such Praise to thee, Most High?
      Should we thy Sounding Organs be
        To ring such Melody?
Our Musick would the World of Worlds out ring   35
Yet be unfit within thine Eares to ting.

Thou didst us mould, and us new mould when wee
    Were worse than mould we tread upon.
      Nay Nettles made by Sin wee bee.
        Yet hadst Compassion.   40
Thou hast pluckt out our Stings; and by degrees
Hast of us, lately Wasps, made Lady-Bees.

Though e're our Tongues thy Praises due can fan
    A Weevle with the World may fly,
    Yea fly away: and with a span   45
        We may out mete the Sky.
Though what we can is but a Lisp, We pray
Accept thereof. We have no better pay.

The Soule Seeking Church-Fellowship.

The Soul refresht with gracious Steams, behold,
    Christs royall Spirit richly tended
With all the guard of Graces manifold
    Throngs in to solace it amended
    And by the Trinity befriended.   5

Befriended thus! It lives a Life indeed
    A Life! as if it Liv'd for Life.
For Life Eternall: wherefore with all heed
    It trims the same with Graces rife
    To be the Lambs espoused Wife.   10

Yea, like a Bride all Gloriously arraide
    It is arrai'de Whose dayly ware
Is an Imbrodery with Grace inlaide,
    Of Sanctuary White most Faire,
    Its drest in Heavens fashion rare.   15

Each Ordinance and Instrument of Grace
    Grace doth instruct are Usefull here.
They're Golden Pipes where Holy Waters trace
    Into the spirits spicebed Deare,
    To vivify what withering were.   20

Hence do their Hearts like Civit-Boxes sweet
    Evaporate their Love full pure,
Which through the Chincks of their Affections reechs

To God, Christ, Christians all, though more,
To such whose Counsills made their Cure.   25

Hence now Christ's Curious Garden fenced in
    With Solid Walls of Discipline
Well wed, and watered, and made full trim:
    The Allies all Laid out by line:
    Walks for the Spirit all Divine.   30

Whereby Corruptions are kept out, whereby
    Corrupters also get not in,
Unless the Lyons Carkass secretly
    Lies lapt up in a Lamblike skin
    Which Holy seems yet's full of sin.   35

For on the Towers of these Walls there stand
    Just Watchmen Watching day, and night,
And Porters at each Gate, who have Command
    To open onely to the right.
    And all within may have a sight.   40

Whose Zeale, should it along a Channell slide
    Not banckt with Knowledg right and Good,
Nor Bottomed with Love: nor wiers ti'de
    To hinder prejudiciall Blood
    The Currant will be full of mud.   45

But yet this Curious Garden richly set,
    The Soul accounts Christs Paradise
Set with Choice slips, and flowers: and longs to get
    Itselfe set here: and by advice
    To grow herein and so rejoyce.   50

26 *Christ's*] PW Christ
38 *Porters*] PW Porter   49 *by advice*] orig: Heavenly wise
50 *and so rejoyce*] orig: it seeks and joyes

The Soul admiring the Grace of the Church
Enters into Church Fellowship.

How is this City, Lord, of thine bespangled
    With Graces shine?
With Ordinances alli'de, and inam'led,
    Which are Divine?
Walld in with Discipline her Gates obtaine   5
Just Centinalls with Love Imbellisht plain.

Hence glorious, and terrible she stands;
    That Converts new
Seing her Centinalls of all demand
    The Word to shew;   10
Stand gazing much between two Passions Crusht
Desire, and Feare at once which both wayes thrust.

Thus are they wrackt. Desire doth forward screw
    To get them in,
But Feare doth backward thrust, that lies purdue,   15
    And slicks that Pin.
You cannot give the word, Quoth she, which though
You stumble on't its more than yet you know.

But yet Desires Screw Pin doth not slack:
    It still holds fast.   20
But Fears Screw Pin turns back or Screw doth Crack
    And breaks at last.
Hence on they go, and in they enter: where
Desire Converts to joy: joy Conquours Fear.

They now enCovenant With God: and His: 25
    They thus indent.
The Charters Seals belonging unto this
    The Sacrament

11 *Passions*] PW Passion   21 *turns*] orig: slips   27 *Seals*] PW Seal's

So God is theirs avoucht, they his in Christ.
In whom all things they have, with Grace are splic'te.   30

Thus in the usuall Coach of Gods Decree
  They bowle and swim
To Glory bright, if no Hypocrisie
  Handed them in.
For such must shake their handmaid off lest they   35
Be shakt out of this Coach, or dy in th'way.

The Glory of and Grace in the Church set out.

   Come now behold
  Within this Knot What Flowers do grow:
   Spanglde like gold:
  Whence Wreaths of all Perfumes do flow.
Most Curious Colours of all sorts you shall   5
With all Sweet Spirits sent. Yet thats not all.

   Oh! Look, and finde
  These Choicest Flowers most richly sweet
   Are Disciplinde
  With Artificiall Angells meet.   10
An heap of Pearls is precious: but they shall
When set by Art Excell: Yet that's not all.

   Christ's Spirit showers
  Down in his Word, and Sacraments
   Upon these Flowers   15
  The Clouds of Grace Divine Contents.
Such things of Wealthy Blessings on them fall
As make them sweetly thrive: Yet that's not all.

   Yet still behold!
  All flourish not at once. We see   20

> While some Unfold
> Their blushing Leaves, some buds there bee.
> Here's Faith, Hope, Charity in flower, which call
> On yonders in the Bud. Yet that's not all.

> But as they stand   25
> Like Beauties reeching in perfume
> A Divine Hand
> Doth hand them up to Glories room:
> Where Each in sweet'ned Songs all Praises shall
> Sing all ore heaven for aye. And that's but all.   30

The Souls Admiration hereupon.

> What I such Praises sing! How can it bee?
> Shall I in Heaven sing?
> What I, that scarce durst hope to see
> Lord, such a thing?
> Though nothing is too hard for thee: 5
> One Hope hereof seems hard to mee.

> What, Can I ever tune those Melodies
> Who have no tune at all?
> Not knowing where to stop nor Rise,
> Nor when to Fall.   10
> To sing thy Praise I am unfit.
> I have not learn'd my Gam-Ut yet.

> But should these Praises on string'd Instruments
> Be sweetly tun'de? I finde
> I nonplust am: for no Consents   15
> I ever minde.
> My Tongue is neither Quill, nor Bow:
> Nor Can my Fingers Quavers show.

> But was it otherwise I have no Kit:
> Which though I had, I could   20

Not tune the strings, which soon would slip
   Though others should.
  But should they not, I cannot play:
  But for an F should strike an A.

And should thy Praise upon Winde Instruments   25
   Sound all o're Heaven Shrill?
My Breath will hardly through such Vents
   A Whistle fill,
  Which though it should, its past my spell
  By Stops, and Falls to sound it Well.   30

How should I then, joyn in such Exercise?
   One sight of thee'l intice
Mine Eyes to heft: Whose Extasies
   Will stob my Voice.
  Hereby mine Eyes will bind my Tongue.   35
  Unless thou, Lord, do Cut the thong.

What Use of Uselesse mee, then there, poore snake?
   There Saints, and Angels sing,
Thy Praise in full Cariere, which make
   The Heavens to ring.
  Yet if thou wilt thou Can'st me raise   40
  With Angels bright to sing thy Praise.

The Joy of Church Fellowship rightly attended.

In Heaven soaring up, I dropt an Eare
  On Earth: and oh! sweet Melody:
And listening, found it was the Saints who were
  Encoacht for Heaven that sang for Joy.
  For in Christs Coach they sweetly sing;   5
  As they to Glory ride therein.

31 *joyn*] orig: Lord, joyn 33 *heft*] orig: thee fly

Oh! joyous hearts! Enfir'de with holy Flame!
    Is speech thus tassled with praise?
Will not your inward fire of Joy contain;
     That it in open flames doth blaze?   10
     For in Christ's Coach Saints sweetly sing,
     As they to Glory ride therein.

And if a string do slip, by Chance, they soon
    Do screw it up again: whereby
They set it in a more melodious Tune   15
     And a Diviner Harmony.
     For in Christs Coach they sweetly sing
     As they to Glory ride therein.

In all their Acts, publick, and private, nay
    And secret too, they praise impart.   20
But in their Acts Divine and Worship, they
     With Hymns do offer up their Heart.
     Thus in Christs Coach they sweetly sing
     As they to Glory ride therein.

Some few not in; and some whose Time, and Place   25
    Block up this Coaches way do goe
As Travellers afoot, and so do trace
     The Road that gives them right thereto
     While in this Coach these sweetly sing
     As they to Glory ride therein.   30

11 *Christ's*] PW Christ

Miscellaneous Poems

[1. When] Let by rain.

Undated. Pub. *W*.

Ye Flippering Soule,
    Why dost between the Nippers dwell?
Not stay, nor goe. Not yea, nor yet Controle.
    Doth this doe well?
        Rise journy'ng when the skies fall weeping Showers.   5
        Not o're nor under th'Clouds and Cloudy Powers.

Not yea, nor noe:
    On tiptoes thus? Why sit on thorns?
Resolve the matter: Stay thyselfe or goe.
    Be n't both wayes born.   10
        Wager thyselfe against thy surplice, see,
        And win thy Coate: or let thy Coate Win thee.

Is this th'Effect,
    To leaven thus my Spirits all?
To make my heart a Crabtree Cask direct?   15
    A Verjuicte Hall?
        As Bottle Ale, whose Spirits prisond nurst
        When jog'd, the bung with Violence doth burst?

Shall I be made
    A sparkling Wildfire Shop   20
Where my dull Spirits at the Fireball trade
    Do frisk and hop?
        And while the Hammer doth the Anvill pay,
        The fireball matter sparkles ery way.

One sorry fret,   25
    An anvill Sparke, rose higher
And in thy Temple falling almost set
    The house on fire.
        Such fireballs droping in the Temple Flame
        Burns up the building: Lord forbid the same.   30

In PW at top of page is written: "******* occurrants occasioning what follow"
Title means: when hindered (from going on a journey) by rain.

2. Upon a Spider Catching a Fly.

Undated. Pub. *W.*

Thou sorrow, venom Elfe.
     Is this thy play,
To spin a web out of thyselfe
      To Catch a Fly?
        For Why?   5

I saw a pettish wasp
     Fall foule therein.
Whom yet thy Whorle pins did not clasp
     Lest he should fling
       His sting.   10

But as affraid, remote
     Didst stand hereat
And with thy little fingers stroke
     And gently tap
       His back.   15

Thus gently him didst treate
     Lest he should pet,
And in a froppish, waspish heate
     Should greatly fret
       Thy net.   20

Whereas the silly Fly,
     Caught by its leg
Thou by the throate tookst hastily
     And 'hinde the head
       Bite Dead.   25

This goes to pot, that not
     Nature doth call.

8 *clasp*] Conj. word torn away in PW. *W* conjectures hasp
17 *pet*] orig: thee ***set   21 *Fly,*] PW Fly.

Strive not above what strength hath got
    Lest in the brawle
        Thou fall.   30

This Frey seems thus to us.
    Hells Spider gets
His intrails spun to whip Cords thus
    And wove to nets
        And sets.   35

To tangle Adams race
    In's stratigems
To their Destructions, spoil'd, made base
    By venom things
        Damn'd Sins.   40

But mighty, Gracious Lord
    Communicate
Thy Grace to breake the Cord, afford
    Us Glorys Gate
        And State.   45

We'l Nightingaile sing like
    When pearcht on high
In Glories Cage, thy glory, bright,
    And thankfully,
        For joy.   50

3. Upon a Wasp Child with Cold.

Undated. Pub. ETG.

The Bare that breaths the Northern blast
Did numb, Torpedo like, a Wasp
Whose stiffend limbs encrampt, lay bathing
In Sol's warm breath and shine as saving,

28 *what*] orig: thy
43 *Cord,*] PW Cord   49 *And*] Conj. W conjectures Yea   1 *blast*] PW blast.

Which with her hands she chafes and stands   5
Rubbing her Legs, Shanks, Thighs, and hands.
Her petty toes, and fingers ends
Nipt with this breath, she out extends
Unto the Sun, in greate desire
To warm her digits at that fire.   10
Doth hold her Temples in this state
Where pulse doth beate, and head doth ake.
Doth turn, and stretch her body small,
Doth Comb her velvet Capitall.
As if her little brain pan were   15
A Volume of Choice precepts cleare.
As if her sattin jacket hot
Contained Apothecaries Shop
Of Natures recepts, that prevails
To remedy all her sad ailes,   20
As if her velvet helmet high
Did turret rationality.
She fans her wing up to the Winde
As if her Pettycoate were lin'de,
With reasons fleece, and hoises sails   25
And hu'ming flies in thankfull gails
Unto her dun Curld palace Hall
Her warm thanks offering for all.

     Lord cleare my misted sight that I
May hence view thy Divinity.   30
Some sparkes whereof thou up dost hasp
Within this little downy Wasp
In whose small Corporation wee
A school and a schoolmaster see
Where we may learn, and easily finde   35
A nimble Spirit bravely minde
Her worke in e'ry limb: and lace
It up neate with a vitall grace,
Acting each part though ne'er so small

11 *in*] orig: and   16 *Volume*] PW Volumn   18 *Apothecaries*] orig: in't
Apothecaries   20 *ailes,*] PW ailes   28 *warm*] Conj.   32 *downy*] Conj.
39 *each*] orig: in ery

Here of this Fustian animall.   40
Till I enravisht Climb into
The Godhead on this Lather doe.
Where all my pipes inspir'de upraise
An Heavenly musick furrd with praise.

4. Huswifery.

Undated. Pub. ETP, *W*.

Make me, O Lord, thy Spining Wheele compleate.
    Thy Holy Worde my Distaff make for mee.
Make mine Affections thy Swift Flyers neate
        And make my Soule thy holy Spoole to bee.
        My Conversation make to be thy Reele   5
        And reele the yarn thereon spun of thy Wheele.

Make me thy Loome then, knit therein this Twine:
        And make thy Holy Spirit, Lord, winde quills:
Then weave the Web thyselfe. The yarn is fine.
        Thine Ordinances make my Fulling Mills.   10
        Then dy the same in Heavenly Colours Choice,
        All pinkt with Varnisht Flowers of Paradise.

Then cloath therewith mine Understanding, Will,
        Affections, Judgment, Conscience, Memory
My Words, and Actions, that their shine may fill   15
        My wayes with glory and thee glorify.
        Then mine apparell shall display before yee
        That I am Cloathd in Holy robes for glory.

40 *Here*] orig: Exactly   41 *Climb*] orig: up Climb
42 *on*] orig: upon

5. Another upon the Same.

Undated. Pub. ETG.

Make me thy Spinning Wheele of use for thee,
    Thy Grace my Distaffe, and my heart thy Spoole.
Turn thou the wheele: let mine Affections bee
    The flyers filling with thy yarne my soule.
    Then weave the web of Grace in mee, thy Loome   5
    And Cloath my soule therewith, its Glories bloome.

Make mee thy Loome: thy Grace the warfe therein,
    My duties Woofe, and let thy word winde Quills.
The shuttle shoot. Cut off the ends my sins.
    Thy Ordinances make my fulling mills,   10
    My Life thy Web: and cloath me all my dayes
    With this Gold-web of Glory to thy praise.

6. Upon Wedlock, and Death of Children.

Undated. Pub. ETP, *W*.

A Curious Knot God made in Paradise,
    And drew it out inamled neatly Fresh.
It was the True-Love Knot, more sweet than spice
    And set with all the flowres of Graces dress.
    Its Weddens Knot, that ne're can be unti'de.   5
    No Alexanders Sword can it divide.

The slips here planted, gay and glorious grow:
    Unless an Hellish breath do sindge their Plumes.
Here Primrose, Cowslips, Roses, Lilies blow
    With Violets and Pinkes that voide perfumes.   10
10 *mills*] PW mulls

Whose beautious leaves ore laid with Hony Dew.
And Chanting birds Cherp out sweet Musick true.

When in this Knot I planted was, my Stock
   Soon knotted, and a manly flower out brake.
And after it my branch again did knot   15
   Brought out another Flowre its sweet breathd mate.
   One knot gave one tother the tothers place.
   Whence Checkling smiles fought in each others face.

But oh! a glorious hand from glory came
   Guarded with Angells, soon did Crop this flowre   20
Which almost tore the root up of the same
   At that unlookt for, Dolesome, darksome houre.
   In Pray're to Christ perfum'de it did ascend,
   And Angells bright did it to heaven tend.

But pausing on't, this sweet perfum'd my thought,   25
   Christ would in Glory have a Flowre, Choice, Prime,
And having Choice, chose this my branch forth brought.
   Lord take't. I thanke thee, thou takst ought of mine,
   It is my pledg in glory, part of mee
   Is now in it, Lord, glorifi'de with thee.   30

But praying ore my branch, my branch did sprout
   And bore another manly flower, and gay
And after that another, sweet brake out,
   The which the former hand soon got away.
   But oh! the tortures, Vomit, screechings, groans,   35
   And six weeks Fever would pierce hearts like stones.

Griefe o're doth flow: and nature fault would finde
   Were not thy Will, my Spell Charm, Joy, and Gem:

17 orig: One ••• knot gave tother tothers place   38 *my Spell*] orig: my Spell, my joy

   Four children are mentioned in this poem: line 14, "a manly flower" (Samuel, born Aug. 27, 1675, survived until maturity); line 16, "another Flowre" (Elizabeth, born Dec. 27, 1676, died December 25, 1677); line 32, "another manly flower" (James, born Oct. 12, 1678, survived until maturity); and line 33, "another, sweet" (Abigail, born Aug. 6, 1681, died Aug. 22, 1682). Taylor's fifth child (Bathshuah, born Jan. 17, 1683/4) is not mentioned; the date of this poem, then, is probably 1682 or 1683.

That as I said, I say, take, Lord, they're thine.
  I piecemeale pass to Glory bright in them.   40
  I joy, may I sweet Flowers for Glory breed,
  Whether thou getst them green, or lets them seed.

7. The Ebb and Flow.

  Undated. Pub. ETP, *W*.

When first thou on me Lord wrought'st thy Sweet Print,
  My heart was made thy tinder box.
  My 'ffections were thy tinder in't.
    Where fell thy Sparkes by drops.
Those holy Sparks of Heavenly Fire that came   5
Did ever catch and often out would flame.

But now my Heart is made thy Censar trim,
  Full of thy golden Altars fire,
  To offer up Sweet Incense in
    Unto thyselfe intire: 10
I finde my tinder scarce thy sparks can feel
That drop out from thy Holy flint and Steel.

Hence doubts out bud for feare thy fire in mee
  'S a mocking Ignis Fatuus
  Or lest thine Altars fire out bee,   15
    Its hid in ashes thus.
Yet when the bellows of thy Spirit blow
Away mine ashes, then thy fire doth glow.

5 *came*] orig: **fell**

8. Upon the Sweeping Flood Aug: 13.14. 1683.

Dated as above. Pub. ETG.

Oh! that Id had a tear to've quencht that flame
    Which did dissolve the Heavens above
    Into those liquid drops that Came
        To drown our Carnall love.
Our cheeks were dry and eyes refusde to weep.   5
Tears bursting out ran down the skies darke Cheek.

Were th'Heavens sick? must wee their Doctors bee
    And physick them with pills, our sin?
    To make them purg and Vomit, see,
        And Excrements out fling?   10
We've griev'd them by such Physick that they shed
Their Excrements upon our lofty heads.

9 *Vomit, see,*] PW Vomit see   *see*] orig: as wee

Glossary

Words and phrases of obsolete, dialectal, or otherwise unusual meaning are listed and identified in this section. Dubious or speculative identifications are queried by a parenthetical question mark: (?)—e.g. *Chase*. Included for the sake of convenience are some proper names, as well as theological terms defined or discussed by Taylor elsewhere in his writings. Words in this latter category appear in small capital letters. The primary sources for glosses are first the *OED*, second, the *EDD*, but these works are cited only when direct or paraphrased quotations are used. Books of the Bible are abbreviated as in the *OED*. For other abbreviations see above, p. ix. References to the text of the poetry are by page and line of the present edition: "12.25," e.g., means page 12, line 25.

Taylor's spellings and punctuation are retained, but his capitalization is disregarded: all words are capitalized initially, but no others unless they are normally spelled with capital letters. Variant spellings as used by Taylor appear in alphabetical order under the word (e.g. *Alembick, Alimbeck*) unless, under this scheme, a little-used spelling would appear first (e.g. *Pother, Poother*).

Nouns and verbs are given in their uninflected form except where it seems preferable for one reason or another to cite them just as they appear in the poetry (e.g. *Almugs*). Taylor is fond of interchanging parts of speech—sometimes by syntactic means alone (e.g. *Cabbinet* used as a verb, 6.17), sometimes by affixation (e.g. *bebride*, 100.14, *Dayify*, 178.13, verbs from nouns; and so on). Such altered forms are not listed unless there is a special reason for doing so.

Abaddon, destroyer, angel of the bottomless pit (Hebrew name—the Greek equivalent is Apollyon: Rev. 9:11)

ADAM. Taylor, like many of his New England contemporaries, considered Adam to be the head of all mankind, and Christ—a second Adam—the head of the elect. "Se[e] hence how God hath Confounded Satan in the greate Design managed by him to the ruine of mankinde. His Design discovers itself—it was to ruine mankinde in the Head of all mankinde [Adam] that was the Originall of all men; and the Head Covenanter for all with God so that overthrowing of him and destroying of Grace in him, all mankinde ever after might never have any such thing as sanctifying grace amongst them. But God hath utterly befoold this subtill piece of hellish policy. For he hath made another Adam to be advanced to be head of his Church, in whom there is a greater Fulness of grace than ever there was in the first, and he is the Head and Originall of all that obtain grace, Their spirituall Head from whence their gracious Nature flows, and their Head Covenanter with God in the New Covenant" (C, Sermon 8)

Adepts, makes adept, makes proficient

ADOPTION. "Adoption is a gracious Act of God, passt upon a true believer in Christ, whereby, translating him out of Satans famaly, as a Childe into his own houshould, he constitutes him a rightfull heire of all the privilidges of his own child" (CR)

Ahone, alas; = *ohone*, Scottish and Irish exclamation of lamentation

Alembick, Alimbeck, apparatus used for distilling

Alkahest, the "universal solvent" of the alchemists (probably coined by Paracelsus, after the Arabic, in medieval Latin)

Almugs, variant of *algums*, i.e. algum trees—variously surmised to be a species of acacia, cedar, or cypress, but probably a kind of sandalwood (said to have been brought from Ophir: cf. e.g. 1 Kings 10:11–12)

Altaschat, Altaschath, Al-tashcheth, i.e. Al-Taschith, Al Tashcheth, literally 'destroy not'; found in the introductory verse to Psalms 57, 58, 59, 75 and probably designates the tune to which the Psalm is to be sung (DB). In Taylor, followed in each occurrence by *Mic(h)tam*, q.v.

Amercement, imposition of a penalty or fine at the "mercy" of the inflicter; hence, an arbitrary penalty or fine

Amoring, aphaeretic form of *enamoring*

Amuse, divert the attention of, be-

guile, mislead

Anakims, anglicized plural of the Hebrew plural *anakim* (singular, *anak*); "an Old Testament race of giants of southern Canaan, who were virtually annihilated by the Israelites. *Josh.* xi.21" (WNI)

Angelica, an aromatic plant used for culinary or medicinal purposes and believed to be a preservative against poison

Angell, English coin (1470–1634) showing archangel Michael slaying the dragon

ANGELS. "Angels are compleat spirits created, probablie in the morning of the first day, with Intellectual faculties to attend the glorious Throne of God, and to be sent out for the good of Gods elect" (CR). ". . . the Holy Angels appearing to do their Messages do attend upon those forms and modes of good manners which are esteemed acts of Honour by those places where they are sent. The Angel doth not come in as a mere Clown, no, but as soon as he is entred, he doth as it were moove his hat and bow his body and say how do you" (HG, 30). "The visibility of Angels is not proper to their own nature for the Angelicall nature is spiritual and Invisible but they appeared visible in an Elementary body which they either assume or make to array themselves withall when they are dispensing their Message, for as an Ambassador coming into another contry arrayeth himself in apparrell suitable to the mode and Condition of those to whom he is sent, but layeth aside the same apparrell when he returns if it is not according to the Custom at home, so do the Angels sometimes array themselves in visible shape when they approach with Ambassies to Men which they lay by when they return into their own Countrie againe" (HG, 16). "Hence se[e] what love God manifests unto his own people. He hath special tokens to send them; a token is from a loving friend. So here is a token, a love token sent out of heaven unto thee, here is love indeed, nay and it is sent by an angel; this much more manifests Gods love, the Angels of God, those Courtiers of glory, that stand attending Gods royall Throne of Glory are not too glorious to be imployed in this work. God sends them with good things in their hands to his people; he spares his own royall Guard for this work! oh! then what love is here! . . . Hence se[e} what excellent wayes the wayes of God are to walk in; here the Angels of God are Conversant; here the soul may meet with the Holy Angels flocking from heaven unto him and may see them herein upon Jacobs Ladder flocking backward and forward in a way of divine favour to the people of God. Hence se[e] what fools all those are that will not walk in Gods way. Oh poore souls! they walk Just in the Divels way; they shall not meet the Holy Angels coming down from God out of heaven with love tokens unto them, but with the wicked angel rising out of the bottomless pit with damnable delusions to tole them on in the wayes to hell and eternall Damnation" (HG, 16)

ANTITYPE, that which is shadowed forth or represented by a type (q.v.) or symbol

Aqua vitae, any brandy or spiritous liquor; originally applied by alchemists to ardent spirits. Taylor often uses it in its literal meaning 'water of life'

Archont, i.e. *archon*, ruler, chief magistrate

Arrians, believers in the doctrine of Arius (4th-century presbyter of Alexandria), who denied that Christ was consubstantial, i.e. of the same substance with God

Aurum vitae red, possibly *aurum potabile* 'drinkable gold'—a blood-red gummy or honey-like substance taken as a medicine and cordial

Awn, "beard" of grain sheath of barley, oats, etc.; often spelled *yawn* as a result of the frequent combination *barley awn*

Baalzephon. See *Hiroth*

Bag, catch, seize (?); or, jilt (dialectal) (?)

Baracadoes, barricadoes, barriers

Barath'rick, adjective coined from *Barathrum* (Greek βαρα θρον) 'pit, gulf; the abyss, hell.' More particularly, the name was applied to a deep pit at Athens into which condemned criminals were thrown

Barjona, patronymic of Simon Peter

Barlybreaks, a game played by six persons, three of each sex, formed into couples. One couple stands in "hell" (a plot of ground between two other plots) and tries to catch other couples as they pass through

Bay, evidently the architectural meaning 'division of a wall or space lying under a gable'

Bdellium, a fragrant gum (also the name of the tree yielding it) used in medicine and perfume; from Hebrew בדלח *b'dolakh*, rendered by Josephus as βδελλα, in Genesis as ἄνθραξ 'carbuncle,' and in Numbers as κρύσταλλος 'crystal' but explained by the Rabbins and Bochart as 'pearl, pearls' (OED): hence Taylor's *pearly Bdellium*

Bear the bell, have foremost position, win the prize, take first place (the phrase, according to the *OED*, represents a merging of two denotations: *bear the bell*, i.e. take first place, as the bell-wether or leading sheep of the flock, which wears a bell on its neck; and *bear*, or *carry away, the bell*, i.e. carry off the prize —perhaps a golden or silver bell presented to a victor)

Bearing blancket, cloth or blanket used to wrap a newborn baby

Bedotcht, soiled, bedaubed (?); origin not known

Beetle, heavy mallet used for driving stakes, etc.

Bell: Bells (noun, 311.30) 'bubbles'— cf. 1576, J. Woolton, *The Christian manuell*, "Mans life flieth away . . . as the bells which bubble up in the water" (quoted in *OED*); *belling* (verb, 279.10) 'bellowing.' See also *Bear the bell*

Bemegerim, inflict with a severe headache (*be-* + *megrim* 'severe headache')

Bepinckt, Bepinkt, cut in small scallops; worked or pierced with eyelet holes. Cf. *pinkt*

Besprindge, variant of *besprenge* 'sprinkle (something) over'. (*be-* + *sprindge*, q.v.)

Bib, drink

Bibble, dabble with the bill like a duck

Bindg'd, past participle of *binge* 'make (a wooden vessel) watertight by filling it with hot water, in order to swell the wood'

Black-Cap, chickadee

Blancht, whitened, made white; (57.2) made pale with fear or awe

Blin, cease

Blodge, possibly *blotch* 'discolored patch; pustule, boil'

Bloomery, the first forge in an ironworks, where the metal is made into blooms (ingots)

Boanerges, a loud, vociferous preacher

Bob, strike, buffet

Boon, favor, gift

Booths. See *Feast of Booths*

Boss: [as noun] a round prominence in hammered or carved work, as in the cover of a book; [as verb] furnish or ornament with bosses

Bowl, Bowle, roll, like a ball in a bowling alley

Bozrah, capital of Edom (Hebrew word for 'sheepfold'). Cf. p. 23, note to line 3

Brancht, adorned with a figured pattern

Brazeel Bow, a bow made of brazilwood, a wood noted for its hardness and red color

Bruddled, Brudled [past participles], *Brudl'st* [2d singular], from *broodle* 'brood over, fondle'

Bubs, pustules

Bucking.tub, a tub used for bucking, i.e. for steeping or boiling yarn, cloth, or clothes in a lye of wood ashes, etc.

Buffe. See *Counter buffe*

Burr'ing, burrowing, sheltering

Buskt, dressed, attired, adorned

Buss, buzz, hum

Butter teeth, buckteeth, large projecting front teeth

Cades, pets (cf. cade-lamb 'pet lamb')

Calamus, sweet calamus, an aromatic plant (cf. Song of Sol. 4:14)

CALLING, EFFECTUAL. "Effectual-Calling is the Regenerating Work of the Spirit of God in the means of Grace upon the Soule, whereby the Soule turning from sin, is inseperably joyn'd unto Christ in a new Covenant. . . . The Principall of the Souls returning to God is the passive principle of Grace wrought upon the Will by the free grace of God" (CR)

Cant, pitch, turn over

Cassia, aromatic wood, ingredient of anointing oil (cf. Ps. 45:8)

Casts (62.34), defeats (in an action at law)

Catholicon, universal remedy, panacea

Catochee, catochus, catalepsy or similar affection

Cawle, caul, net, spiderweb; *anat.,* any investing membrane. Taylor probably used the word in the anatomical sense in the phrase *Cawle-wrought Case*

Chalybdine, of steel, steely. From Greek χαλυβδικos or χαλυβικos (derived from the name of an Asia Minor nation famous for iron working) with the adjectival suffix *-ιvos*

Chase, box or setting for gems; grooves (?), stone troughs used in cider-making (?)

Chat, small branch used for kindling

Cheape. See *Good cheape*

Checkling, chuckling

Chokewort, chokeweed (a weed which chokes other plants)—a species of Broomrape

Chuffe, swollen, puffed out as with disease

Cittern, a guitar-like instrument, the Tyrolean zither

Clagd, Clag'd, bedaubed with some sticky substance

Clew, ball, round bunch, cluster

Clout, cloth

Collops, thick folds of flesh on the body evidencing a well fed condition

Concoct, digest

Conjue, congee, bow

Consents (333.15), concents, harmonies

Consonant, harmonious

Cony cut, probably 'rabbit run' (*cony* 'rabbit,' *cut* 'way, passage'—cf. *short cut*)

Cordilera, Spanish for 'mountain chain'; the Spaniards applied the plural form *Cordilleras* originally to the parallel chains of the Andes in South America and later to the same system through Central America and Mexico as well

Corinthian brass, "an alloy, said to be of gold, silver, and copper, produced at Corinth, and much prized in ancient times as the material of costly ornaments" (*OED*); figuratively, 'effrontery, shamelessness'

Counter buffe, in a contrary direction

Coursey park, course-a-park, a country game in which a girl calls out a boy to chase her

COVENANT OF GRACE. Taylor believed that the Covenant of Grace became operative after the fall, when God promised that the seed of Eve would bruise the serpent's head. This new covenant, which supplanted the Covenant of Works, was made out of the free grace of God with sinning and undeserving man. "God doth forthwith plight a New-Covenant with all mankinde in Adam, Gen. 3.15. The seed of the Woman shall breake the serpents Head. Herein God did Confound the Master piece of Hellish Policy, And translate his Dispensations towards man, from the First Covenant Administrations to the New . . . and so . . . shewing signalls of his Favours to his own people, As the Blessing of Abraham, His presence with Moses, and his Advancing of David" (C, 85–86). The Covenant of Grace left man unable to be saved by his own efforts. "Whether or no a man be able of himself to come up to the terms of the Covenant. He is not able . . . from the Condition in which hee lieth till a Change be wrought . . . he is without strength" (DTP). The Covenant of Grace in New Testament times is not confined to the elect; a man under the Covenant of Grace may fall away from Grace and so be damned. "Whether or no the Covenant of Grace in new Testament times be restrained onely to the Elect. Answer: It is not . . . Because Gods call in New Testament times is of far greater latitude than the Grace of Election" (DTP). In commenting on Matt. 3:10 Taylor writes: "there are many in Covenant Relation unto God that bring not forth

good fruit . . . Such as bring not
forth Good fruite Gods judgments
shall advance against . . . Gods
judgments which he advanceth
against a people in Covenant Re-
lation to himselfe are Compared
unto a Sharp Ax . . . those that
are Cut off by Gods Ax from the
Root of their Relation to God shall
be Cast as fuell in Gods fire or hell"
(HG). For further explication of
the covenant see below, OLD AND
NEW COVENANT

COVENANT OF WORKS. "The Covenant
of works with Angels and Men is
Gods tr[a]nsacting with them upon
their Creation, in put[t]ing them
into his service, whereby he gave
them his Law as the condition of
injoying life, binding of them to
perfect Obedience upon pain of
death and for the confirmation of
mans faith therein he instituted
the tree of Knowledge and Life to
be the Sacramentall Seales thereof"
(CR)

Cribb, house, lodgings

Crickling, small, wrinkled, dried
apple (dialectal variant of *crinch-
ling, crinklin'*)

Crincht, cringed

Crosswort, name for various plants
having leaves in the form of a cross

Crouce, pert, brisk, lively, jolly

Cue, one-half pint of beer or cider
(DAE); Taylor uses it to mean *cue-
cup,* a cup which holds this amount

Cupping glasses, glass vessels applied
to the skin during the operation
of cupping, i.e. scarifying the skin
and applying to the opening a
vessel having the air within it rare-
fied

Dead head, the residuum remaining
after distillation or sublimation;
figuratively, worthless residue

Declensions, falls

DECREES OF GOD. "The Decree is an
Internall Act of God, whereby hee

hath for his own Glory appointed
whatsoever should come to pass
from all eternity" (CR). "Hence
he saith Counsill is mine and Pru-
dence is mine, and the Lord pos-
sessed me in the begining of his
Way, before his Works of old, be-
fore there was any time, before the
world was I was anointed, before
the beginning. . . . It hath drawed
out as a map, an Exemplar of all
things whatsoever from the Highest
Heavens to the lowest dust of the
Earth, yea and from the brightest
Angell in Celestiall Glory to the
smallest nit in animall Nature" (C,
80–81)

Delph, quarry, mine

Dide in grain, dyed in fast colors

Distraint, (law) action of distraining,
i.e. forcing a person to perform an
obligation by seizure of a chattel
or thing

Divells bit, devil's-bit, a meadow plant

Dozde, Doz'de, Dozed, Dozie, dozed,
dozy 'in a state of incipient decay
[of timber]'; refers in 195.19 to the
cold light given off by rotting wood

Dragons (184.14), dragonwort, plant
of the genus *Araceae*

Drugstery, drugs (?); cf. the *-ery* of
Rantery, q.v.

Dub, array, adorn; (84.35) strike

Dunce, puzzle

Edom, mountainous country south-
east of Palestine, about 100 miles
long and 20 miles broad

Effectual-Calling. See CALLING, EF-
FECTUAL

ELECTION AND THE ELECT. According
to Calvin's and Taylor's thinking,
the elect are chosen by God to be
saved and glorified, the choice be-
ing made before the foundations
of the world were laid and without
foresight of the good works or faith
of the elect. "Whether God of his
good pleasure doth elect some to

life eternall, or of foreseen Faith and good Works, or of foreseeing some good in the Creature. Answer. It is of Grace . . . Rom. 9.11. . . . Because God could foresee no good in us but what he himselfe had determined to worke in us. . . . Because the end is alway[s] in intention before the means. But Gods will to elect men to glory is his end and therefore is intended, and goes before his calling them to faith and good works . . ." (DTP). The elect may be assured of salvation. "Whether or no a man may be assured in this life he is Elected. [Answer] He may be assured of it and it is proved by Scripture 2 Pet. 1.10 . . . its assured by the testimonies of our own spirit as our spirit witnesseth with Gods spirit and this is two ways: 1. By inward tokens, as sorrow for sin, faith in Christ . . . love of Righteousness and praying for pardon. 2. By outward fruits, as a holy life and Conversation" (DTP). Taylor, of course, was not a universalist. "Whether or no Christ in the intention of his Father did die for, and redeem all men. Answer: Christ did not die for all . . . Because of the absurdity which will follow if we grant he died for all, as That Christ did actually shead his blood in the last age of the world for them that were damned in hell in the first age of the world as Kain, etc. Christ calls all with a Common call in regard of the means. But the Elect onely with a speciall call in regard of the effectual working" (DTP). "Art thou an Elect vessell? oh! Gods providences are signall touching thee. Looke on Moses, and you shall finde he and all other Males of the Israelites are under a Decree of Death to be executed upon them as soon as they peep out into the World at their birth. Well, Provi-

dence hides him in a boate of Bulrushes: Pharoah's Daughter findes him and will fauster him as her own son, puts him to Nurse to his own Mother, takes him and trains him up with all the Wisdom of Egypt, then Providence banishes him into the land of Midian and there Calls him and makes him Greate" (C, 86). The number of the elect compared with the number of the non-elect are few. ". . . there are but some of Israels unconverted Children brought up to the Lord their God by the means of Converting Grace allowed them . . . hence saith Christ few enter into the streight gate Mat. 7.13.14. and Paul calls them a remnant Rom. 9.27" (HG, 21). The Calvinist preacher, although in theory he believed that man was incapable of achieving saving faith through his own efforts, nevertheless in practice, that is in his sermons, preached as if man could make an effectual effort to achieve saving grace, and he held man morally responsible if he did not make the effort: "O most lovely Jesus! O most wonderfull One. O most necessarie unto the sons of men. There is no Life but what is in thy hand, and comes from thee. But o the folly and Hellish folly then in men, before whom thou art propounded as Life, as life for them, as the Way of Life to them: and without whom they are dead, and shall possess Eternall Death, Death the Death of Death to all Eternity, and yet they will not come to Christ. Ye will not come to mee that you may have a Life. O their folly shall be written in letters as black as Eternall Death and imbellished in the fire of Hellish flames for ever" (C, Sermon six)

Eliakim. See p. 254, note to line 25

Elim, second encampment of the Is-

raelites after passage of the Red Sea
(Exod. 15:27)

Emmet, ant

Empon'd, past participle formed from
pond 'store up, dam' (*em-* + *pond*
+ *-ed*); *up Empon'd* 'stored up, as
by damming' (*up* placed before
Empon'd for metrical reasons)

Empt, empty, exhaust

Engedi's Vineyard, an oasis celebrated
for its palms, vineyards, balsam, and
rich tropical vegetation, created
by hot water from the fountain
Engedi (in the town of the same
name) on the west shore of the
Dead Sea (*WDB;* cf. Song of Sol.
1:14)

Enkentrism, a Greek-derived coinage
describing a theological conception
of the Trinity with Christ at the
center (?); or *Encratism,* doctrine of
an early Christian sect whose mem-
bers abstained from flesh, wine, and
marriage (?)

Enrin'de, past participle formed from
rind "To prepare . . . for preserva-
tion by melting and clarifying; to
render; to melt" (OED) (*en-* +
rind + *-ed*)

Enucleate, extract the kernel from;
hence, lay open, make clear, ex-
plain

Epha, a Hebrew dry measure, 4½ to
9 gallons (*DB*) (cf. Exod. 16:36)

Ephods shoulder piece. An *ephod* was
a sacred garment worn by the high
priest, with the shoulder piece held
by an ornamental stone. Attached
to the ephod was a breastplate set
with 12 precious stones, in four
rows, symbolizing the 12 tribes of
Israel; each was engraved with the
name of one of the children of
Israel. These stones constituted the
Urim and Thummim (q.v.) and
symbolized the glory of the New
Jerusalem

Epinicioum, song of triumph, ode in
honor of a victor

Eshcol's Grapes, the celebrated grapes

from Eshcol valley, near Hebron
(*WDB*) (cf. Num. 13:23)

Etham, first encampment of the Is-
raelites after leaving Succoth (q.v.)
(cf. Exod. 13:20)

Euxine, Black Sea

Facete, elegant, graceful, polished

FAITH. "Faith is the first saving act of
Reversion, wrought in the heart by
the spirit of God in its effusing the
principle of Grace therein whereby
the soule doth inseperably cleave
unto Christ Jesus his Saviour for
life and salvation" (CR)

FALL OF MAN. "The Fall itselfe is a
Consequence of the Covenant of
Workes consisting in a Volentary
disobedience unto the Command
through the instigation of Satan, by
eating the forbidden fruit, whereby
all mankinde fell from God into a
State of Sin" (CR)

Fardells, bundles, especially burdens
or loads of sin (cf. *Hamlet* 3.1.76,
"Who   would   these   fardels
bear . . . ?")

Fat, vat

Fawnbain, a plant (species unknown)
which is harmful to fawns

Feast of Booths. See p. 125, note to
line 26

Ferula, giant fennel (see p. 216, note
to lines 1–2)

Fet (264.35), fetched

Filberd, filbert, fruit or nut of the
hazel

File, polish

Fillitted, bound or girded as with an
ornamental band

Fincht. See *Gold-fincht*

Finde, fined, brought to an end

Fistula'es, long, narrow suppurating
canals of morbid origin

Fleer, Fleere, make a wry face, laugh
in a coarse manner; mock, sneer;
flare

Flippering, crying (?); swinging, flut-
tering in the air (?)

Florendine, pie, tart

Flory, showy, flowery

Flout. See *May game flout*

Flur, Flurr, scatter; flutter

Flyer (343.3), the part of a spinning wheel that twists the thread as it leads it to the bobbin

Foil, apply a thin sheet of metal to; see also p. 17, note to line 16

Foist, stink, musty smell

Fox and geese, a boys' game played with marbles or pegs

Frame (277.13), constitution, nature

Freestone, any fine-grained sandstone or limestone

Frim, vigorous, flourishing, luxuriant

Frize, frieze, a kind of thick, warm woollen cloth used for rough outer garments

Frob, variant of *throb*

Frog, disease of the throat or mouth

Froppish, froward, fretful, peevish

Fude, feud

Full, beat (cloth) with wooden mallets and cleanse it with fuller's earth or soap. *Fulling mill*, mill in which cloth is fulled

Furrd, trimmed, covered

Fustian, thick twilled cloth

Gam-Ut, musical scale; technically, the "Great Scale," consisting of all the recognized notes used in medieval music

Garland tuns, probably tuns with garland insignia

Garnisht, adorned

Gastard, Gasterd, astonished; terrified; struck with amazement

Gayes, toys, childish amusement

Geer, Geere, gear, apparatus; matter, stuff

Gilgal, first encampment of Israelites west of the Jordan, where those born during the march through the wilderness were circumcised; cf. *Gilgal's Razer*. See p. 97, note to Med. 10

Giliad, Gilliad, mountainous country east of the Jordan, where the famous balm grew. *Giliads Balm*, Balm of Gilead, or Mecca balsam, which exudes an agreeable balsamic resin

Gird, strike, smite; bind tightly

Girths, tight bands

Glaver, flatter

Glore, Scottish form of *glory*

GLORIFICATION. "Glorification is a Reall Change of State whereby a Person is translated out of a state of misery into a state of felicity that shall be compleated in the full fruition of heavenly Glory to all eternity" (CR)

Glout: [as noun] frown, sullen look; [as verb] frown, look sullen

Gold-fincht, having a golden streak on its back (*gold + finched* 'streaked along the back')

Good cheape, a cheap market

Goshen, the part of Egypt where the Israelites dwelt throughout their sojourn in that country

GRACE. The effect of the working of God's free grace upon the soul was a very real experience to Taylor and resulted in some of the most moving passages in the Meditations as well as eloquent passages in prose. "What can all the Powers of Hell and Darkness do or Effect, think you, against God? If God be for us who can be against us? The sweetest Consolation attainable for man comes in with this Relation. Oh! with joy shall you draw water out of the Wells of Salvation. What Comfort is here for all in Christ. All God is in Christ, therefore all Comforts of God are in Christ. If the Influence of God in the outlets of his providence, makes a Pinke, A Rose, a Violet so sweet to us, if a touch of such influences make the liquour of the Grape, the fertility of the Field, the Cookery of our food, the Labour of the Bee. the sati[s]faction of the Cane juyce, yea

and the Influences of a sorry mor-
tall acting gratefully, leave such a
Delightsomeness upon our spirit
and senses and are so Edulcorated
for us, What then are the sweet
heart enravishments of the Consola-
tions that are Contained in the
Godhead itselfe from a little vent
of whose influences these things are
made so sweet unto the hearts of
saints in Christ?" (C, Sermon 1).
"O let this stir up all to be bathing
their souls in this sunshine; all
heavenly Excellencies are here to
be had; here is Warmth to revive
thy soule; Life to Enliven thy dead
soule; Light to Enlighten thy
Blinde soul, and to direct it in the
right Way and Glory to make all
glorious thy black deformed soule!
Oh what would thou have more;
nay here is a glorious golden scaling
Ladder made of this shine to carry
thy soul up into the Body of the
son of Righteousness and so into
the Throne of Eternall Glory" (HG,
6). The saving grace of Christ is im-
parted to the elect and the elect
only. "But oh how doth he . . .
worke Graciously to and for his
own people? This lies as a founda-
tion for all that he hath done and
suffered for them. His Grace and
Favour to them lies as the Corner
Stone that bears up the Whole of
this building. His undertaking the
work lies upon this rock. His suffer-
ings ly upon this bottom. Because
he hath a Favour for them, he died
for them, and he pours out his
prayers to God for them, yea and
Conferrs all Grace in them and on
every one of them and advanceth
every one of them into Eternal
Glory" (C, Sermon 8). "Grace,
furnishing the soule for glorie and
Glory the Felicity and Reward of
Grace. O! what Comfort and Con-
solation is here. Hands off: its Chil-
drens bread; a Crumb of it may not

fall to dogs. But all of it belongs
to every Child in the Family" (C,
Sermon 8)

Grain. See *Dide in grain*

Grindlestone, dialectal form of *grind-
stone*

Grudgens, gurgeons, coarse meal

Gudgeon, bait

Gum'd Taffity. See *Taffity*

Gust: (24.20) blow; taste

Halls (267.22), hauls

Hanck, hank, fasten by a loop or
noose; entangle

Harish, mad

Harle, filament or fiber of flax or
hemp; tangle, knot, confusion

Haump, smock-frock (Yorkshire: "a
hardin' hamp" *EDD*)

HEAVEN. Taylor had a literal concep-
tion of heaven, typical of the Puri-
tan idea of his time. ". . . what
transporting contentment will it
yield? to se[e] God face to face, to
se[e] Jesus Christ, to se[e] the wayes
of God · in the World! to se[e] the
Golden Checker work of the Draw
net of Providence hung open before
the view of the soule, to behold
how in the Mashes of the same the
Saints are Cought and carried to
Glory and the Sinners cought and
Cast into hell . . . to see the glori-
ous outgoing of Gods Essential
Properties . . . oh how will this
amount the Soule . . . it sets the
Soule a singing forth the Praises of
the Lord God having made the
soule such a glorious Musicall In-
strument of his praise, and the holy
Ghost having so gloriously strung
it with the golden Wyer of Grace
and heavenly Glory, having screw'd
up the strings to sound forth the
songs of Zions King; the pouring
forth of the Influence of Glory play
upon the Soule Eternall praises
unto God, and Now the soule be-
gins to sing forth its endless Halle-

lujahs unto God; if it were possible it would fly in pieces under its glory, if this glory got no vent; and therefore it being filled with glory for Gods glory it falls to singing most ravishingly out the Glory of God in the highest strains" (CR)

HELL. Taylor had a very literal and vivid conception of this place where the wicked are tormented: "The sentence is thus given Depart from me, thou accursed into eternall flames . . . the place where the Damned and Divels are tortured forever . . . oh this must needs be a dreadfull, dolefull, darksom, gloomy, dismall, and Deadly place indeed; it is called in scripture utter darkness; Hell fire; Wrath to come; a Lake of fire and brimstone; Everlasting Distruction; Everlasting torment and everlasting flames. Whether by this fire or flame is intended the Pure wrath of God as some, or also material fire as most probable I shall not determine, yet this is plain, it doth import the most extream tormentor which is, for nothing acts more furiously than fire upon any thing. Hence this place is the most terrible, torturing, tormenting, burning, scalding, Enfiring, stincking, strangling, stifling, Choaking, damping Dungeon immaginable" (CR)

Henbain, henbane, common name of a certain weed having an unpleasant smell and narcotic and poisonous properties

Herba Trinitatis, an herb; old name for pansy or anemone hepatica

Herb-a-grace, herb of grace, an old name for the herb rue; in a general sense, an herb of virtue or valuable properties

Hesbon, Heshbon, city of Sihon (cf. Song of Sol. 7:4)

Hift [noun, verb], heft, lift, help, heave

Hilt, foil

Hin, Hebrew liquid measure, a little over a gallon

Hint, occasion, opportunity (cf. *Othello* 1.3.142, "It was my hint to speak")

Hiroth, Pi-hahiroth, site of the last encampment of the Israelites before they left Egypt, between Migdol and the sea, near Baal-zephon (Exod. 14:2)

Hopple, fasten together the legs of an animal to prevent it from straying; fetter, hobble

Hopt, happed, covered, wrapped

Horeb, the mount of God in the peninsula of Sinae where the Law was given to Israel (*WDB*)

Hurden, harden, a coarse fabric made from the hards of flax or hemp; often used attributively, 'coarse'

Hyssop, small herb used by Hebrews to sprinkle blood on door posts during Passover

Ignis lambens, a lightly licking fire

Iliak, Illiak, ileus, a painful affliction caused by intestinal obstruction; also called *iliac passion*

Imply, employ

Issick Bay, a bay in the northeast corner of the Mediterranean

I'st, I shall (*I* + *'st,* reduced enclitic form of *shall*)

Jet, swagger

Jews trump, Jew's harp

Jing, Jinks, Jink Game—a card game derived from Spoil-five

JUDGMENT DAY. "The day of Judgment is the Generall Assise of Jesus Christ who summoning all sinners to appeare before his Tribunall shall in a glorious manner render to every one exactly according unto their Deeds" (CR). In CR there are seven and a half folio pages of very close, minute writing by Taylor describing this great event, much of it reminiscent of Wigglesworth's "The Day of Doom." For example: "The

Arreignment of the Miserable Miscreant and Damnable wretch who shall stand in his sin and guilt and ugliness and filth trembling and that every one of them, not one whether wicked men or Divells, none over-lookt, none omitted; none can get away from the wrath of the judge, or make an Escape." See also above, HEAVEN; HELL

JUSTICE. With respect to the non-elect, that is the majority of mankind, God's justice takes precedence over his mercy. Like Jonathan Edwards and other Calvinists, Taylor preached that Christ would take a just and terrible vengeance on his enemies: "What a terrour will it be to thee to have Christ thine Enemy that is Almighty? O think of this. No terrour on this side hell like this. Can thy heart endure or thine hands be strong in the day that he shall deale with thee? Alass, if he come against thee in the form of a Lamb, though thou was the greatest Monarch or Mightiest mountain on earth, thou wouldst be ready to run into [a] mouse hole to hide thyselfe from his Wrath . . . He will put on Might as a garment and Majesty and strength as a Robe. He will array himselfe With glory and come in flames of fire to take Vengeance of his Enemies and revenge upon his Adversaries, to render his anger with fury and his rebukes with flames of fire. Now then what a terrour wilt thou be in when he shall thus come to deale with thee? Thinke of it. His Maje[s]ty shall bee so greate that the Angells of Glory Will shout at it, the Heavens Will ring again, the Aire and skies filld with his host will Quaver and the earth Will tremble, and now the most amazing sight that poor sinners set their Eyes on will appear before their eyes to their utter Con-

fusion. Thou mayst as easily toss away the earth as a tennis ball or turn the World out of doores as a puppy dog or Pull down the Heavens over the heads of all things as a tilt Cloath, as easily recover the time that is passt away, Weigh the Whole Empyreall battlements in a pair of Gold Scales, Contain the Winde in the Hollow of thy hande and lade the Sea dry with an acorn bowle as stand before the Lord Jesus Christ who is Almighty and thine Enemy" (C, Sermon 7)

JUSTIFICATION. "Justification is a gracious sentence of God passt upon a true believer in Christ whereby on the accou[n]t of Christs Righteousness, he being freed from guilt of sin, is pronounced truely Righteous in the sight of God eternally" (CR). Taylor, like all Calvinists, believed that man was justified by faith alone, and not by works. "Whether or no we be justified by Faith alone. Answer: We are justified by Faith alone" (DTP)

Keck, retch, reject with loathing
Ken, catch sight of, discover by sight
Kerfe, incision
Kid, faggot or bundle of twigs, brushwood, etc., either for burning or for embedding in sand to give it firmness
Kit, small fiddle
Kit-cat, a boys' game rather like baseball on a small scale
Knops, knobs, ornamental studs, bosses
Knot, flower bed

Lade, take up or remove water from a river, vessel, etc.
Lake of Meris, Lake Moeris, an artificial lake in Middle Egypt (*Cent. Dict.*)

Lather, ladder

Layes, layers or courses (of masonry)

Learch, lurk

Let, hindrance

Lign aloes, the aromatic wood of the Agalloch, noted for its fragrance (cf. Song of Sol. 4:14)

Lignum vitae, wood of life; wood from the *Guaiacum* tree

Linsy-Wolsy, an inferior material of wool and cotton

Lug, pull, as by the ear

Lythargy, lethargy

Macie, mace-like; adjective formed from *mace*, the spice consisting of the dried outer covering of the nutmeg

Mammocks, scraps, shreds, broken pieces

Mammulary, nipple, breast. See also p. 7, note to lines 18 ff.

Mara, fountain of bitter water (Exod. 15:23)

Mates, pairs

Maukin, scarecrow

May game flout, a flout (i.e. butt or object of flouting, mocking) in a May game

MEDIATION. "The Mediation itselfe is Christs appearing before his Father on the account of his people who by making full satisfaction to Justice itselfe, hath purchased them unto Eternall Salvation" (CR)

Mence, adorn, grace

MERCY. With respect to the elect God's mercy takes precedence over his justice. "Now by Mercy we are to understand that speciall Favour which God doth bestow upon his own people for here in our Text [Luke 1:50] all other are exempt from it . . . onely those that are the true fearers of God in any generation have a right propriety in the Mercy of God" (HG, 44). God's mercy will sustain the elect, and

even satan is powerless against it: "Satan by all his Wiles and Temptations can't . . . touch them. He is a Conquer'd Enemy. He is cast down out of his throne, out of his first habitation. Those Starrs that are struck down by his Taile out of Heaven were but Wandering stars for Whom is reserved the blackness of darkness for ever. None in Christ be harmed by this Enemy of Christ . . . Christ is Almighty and Will blow the old Serpent and his Serpentine subtilty away as a feather in the Winde. Now is not this sweet Comfort?" (C, Sermon 7)

Meris. See *Lake of Meris*

Michtam, Mictam, term applied to certain psalms to indicate their musical character; in the phrase *Michtam-David*, apparently 'psalm.' Usually preceded by *Altaschat* (etc.), q.v.

Migdol. See Hiroth

Minced, chopped

Miserere mei, name for iliac passion (see *Iliak*)

Morrice, Nine Men's Morris, a game rather like checkers or chess, but played in a field (or on a table or board); cf. *Midsummer Night's Dream* 2.1.96-98, "The fold stands empty in the drowned field, / And crows are fatted with the murrion flock; / The nine men's morris is fill'd up with mud"

Mullipuff, fuzz-ball (used as a term of contempt)

Mummy, a medicinal preparation of the substance of mummies

Muscadalls, the grapes from which muscatel wine is made; or the muscadell pears

Neatly, finely

Neckt, dialectal pronunciation of *naked*

New Covenant. See OLD AND NEW COVENANT

Nine holes, a boys' game played with a ball and nine round holes in the ground (or in a board)

Nine pins, skittles, a bowling game played with nine pins

Ninus, Nineveh

Noddy, a card game like cribbage (ETG)

Non-suites, subjects to a *nonsuit,* "the stoppage of a suit by the judge, when, in his opinion, the plaintiff fails to make out a legal cause of action or to bring sufficient evidence" (*OED*)

Note, sigh, token, indication

Nymps, imps

Obsignation, ratification, action of sealing

Oculated, observant

Officine, workshop, laboratory; office in a monastery (cf. medieval Latin *officina,* "applied to a store-room of a monastery, in which medicines, etc. were kept"—*OED*)

OLD AND NEW COVENANT. Taylor defines the differences between these in his theological notes (old refers to Old Testament times, new to New Testament times)

SIMILARITIES:

"1. In the Authour of them, which is God.

2. In regard of the Mediator of them, Christ. Moses indeed was called a Mediator of the old Covenant, but he was but Typical.

3. In regard of the parties accepting of them, i.e., man.

4. In regard of the moving Cause, to wit Free-Grace.

5. In regard of the Conditions of them for they are the same.

1. On Gods part, as remission of sins and happinesse.

2. On Mans part, As Faith and Repentance."

DIFFERENCES:

"1. In their extent and latitude. For the old Covenant received onely the Jews, but the new, all Nations.

2. In the parties impl[o]yed in the administration of them. The old Covenant was administred by Priests and Prophets, but the New by Christ.

3. In their Duration. The old had its date and time, but the New continues to the end of the world.

4. In the Seales annext to them. The old had Circumcision and the Passeover, but the New Baptism and the Lords Supper.

5. In the Way of Consecrating of them. The old by the blood of Bulls and Goats, etc., the New by the blood of Christ.

6. In their Clearenesse of the Doctrine of Salvation; it is more cleare and distinct by Christ than before.

7. In the time of the Exhibition of Christ; in the old there were onely Christ in a promise, but in the New he is set forth as already come.

8. In the liberties injoyed under the New Covenant above what was under the old. For those under the New lie not under the yoake of Ceremoniall bondage.

9. In the large effusion of the spirit under the New above what was under the old. For the application of the spirit is more effectuall and his gifts more perfect under the New than under the old" (DTP)

Olivant, horn of ivory

One-and-thirty, a card game resembling vingt-un

Ophir, a place of uncertain locality. mentioned in the Old Testament (e.g. 1 Kings 10:11), where fine gold was obtained

Ophthalmicks, medicines for the eye

ORIGINAL SIN. "Originall Sin . . . is the want of Originall Righteousness together with a strong inclination unto all actuall evill flowing from the guilt of Adams first Sin over all his posterity descending from him by ordinary generation, and is the spawn and spring of all Actuall transgressions" (CR). The guilt of original sin extended to children. "Whether or no Infants, and so all men bee borne guilty of Originall Sin? Answer: All men by nature are sinners. . . . Children are part of the world, and if so then guilty of sin before God" (DTP). Man in a state of sin is completely helpless without the free grace of God: ". . . we may see what an accursed, poisonous, ruinating Evill thing Sin is, and what a dismall, Woefull, Miserable, and forlorn Condition man is cast into by Sin. The Case is such that the Elect of God, the Object of Gods Everlasting Love are sure on the account of sin to sustain the Vengeance of Gods Everlasting Wrath, and the torments of Eternall flames in hell unless they be relieved and their condition is so Execrable that it is beyond the relief of all Created help whatsoever. None But the Eternall son of God could succor them. There is no remedy the whole world can procure them: All man Kinde is lost, and beyond its own Reliefe. His state is remediless; as to the Holy Angells of God—No help in their hand. Its onely Godhead Power that could do it" (C, Sermon 1)

Paintice, penthouse, a sloping roof, awning, canopy, shed, etc.

Palate fallen, relaxed uvula (1664, Pepys Diary, 23 Sept., "the palate of my mouth falling, I was in great pain"—quoted in *OED*)

Pald, enclosed with pales, surrounded, fenced in

Palma Christi, the castor oil plant

Panchins, pancheons, circular pans made generally of earthenware

Parg'd, covered with parget or plaster

Pargings, pargeting, ornamental work

Passover, Passo're. See p. 119, note to line 10

Patmos Ile, the island in the Aegean Sea to which St. John was banished and where he saw his vision

Peare, aphaeretic form of *appear*

Peart, Piert, quick to see, sharp (of the eye); lively, brisk (of a person)

Peckled, speckled

Peere, (be the) equal (of)

Pegs, pins or points of the rowel of a spur

Pensile orchards, hanging gardens

Peps, pepse, pelt, throw at

Pericarde, Pericordium, pericardium, the sac which encloses the heart

Petro oyle, probably Peter's oil

Phlebotomized, bled by having a vein opened

Pia-mater'd, covered with a pia mater, i.e. with "a delicate fibrous and very vascular membrane which forms the innermost of the three *meninges* enveloping the brain and spinal cord" (*OED*)

Pick, pitch (cf. *Coriolanus* 1.1.204, "As high as I could picke my Lance")

Pickpack, pick-a-back, on the shoulder or back, like a bundle

Piert. See *Peart*

Pild, tipped with a pile, i.e. "the pointed metal head of a dart, lance, or arrow" (*OED*)

Pillard, one who is peeled or stripped (from the obsolete verb *pill* 'peel'; Taylor also uses *pilled* 'peeled' in his diary)

Pimping, small, petty, mean, insignificant

Pinck, Pink, peep, blink, wink; *pin(c)ked, pin(c)kt* 'adorned,' see also *Bepin(c)kt*

Pincky eyes, small, narrow eyes; cf. *pinkeny* 'blinking, peering eye' (17th-century usage)

Pingle, small piece of enclosed ground

Pink. See *Pinck*

Pipkin, small earthen pot or glazed earthenware saucepan

Plastrum Gratiae Dei, plaster of the grace of God

Pledgets, small compresses for applying to wounds

Plites, plights, conditions, states, moods

Pomills, ornamental knobs on a chair

Poole of Shiloam, pool built by Hezekiah on the west side of Jerusalem, to which sick persons were brought to bathe in Jesus' time (cf. John 9:7–11)

Poother. See *Pother*

Posamnitick's Labyrinth. See *Psammitich's Labyrinth*

Post-and-pare, a card game played with three cards each in which the players bet on their own hands

Pother, Poother: [as noun] commotion, tumult; [as verb] move, pour, or roll in a cloud, as smoke or dust

Pottinger, porringer, small soup bowl

Pounderall, pounder, pestle, instrument for crushing

POWER. Taylor emphasizes God's use of his power in punishing sinners and rewarding saints. ". . . hence this power which is matter of joy to Gods people, is matter of amazing Astonishment to the wicked; as sure as God is a God of power he will put forth his Power in scattering the Wicked before him, and in succoring his own people. Oh then all the Enemies of his people comming out as a mighty host against him shall not be able to stand before him; but he will breake all their Ranks and scatter

their power into the four winds togather. But oh! the joy then of his own people! Oh happy day!" (HG, 45)

Pranck, caper with an arrogant air

Print: [as noun] an image or character stamped on the mind or soul, especially the divine likeness; [as adjective] perfect, neat, precise, hence *in print* 'in a precise and perfect manner, to a nicety'

Pritch, grudge, spite

Propence, inclined

PROVIDENCE. "Providence in Generall is an externall worke of God whereby he disposeth of all things with all their Actions" (CR)

Psammitich's (Posamnitick's) Labyrinth, labyrinth built by Psammetichus, an Egyptian ruler of the 13th dynasty (*Cent. Dict.*)

Purdue, perdue, concealed

Purse, scrotum

Pursevant, pursuivant, messenger

Put, a card game

Quaver, a shake or trill in singing

Quicken'd metall, probably quicksilver

Quill, piece of reed or other hollow stem on which yarn is wound

Quilting, blanketing, (all-)covering (?)

Quinsie throate, inflammation of the throat; tonsillitis

Quintesses, quintessences

Quorn, quern, a simple mechanism usually consisting of two stones, the upper one turned by hand, for grinding corn

Radien, radial, pertaining to light in the form of rays

Ragnell, coinage meaning vagrant (?)

Ragwort, an herb of a bitter, cleansing quality

Rameses, Ramesis, town in Goshen (q.v.), starting point of the Exodus; first stage of the journey was from here to Succoth

Rantery, ranting (cf. the *-ery* of *Drugstery*)

Recepts, receipts

REDEMPTION. "Redemption is the first part of the Recovery of the Elect out of the Fall by the Redeemer, Who laying down for them the full price satisfactory to justice itselfe, hath purchased them unto eternall salvation . . . Christs Humiliation is the first part of Redemption whereby yielding obedience unto the whole Law of God perfectly satisfactory to justice itselfe, he hath purchased eternall salvation for his people" (CR)

Reech, reek, odor (either sweet or bad)

Reev'd, intertwined, wreathed (?)

Refelld, repelled

REPROBATION. "Unbeliefe and bad works are the Cause of Damnation, but not of Reprobation. Because sin doth not go before but follows after Reprobation. For we must distinguish between the Decree and the Execution of it. The Decree is eternall and before sin. The Decree respects man in generall as a Creature; the Execution looks on man as he is in sin" (DTP). Like Calvin, Taylor found it difficult to resolve the conflict between man's moral responsibility and the decree of Reprobation, and like Calvin he insisted that in spite of the Decree, God was not the author of sin. The following verbal quibbling by Taylor is typical: "Objection: Reprobation brings men into a necessity of sin[n]ing; therefore God is the Author of Sin. Answer: Gods Decree infers no necessity of constraint but onely of immutability" (DTP)

Riggalld, verb formed from the noun *riggal* 'ring-like mark' (or 'groove in wood or stone'?)

Rinde, strip the rind or bark from

Rive, pierce

Rowell, spur with a rowel

Rowle upon, meditate on; *Rowle oneself upon,* entrust oneself to. The word occurs in the poetry of Taylor's contemporary Anne Bradstreet:

> Hide not thy face from me, I cry'd,
>> From Burnings keep my soul;
> Thou know'st my heart, and hast me try'd;
> I on thy Mercyes Rowl.
>> (From "For Deliverance from a feaver")

> O stay my heart on thee, my God,
>> Uphold my fainting Soul!
> And, when I know not what to doe,
> I'll on thy mercyes roll.
>> (From "In my Solitary houres in my dear husband his Absence")

Mrs. Bradstreet's 19th-century editor J. H. Ellis offers an interesting interpretation of the expression:

This singular expression . . . is probably taken from Ps. xxii.8, —"He trusted on the lord *that* he would deliver him: let him deliver him, seeing he delighted in him"; or from Ps. xxxvii.5, —"Commit thy way unto the Lord; trust also in him; and he shall bring *it* to pass." The marginal reading for "trusted on" is *"rolled* himself," and for "Commit thy way unto," *"roll thy way upon."*

The "Bay Psalm Book" translates the former verse as follows:
Vpon the Lord he rold himself, let him now rid him quite: let him deliver him, because in him he doth delight.

Winthrop uses the same expression in a letter to his son ("Life and Letters," p. 250).

But such as will roll their ways upon the Lord, do find him always as good as his word.

J. H. Ellis, *The Works of Anne Bradstreet* (Charlestown, 1867), pp. 35–36 n.

Rubston, rubstone, a kind of whetstone

Ruff-and-trumpt. Ruff, "a former card-game. . . . The act of trumping at cards, esp. in whist" (*OED*)

Sabellians, followers of Sabellius (3d century), who believed that the Father, Son, and Holy Spirit are merely different modes of one divine being

SACRAMENTS. The New England Puritans had two sacraments, the Lord's Supper and Baptism. "The Seales of the Covenant of Grace (called the Sacraments) are means instituted of God whereby the benefits of Redemption by outward signs represented are sealingly applied unto believers, as in Baptism and the Lords Supper" (CR)

Saints Johns Wort, plants of the genus *Hypericum*

Salamanders Woole, asbestos

Sampler, an example to be imitated; model, pattern, archetype

SANCTIFICATION. "Sanctification is a Reall Change of State whereby the Person being cleansed from the filth of sin, is renewed in the likeness of God by the graces of the Spirit" (CR)

Saphrin, sapphirine, sapphire-like

Sapphick, seraphic (?)

Sawceboxes, persons addicted to making saucy or impertinent remarks

Scar-fire, scare-fire, a sudden conflagration

Searce, Seirce: [as noun] sieve, strainer; [as verb] sift, strain (past participles *searcde, searst*)

Secundine, placenta

Sedan, carry, as in a sedan

Seirce. See *Searce*

Selvedge, border, edge; literally, edge of woven material finished to prevent ravelling out of the weft

Set, at a, at a standstill, in difficulties, nonplused

Shab, get rid of, get (a person) out of the way

Shackeroon, -oon variant of *shackerell* 'vagabond'

Shalm, Shawm, a musical instrument

Sheed, variant of *shed* 'cause (blood) to flow, by cutting or wounding'

Shew-bread, "the twelve loaves that were placed every Sabbath 'before the Lord' on a table beside the altar of incense, and at the end of the week were eaten by the priests alone" (*OED*)

Shiloam. See *Poole of Shiloam*

Shittim wood, a species of acacia—supposed to be hard, resistant to insects, and not subject to rot—of which the ark of the covenant was made. Cotton Mather judged it to be the black acacia: see *Philosophical Transactions of the Royal Society of London, 29* (1714), 63

Shivers, splinters, fragments

Shooclout, shoe cloth, cloth for wiping the shoes

Shory, shorry, short pole

Shoshannim, probably a stringed instrument (*DB*). Word occurs in Psalms 45 and 69

Shulamite, woman of Shulem (cf. Song of Sol. 6:13)

Shutts, shutters

Sibma, Sibmah, 'balsam-place'—a town east of the Jordan famous under the Moabites for its grapes (*WDB*) (cf. Isa. 16:8–9)

Sillibub, Sillibubb, Syllabub, "a drink or dish made of milk or cream, curdled by the admixture of wine, cider, or other acid, and often sweetened and flavoured" (*OED*)

Silverlings, shekels

Simnill, simnel, "rich currant cake, usu. eaten on Mid-Lent Sunday in certain districts [of England]" (*OED*)

Sin-falling mallady, probably epilepsy (the "falling sickness"—*OED*)

Sippits, small pieces of toasted bread, often served in soup

Skeg: (74.1) variant of *keg* (?); (175.12) wild plum

Slatch, lazy idle vagabond

Slickt up, made elegant or fine

Slops, food

Slunk, cast

Snick-snarls, tangles

Socinians, members of a sect founded by Laelius and Faustus Socinus (16th-century Italian theologians), who denied the divinity of Christ

Sockage, socage, tenure of land; most usual in the phrases *free socage* and *common socage*

Sogd, soaked, steeped, saturated

Sory, a kind of mineral ore yielding vitriol; a kind of vitriol

Soul Blindness, defective power of recognizing objects seen, caused by cerebral lesion, without actual blindness and independent of other psychic defect (*Cent. Dict.*)

Spagyrist, alchemist

Spermodote, giver of seeds

Spic'd, seasoned

Spicknard, spikenard, the aromatic plant *Nardostachys Jatamansi* of North India

Spiles, spoils

Spiricles, diminutive form of *spires*

Sprindg, Sprindge, variant of *sprenge* 'sprinkle; scatter, disperse, spread about'

Spruice, brisk, smart, lively

Sprunt, struggle, lash out, kick

Squibd, attacked as with a squib, i.e. with a sarcastic hit or lampoon

Squitchen, variant of *scutcheon* 'piece of bark used in grafting' (?)

'St, reduced enclitic form of *shall;* see also *I'st*

Stale, butcher's stall; lure

Standish, inkstand, inkpot

Stem (56.24) shoot, as advanced by a growing plant

Stob, stab

Stoole (314.18) head of a tree stump, from which new roots are produced

Stowhouse, variant of *stovehouse* 'hothouse (for plants)'

Stranging, wondering

Strout, strut

Stut, stutter

Sub Forma Pauperis, in the form of a poor person exempted from liability to pay the costs of a legal action

Succoth, sukkoth, Hebrew holiday also known as the Feast of Booths (see p. 125, note to line 26). See also *Rameses*

Surdity, deafness

Swash: [as noun] swaggering; [as adjective] showy (cf. printing: swash letters, capital letters made with flourishes)

Sweetspike, the sweet flag, a rush-like plant with sword-shaped leaves, from whose roots *Calamus aromaticus* (a stomachic) is extracted

Syllabub. See *Sillibub*

Syncopee, heart failure

Tabber, tabor, drum; *tabber stick,* drumstick

Taffity, taffeta; *brancht taffity,* taffeta adorned with a figured pattern; *gum'd taffity,* taffeta stiffened with gum

Tag'd, fitted with ornamental ends or points of metal

Tantarrow'd, verb formed from *tantara* 'trumpet flourish.' Cf. PW, Canticle 3, item 32, appendix 2: "I trumpet out tantarroes"

Tazzled, tangled, fuzzy, twisted, knotty (from *tazzle,* dialectal form of *teazle* 'entangle')

Tenent, tenon, join together with tenon and mortise

Tent: [as noun] probe; [as verb] (74.6) reside, (84.4) past participle of *tend* 'kindle, light, set fire to'

THEANTHROPY, THEANTHROPIE, the fact of being both God and man; the union of the divine and human natures in Christ

Thresher, or thrasher, a shark which attacks with its tail

Thrum, fringe of warp-thread ends remaining on the loom when the web is cut off

Thrump, variant of *frump* 'mock, flout'

Thummim. See *Urim*

Tilt-clothe, awning, canvas; tent, tabernacle

Ting, ring

Tipple, topple

Tole-Dish, toll-dish, vessel of the proper dimensions for measuring the grain which is the miller's fee for grinding

'*Tony Cross,* St. Anthony's Cross, the *crux commissa,* in the shape of the letter T; so called because it was supposed to have been worn on the cope of Sir Anthony, who suffered from frequent temptations of the devil (John McClintock and James Strong, *Cyclopaedia of Biblical, Theological, and Ecclesiastical Literature,* 12 vols. New York, Harper's, 1894–96).

Topping, ascending

Trancifide, put in a trance

Tread, cicatricula, the round white spot on the yolk bag of a bird's egg, consisting of the germinal vesicle

Trig, trip

Trine, group of three, threefold

Tuck up, enclose, fold in

Tumberill, tumbrel, tumbril, "A cart so constructed that the body tilts backward so as to empty out the load; *esp.* a dung-cart" (*OED*)

Turn, Turns, a brain disease characterized by giddiness

Type, analogy, foreshadowing; "a person, object, or event of Old Testament history, prefiguring some person or thing revealed in the new dispensation; correl. to *antitype*" (*OED*). In 83.13, 19 possibly used in the more general meaning 'symbol, emblem—especially of something or someone yet to appear'

Ubiquitarians, believers in ubiquitism, the doctrine of the omnipresence of Christ's body

Ubiquity, the omnipresence of Christ or his body

Unguent Apostolorum, unguent of the Apostles

Unlute, remove lute—tenacious clay or cement used to stop an orifice —from a vessel

Urim and Thummim. Taylor believed that the Urim ('light'?) and Thummim ('perfection'?) were used to determine the will of God—that God spoke through them: ". . . for in the Temple God did discover his minde by Urim and Thummim but probably the Urim and Thummim there were burnt when Solomons Temple was burn[t] or left in the Captivity" (HG, 15); "that God sometimes doth reveale his will unto his people worshiping him, not according to the manner of his own Institution . . . the way wherein he gave forth Oracles in his Temple was by Urim and Thummim" (HG, 17). See also *Ephods shoulder piece*

Varnishing, polishing

Verjuicte, sour; past participle from *verjuice* 'acid juice of unripe fruit; make sour'

Wamble, feel nausea; *womble-crop* 'nauseate, make sick,' formed from the phrase *wamble-cropped* 'affected with nausea, sick'

Wards, ridges of a lock

Wash (277.14), swill

Waybred, Waybred Leafe, plantain, an herb used medicinally

Wedden, wedding

Welt, roll

Welted, adorned or trimmed as with welts, i.e. borders or fringes

Whelm'd-down, turned with the concavity downward; buried under a load

Whiffle: [as noun] trifle, insignificant thing; [as verb] blow or puff about as by slight gusts

Whimsy, dizziness

Whorle, small flywheel on a spinning wheel

Wisp, small bunch of straw, etc. used to wipe something dry or clean

Womble-crops. See *Wamble*

Wooling, woolgathering

Writh, writhed, wrenched; wreathed

Yawn. See *Awn*